Divine Progr

Divine Programming

*Negotiating Christianity in American
Dramatic Television Production 1996–2016*

CHARLOTTE E. HOWELL

OXFORD
UNIVERSITY PRESS

OXFORD
UNIVERSITY PRESS

Oxford University Press is a department of the University of Oxford. It furthers the University's objective of excellence in research, scholarship, and education by publishing worldwide. Oxford is a registered trade mark of Oxford University Press in the UK and certain other countries.

Published in the United States of America by Oxford University Press
198 Madison Avenue, New York, NY 10016, United States of America.

Library of Congress Control Number: 2020931223

ISBN 978–0–19–005437–3 (hbk)
ISBN 978–0–19–005438–0 (pbk)

To my parents

Contents

IV. ACKNOWLEDGING CHRISTIANITY IN
THE ERA OF PEAK TV

List of Figures

Acknowledgments

This book could not have existed without Alisa Perren's guidance, mentorship, and support. I could not have asked for a better advisor to help me figure out what this project would eventually become. Kathy Fuller-Seeley, Tom Schatz, Jorie Lagerwey, and Horace Newcomb all made this book better by giving me feedback, asking the important questions, and making sure this project could live up to the promise of its idea. I also thank Cindy McCreery, Cully Hamner, and all the other generous people who put me in touch with their colleagues, friends, and friends of friends to make this work possible. Many thanks to my professors who helped me learn how to think and be critical of the things we love: Mary Celeste Kearney, Michael Kackman, Suzanne Scott, Ted Friedman, Alessandra Raengo, and Thomas A. Tweed. I am incredibly grateful for the supportive Television Studies community, which kept me up to date through Twitter and challenged and invigorated by their research. To my Boston University colleagues, department, and students: you gave me the space, support, and energy to get this book over the finish line. Thanks especially to Deborah Jaramillo, Lindsey Decker, Roy Grundmann, and Paul Schneider for believing in me. Thanks to Norm and Lauralee and everyone at OUP who shepherded this project through the years.

I dedicated this book to my parents, but they deserve my thanks as well. My mother, Joyce, and my father, Hank, who acted as cheerleaders, sounding boards, first readers, and occasionally necessary distractions. My brother, Walter, and my sister-in-law, Mary Katherine, provided a perspective to my work that was desperately needed as I was formulating my terms and argument. I will always be grateful for my family's love and belief in me.

I have been incredibly lucky to find and maintain friendships with some of the most wonderful, smart, strong boss ladies I have ever known. Liz, Brittany, Jenna, Aliya: thank you for helping me stay grounded and for being there for me over the many years of our friendship. I am so grateful for Caroline Leader and Sarah Murray's support through our MA, PhD, and TT adventures and all the adventures and fun we have outside of academia. Carolina Hernandez, Jessalynn Keller, Amanda Landa, and Morgan Blue showed me how to be a generous, supportive, feminist scholar and peer.

Emily Kofoed, Laurel Ahnert, Lauren Cramer, Jing Zhang, Daren Randall Fowler, and J. Derby challenged my thinking in the best way possible in Georgia and continue to do so at conferences or around the campfire. Laura Felschow, Jackie Pinkowitz, and Annie Major kept me sane when it seemed impossible and made me feel that I had roots in Austin again. Nancy, Leah, the Cindys, Sherri, MaryJo, Darcie, Barb, Eileen, and all of my soccer ladies, thanks for getting me out of the house weekly and always being ready with positive energy and booze. Thanks to Emily H. and Lauren KN, my Boston buds. And thank you to my rescue dog, Zoya, for the constant reminder to play.

Introduction

Christianity, Religion, and Hollywood Television Production Cultures

TWO PREACHERS, 2016 AND 1996

In late May 2016, AMC, a cable network known for its quality dramas and the runaway success of its zombie comic book adaptation of *The Walking Dead* (2010–), was gearing up to premiere its latest attempt to recapture *The Walking Dead*'s success: *Preacher* (2016–2019). Like *The Walking Dead*, *Preacher* is a serial drama adapted from an adult-oriented cult hit comic book series. Unlike *The Walking Dead*, *Preacher* had already failed to be adapted to television in 2008, when it was deemed too controversial even for premium cable giant HBO.[1] Perhaps because of the memory of this past riskiness, *Preacher*'s basic premise leading up to its premiere remained ambiguous in promotional materials. For more than two years prior to the show's premiere, reports and interviews focused on the show's potential fidelity to its comic book source. The *Preacher* that ultimately premiered differed from the source text in a fundamental way: unlike the comic, which revolved around the titular preacher Jesse Custer's life after he had left his parish (he was a preacher who no longer consistently preached), the show revolved around the vocation of the eponymous preacher. The sum total of comic book parallels over the course of the ten-episode first season amounted to fewer than ten pages of the first issue of the comic. Fidelity clearly was no longer the goal by the time the series started production. By virtue of this shift in emphasis, religious representation became more central to the narrative throughout its first season. Such a change over the years of preproduction and publicity until premier illustrates a trend chronicled in *Divine Programming*: that religion-qua-religion only since the mid-2000s has become an acceptable subject of dramas aimed at elite audiences.

Divine Programming. Charlotte E. Howell, Oxford University Press (2020).
© Oxford University Press.
DOI: 10.1093/oso/9780190054373.001.0001

Making religious representation a central part of a show's narrative is not, in itself, surprising or unusual. Preachers and other overtly religious protagonists—from flying nuns to angels and even the Devil—and corresponding religious narratives always have been a part of American television dramas, although they were relatively small in number prior to the twenty-first century. But Jesse Custer is not a typical religious protagonist. Rather, he is a foul-mouthed, rage-filled minister with an extremely disturbing past. Custer is an edgy version of a man of God, and, as such, is highly atypical for television. Combining religious representation with "edge"—that is, marketable controversy—is newly acceptable. Such a mode of representation has become a way for the certain companies, executives, and creatives in the contemporary US television industry to differentiate their shows in an age of Peak TV, the era in which hundreds of scripted series available each year through multiple broadcast, cable, and streaming options, a phase that began in the mid-2010s.[2] When *Preacher* showrunner Sam Catlin described Jesse Custer as a "spiritual sheriff for the town" in which the series is set, he linked Custer to other fictional television preacher-protagonists who have provided spiritual leadership for their fictional communities and whose vocation has served as a show's narrative basis.[3] A notable example of a preacher as main character is *7th Heaven*'s Reverend Camden, a mild-mannered and wholesome patriarch character who provided religious and familial leadership on that WB drama. Certainly, there are substantial differences between *7th Heaven* (the WB/CW, 1996–2007) and *Preacher* in terms of style, characterization, narrative structure, and tone. But more significant than such aesthetic and tonal differences are the different conditions in the television industry from which each of these shows arose. The two shows come at the beginning (for *7th Heaven*, the mid-1990s) and the end (for *Preacher*, the mid-2010s) of a period when religious content in television dramas dramatically expanded. Additionally, Pew research has noted a rise of those who claim they don't practice any particular religion in the United States in the 2010s.[4] This demographic shift coincides with a downturn in individuals belonging to white Christian denominations. Non-affiliation doesn't mean that these Americans aren't spiritual or religious in a broader sense, and in fact, more than two-thirds of the "unaffiliated" say they believe in God.[5] The non-affiliation of the nones is overwhelmingly skewed toward white liberals under thirty years old, who, significantly, are a key part of the target upscale demographics of many television dramas discussed in this study.[6] Indeed, the cultural and industrial contexts altered considerably during the course of the two decades marking each show's premiere. This book analyzes the shifts in these changing industrial and cultural contexts—contexts that made the emergence of a show like *Preacher,* with its cultivation of religious edginess and appeal to quality audiences, not only possible but even logical by 2016. However, it took two decades to make this transition, and uniting acknowledged Christian representation and edgy appeal remains rare at the end of the 2010s. To comprehend this long-standing hesitation and the legacy practices and assumptions that continue to shape production culture discourse around Christian representation, we must analyze how Hollywood production cultures position Christianity relative to the work they do.

Divine Programming chronicles the negotiation of religion within the Hollywood television industry from 1996 to 2016, specifically between the simultaneous naturalization of Christianity as American mass culture and the increasingly significant industrial imperative to appeal to elite audiences. I argue that the gap between what is represented and how industry creative workers discuss the representation of Christianity exists in order to contain the middlebrow associations of white Christian television representations in order to better appeal to upscale audience tastes. This is a necessarily culturally specific argument, as the American television context contrasts significantly with other cultures, such as Latin American telenovelas or British comedies that have specific cultural reasons for including more in-depth approaches to Christianity within their television shows. For a variety of reasons—a more broad and varied television audience, commercial appeal as the primary goal, the particular American definition of public interest guiding broadcast norms, and American religious pluralism that often assumes Christianity without specificity—American television culture has had a tentative approach to representing Christianity overtly.

This study begins in 1996 because the 1996–1997 TV season reflected the effects of the repeal of the FCC's financial and syndication rules in 1995. The rules had sought to limit vertical integration—the structure in which one company owns or controls multiple stages of production and, especially in media companies, distribution—within the broadcast television industry since the 1970s. The 1996–1997 television season was also the first full season for the new networks created to profit from vertical integration: the WB and UPN, owned by Warner Bros. and Paramount, respectively, and meant as key distribution outlets for programming made by those studios. These shifts—new, smaller networks that had to target audiences more specifically and on a smaller scale than the established networks did and the reliance on vertical integration to keep costs down for programs that attracted a few million viewers instead of tens of millions of viewers—laid the groundwork for the increased nichification that would drive television programming for the next two decades. They also marked a dramatic increase in the hours of scripted television produced, a growth that only increased in the subsequent twenty years. By 2016, this drive to attract more distinct taste groups within an increasingly crowded (and still highly vertically integrated) marketplace resulted in Peak TV with its overabundance of scripted programming produced per year. Within Peak TV, upscale viewers who can afford multiple subscription packages, who have high-speed internet and unlimited phone data, who are valued by advertisers and media companies, and who have the leisure time to view that much television have become the new center of the television industry. Although there may be occasional exceptions like the revival of *Roseanne* (ABC, 1988–1997, 2018), the presumed Christian and white mass audience has lost its dominance since the mid-1990s.

During this twenty-year span, Christian representation became, at least in the framing of many US television creatives, a narrative tool unconnected to religious practice as a way to contain an industrial perception of risk. I analyze this shift through case studies of the development, writing, producing, marketing, and positioning of key series that feature mainstream Christianity as a core narrative element for at least one season. This criterion limits the study to a manageable size by excluding programs that relegate religion to a single character. Jed Bartlet's (Martin Sheen) Catholicism on *The West Wing* (NBC, 1999–2006) was key to his character and some plotlines, but it was centered on Jed as an individual and didn't rise to the level of season-long serial plots. Similarly, the teen daughters on *The Good Wife* (CBS, 2009–2016) and *The Americans* (FX, 2013–2018) both defied their parents' atheism to become devout Christians—at least for a time—but it wasn't central to the premise, milieu, or narrative foundation for at least a season. These constraints also exclude a number of shows like *Justified* (FX, 2010–2015), *Big Love* (HBO, 2006–2011), and *True Detective* (HBO, 2014–) in which Christianity was represented through fringe practices or cults. The ability for mainstream white Christianity to be normalized and thus more easily rendered invisible is necessary for the kinds of denials I heard.

The series comprising my case studies, combined with my focus on development, writing, producing, marketing, and positioning of these series, require of their production cultures' significant engagement with Christianity as a religion that reflects in some way the Christianity that the majority of

Americans practice. Thus, on the basis of case studies including *7th Heaven, Friday Night Lights* (NBC, 2006–2011), *Rectify* (SundanceTV, 2013–2016), *Supernatural* (the WB/CW, 2005–2020), *Jane the Virgin* (The CW, 2014–2019), *Daredevil* (Netflix, 2015–2018), and *Preacher* (AMC, 2016–2019), I determined that as Christian content expanded across American dramatic television since 1996 (see Table I.1), corresponding with it was a deep ambivalence among television production cultures with regard to the subject. Religious representation's proliferation coincided with the period's overall growth in scripted programs, but the hesitance attached to Christian narratives and tropes indicated that religion was operating differently in this changing landscape, more beholden to legacy ideologies than other expanding representations were.

The shifts examined in this book exemplify the effect of two important industrial trends shaping television since the 1990s. First, since the late 1990s, the television industry has increasingly sought upscale audience niches, even on broadcast channels. Such a strategy de-centered the mass, middle-American audience that had dominated television taste since the 1950s. Second, those upscale audience niches aligned with the perceived tastes of affluent, educated, multicultural, and—importantly—secular elites. Assumptions about the taste of upscale audiences shaped how religion was represented as such storylines increased, as this book demonstrates.

Understanding Religion in Hollywood's Production Culture

One way to understand the occupation and simultaneous distancing of Hollywood's television production culture is as an expression of post-Christianity, and a particularly American articulation of post-Christianity at that. A post-Christian sensibility illustrates a normalizing of Christian tropes in a culture seen as increasingly non-Christian after a period of dominant Christendom. Post-Christianity is not an overcoming of marginalization but instead a distancing from a (past) hegemonic structure. One of the ironies of the post-Christian sensibility is that Christianity is more represented than ever on television not aimed at the devout Christian population, as evident in the twenty-first-century boom of US religious programming investigated in this book. A simultaneous denial and renewal of religion is one of the foundational ideas of post-Christian theory.[7] That paradox also positions it well within the dominant non-Christian culture of Hollywood.

Table I.1 Mainstream religious programming in neo-network, post-network, and Peak TV eras

	Neo-Network Era (late 1980s–early 2000s)	Post-Network Era (early 2000s–present)	Peak TV (2015–present)
Dramas featuring season-long Christian narrative or context (* indicates broadcast)	• *7th Heaven* (WB/CW, 1996–2007)* • *Brimstone* (Fox, 1998–1999)* • *Father Dowling Mysteries* (CBS, 1989–1991)* • *Highway to Heaven* (NBC, 1984–1989)* • *Nothing Sacred* (ABC, 1997–1998)* • *Promised Land* (CBS, 1996–1999)* • *Touched by an Angel* (CBS, 1994–2003)*	• *American Horror Story: Asylum* (FX, 2012–2013) • *Battlestar Galactica* (SciFi, 2003–2009) • *Believe* (NBC, 2014)* • *Big Love* (HBO, 2006–2011) • *Carnivàle* (HBO, 2003–2005) • *Constantine* (NBC, 2014–2015)* • *Dominion* (Syfy, 2014–2015) • *Eli Stone* (ABC, 2008–2009)* • *Friday Night Lights* (NBC, 2006–2011)* • *GCB* (ABC, 2012)* • *Jane the Virgin* (The CW, 2014–2019)* • *Joan of Arcadia* (CBS, 2003–2005)* • *John from Cincinnati* (HBO, 2007) • *Kings* (NBC, 2009)* • *Lost* (ABC, 2004–2011)* • *Miracles* (ABC, 2003)* • *Penny Dreadful* (Showtime 2014–2016) • *Rectify* (SundanceTV, 2013–2017) • *Resurrection* (ABC, 2014–2015)* • *Saving Grace* (TNT, 2007–2010) • *Sleepy Hollow* (Fox, 2013–2017)* • *Supernatural* (the WB/CW, 2005–2020)* • *The Bible* (History, 2013) • *The Book of Daniel* (NBC, 2006)* • *The Leftovers* (HBO 2014–2017)	• *A.D.: The Bible Continues* (NBC, 2015)* • *Damien* (A&E, 2016) • *Daredevil* (Netflix, 2015–2018) • *Dig* (USA, 2015) • *Evil* (CBS, 2019–)* • *Filthy Rich* (Fox, 2020–)* • *Greenleaf* (OWN, 2016–) • *God Friended Me* (CBS, 2018–) • *Hand of God* (Amazon, 2015–2017) • *Lucifer* (Fox/Netflix, 2016–2020)* • *Of Kings and Prophets* (ABC, 2016)* • *Perpetual Grace, LTD* (Epix, 2019–) • *Preacher* (AMC, 2016–2019) • *The Dovekeepers* (CBS, 2015)* • *The Exorcist* (Fox 2016–2018)*

Other prime-time religious (including non-Christian faiths) scripted programs

- *Amen* (NBC, 1986–1991)*
- *Oz* (HBO, 1997–2003)
- *Teen Angel* (ABC, 1997–1998)*

- *The Librarians* (TNT, 2014–2018)
- *The Secret Life of the American Teenager* (ABC Family, 2008–2013)
- *True Detective* (HBO, 2014–)
- *Wonderfalls* (Fox, 2004)
- *Aliens in America* (The CW, 2007–2008)*
- *Dead like Me* (Showtime, 2003–2004)
- *Enlightened* (HBO, 2011–2013)
- *Homeland* (Showtime, 2011–2018)
- *Life* (ABC, 2007–2009)*
- *Sleeper Cell* (Showtime, 2005–2006)
- *Transparent* (Amazon, 2014–2019)
- *Vikings* (History, 2013–2020)

- *The Handmaid's Tale* (Hulu, 2017–)
- *The Messengers* (The CW, 2015)*
- *The Young Pope* (HBO, 2016–)
- *Angel from Hell* (CBS, 2016)*
- *Living Biblically* (CBS, 2018)*
- *The Good Place* (NBC, 2016–2020)
- *Impastor* (TV Land, 2015–2016)
- *Perfect Harmony* (NBC, 2019–)*
- *The Real O'Neals* (ABC, 2016–2017)*
- *The Righteous Gemstones* (HBO, 2019–)

Post-Christianity theorists like Jean-Luc Nancy and Rudolph Binion argue that living within a cultural environment in which Christianity is a key meta-narrative of the culture is necessary to this concept.[8] That this is true even if it is framed as historical or predominantly attached to a conservative "other" as it is with Hollywood production cultures, indicates an alacrity of understanding and legibility for Christianity that persists beyond its belief system and adherents. Christian tropes are known, recognizable, and generalized beyond denominational schisms. Media theorist Stig Hjarvard conceptualizes how these tropes are mediatized, creating what he calls "banal religion." Hjarvard writes,

> Banal religion may consist of elements taken from institutional religion, such as crosses, prayers and cowls as well as elements usually associated with folk religion, such as trolls, vampires and black cats crossing the street. . . . The iconography and liturgical practices of both institutionalized and folk religions become stockpiles for the media's own production of factual and fictional stories about the world. . . . Owing to their industrial nature, the media talk about the world through generic conventions and accordingly the media's banal religious imaginations become moulded according to popular genres.[9]

Hjarvard offers banal religion as a framework for understanding the post-modern bricolage of meaning in which religious significance can be subsumed into secular media constructions. Although banal religions is applicable to a variety of cultures, the multitude of American Christian denominations—as opposed to the dominance of Catholicism or Anglicism in Latin American and Britain, respectively—and the heightened visibility of Christian conservatism through the televangelism of white evangelical Christianity since the 1970s, the US expression of post-Christianity also folds in specific cultural and political denial and distancing in a liberal-leaning Hollywood context. Lucifer and the Four Horsemen of the Apocalypse, for example, are recognizable characters with stories familiar even to people who grew up in or adhere to non-Christian religious systems within the American cultural milieu, but on shows like *Supernatural* or *Dominion* (Syfy [formerly SciFi], 2014–2015) these Christian figures become fantasy-horror genre tropes instead of heralds of the biblical apocalypse. Denial makes it safe both culturally and politically, and that safety allows for more representation. This logic is predicated on the fundamental shared understanding that Christian tropes, when used as pure entertainment, are no longer Christian. They may not even be religious at all, at least according to those creating and framing the work. One consequence of this denial, however, limits and ostracizes religious readings of those narratives. While I discuss this result mainly as legacy practices and understandings, it could also be understood by using Tim Havens's definition of "industry lore," "any *interpretation* among industry insiders of the material, social, or historical realities that the media industries face . . . serv[ing] as a 'regime of truth' that makes the chaotic waters of global cultural diversity and mysterious viewer tastes seem navigable."[10] However, the containment discourses that dismiss or don't even consider the religiousness of Christian narratives are not as solid or cogent as the term "lore" implies nor do they have long histories specific to this trend, so I prefer to describe the practices and discourses as such.

In the critical study of religion in media culture, identifying where religion is avoided can be more useful than exploring religious variety. Thus, this study focuses on US shows that represent Christian narratives and tropes and their relationship to the broad concept of religion but does not examine the representation of non-dominant religious traditions that cannot be subsumed into the wider American culture. While there has also been an increase in more deeply engaged representations of other religions, such as Judaism in *Transparent* (Amazon, 2014–2019) and Islam in *Homeland* (Showtime, 2011–2019), these religions are understood and framed as religions within the television discourse. Only the hegemonic position of Christianity allows for the denial of its religiousness, making it more pliable, adaptable, and deniable. Christianity and a more general sense of religion can become conflated. Given its post-Christian context, when religion is discussed in American television production cultures, it can mean either an abstracted religiousness or Christianity, while that same generalization is not available to other religions. This dichotomy explains why many creatives I interviewed understood religion to mean Christianity, or at least implied as much through their discourse of denial. Such conflation also perhaps helps to explain why the religiousness of Christianity in particular so often required containment or outright denial.

Divine Programming maps a shift in Christian representations from safe, inoffensive religiousness exemplified by *7th Heaven* and its Reverend Camden to diverse, sometimes challenging, and even edgy representational modes as with *Preacher*'s Jesse Custer, even if those representations generally weren't discussed as religious by creatives. By focusing on a variety of US shows featuring Christian representations from the neo- and post-network eras, this book explores the shifting parameters within which religion was contained discursively and enabled representationally. It does so by analyzing both how Christianity has been represented and how executives, producers, and writers who have created and positioned its representation have understood their work with regard to religion. Both the representation of religion and the understanding of it have been affected by production culture ideologies formed through long-standing legacy practices, established genre expectations, and assumptions by creatives about perceived target audiences. As media scholar Herman Gray stated in his study of race on television, "In order for television to achieve its work—that is, to make meaning and produce pleasure—it has to draw upon and operate on the basis of a kind of generalized societal common sense about the terms of the society and people's social location in it. The social ground and the cultural terms on which it works depend on the assumptions about experience, knowledge, familiarity, and the accessibility of viewers to these assumptions."[11]

Focusing on religious content reveals a pattern of industrial practices and attitudes that endured across a variety of genres and outlets. Specific cultural conditions constrained how the industry both presented and discussed religion. This was the case even as other topics deemed edgy at the time, such as homosexuality and queer representations, became increasing viable. Gay representation gained quick acceptance within the industry, as it was categorized as a way to appeal to socially liberal urban-minded professionals, an upscale taste market.[12] Christian representation, however, is largely ideologically contained within the cultures of production because of its association with conservative politics and middlebrow tastes. The gap between religion and other topics used for marketable edginess relies heavily on the history of religion on television and the various associations that became attached to it from the 1950s through the 1990s. I will discuss this history and the establishment of Christianity's middlebrow associations in Chapter 1, then explore anchoring examples of the attitudes expressed in later industry assumptions. The majority of this book examines the period of accelerated change in the twenty-first century, the post-network era that includes the further amplification of those changes in Peak TV.

The Boom in Religious Representation in the Post-Network Era (Early 2000s–2016)

Although the 1990s featured *Touched by an Angel* (CBS, 1994–2003) and *7th Heaven* as prominent, successful shows featuring Christianity (and *Nothing*

Sacred [ABC, 1997–1998] as a notable failure), the still somewhat hesitant shift to overt religious representation prior to the 2000s gave way to a dramatic increase in such programming after 2003. This boom in religious representation, which was due to post-network industrial changes such as the fracturing of the audience and resultant expansion and nichification of the television landscape as well as the increased attention to religion in the greater American culture, was characterized by a marked increase in ongoing religious narratives in prime-time dramas (see Table I.1, above). Despite this increase, there were certain types of representation that dominated. Following from *Battlestar Galactica*, fantastic (fantasy, science fiction, and horror) genre modes of religious representation were and continue to be the most prolific, and because of generic containment of religion within supernatural unreality and increased attention to fan audiences as an upscale niche, the fantastic genres continue to dominate. The fan audience for fantastic genre shows has been gaining prominence for decades as a devoted viewer base with money to spend. However, in the post-network era, according to scholar Matt Hills, fans now "make up the entirety of a niche audience" with the attendant cultural power.[13] Moreover, the practices of fan audiences are becoming increasingly mainstream and are particularly visible to marketers, advertisers, executives, and creatives as (anecdotal) proof of audience engagement with a show and/or its brand.[14] The upscale fan audience overlaps with the quality audience significantly in terms of class, race, region, gender, and their supposed secularism. To target a program to either audience is to target an upscale niche, and both audiences have gained significance in the post-network television industry to the detriment of the atavistic mass audience.

This study maps the ways that different means of representing religion emerged over this time span while the ways creatives spoke about that representation continued to be shaped by hesitation until the 2010s. The post-network boom included several genres—from *Battlestar Galactica*, *Dominion*, and *Preacher* among its fantastic genre examples to *Friday Night Lights* (NBC, 2006–2011) and *Rectify* (SundanceTV, 2013–2016) as its realist genre examples. It also spanned distribution outlets, appearing on a wide range of broadcast, basic-cable, premium, and streaming platforms. Significantly, this boom was, for many years, identified only through shorter cycles of programming trends, attached to exceptional shows, and focused on the broader concept of spirituality instead of Christianity.[15] Even though the series under discussion here engaged with Christianity and its tropes for at least a season, for the most part, they were discursively characterized by traits other than Christianity. Realist dramas were not labeled religious; they merely portrayed an authentic American South or nonwhite culture that included Christianity. Generically fantastic dramas could use religion as part of a fantasy or science fiction world removed from traditional Christian connotations and groupings. The boom extended across generic categorization within dramatic television, spanned approximately thirteen years (2003–2016) and each major mode of television distribution, but was rarely discussed within the industry or in the wider culture as the diffuse, sustained, and extensive expansion of religious representation that it actually was.

As alluded to above, the boom began with the December 2003 premiere of SciFi's *Battlestar Galactica* three-hour miniseries that would become the first installment of a five-season-long drama. The series followed from and reimagined aspects of the original science fiction series of the same name that had aired on ABC in 1978–1979. The twenty-first-century version of *Battlestar Galactica* was packaged as a quality science fiction series, dealing symbolically and allegorically with contemporary political, cultural, and social anxieties through the displaced reality of science fiction. It was praised by critics for its realistic, flawed characters and its critical dialogue with post-9/11 American culture and the War on Terror.[16] The pervasive fear following the 2001 terror attacks had created a culture of paranoia and religious profiling. The year 2003 marked a pointed shift in American foreign policy, with the US government moving from fighting Al-Qaida, the terror organization responsible for the 9/11 terrorist attacks, toward presenting itself as fighting a more generalized and worldwide definition of terror that included Saddam Hussein in Iraq. These political, cultural, and social anxieties manifested explicitly in shows like *Battlestar Galactica* and *24* (Fox, 2001–2010). Whereas *24* dealt with religion only superficially as it showed America fighting Islamic terrorists, *Battlestar Galactica* dived deeply into the existential questions wrought by a religious war.

In the immediate post-9/11 environment, both within and outside the United States, there was strong sympathy for, and loyalty to, American culture and foreign policy shifts.[17] In contrast to a growing nationalism evidenced in the wider culture, increasing questioning of American righteousness and crusading began in the media industries in 2003. Much of this challenge was focused on the political sphere, in the sense that the War in Iraq was motivated by political and capitalistic reasons more than actual global threat. This questioning was particularly marked among liberal elites like creatives in Hollywood. Although Ronald D. Moore, the showrunner of *Battlestar Galactica*, claimed no direct influence of 9/11 on the development of his show, the climate created following the attacks clearly shaped the series' critical focus on terrorism, torture, insurgency, and military leadership.[18] Moreover, the specifically religious character of the September 11 attacks and subsequent war(s) that followed brought religion—both Islam and Christianity—to the forefront of American cultural discourse. This is a crucial factor that played a role in the religious representational boom of the 2000s.

Following *Battlestar Galactica*, several other series premiered that featured religious narratives in ways distinct from the 1990s middlebrow mode. *Lost*, a fantasy adventure series that followed the survivors of a plane crash on a mysterious island, premiered on ABC in 2004 and ultimately became the show most often compared to *Battlestar Galactica* with regard to its religious narrative.[19] *Supernatural* premiered on the WB in 2005 and by the end of the decade displayed some of the most overt—and most challenging—representations of Christianity on television. The following year, *Friday Night Lights*, a drama centered on high school football in a small Texas town, premiered on NBC and moved religious representation into a realist genre. Each of these shows serve as case studies of the boom studied in the pages that follow: each was a successful, multi-season show in which religious representation was central to the show's narrative. Although *Battlestar Galactica* began the boom, each of these mid-2000s shows provided a different shading and approach to its uses of religious representation. These four shows—along with a variety of failures that premiered and disappeared relatively quickly in the 2000s, such as *Miracles* (Fox, 2003), *Revelations* (NBC, 2005), *Point Pleasant* (Fox, 2005), *The Book of Daniel* (NBC, 2006), *Eli Stone* (ABC, 2007–2008), and *Kings* (NBC, 2009)—represent the first wave of the boom, tied to the rise of religious cultural discourse in the wake of 9/11 and launched during the height of the War on Terror. Despite the rise in the broader culture's attention to religion during this period, the subject nonetheless remained a risky one for creatives to be associated with. After all, the main associations that came with religion at the time were a new-millennium crusade in the Middle East and a vocal nationalistic, conservative culture within America, both of which contrasted with the post-Christian mentality that dominated in liberal enclaves.

The end of the decade renewed the centrality of religion in the wider American cultural discourse. This renewal involved the rise of the ultraconservative and largely evangelical Christian Tea Party movement. This movement became overtly inscribed in culture during the 2010 midterm election. The Tea Party movement arose following Barack Obama's historic election as president in 2008 and centered on both anti-tax fiscal conservatism and evangelical moralism, with almost half of its members identifying as born-again Christian.[20] Beyond its members' self-proclaimed ideologies and motives, the Tea Party in the early 2010s was strongly associated with racism and white nativism in addition to evangelicalism.[21] The movement was exceptionally visible in the news and within the culture of the time. The cultural construction of Christianity tied to social conservatism as much as or more than religious practice gained prominence in America in relation to the post-Christian sensibility increasingly visible in entertainment cultures. This construction corresponds to the 2010s acceleration of the boom in religious representation and the premieres of shows that approached Christian content in increasingly varied ways: for example, *Sleepy Hollow* (Fox, 2013–2017) featured Ichabod Crane fighting off the biblical apocalypse; *Rectify* (SundanceTV, 2013–2016) focused on a man released from death row in Georgia; *The Leftovers* (HBO, 2014–2017) was a tense drama about the aftermath of a Rapture-like event; *Dominion* centered on warring angels; the comic book adaptation *Constantine* (NBC, 2014–2015) displayed a demon-fighting occultist; and procedural *Lucifer* (Fox/Netflix, 2016–2020) demonstrated the Devil solving crimes. All of these shows used Christianity—sometimes even through biblical literalism—as a foundation for their narratives.

In these shows, as well as in the shows from earlier in the 2000s, although the religious content featured expands, this expansion corresponds to their creatives' ongoing denial, distancing, and displacement of the term "religion." Throughout the boom, although religion became a main part of the dialogue in the public sphere it often came in close association with social and cultural conservatism, xenophobia, self-righteous nationalism, and hawkish, interventionist foreign policy. Religion thus had associations in the wider public sphere that were polarizing for liberal cultures dominating media production, making acknowledgment of religion potentially dangerous. This dynamic figured into the repeated denial and displacement by creatives and helps explain why the mainstream and trade press for the most part failed to identify this as a tendency. All combined, religion, and religious audiences, were constructed over the span of the boom as something to avoid among the elite, liberal culture of mainstream prime-time Hollywood television production.

Religion among Expansive Options: Toward Peak TV (2015–2016)

During this boom period, and concurrent with these larger cultural and political shifts, the television industry was undergoing its own transformation toward Peak TV. As the post-network era began in the early 2000s, for the first time, cable television surpassed broadcast network television in the ratings.[22] As Amanda Lotz argues in *The Television Will Be Revolutionized*,

> Changes in television have forced the production process to evolve during the past twenty years so that the assorted ways we now use television are mirrored in and enabled by greater variation in the ways television is made, financed, and distributed . . . Consequently, the industrial transformation of U.S. television has begun to modify what the industry creates.[23]

More distribution outlets, greater reliance on narrow upscale audiences, and shifts in patterns of creative agency all contributed to both the boom in religious content and the precariousness of speaking about the choices involved in religious representation. The elevation of the upscale niche audience along with quality-audience targeting created conditions favorable to the boom as well as creatives' tendency to displace religion in their discussions of their work within the boom.

In the post-network era, the mass audience has largely yielded to a variety of niches, affecting all aspects of the television industry and creative production from story development to reception. We can consider this process of industrial transformation to be a defining paradigm of twenty-first-century media and a key element to understanding how and why religious content began appearing with greater frequency in mainstream television during the 2000s and 2010s. At this time, the risk of incorporating religious representation (at least when ideologically contained, in ways addressed throughout this book) began diminishing, largely because of the more precise and narrow targeting of upscale niche audiences in the post-network era than had been the case in previous eras. Various new technologies of audience targeting favor upscale audiences and further the post-network era's emphasis on coalitions of upscale audiences over pure ratings or broad demographics.[24]

Once the post-network refinement and expansion of niche strategies had been adopted across much of the television industry, the appropriate identification, targeting, and—increasingly—measurable engagement of these desirable audiences became the dominant, popular logic of the industry. As Philip Napoli notes, "A media environment in which audiences' engagement in, and appreciation of, the content they consume is as valuable (or perhaps even more so) as the size and demographic composition of the audience is one that has the potential to support content forms that resonate powerfully with segments of the media audience that would otherwise be too small to encourage the production of content serving their particular needs and interests."[25] This emphasis on engagement and niche targeting aligns with the increased attention to upscale audiences in both their quality and fan constructions. During this time, in conversation with shifts in the public sphere discussed above, imagined upscale audiences and creatives working in shows pursuing those audiences construed their viewers as resistant to religious representation in particular ways. The increased attention to these demographic and taste cultures by television industry creatives, executive, and marketers contributed an imagined entity to be pursued. Yet this liberal, affluent, and coastal taste culture is perceived to be averse to religious content. Such constructions of the audience imaginary by creatives may be influenced by the new technologies and metrics available to measure them in the post-network era. However, as I discovered through the course of my study, a legacy of internal practices and attitudes has had a more obvious impact on when religion is—and is not—depicted in primetime mainstream serial dramas.

The fractured and increasingly niched audience paradigm of the post-network television industry coincides with rise of new distribution outlets and their shifting models of acquiring and producing television. As Horace Newcomb argues, television in the post-network era "functions [less like the "cultural forum" in the classic network era and more] as a bookstore, a newsstand, or a library. Programs are available for purchase or on 'loan for fee,' as in subscription libraries . . . [that] predated the modern 'free public library.'"[26] This "logic of publishing" has been pushed forward by the rise of streaming video on demand (SVOD) outlets like Netflix but has influenced the whole of the television industry.[27] Within the logic of publishing as it shapes television in the post-network era, the quest for prestige—and thus appeal to upscale audiences that will pay for the content—has become a dominant mode of program branding. In an attempt to attain prestige programming and audiences, studio financiers and program distribution outlets have had to experiment. Through their experimentation within an industry composed of fractured niches of the audience, there has been a marked rise in the quantity of fictional television production.[28] Beginning in 2015 and continuing to the end of the 2010s, this rise in productions to fill the multiple niche outlets and content libraries—both in terms of SVOD licensing and of the figurative model of publishing—has yielded what has come to be called Peak TV by some critics, journalists, creatives, and executives.

Peak TV describes the current preponderance of scripted series on television across all outlets, from broadcast networks to streaming platforms. In 2015, the term was coined by FX president, John Landgraf, to describe an industrial context that yielded over 400 scripted programs that year.[29] Beyond mere quantity, Peak TV is shaping all aspects of the industry, leading to greater experimentation in content that has allowed for a new stage of representing religion. But industrially, the capital going into Peak TV is generally allocated to the top creative talent, as studios and distributors seek to separate their signal from the noise of the 400-plus other shows on television. Journalists Josef Adalian and Maria Elana Fernandez explain the market model of Peak TV:

> Overall spending is way up, but like the broader national economy, the wealth isn't being distributed equally. Movie stars are getting offered $5 million to do a single ten-episode season of a show, even as studios slash budgets for lower-level actors. Writers have plenty of job opportunities, but shorter seasons have meant more career volatility. Experienced showrunners are in high demand, yet they're unlikely to ever become as rich as a Dick Wolf or Norman Lear.[30]

There are shifting notions of creative agency in the era of Peak TV corresponding to the industrial shifts discussed so far. The increased reliance on top-level talent has granted relatively new status for the figure of the showrunner. Concurrently, mid-level job precarity remains, a point especially notable in this study in terms of staff writers. For dramas that feature religious narratives, this uncertainty means that staff writers, who operate on season-to-season contracts, are beholden to the ideology and culture of the dominant creative voice(s) of the showrunners in the writers' rooms and executive offices. A relatively recent construct within the television industry, the contemporary showrunner takes on the dual roles of head writer and executive producer. He (usually, he) leads the writers' room by guiding the writers through creating season-long narrative arcs, assigning writers to scripts, managing outlines and network notes on them, and ultimately being the centripetal and centrifugal force associated with the show. He dominates the space of the writers' room and is the one with enough power to negotiate with the studio and distributor if need be. In addition, he is increasingly the voice for the show with both press and fans. The showrunner gained prominence in the post-network era as a means of managing and elevating a program's brand.[31] The showrunner's voice dominates industry discourse about the show—particularly for upscale dramas—and sets the tone for the culture of the writers' room and the type of audience that will be targeted.

Given the showrunner-staff power dynamic, if a showrunner associates religion with Tea Party conservatives or middlebrow tastes connected to the mass audience, it is likely there will be a production culture in which religion as both a term and a subject is to be avoided. When the topic is not avoided, it must be contained. Such containment works to clearly distance a creative or show from what are perceived as dominant, adverse cultural discourses about religion. This way of thinking about religion among many television creatives frames the paradoxical relationship between the 2003–2016 boom in religious content and the persistent disavowal of religion among creatives throughout much of this boom.

However, despite the persistent hesitancy that has characterized creatives' discussion of religion in the post-network era, the increased power and individual creative agency for the showrunner figure in the context of Peak TV has also allowed for a gradual shift in that hesitancy of discourse. Although programming has reflected a shift in religious representation since 2003, it is only since 2015 or so that creatives—particularly showrunners—have expanded the ways in which they approach and discuss religion's place in their work. For showrunners like Ben Watkins on *Hand of God* (Amazon, 2015–2017), Steven DeKnight on the first season of *Daredevil* (Netflix, 2015–2018), Craig Wright on *Greenleaf* (OWN, 2016–), and Sam Catlin on *Preacher* (AMC, 2016–2019), their willingness to discuss, fight for, or frame their stories in terms of religion both in their writers' rooms and the press illustrates a relatively recent change. The creatives working on these shows discuss religion differently from how they or their counterparts discussed the topic in the dozen years before the 2015–2016 season. In their emergent discourse, they push through the legacy of hesitation and distancing, engaging in franker discussions of religion and providing edgier representations of it. Such changes, as will be illustrated in detail in the chapters that follow, have been made possible by the dynamic interplay between cultural and industrial changes since 1996. What's more, these discourses and depictions have been greatly amplified—along with television production more broadly—in the 2015–2016 television season. This is where I end my study, with the beginning of Peak TV. Through this exploration of Christianity in serial dramas, *Divine Programming* provides an extensive look at the transition from the mass-oriented neo-network era to the myriad and narrowing audience niches of Peak TV.

METHODS AND CHAPTERS

In the earlier sections of this introduction, I discussed my selection of case studies within the larger context of neo-network and post-network television. To understand their discourses around Christian representation, I include as my primary sources for research interviews with writers, producers, executives, and marketers who worked on American prime-time dramas that featured Christian and Christianity-inflected narratives. That is, the programs comprising my case studies had to have Christian narrative arcs (whether overtly or through use of identifiably Christian tropes) or explicitly Christian contexts that lasted for at least a season. From that bank of possibilities, I interviewed people whose work constructed, framed, or shepherded these creative decisions for shows that met that criteria. I call these workers, as a collective, creatives for both brevity and to focus on their work within the narrative and framing structures of television production. I draw on scholars like John Caldwell, Elana Levine, Vicki Mayer, Laura Grindstaff, Catherine Johnson, David Hesmondhalgh, and Sarah Baker as models for this kind of production studies work.[32] I used snowball sampling, requesting that people I interview suggest other workers they know for interviews, to make contact with creatives, thus yielding twenty-one interviews, most occurring over the phone, along with three interviews via email correspondence. I asked the same basic questions of the interview subjects. My focus was on the individuals' work and history within the television industry, not on personal subjects such as their religious backgrounds. I took this approach for a few reasons: (1) it provided me with a more holistic view of their work within the television industry, allowing me to better understand how religion operated in the general production culture; (2) religion is a contentious personal subject, and I didn't want to create a sense of defensiveness on the part of the interviewees; (3) those who wanted to discuss their personal beliefs did so freely within the context of answering other questions; and (4) it eased interviewees into a flow so that their answers to my questions about their work with religion might be more candid. Of course, because all of my interviews were with above-the-line creative workers, almost all of whom chose not to be anonymous, these interviews are shaped by a savvy understanding of television publicity and the desire to represent their work in the best possible light. I understood that those I interviewed would likely be timid in their critique of the industry, since all those creatives were still working in it. However, because I sought to understand the television production culture through its discourse and output, I also recognized that these limitations in the interviewees' candor traced the boundaries of acceptability and value within the corporate and creative cultures of television production. These understandings shaped my analysis of these interviews and what they revealed (or didn't) about the television industry.

Each interview lasted between twenty minutes and an hour and a half, with most being an hour long. In addition to these personal interviews, I occasionally used publicly available interviews published in popular or trade press. These were especially useful for accessing perspectives from a few showrunners I did not manage to personally connect with but who have enough industry capital to speak openly about religion on their shows in publicly disclosed texts. The unpublished interviews provided a wealth of information beyond that available solely in published materials. Very early on, I began recognizing patterns of containment that I found to reside at the heart of how religion operates within the Hollywood TV industry's production cultures. It is worth emphasizing that very few interviewees acknowledged their role in this act of containment, leaving it to me to identify this practice on the basis of an analysis of their discourses along with the corresponding programs.

I interviewed producers and writers who had worked on a variety of shows that centered Christianity in their narratives, but not all of those shows proved useful case studies. Often these shows and the people who worked on them reproduced the discourses of other shows that proved more interesting or illustrative of these discursive and narrative patterns. Thus, the selection of case studies for this project occurred at the intersection of a number of factors: access, familiarity, and relevance. I am not a member of the production cultures that I am studying; thus, I was reliant on snowball sampling and contacts of contacts to initiate these interviews. Aside from the chapter on nonwhite Christianity that I felt needed to be part of the conversation, access was the foundation of case study selection. The next factor was familiarity both for myself and in wider discussions: Did these shows crop up in discussions of religion on television? For the more recent shows, proximity established that for even canceled series like *Dominion* or *Constantine*. Finally, as implied above, some shows like *Eli Stone* or *Resurrection*, to which I was lucky enough to gain access, did not, to my mind, add significantly enough to the interviews I had already conducted to merit in-depth discussion as a case study. These interviews—as well as all programming that could have fit this study—certainly inform this book and will be referenced when appropriate, but for the reasons mentioned above did not become case studies.

Beyond interviews, I also analyzed marketing materials and articles in trade press (e.g., *Variety, Hollywood Reporter, Deadline*) and industry-focused popular press publications (e.g., *New York Times, Los Angeles Times*). These publicly disclosed and semi-embedded deep texts of the industry aided in my understanding of how the shows were positioned within the television industry and marketplace.[33] Particularly useful were marketing and promotional materials circulated through popular entertainment news websites that used religious iconography like *The Last Supper* to nod to the religious narratives of certain shows such as *Battlestar Galactica* (Figure I.1) and *Lost*

Figure I.1 *Battlestar Galactica* promotional photo, season four

(Figure I.2). These images appeared only in the marketing materials once the religious narratives had been accepted by the upscale target audiences and could thus stretch the bounds of their containment. Combined with my personal interviews and textual analysis of the shows featured as case studies, these promotional materials and press articles provided a broad discourse of television production cultures for me to analyze.

Finally but importantly, I perform textual analysis of the religious representations and narratives in each case study. I use ideological and genre analysis to gain a better understanding of how religion is represented and contained, as well as how it interacts with assumed audiences on the basis of genre conventions.[34] Overt and acknowledged representations of Christianity without patterns of containment—as featured in Part I—merit less in-depth textual analysis than the other case studies in which I must show how Christianity appears in the programs in order to analyze the discourses that deny or reframe the religion. A disavowal of religiousness becomes more legible as a discursive process when juxtaposed with the way, for example, Heaven appears within the show. In this project, both ideological and genre textual approaches are consistently placed in conversation with an analysis of industry context and production discourses. The core of my study examines how the production practices of containment, abstraction, and disavowal

Figure I.2 *Lost* official cast photo, season six

shape representations of religion on prime-time television, with careful attention to the surprising contradictions between the representation and its discursive framing. I look at texts and how meaning is encoded within them; reception of religious representation and decoding are beyond the scope of this study. The religious representations articulated through the television programs are affected by the production practices of containment, but it is worth underscoring that the representations themselves are not explicitly—nor even predominantly—understood by viewers as contained. Religious viewers may see these representations as thorough, true, and fully religious cultural objects. Secular viewers may consider them mere fantasy. The polysemy of the religious representations I study does not impact my argument. I use the theoretical and cultural understanding of religion in post-Christianity to identify and analyze these religious representations *in order to* gain a greater understanding of how the production cultures' practices of containment affect their creative output and how the television industry perpetuates an ideology of religion as risky within industry assumptions and perpetuated by individuals' decisions despite the greater creative freedoms that characterize the post-network era.

Despite the perceived risk—or perhaps because of the success of containment—most of the people that I interviewed for this book allowed me to use their names; those who granted consent to be identified by name were primarily creatives who had attained a certain level of status in the television industry. The few individuals who requested anonymity were all staff writers; these lower-level creatives felt they had to be exceptionally careful in terms of what they disclosed because of the greater precariousness of their positions. Anonymous or not, most of the creatives I spoke to relied on vague abstractions or evidenced outright denial when discussing their use of religious narratives. There was, however, one exception to this pattern of discursive distancing. One anonymous staff writer was especially candid and clear about the dominant ideology within that writer's production culture. This person believed there was a clear "taboo about touching any religion except [when] Muslims [appear] in a bad light."[35] This writer told me about writing a pilot in the late 2000s that utilized religion but couched it within supernatural genre elements. When it was pitched, this person described the response: "My agents' heads exploded."[36] The writer then told me another story about an extremely well-known writer, Aaron Sorkin (*The West Wing*), who pitched a show with this writer's friend in the mid-2000s. Their show had an overtly religious narrative, and when they pitched it to HBO, they didn't even get halfway through their delivery to the pay-cable channel before executives told them, "We don't touch religion."[37] Just like that, their project was dead.

These anecdotes are dramatic and specific illustrations of a concern regarding the acknowledgment of religion that my study affirms has been a consistent fear and worry, and a pervasive avoidance pattern within the television industry since the mid-1990s. As a result of this fear, during the time under examination, creatives have largely sought to distance themselves from their work in religious representation and narratives. This pattern of containment through discourse and representational practice was enacted again and again by the creatives with whom I spoke. My findings nuance one of the dominant scholarly and critical conclusions about television in the post-network era: that the changes in technology, distribution, business models, production, and consumption since the early 2000s, in the words of Amanda Lotz, have "created opportunities for stories much different from those [possible] in the network era."[38] The possibilities may have been there, but they were consistently contained through textual strategies that allowed for new, more complex modes of religious representation while also creating a context in which they could be downplayed as religious. The religious aspects of those stories, which were part of a matrix of innovative stylistic and narrative elements, were avoided in creative discourse because they did not adhere to the culture and politics of both television production and upscale audience tastes. Instead of heralding these changes in acceptable content regarding religion, creatives avoided the notion of their newness. Only in 2015 and 2016 did creatives begin to shift how they discussed religion as a subject of their narratives: while certain discursive containment strategies remained, new distribution outlets and a more fragmented media marketplace enabled space for both edgier representations of religion and greater creative acknowledgment of religion. In 2016 there was finally more room for "much different" religious stories and storytelling, but as this book demonstrates, they did not arrive at this point in a straightforward manner. Whereas other types of "edge" (such as race, language, sexuality, and sex) emerged much earlier in television—and were promoted as edgy in marketing and by creators—it took much longer for religion to appear or be talked about as such.

Divine Programming covers four strategies for understanding religion throughout this time period, explored through chapter pairings grouped thematically. Although this book presents a progression, it is one of eras and themes—from neo-network to post-network and Peak TV, from little to no containment of Christianity to distancing, displacement, outright dismissal, and finally acknowledgment and utilization—instead of chronologically. Part I illustrates the ways that white Christianity's middlebrow associations were solidified in the 1990s and their incompatibility with post-network-era industrial structures and desires. Part II maps the use of place and race in realist dramas to distance Christianity from those middlebrow tastes. Part III analyzes the ways that fantastic genre conventions have been utilized to displace religion from its middlebrow associations. Finally, Part IV examines the ultimate acknowledgment of religion in order to use it for distinction in the era of Peak TV, affirming the solid boundaries between upscale audience niches and the diminished middlebrow audience. Altogether, these four sections also perform a loose chronological narrative of the progression of Christian representation and how creatives discuss it. With each chapter focusing on a cluster of shows, the seven chapters demonstrate how both the representation of and creatives' understanding of religion are affected by legacy ideologies and practices. These ideologies and practices, including genre expectations and assumptions by creatives about target audiences, shape how religion and its representations are positioned within prime-time television's production discourses. Cumulatively, these discourses show that religion, even as an abstraction, was anomalous to the representational and production practices within the contemporary television industry, which otherwise seems to be characterized by greater openness and textual possibilities in the first dozen years of the post-network era. In the 2015–2016 season, the confluence of both industrial and cultural changes over the course of a dozen-year boom led to a shift closer to the positioning of other contemporary post-network-era subjects such as sex, violence, and explicit content.

Chapter 1 presents a brief history of representing religion on television before focusing on two 1990s shows, *Touched by an Angel* and *7th Heaven*. This chapter demonstrates how, during the neo-network era, Hollywood TV's creatives and executives linked Christianity with a middlebrow mode of representation that worked in the 1990s but became perceived as atavistic as nichification progressed. The naturalized ideology equating religious and middlebrow underlies the habitual practice of later creatives who avoided having their shows labeled "religious" or even discussing religion-qua-religion. *Touched by an Angel* featured moralistic episodic adventures of guardian angels helping those in need. Its star (Roma Downey) and executive producer (Martha Williamson) were both evangelical Christians, further strengthening the equation of religious representation with Christian messaging and appeal. Industrially, during its initial run, *Touched by an Angel's* positioning by CBS marketers and in syndication on "God-flavored" PAX-TV reinforced its Christianity in both representation and audience targeting.[39] The series *7th Heaven*, meanwhile, was a family drama that centered on the reverend of a suburban town, his wife, and their many children. Each moral lesson learned by the Camden family was framed by Reverend Camden's vocation, and many episodes featured his Sunday-morning homilies. Although *7th Heaven* was not positioned to be as overtly religious as *Touched by an Angel*, both shows treated religion as inoffensively as possible, while creatives also sought to highlight the shows' ability to appeal to a broad audience. This treatment contrasts with that of *Nothing Sacred*, an edgy drama about a Catholic priest, which both lacked ratings and faced significant backlash for its challenging approach to Christianity. Both *Touched by an Angel* and *7th Heaven* represented a moment in the history of American prime time in which a mass-like audience was still sought. As a result, both shows' religious representations were deliberately uncontroversial so as not to alienate the assumed-religious middlebrow audience that still dominated industrial thinking about viewers in the 1990s. By analyzing these shows, their industrial positioning as bound to their time, and the discourses creatives perpetuated about them, Chapter 1 demonstrates how these Christian shows illustrate later creative understandings of mainstream religious television series.

However, these mass-appeal faithful shows did not disappear in the post-network era either; rather, either they moved to religious-oriented outlets such as GMC/UP and the Hallmark Channel or, more conspicuously, their approach reappeared on mainstream television in the form of highly promoted biblical adaptations. Chapter 2 examines how these 1990s Christian shows' post-network descendants in the form of biblical adaptations solidified the assumption that religious programs attracted a middlebrow audience that alienated upscale viewers. This chapter analyzes the continuation of the approach to production, content, and audience targeting that characterized the religious dramas of the 1990s in the biblical miniseries of the 2010s. Roma Downey, the evangelical former star of *Touched by an Angel*, her husband Mark Burnett, and their production companies created a grouping of Bible adaptation dramas including *The Bible* (History, 2013*)*, *A.D.: The Bible Continues* (NBC, 2015), and *The Dovekeepers* (CBS, 2015) for cable and broadcast outlets. This second round of overtly Christian dramas enabled a discursive linkage between religious motives and Christian representation beyond the 1990s. Moreover, the discourses of failure—or at least underperformance—on broadcast television after the initial niche cable success further emphasized the diminished power of the middle-American audience in the post-network era. The persistence of linkage between mass, middle-American, faithful ideology and undesirable audiences shaped the production cultures that required religion to be both abstracted conceptually and contained by a variety of distancing or displacement strategies.

The next two chapters, Chapters 3 and 4, examine how notions of Christian culture couched in otherness from production cultures and the presumed geography and identity of upscale viewers allowed for representations of Christianity as religion within realist (non-fantastic) regimes. Chapter 3 focuses on two realist television dramas from the post-network-era boom that attempt to cultivate quality claims and audiences: *Friday Night Lights* (NBC, 2006–2011) and *Rectify* (SundanceTV, 2013–2016). These two shows represent religion—that is to say, Christianity—realistically and specifically. But more importantly, each show represents Christianity as both the dominant faith of their characters and as a characteristic part of Southern culture. The quality claims sought were incompatible with religion-represented-as-religion, given the fear of middlebrow associations within the culture of Hollywood production. Realist genre religion, therefore, required some distancing strategy, and in the examples of Chapter 3, that was the displacement of religion into an othered culture. Situated as a part of Southern culture, religion is safely incorporated into regional representation. Creatives used the milieu of the American South to shift religion away from themselves and their quality-audience expectations, maintaining their acceptability within the dominant non-Christian culture of television production. Creatives othered American Southern culture in order to explore the religious other of Christianity within it. This displacement safely contained religion within the creatives' production culture, allowing them to acknowledge religious content but only within the particular peculiarities of the American South.

In Chapter 4, I analyze the displacement of religion onto the otherness of race. This approach to religious representation allows for engagement with Christianity as a religion and, similar to Southern Christianity in Chapter 3, a cultural, lived religion. Two prime-time dramas focusing on casts and characters of color act as my case studies: Latinx Catholicism in *Jane the Virgin* (The CW, 2014–2019) and black megachurch evangelism in *Greenleaf* (OWN, 2016–). For both shows, industrial discourses actively highlight and praise their portrayals of Christianity as a means to appeal to upscale audiences for whom these raced religions are presumed wholly other and therefore interesting. These plaudits highlight the relative dearth of such strategies concerning white Christianity. Through the contrast in how Christianity is represented and discussed when it is not *white* Christianity and the parallels with the geographic othering for the sake of authenticity found in Southern Realist dramas, we gain better understanding of the role that cultural normalization and the discourse that white Christianity equates with middle-American taste, class, and values. These two approaches to realist representation of Christianity contrast with the disavowal discourses that are used to frame fantastic genre representations of a general, normalized Christianity, which are discussed in Chapters 5 and 6.

Chapter 5 explores how quality positioning affects the representation of religion within fantastic genres of fantasy, science fiction, and horror. This chapter focuses on four shows from the boom in religious content: *Battlestar Galactica* (SciFi, 2003–2009), *Lost* (ABC, 2004–2011), *The Leftovers* (HBO, 2014–2017), and *Preacher* (AMC, 2016–2019). Unlike realist dramas, fantastic genre shows can displace religion through their generic unreality. These dramas do not represent religion as traditional religion within our familiar culture, but rather they present recognizably religious and Christian elements in the functioning of belief systems with deep meaning for characters. Like the realist dramas, each of these four series was positioned and categorized as a quality drama, and so Christian elements required containment. Within the production culture for fantastic series, religion is acknowledged but contained. The fantastic genre context allows for distancing content from traditional religious narratives and distances characters' beliefs from specific religious creed, instead labeling religion as spirituality. Religious content in these fantastic series—albeit as abstracted spirituality—is acknowledged in their production cultures. This acknowledgment distinguishes these programs from the other fantastic dramas in Chapter 6. Creatives working on these four fantastic genre quality shows were relatively free in their discussion of religious representation largely because of the generic distancing from Christianity. On the spectrum of religious representational containment strategies and how creatives discuss religion, religion-as-spirituality in quality fantastic dramas occupies the midpoint between religion-as-religion and religion-as-mythology.

Chapter 6 investigates eschatological dramas in three programs that use the biblical Book of Revelation as their premise: *Supernatural* (the WB/CW, 2005–2020), *Dominion* (Syfy, 2014–2015), and *Constantine* (NBC,

2014–2015). Despite the direct connection with the New Testament, the shows' creatives disavow the religious nature of their narratives. All use the Bible as the basis for what they assert is supernatural mythology. Instead of spirituality, which maintains some sense of religious functioning, mythology is used by creatives as a specifically nonreligious term. Such a strong disavowal of religion is especially necessary for creatives working on these three shows: they had a particularly strong fear of being associated with religious culture and audiences because their narratives are so closely tied to the Bible. When dramas hew as close to biblical literalism as these three shows do, the distancing from Christianity requires an equally extreme but opposite reaction: constructing their work in religion as wholly areligious or even antireligious. The pushback against religion aligns with the assumption that the upscale fan audience these shows target is nonreligious.

The final chapter, Chapter 7, examines religious representation and creatives' understanding of it within the new realm of original programming on streaming television. This chapter's case studies of Netflix's *Daredevil* and Amazon's *Hand of God* point us to the most notable shifts thus far in the discourse and depiction of Christianity on mainstream television. Here we can see clear evidence of how changing industry context, cultural conditions, audience engagement, and continued fragmenting into niche taste cultures coalesce to lead to greater diversity and increasing—if slowly— acknowledgment of white Christianity's use in prime-time dramas. These most recent case studies illustrate how combinations of containment strategies and claims of abstraction analyzed in the earlier chapters create production environments in which religion is still risky but that risk is far less rigid than it has been throughout most of the post-network era. Along with AMC's *Preacher*, these two streaming dramas represent religion-as-religion within industrial practices that position even traditional religion as part of their edgy and quality claims. The assumed audience for these shows is still perceived as nonreligious, but after a dozen years of the boom, they are no longer imagined as wholly oppositional to religious representation. All that matters is that they steer clear of the middlebrow, direct-but-bland approach to religion.

In conclusion, I discuss how this project's focus on 1996 to 2016 represents a particular historical moment for the TV industry and its production practices, from the end of the era of mass appeal to the increasingly narrow niches that characterize Peak TV. The changing representation of white Christianity—from faithful and mass oriented to faithless for secular niche appeal—since the 1990s illustrates the waning dominance of the once sacrosanct taste culture: white, middle-class Americans. It is not that that audience has disappeared or even seen significantly less programming made for it, but instead that prime-time television aimed at upscale tastes has become central to the discourses of television. Over the previous twenty years, Christian representation largely stopped focusing on being faithful and inoffensive in prime-time dramas, and instead, religion became a post-Christian narrative tool with little connection to lived religion. At the end of the twenty-year span, this trend began to shift somewhat back toward situating Christianity as a lived religion and faith culture in television dramas because of the exponential growth of television content. I end the book by speculating briefly on the future possibilities for religious representation as Peak TV continues and eventually wanes. The duality (Christian in message and appeal for middlebrow audiences and post-Christian denial of religiousness for upscale audiences) that has been negotiated over the twenty-year period of this study has continued and heightened in late 2010s polarization in such a way that the dualism of approaches may diverge instead of continuing to be negotiated, or it may make space for an upscale variation on a Christian audience.

PART I

ESTABLISHING WHITE CHRISTIANITY'S MIDDLEBROW ASSOCIATIONS

From researching television industry production cultures for this study, a surprising pattern emerged: among shows with obviously religious narratives, the writers, producers, and executives working on them regularly labeled them as "not religious." This pattern led me to wonder what "religious" meant and means to key creative figures within the contemporary Hollywood television industry. For the writers I spoke to, their shows weren't religious and were often somewhat surprised that I asked about their religious narratives. Their unwillingness to call their shows religious or to view them as part of a history of religious television is directly related to a set of assumptions about religious representation on television, and associated assumptions about audience, genre, and production. The formation of these assumptions is exemplified in discourses around 1990s shows that were religiously didactic: evangelical, white, Christian religious messages motivated the show's creation (e.g., *Touched by an Angel*) or became associated with the show (e.g., *7th Heaven*). These kinds of shows employed overt moralizing, a religiously slanted lesson learned by both characters and viewers at the end of an episode, which in turn would resolve ongoing conflict or dramatic tension. Moreover, the shows' creative and marketing discourses did not shy from the Christian aspects, assuming the mass audience was majority Christian and thus welcoming of or at least indifferent to Christian representation. The concept of middlebrow tastes indicates blandly inoffensive creative productions associated with mass appeal.[1] The shows are well crafted but take few risks in terms of style or story, especially with regard to the Christian elements. They are meant to appeal to the broadest range of people and thus take great care to not offend or alienate any potential viewers by deviating from aesthetic or content norms. The audience targeted by these Christian shows was subsequently constructed as middlebrow. Such shows are incompatible with upscale television from the perspective of key creative and executive figures in the 1990s and beyond.

Part I of this book tracks the establishment of assumptions about religion and television dramas in the 1990s. The premises of these shows—a reverend's family life, angels helping people, adaptations of biblical stories— are the Christian foundation of their religious representations and importantly are mostly uncontained. Instead, the Christian aspects are framed as part of the appeal or at least neutrally similar to how Christianity had appeared on television before. Thus, the Christian representations in the text will receive less attention than case studies in later chapters. Part I examines the legacy of these shows as exemplars of how Christianity on dramatic television was understood before the twenty-first century and how the changing television landscape further highlights their approach as atavistic. The following two chapters demonstrate how in the American television industry a link between overt Christianity in prime-time dramas and middlebrow tastes solidified in internal logics and resulted in changes that in subsequent decades made an overt, faithful approach to Christianity significantly less viable outside of the Christian audience niche. While subsequent parts of this book focus on the ways that Christianity is narratively and discursively contained in prime-time dramas since the 1990s, this first part focuses on the type of programming that acts as the industry imaginary against which those later series are positioned. Although the shows discussed in this section are rarely evoked by name, the effect of their popularity and their usefulness as exemplars of the kinds of attitudes implied in industry discourses that already tended to shy from overt discussions of Christianity remains useful. Once the connection between middlebrow tastes and Christian representation had been established, it provided the baseline for differentiating the use of Christianity in programs targeting upscale audiences.

1

Christianity's Broad Appeal in the 1990s

Touched by an Angel and 7th Heaven

A BRIEF HISTORY: ESTABLISHING THE NORMS OF REPRESENTING CHRISTIANITY ON AMERICAN TELEVISION

Religious representation has always been a part of fictional television, albeit a small part since the early days of the medium in the classic network era. The classic network era is characterized by the oligopolistic control of television by NBC, CBS, and ABC, the three broadcast networks that controlled television as a medium, technology, and industry from the mid-1950s to the rise of cable in the mid-1980s. Television in the classic network era sought the most viewers possible to watch any given program because it was an advertising-based industry. The more viewers a show regularly had, the more the viewership could allow the networks to charge more to the sponsors, who wanted the most potential customers to see their advertisements. Advertising revenue is how broadcast networks made money. It was also how the myriad local affiliates for each network that actually broadcast the over-the-air signal gained revenue. This era of television generally sought to appeal to the most people it could and minimize the potential for viewers, local affiliates, and advertisers to be offended by network television programming. Thus, the mass audience and their perceived tastes—including what might offend them—were central to decisions about programming acceptability. This included the portrayals of religion.

From *The Goldbergs* (CBS/NBC/DuMont, 1949–1956) to *The Flying Nun* (ABC, 1967–1970) and *The Thorn Birds* (ABC, 1983), visible, overt depictions of religion have appeared throughout television history. However, when religion did appear, as in *The Flying Nun*, it was benign, designed to keep the mass audience and the advertisers free from controversy or alienation. As the classic-network era came to a close in the 1980s, however,

Divine Programming. Charlotte E. Howell, Oxford University Press (2020).
© Oxford University Press.
DOI: 10.1093/oso/9780190054373.001.0001

competition between the broadcast networks and emerging cable channels allowed for the networks to take more risks in attempting to lure an increasingly fragmented audience.[1]

In the 1980s, the television industry began to manifest the neoliberal market logic that would carry it through the next twenty-plus years.[2] Conglomeration, deregulation, and the diffusion of cable contributed to a period of greater content diversity. Michael Curtin refers to this period as the neo-network era to indicate the dialectic of both older network models and newer flexibility and industry adaptation.[3] Curtin describes the neo-network industry structure in relation to target audiences: "One of the consequences of this new environment is that groups that were at one time oppositional or outside the mainstream have become increasingly attractive to media conglomerates with deep pockets, ambitious growth objectives, and flexible corporate structures."[4] In terms of programming strategies, this consequence meant across-the-dial attempts on the part of networks and cable channels to attract the still-viable mass audience with general programming and also appeal to an affluent niche audience availed of many choices and thought to be seeking programs that had what Curtin identifies as "edge."[5]

Throughout the 1980s and 1990s, television as a medium continued to fracture. As Ien Ang argues, "The 'revolt of the viewer' [in the 1980s], then, is not some sort of romantic eruption of viewers' rebellion on the basis of their 'authentic' needs and desires, but is brought to the surface by the very technological changes introduced by the television business itself," such as the VCR, remote control, and rise of cable.[6] Aided by these industrial and technological shifts, television and its perceived audience began more extensively fracturing along taste lines. The threat of alienating the vestiges of the mass audience without finding an appropriate niche to replace it became even more pronounced as more and more options were presented to viewers. Moreover, the particularly marketable niches of the television audience were still being fought over by the broadcast and cable channels.

It was at this time in the 1980s that the notion of quality became attached to affluence and elite taste cultures, often called "upscale" by advertisers. The upscale quality audience, according to Joseph Turow, "suggested a large and growing portion of society with a disposable income that represented a marketers' dream."[7] Neo-network-era shows that sought to appeal to these upscale audiences included *Hill Street Blues* (NBC, 1981–1987), *Northern Exposure* (CBS, 1990–1995), *ER* (NBC, 1994–2009), and *Homicide: Life on the Street* (NBC, 1993–1999). On neo-network-era broadcast television of the 1980s and into the early 2000s, controversial subjects such sex, drug use, and violence became increasingly present as part of the appeal to an edgy upscale audience. Quality in this context is meant to indicate perceptions of "good" television in largely formal-aesthetic terms. John Caldwell examined the stylistic shifts toward cinematic forms on broadcast television in the 1980s, coining the term "televisuality."[8] Jason Mittell has recently written about "complex television" and its rise to prominence since the 1990s, citing narrative, aesthetics, and authorial practices cohering to form quality television.[9] For dramas, the criteria for quality currently imply cinematic aesthetics, complex characters, serial narrative structures, high production values, and often realist genres.[10] Many critics and scholars trace the current iteration of quality television to HBO's positioning of *The Sopranos* (1999–2007) as the foundation of its quality brand as "not-TV."[11] Quality television is generally understood as different from, and thus better than, regular television. The distinction constructs a raced, classed, and gendered hierarchy of power and taste. As Newman and Levine argue, "TV becomes respectable through the elevation of one concept of the medium at the expense of the other," generally at the expense of women and minority perspectives.[12] Quality, in its separateness from regular television, also operates counter to middlebrow tastes.

Concomitant with this turn toward slightly more niched approach to broadcasting was, as Ron Becker argues in *Gay TV and Straight America*, the rise in gay representation as a way to appeal to a socially liberal, urban-minded professional ("slumpy") taste culture of upscale viewers favored by advertisers in the 1990s.[13] More gayness on television "was convenient because, as a cultural category, homosexuality fit so comfortably with the socially liberal, fiscally conservative politics many 'sophisticated,' well-educated, and upscale American found resonant in the neoliberal political climate of the 1990s."[14] More recently, Julia Himberg has "push[ed] beyond the critique of LGBT television representations as only commodified, homonormative, and assimilationist, in order to identify spaces of contradiction and intervention" in the contemporary television industry.[15] Through her interviews with LGBT industry workers, Himberg discovered that "many openly gay and lesbian workers in positions of power have been able to navigate and operate within the corporate media industry space in explicitly political ways."[16] Gay representation is valued in its appeal to upscale audiences, and LGBTQIA (lesbian, gay, bisexual, trans, queer or questioning, intersex, asexual) identities are acknowledged and accepted within the cultures of American television production.

In contrast to the hip and edgy rise in representations of LGBTQIA identities since the mid-1990s, Christianity was associated with the mass audience who loved wholesome but banal shows like *Touched by an Angel* (CBS, 1994–2003). The two audience identities were often pitted against each other. According to Becker, CBS's "'Welcome Home' campaign unveiled in September 1996 sent a clear message that CBS was the network for . . . those older, more rural, more conservative viewers turned off by the New York sensibilities of slumpy TV."[17] Gay representation was to be lauded as progressive and appealing to quality audiences, but Christian representation was to be avoided as industrially and culturally regressive unless it could be reframed for these progressive upscale audiences. This reframing often occurred through discursively distancing the production of Christian narratives from their religiousness.

Those who are targeted by the television industry hold a degree of power. Within this study, quality audiences act as the paragon of upscale target audiences to which many of the post-network case studies are appealing, but they have been constructed within the industry as oppositional to religion. Thus, the imaginary of the quality audience—and upscale audiences more generally—is one of the key factors assumed by prime-time production cultures, a factor that necessitates that religion be contained in both practice and representation.

Throughout the neo-network era, religion remained a minimal, strictly contained topic on commercial TV, even as it became more prominent in wider cultural conversations. The 1980s marked the end of silence for the so-called Moral Majority, and thereafter religion became more prominent culturally. Part of this expansion included the growth of media made by and targeted to evangelical audiences, entertainment that adhered to the moralism of conservative Christians who felt that they were at odds with mainstream media.[18] While the evangelical media industries grew parallel to mainstream media, starting in the 1980s, they were not designed to be exclusive. Part of evangelizing is reaching out to religiously bear witness for Christianity to the wider culture.[19] The religious media culture of the televangelists was fundamental to this shift, spreading their message beyond the boundaries previously separating mainstream and religious media and culture. As Robert Wuthnow explains in *After Heaven: Spirituality in America since the 1950s*, "Religious leaders who advanced a conservative moral agenda, such as [Jerry] Falwell and [Pat] Robertson, attracted a great deal of media attention in the 1980s . . . Capitalizing on Americans' sense of spiritual homelessness, they argued for a return to absolute moral principles, deep faith, and personal discipline in matters of the spirit."[20] The evangelical voices of these leaders expanded beyond their televangelical pulpits and into the general public sphere. In translating their religious concerns into political ones, they initiated a cultural moment in which American Christianity played a larger role in American society, beyond the church and chapel.

Although religion may have gained greater prominence in American culture in the 1980s and 1990s, on prime time, scripted television religion was still generally avoided or presented vaguely and minimally. This was the case even for neo-network-era quality television. In his analysis of religious representation on *Northern Exposure*, considered a quality drama, Stuart M. Hoover explains the rationale for just such a vagueness when he writes, "The salient images of traditional religion do not hold sway in an era when the authorities that support those images are in decline. A new kind of religion—and a new iconography—must emerge," an iconography of individualistic and new-age spirituality.[21] Horace Newcomb further articulates the logic driving the vagueness of religious representation in the 1980s and 1990s when he writes, "Producers avoid the specifics of belief, the words of faith, and concrete images of the transcendent like the plague. Such specificity could cost them audience. In the meantime, we are given the deeply, powerfully embedded notions of the good that must come from . . . somewhere."[22] Newcomb articulates an assumed sensibility about religion held by creatives in the neo-network era: Religion is risky and thus must be held at a distance. Specificity was perceived as particularly dangerous because it could offend large swaths of the audience who held (or did not hold) that specific belief, a prospect especially germane, given the lingering attention to the mass audience at the time.

In the 1980s, overt religion was not considered a marketable audience category. While sex, violence, extreme language, grittier and more realistic styles, and even racial diversity became markers of differentiation designed to appeal to desirable niche audiences, religion was viewed as likely to turn off those same viewers.[23] As Joseph Turow argues, "The bulk of distinctions that people from the marketing and media worlds grappled with during the '80s and early '90s revolved around five categories: income, gender, age, race, and ethnicity."[24] Overt Christianity remained mostly relegated to the Christian lifestyle industry that had begun in the 1970s.[25] Mainstream fictional television in the 1980s and through the 1990s did produce a small number of shows with overtly Christian content, such as *Amen* (NBC, 1986–1991), *Father Dowling Mysteries* (NBC/ABC, 1989–1991), *Highway to Heaven* (NBC, 1984–1989) and *Touched by an Angel* (CBS, 1994–2003), but such shows largely relied on a vague set of religious signs and symbols. The most popular trope involved do-gooder angels, which existed without any ostensible connection to a particular scripture or dogma. However, as I argue in this chapter, the mode of angelic help presented is inherently Christian and can be understood as vague nondenominational representation in the American cultural context precisely because of Christianity's dominance.

While *Touched by an Angel* and *Highway to Heaven* presented a vague morality that was implicitly linked to Christianity, another show was more directly associated with the institutional construction of belief and became one of the most well-known mainstream/religious crossover successes on television: *7th Heaven* (the WB/CW, 1996–2007). The series was a teen-oriented melodrama focused on a Protestant minister and his family that was the WB's top program from 1999 through 2006. Despite the show's longevity and ratings success, the WB did not develop other shows that shared its wholesome Christian elements. Although the potential for a religious audience was increasingly visible and relevant for mainstream media from the 1980s through the end of the twentieth century, given the rise of the Moral Majority in the wider culture, industry executives and advertisers still did not perceive them as an identifiable or desirable niche for mainstream television. Thus, this audience was rarely catered to in mainstream television. Furthermore, the appeal of religiously themed content to a secular audience remained uncertain.

THE NEO-NETWORK LEGACY: DEFINING AND AVOIDING "RELIGIOUS TV" WITHIN MIDDLEBROW APPEAL

The linkage between middlebrow tastes and television's mass-appeal orientation in the twentieth century began at the inception of television. In her book *Heartland TV* Victoria E. Johnson states, "Midwesternness was the frame through which television was introduced [by Westinghouse at the 1939 World's Fair], through which its uses were imagined, and through which its ideal audience was represented. Regional appeals were invoked to ally television and its uses with national, consensual ideals and values."[26] Uniting these ideals and values was a basic sense of middlebrow taste: that is, conserv-ative in that it reinforced social norms instead of challenging them. Darrell Y. Hamamoto wrote that the sitcom was the most televisual genre because it reverted to the status quo by the end of each episode, reinforcing narrative and thus ideological conservatism.[27] If middlebrow tastes can be fundamen-tally identified as inoffensively "normal" or at least an unchallenging habitus between elite and lowbrow tastes, those tastes have dominated television's programming and identity since its beginnings as long as it remained a me-dium oriented to the generalized, mass identity of the United States.

The geographical imaginary of the Midwest as the "heartland" of the United States is characterized by a broader "centrist—and, increasingly, post-1960s, neoconservative—traditional cultural values and 'mass,' 'low' market dispositions."[28] Johnson's argument focuses on specifying geographical influ-ence over these broad ideas about the television audience as they have shaped television. And certainly the particular characteristics—homogeneous, conservative, and white, for example—of the Midwestern United States still shapes cultural and political ideologies, but they continue to also be the con-centrated "heart" of more general ideas of America and its citizens unaltered by the multicultural globalism of urban centers. Of course, the idea of unal-terability, of a true "core" of Americanness, is itself facing challenges and struggles in the twenty-first century. The American Midwest has, in the 2010s especially, become a site of creeping demographic change as urban popula-tion density has increased and affordability has decreased.[29] The heartland represents a synecdoche for the general idea of "America" that reinforces associations among middlebrow, white, and Christian characteristics.

Whiteness is a key attribute of this idea of the American heartland, and one that has only since the late 2000s re-entered into broad cultural discussions about who counts as America. With regard to this idea of America's heart-land, Johnson argues, "the persistent association of 'midwesternness' *as* 'white' is critical to the region's revaluation—particularly in moments of so-cial upheaval and trauma—as 'home' of 'authentic' cultural populism and traditional U.S. values."[30] This whiteness, however, is the largely unmarked and unacknowledged whiteness of America's vast middle class. It is not nec-essarily the poor whiteness often associated with the South (discussed more in Chapter 3) or the upper-class whiteness of so-called coastal elites, nor is it whiteness highlighted in contrast to nonwhiteness (which I will discuss in Chapter 4). The normalized whiteness of the American heartland-*qua*-"au-thentic" America is perpetuated in representations targeting this middlebrow audience. As Richard Dyer writes in *White*, "Whites are everywhere in representation. Yet precisely because of this and their placing as norm they seem not to be represented to themselves *as* whites but as people who are variously gendered, classed, sexualized and abled. At the level of racial representation, in other words, whites are not of a certain race, they are just the human race."[31] Normalized whiteness, a racial identity that structures much of American society and dominates in terms of media representation, is especially valuable to middlebrow tastes because of its invisibility as a specific identity. In the 1990s this identity was especially true as cable channels—and eventually broadcast networks—began, as Jennifer Fuller argues in her article, "Branding Blackness," using racially diverse casts to target upscale audiences.[32] Nonwhite racial representation became another way to be edgy in contrast to normal television. The use of blackness to appeal to elite tastes further solidified the connection between whiteness and middlebrow tastes.

For Christian-themed shows like *7th Heaven* and *Touched by an Angel*, the white and middlebrow characteristics of the mass American audience intersected overtly with the understanding of that audience as Christian. Richard Dyer identifies the ways that Christianity, while not inherently white, has been shaped by whiteness for centuries, including "the role of the Crusades in racializing the idea of Christendom (making national/geographic others into enemies of Christ); the gentilising and whitening of the image of Christ and the Virgin in painting; the ready appeal to the God of Christianity in the prosecution of doctrines of racial superiority and imperialism."[33] As discussed in the introduction to this book, representations of religion had been relatively rare on television, but much of television's programming in the twentieth century has been guided by the idea that white, middlebrow culture in America is predominantly Christian, and thus structured to avoid offending white Christian sensibilities. Such thinking further reinforces the idea of middlebrow audiences as desirous of unchallenging stories that reinforce the cultural status quo. When the neo-network religious dramas articulated that, it occurred through Christian moralizing that was understood as connoting religiousness.

Both *7th Heaven* and *Touched by an Angel* had a significant impact in the industry as examples of mass-audience-oriented successes on broadcast outlets.[34] Both shows helped fledgling networks establish their brand and build their audience, the WB network and PAX-TV (the small network anchored by *Touched by an Angel* reruns), respectively. Significantly, *7th Heaven* and *Touched by an Angel* were the longest-running and most commercially successful religious dramas in the neo-network era. These family-friendly moralizing dramas were highly successful and moreover served as key points against which later shows and creatives reacted in the post-network-era boom in religious programming. Within the television industry, however, their moment of peak popularity and commercial success is also the moment when Hollywood creatives turned away from embracing the notion, if not the reality, of representing religion on television. That is, "religious" became associated with Christian moralizing, which was creatively undesirable. Following that association, creatives and executives avoided acknowledging religion within their work on dramatic shows. Such an industrial logic appeared to be buttressed by the backlash, boycotting, and cancellation of ABC's overtly religious one-season drama, *Nothing Sacred*, which focused on a Catholic priest working on his own human flaws and serving his inner-city parish; in melding the murky morality of quality dramas and a thorough depiction of the realistic trials of priesthood, *Nothing Sacred* did not appeal to the middlebrow audience but preceded the turn to using religion to appeal to upscale audiences.[35] Its failure affirmed the believed gap between religious television and upscale audiences in the 1990s. This was the case even as representations of religion began appearing more frequently on prime-time dramatic television, starting in 2003.

This chapter investigates these Christian television shows of the 1990s and situates them in their historical, industrial, and discursive context. In so doing, I can establish key reference points for later attitudes of creatives with regard to the presentation—or avoidance—of religion on scripted television. A certain set of assumptions among creatives about religious representation in prime-time American dramas has developed in the twenty-first century, and many of these assumptions are in response to the terms set by the two shows that are the focal point of this chapter: *Touched by an Angel* and *7th Heaven*.

OLD NETWORKS AND NEW NETLETS: BROADCAST IN THE NEO-NETWORK ERA

The 1990s stand out in television history as a time during which broadcasting dramatically transformed in both structure and representation. A range of new cable channels and systems launched and expanded, and two new major broadcast channels (the WB and UPN) were launched during this time as well. A few years earlier, Fox had been the first new "fourth" broadcast channel to appear in almost fifty years, challenging the monopoly held by the three major networks. In general, the desirable audience for the "Big Three" of CBS, ABC, and NBC was the mass audience.[36] These conditions shaped the broadcast networks' programming strategies in the 1990s. For the most part, CBS continued with the least objectionable programming strategy of mass appeal that had driven much of its classic-network-era programming. Although CBS turned to quality sitcoms in the 1970s and continued to produce the occasional quality drama like *Northern Exposure, Touched by an Angel* represented CBS at its most mass philosophy. CBS in the 1990s generally courted the heartland audience.[37] Some of their programs, including *Touched by an Angel*, represented the height of middlebrow inoffensiveness, which I see in terms of style, genre, narrative, and character.

ABC, meanwhile, succeeded with the popular thank-goodness-it's-Friday (TGIF) family comedy block (e.g., *Step By Step* [1991–1998], *Family Matters* [1989–1998], *Full House* [1987–1995]), as well as its newly formed industrial ties to Disney, which purchased ABC in 1995. ABC positioned itself as a "family-friendly" network, a designation that remained even after they canceled their TGIF block in the mid-1990s, around the time of the WB's launch. NBC, in contrast, gained prominence in the 1990s for its quality "Must-See TV" block of upscale Thursday night comedies, which included the sitcom *Seinfeld* (1989–1998) as well as its tent-pole medical drama, *ER* (1994–2009). Fox's youth—both in terms of the age of the network and its primary target-audience demographics (both younger and more diverse than the "Big Three")—led it to pursue narrower strategies of audience targeting and exhibit a greater reliance on "edge" to set their programs apart from the other broadcast networks. Into this landscape, in 1995, two new networks sought to find their place as "netlets" that bridged broad- and narrowcasting strategies. These netlets were the WB and UPN.

The WB and UPN both emerged in January 1995 and, from their inception, shared a number of characteristics: both used Fox's early years and programming strategies as a model; both were distribution arms of television production studios, Warner Bros and Paramount, respectively; both vied for the same local affiliates to carry their new networks so that they could reach a level of market "clearance"; and both narrowed the broadcast idea of "mass" audience to a more youth-oriented but still broader-than-niche-cable appeal while trying to figure out how they could fill key programming gaps left by the major networks.[38] At the WB's first presentation at the "upfronts,"

WB executives told the room of advertisers present that "they were taking 'dead aim' at the kids, teens, and young adults ABC had left behind with the dismantling of its 'TGIF' Friday comedy lineup."[39] The WB launched with original comedy programming (such as *Unhappily Ever After* [1995–1999], a *Married . . . with Children* [Fox, 1987–1997] clone) and the rejected-at-NBC *The Wayans Bros.* (1995–1999). During its second year, WB executives turned to legendary producer Aaron Spelling (*Charlie's Angels* [ABC, 1976–1981], *Dynasty* [ABC, 1981–1989], *Beverly Hills 90210* [Fox, 1990–2000]) to help them create a "light family drama" that executives believed "was not like anything else on the air."[40] They were deliberately targeting the audience that mass-appeal sitcoms had succeeded with, but in an hour-long format. This program became the WB's most successful drama in the life of the netlet: *7th Heaven*. It targeted certain segments of the mass audience that were perceived to be largely abandoned as a result of the shifts at the broadcast networks taking root in the 1990s. As the netlets further developed their programming, they would continue to narrow both their genre offerings and their target audiences, meaning that the narrative and stylistic features of middlebrow fare like *7th Heaven* became outliers to their brand identities.

A few years after the launch of the WB and UPN, PAX-TV came on the scene as a much smaller over-the-air network. PAX-TV was launched in 1998 by the "media magnate and professed born-again Christian Lowell White 'Bud' Paxson" to appeal to those for whom God was part of their everyday lives.[41] The netlet favored carefully curated second-run syndication deals that fit their brand, rather than opting for original scripted fare. PAX-TV had far fewer affiliates than any of the major networks and netlets, and a much smaller audience than even the WB or UPN. PAX-TV created a brand focused on appealing to the middlebrow audience and its attendant "God-flavor."[42] When it launched in 1998, PAX-TV used reruns of *Touched by an Angel* as both a programming anchor and an indicator of brand identity through its appeal to middlebrow, religious audiences. In addition to *Touched by an Angel*, which was already a big hit on CBS, PAX-TV's stable of reruns relied on other CBS productions such as *Diagnosis Murder* (1993–2002) and *Dr. Quinn, Medicine Woman* (1993–1998).[43] PAX-TV's programming aligned with the output of CBS's in-house production studio at the time, since both CBS and PAX-TV were marketing themselves as "explicitly *broad*casters catering to a multigenerational family audience that is, in their vision, ideally middle American," which includes Christian morals and middlebrow tastes.[44]

One thing that these new networks of the 1990s shared was a heavy reliance on favorable affiliate relations. ABC, NBC, CBS, and, to a lesser degree, Fox all had established affiliates in place by the mid-1990s. In the preceding decades, a system had emerged in which affiliate separation from the parent network was largely not done. However, with the advent of new networks, the threat of losing affiliate stations loomed. The newly launched netlets of the WB and UPN were both scrambling to affiliate with the same one or two independent stations within a television market or, in the case of PAX, relegated to lower-quality UHF frequencies. Within this context of competition, offending even one affiliate by airing controversial or edgy fare could be disastrous. Thus, strategies of containment for potentially controversial fare were a market imperative.

RELIGIOUS MESSAGES AND THE MIDDLEBROW AUDIENCE: *TOUCHED BY AN ANGEL*

In the mid-to-late 1990s, *Touched by an Angel* presented a mode of storytelling that was unusual for network broadcast television: a drama with a religious agenda. The show's executive producer, Martha Williamson, and stars, Roma Downey and Della Reese, were all devoutly Christian and were open with the press from the time of the show's inception about how their religion shaped the content. As Victoria Johnson notes in her study of CBS, PAX, and *Touched by an Angel*, the show was key to CBS's 1996 "Welcome Home!" marketing campaign and programming strategy. *Touched by an Angel*'s significance within the spectrum of neo-network broadcasting was underlined when its reruns were used to anchor the heartland-oriented upstart broadcast network PAX-TV in the late 1990s.[45] Johnson argues that PAX-TV made explicit the connections between heartland audiences and religious belief, writing, "CBS's and PAX's institutional identities are premised on the profitability of three concepts . . . home, the nuclear family, and belief in God."[46] This belief in God is contextualized within American Christian norms assumed about the mass audience that enjoyed *Touched by an Angel*. The show featured a trio of helpful angels, moving through American society, and helping those who need it. They are benign and largely unencumbered by obvious evangelism, but they are still angels and situated within a Christian context.

From the first episode of the series, "The Southbound Bus," the Christian angelic frame is strongly hinted at even before the first words of dialogue are spoken. The camera pans across a desert setting through which Monica (Roma Downey) walks barefoot, untroubled by the rattlesnake nearby. She takes off her white scarf and lets it fly in the wind, where it transforms into a white dove, a symbol of the Holy Ghost within the Christian Holy Trinity. She walks up to Tess (Della Reese), who is singing "I am thankful for this beautiful day," with a cadence that echoes Southern black church songs. Monica and Tess are presented as otherworldly, alerting the audience that these are the titular angels of the show. The series' general plotline then launches as Tess tells Monica that she has been moved from Search and Rescue to Case Work. These characters are angels, serving God, working to help humans through their case work. Tess says, "Somebody—and I do mean Somebody—has decided to give you a promotion." To which Monica responds, "Hallelujah, I'm a case worker!" With the emphatic second use of "Somebody," Tess points up at the sky, indicating that individual is God, or at least a member of the Heavenly Host. The two angels discuss the bravery it takes to be human; "And they don't even know what we know," Monica says. "God help them," Tess responds before giving Monica advice about taking on a human form long-term. These exchanges, particularly the last—and final, most overt—invocation of God, are expressed with sincerity. There is no winking or tongue-in-cheek distancing. This opening scene sets the dominant tone for the series: joyful, grateful, optimistic, Christian.

Such is the attitude of the angels who are the central characters of the series, but throughout the series, they must deal with the modern doubters as well. The show's episodic narrative structure allows for the angels to time and again bring doubters into the fold, to reveal to them God's love. Later in the first episode, for example, Monica reveals herself to be an angel to Christine, a woman who left her family after her youngest child died in her crib. She tearfully and angrily asks Monica, "You're an angel? So what? What are you doing here now? Where the hell were you a year ago? Where was the angel when my baby died alone in her crib?" As Christine breaks down sobbing, the light around Monica brightens to the point of saturation as the high notes on a harp are strung. Monica tells her there was an angel with her baby that night and that angel remains with her child in heaven. Christine looks into Monica's face, and an image and sound of a laughing baby is superimposed as Monica says, "God loves you, Christine, so much you can't even imagine. And so do I." After Christine leaves, overwhelmed, Monica gets down on her knees and prays to God for help. Faith, particularly that of traditional Christianity, is the moral, narrative, and emotional guiding force for the series, made evident and overt in its first episode, and it carries through the entire series. The sincere, unambiguous, central appeals to God and God's work through the angels don't shy away from—and in fact embrace—Christian moral lessons such as forgiveness, love, repentance, and often the ideal of a unified nuclear family. It is not that these lessons are necessarily Christian, but in the context of *Touched by an Angel* (and also *7th Heaven*) they are framed in terms of Christian teachings and culture.

Although *Touched by an Angel* appealed to religious audiences, it was not explicitly targeted toward them. The religious appeal was largely a by-product of the show's middlebrow moralizing within a slightly abstracted Christian imaginary of the mass American audience. That is, there was nothing potentially alienating or challenging about the show's representation of religion, its storytelling, or its style. It was a mainstream episodic drama with an uplifting message at the end of each episode. Moreover, in the summer of 1996, when *Touched by an Angel* was positioned at the core of CBS's "Welcome Home!" programming slate, it aired on Sunday nights preceding family films like *Tuesdays with Morrie* on "America's Night at the Movies."[47] This programming decision by CBS anchored *Touched by an Angel* on the family night, Sunday, and aligned it with similar moralizing telefilms with their own bit of "God-flavor." Its generally unremarkable style and storytelling are key to *Touched by an Angel*'s middlebrow associations.

Middlebrow is primarily a designation of audience, but like quality, that audience taste culture is an imaginary created by content producers and the various television industry intermediaries that influence the system of audience targeting. *Touched by an Angel*'s normal genre, style, marketing, storytelling, and audience exemplify the multivalent connotations of middlebrow that are attached to it. Middlebrow is one way of talking about taste, somewhere between elite and low-taste cultures; it occurs only in relation to highbrow and lowbrow designations and is defined mainly by defying classification as either. As Pierre Bourdieu argued, "Taste classifies, and it classifies the classifier. Social subjects, classified by their classifications, distinguish themselves by the distinctions they make, between the beautiful and the ugly."[48] That is, middlebrow is a taste culture defined by that which it is not: highbrow (in television, elite and its subdivision quality) or lowbrow (trash television), neither beautiful nor ugly, merely inoffensive. In the neo-network era during which broadcasters were starting to shift away from the idea of a mass audience, and particularly rejecting the tastes associated with mass appeal attained through middlebrow programming, the seeds of post-network-era avoidance of such middlebrow appeal were sown.

Touched by an Angel's industrial positioning as a comforting, religious show and outlier to the rise in quality programming was the basis for CBS's and PAX's marketing. Both CBS and PAX still sought a broad audience as opposed to quality audiences and their linkages to urban, affluent, white, and coastal elites. The connection between religious programming and middlebrow audiences solidified around *Touched by an Angel*. Johnson states, "CBS and PAX thus argue that they are the last true, populist, democratic American broadcasters whose mission is to serve a core audience of real, God-fearing Americans who have otherwise been 'forgotten' by America's 'elite' popular producers."[49] This "core audience of real, God-fearing Americans" is the basis of the mass audience imaginary. The construction of mass and the appeal to it, placed in opposition to quality elites, allowed emerging neo-network-era broadcasters to acknowledge these viewers within a system that was "forgetting" the mass audience. Within the context of networks shifting toward more quality programming, practices such as employing overt religious representations, such as angels and explicit prayer, could signify acknowledgment of the middlebrow audience that other networks left behind in favor of edgy programming that did not align with the mass audience's assumed Christian cultural values.

Edgy and quality programming had been part of the broadcast landscape since at least *Hill Street Blues* in the 1980s, but a tipping point was being reached due in part to the influence and success of NBC's Must-See TV programs as well as some of cable's early, critically acclaimed original programming such as *The Larry Sanders Show* (HBO, 1992–1998) that was competing for the quality audience. *Touched by an Angel* represented a major television ratings and commercial success that featured religious representations at the core of its narrative. During its third through sixth seasons, it was in the top ten of Nielsen ratings.[50] In turn, it can be placed in contrast to the rising prominence of elite tastes, audiences, and programs. Within the industry, CBS and PAX programmers and marketers defined *Touched by an Angel* in ways that were not only outside of strategies of edge and upscale quality-audience appeal, but also antithetical to such strategies.[51]

For the idea of the audience that CBS and PAX were targeting via *Touched by an Angel* in the 1990s, quality equated with elitism. This popular versus elite binary was increasingly politicized not only in this case; more broadly, this was becoming one of the foundational tensions of the post-1980s culture wars in America, fanned by the rise of the Moral Majority. While the distinctions between high and low culture and the populations to which these forms appeal were far from new even at that time, the antipathy with which each side treated the other became increasingly aggressive and hostile in the 1990s. Certain types of popular, low-, and middlebrow culture became rallying points for conservative Americans who saw American culture generally being led by the coastal elites toward a too-speedy shift in what it meant to be American, toward multiculturalism instead of the assimilationist melting pot, and toward nonbelief instead of one nation under God. *Touched by an Angel* spoke to a certain (white, Christian, lower-to-middle class) group's sense of being left out of the mass medium of television and provided a space for their perspective (and faith) to be heard and venerated.

The appeal to middle America and its middlebrow, conservative faith and tastes made commercial sense in the 1990s industrial context. Johnson notes that CBS's and PAX's success in the late 1990s were "as the only media outlets that speak for the post-1960s 'silent majority', those presumed to occupy a figurative and literal, ideological and geographical, affective, tangible, devout American middle."[52] *Touched by an Angel*'s 1990s popularity and success, as well as its industrial position as anchor for both CBS and PAX-TV's middlebrow appeal in the neo-network era, situate it as a key turning point in how religious television was understood within the industry. Namely, it was linked to that "devout American middle," a middle that was losing its value to marketers relative to other more finely tailored demographics. The show's articulation of religion through overt but vague (talk of God but not Jesus) religious messaging, aided by its "out" Christian creatives, was the basis for marketing it to religious audiences in opposition to elite audiences. The show marks a moment when the religious audience began to be cast as outsiders to the mainstream of television production and journalistic discourse about the industry. Then along came their own niche broadcaster in the form of PAX-TV, which was able to reclaim as religious a program not originally marketed as overtly religious when it aired on CBS. A similar set of circumstances—in which religion was a subject (and an audience) cast as outside of mainstream television production—recurs but with different resonances, in relation to *7th Heaven*.

ATTEMPTING TO AVOID "PREACHY": *7TH HEAVEN*

The series *7th Heaven* (the WB/CW, 1996–2007) was the WB's top-rated program from 1999 to 2006, reaching as many as 12.5 million viewers, although this viewership still usually placed it out of the top one hundred in Nielsen ratings.[53] As noted above, at the time of its premiere in 1996, netlet WB was reaching a narrower broadcast audience than its competitors and providing a more limited programming schedule. In addition, it was networked to fewer affiliate stations than the major broadcast networks. The WB, like the other young networks of the 1990s, built its success by appealing to a niche-mass-hybrid audience, i.e., young adults. Jordan Levin, an executive at the WB while *7th Heaven* was developed and aired, described the show as a family series first and foremost. But, as he acknowledged, using the term "family" to market a drama was risky at the time. However, with *7th Heaven*, the WB found a successful family drama in the lower-stakes world of netlet television broadcast.

A teen-oriented family drama, *7th Heaven* was focused on a Protestant minister and his family. Eric Camden (Stephen Collins), his wife, Annie (Catherine Hicks), and their five (later, seven) children provided ample fodder over the course of eleven seasons of episodic narratives to tackle a variety of dramatic and topical storylines. The Camden children and their friends struggled—usually only for the length of an episode—with issues such as alcohol and drug use, sexual harassment, homelessness, abuse, and teen pregnancy. Unlike *Touched by an Angel*, *7th Heaven* did not make its overtly religious frame obvious in the first minutes of its pilot. Rather, the series' first episode spends its first act establishing the domestic setting and family dynamics: the romance between the parents, the angsty teenagers and puckish children, and the fact that this family is functional, as evidenced by shots of them saying grace and eating dinner together. Eric's vocation as a Protestant minister doesn't get mentioned until almost halfway through the episode, at which time it is treated like a reveal as a shot begins at the reverend's shoes and then pans up as he begins delivering a sermon. Many episodes of the series, especially in the early seasons, tended to include at least one scene in the church. As Richard Wolff points out, "The role of the church was presented as a normal, everyday part of the Camden family life."[54] Most episodes centered around the Camden children—teenagers fitting the brand and demographic targeted by the WB—but with Annie and Eric as strong guiding figures. In fact, *7th Heaven* was a family drama first, a show about a reverend second but still significantly. These scenes usually had Reverend Camden delivering a homily from the pulpit in his church to tie into the lessons learned by the Camden children (and the show's viewers). Like *Touched by an Angel*, the moralizing offered by each episodic narrative is framed by Christianity and its teachings, unlike lessons learned from other family dramas like *Gilmore Girls* (the WB/CW, 2000–2007). The use of the space of the church and a vestment-clad reverend moves the moralizing into a clearly religious context, albeit one based in that reverend's family life. However, *7th Heaven*, unlike *Touched by an Angel*, used the family drama elements as its main narrative frame, with Christianity infused in subtle ways that more clearly reflected religious lived experience. Christianity was clearly a strong thread in the life of the Camden family, but it didn't define the Camdens in the same way that it did the angels of *Touched by an Angel*. Of course, this is also the difference between a drama focused on supernatural figures like angels that are foundationally religious and a family drama more realist in its orientation.

Sometimes, the church aspects of the show drive an episode's plotline, as in episodes featuring the aftermath of arson at a nearby black church in the first-season episode "The Color of God"; when one Camden daughter begins researching other religions in the first-season episode "Choices"; or when Reverend Camden's church's services are set to be televised in the second-season episode "Lead, Follow, or Get out of the Way." These episodes, and the centrality of the church in their narratives, are exceptions to the general thrust of the show's episodic narratives. The thread of religion persists enough to make these episodes normal for the series and its characters but not the norm for the series as a whole. However, when a moral lesson is learned, whether in these more religiously oriented episodes or more standard storylines, especially one that is particularly controversial or clearly meant to be a moral message, it is often done in relation to Christianity. The religious framing gained by Reverend Camden's literal preaching turns after-school-special type of moralizing into preachy messaging in the discourse about the show.

While family-based television comedies such as the TGIF block on ABC in the early 1990s were extremely successful, Levin argued that producing a family drama was innovative and thus risky for the fledgling the WB network. He said, "We knew we had to have a family series [but at that moment] family was a dirty word. It was considered a turn-off in that a family hour had not worked on television in over a generation."[55] However, the WB benefited both from its industrial position as a new netlet with lower ratings expectations than other networks had and from the support of its Warner Bros. parent company, which helped defray costs of production through vertical integration. Nonetheless, the association between religion and middlebrow tastes established by *Touched by an Angel* had the potential to alienate the key target demographic of the WB: young, white adults. As noted above, religion already had become associated with middlebrow audiences and thus was perceived by creatives and executives as counter to the prevailing desire for edgy programming as it was developing in the neo-network era. With this show or others, the WB *could* have been a site for negotiating a new way of representing religion. Yet even representing religion in the least objectionable middlebrow mode was seen as risky at the time for a new netlet largely dependent on affiliate cooperation and targeting a smaller but more affluent viewership. The WB did not want to alienate its affiliates in religious markets by presenting edgy religion, but its executives also did not want their youth-oriented channel to be perceived as similar to CBS in its programming or audience.

To further help mitigate any potential risk associated with broadcasting a "religious show," the WB executives brought Aaron Spelling in to serve as producer. Then the WB executives sought a writer to package with him for the project. Levin thought Brenda Hampton (who wrote for *Mad About You* [NBC, 1992–1999]) would be a good choice because her history with sitcom writing would contribute character and humor as well as drama. Moreover, Levin states, "I knew she was from the South, from Georgia. I thought that sensibility would be important" and mesh well with Spelling, who was a Texan.[56] Even though the show was not set in the American South, Levin sensed that being Southern would help when crafting this family series. He doesn't say that he thought that because he associates Christianity or "heartland" values with the South, but it was implied in the context of our conversation.

The use of the American South as a touchstone in *7th Heaven*'s development became evident when Levin cited *The Andy Griffith Show* as a model for the show despite the fact that the Camdens did not live in the South. The creatives developing the WB's new family drama liked that Andy was both a father at home and a father figure to the town in his role as small-town sheriff, and that balance between familial and social patriarchal roles was the core dramatic tension they wanted *7th Heaven* to explore. Through this confluence of Southernness, religion, and the presumed middlebrow family audience, the WB contributed to cultivating a production environment open to representing Christianity on television, but only within a certain context: namely, as non-edgy (no cursing, little to no violence, traditional soundstage-based aesthetics), thereby linking this program to older models of TV religion, including the contemporaneous hit *Touched by an Angel*. The association of religion and Southernness cued by the interest in *The Andy Griffith Show* continued in the post-network era with Southern realist dramas that reacted in opposition to this earlier means of presentation and will be examined in Chapter 3.

Within this industrial and creative environment, Jamie Kellner, the CEO of the network at the time, introduced *7th Heaven*'s main religious element: that the patriarch of the family be a pastor. Levin described how the premise developed from there:

> We pitched that to Brenda and Aaron, not knowing what they'd think. We said, "We don't want this to be a *preachy* show with a religious agenda. We just think it's an interesting juxtaposition to have this dad struggling with just being a father while also being viewed as someone who, in people's eyes, is supposed to be held to a higher standing." We didn't know how [producers Aaron Spelling and Brenda Hampton] would react. Brenda said, "Well, can I write the character in a way that I really want to? [Do you want] this character to be very upright and upstanding? Is this a religious motivation, or is this purely dramatic?" [the WB executives responded,] "It's purely dramatic."[57]

This neo-network-era negotiation of preachiness highlights a number of themes about religious representation that recur in the discourses about producing religious representation on television throughout this study, at least until around 2015. There was and generally remains a fear on the part of creatives and executives of a negative reaction from the public: fear of being seen as disrespectful to believers, fear of alienating young and hip viewers, and fear for the writers of being seen as less creative if their work is religious. This was and remains the case even for writers who are Southerners and therefore presumed familiar with the Christian context (in contrast with the assumption of secularism in coastal cultures, a microcosm of the larger cultural presumptions that undergird my argument). Brenda Hampton is just one example. Similarly, executives voiced concern about the producers' reaction, indicating that religion's risky status in the Hollywood television industry had already taken hold by the mid-1990s. The perception that being seen as preachy (which is necessarily couched in overt Christianity) is dangerous and to be avoided was already a part of the naturalized ideology affecting dramatic television production by 1996—a point that is somewhat surprising, given that the development of *7th Heaven* overlaps with *Touched by an Angel*'s first seasons. The connection between preachy and religious messaging, and the implication that such messaging was antithetical to good dramatic writing, can be strongly inferred from Brenda Hampton's reaction. In many ways, this one anecdote told by Levin captures and illustrates a chain of logic that recurs in prime-time Hollywood dramatic storytelling for the next several decades: religion automatically makes writers and executives think of preachiness; being preachy is bad, as it is associated with a faith-based religious agenda and antithetical to what constitutes good drama; and being preachy is risky because most writers, producers, and executives are likely to worry about one another's reactions to using religion in a dramatic narrative. And preachiness and Christian religiousness are closely linked. The majority of writers and executives I spoke to had already internalized the ideology of religion as taboo at most, and risky and needing distancing at least. There is little sense of what these creatives think would be the result of using religion or being seen as religious within their industry communities, merely that it was and remained something to be avoided.[58]

7th Heaven's success countered the assumed risk Levin discussed of producing family dramas and dramas with a religious element to their premise. The religious risk, though overcome in the exemplary case of *7th Heaven*, was not built upon in the WB's subsequent programming, whereas family dramas such as *Gilmore Girls* (2000–2007) and *Everwood* (2002–2006) would become key to the WB's brand alongside the fantasy hits like *Buffy the Vampire Slayer* (the WB 1996–2001, UPN 2001–2003) and *Charmed* (1998–2006) that used the occult but largely avoided Christian theology. Although *7th Heaven* was a success, it was one that contrasted with the hegemonic ideology and thus was not incorporated into dominant practices and tastes.[59] Indeed, religion continued to be perceived by executives and creatives alike as a risky subject. Levin said of his experience of producing religion on television in the 1990s and broadcast television more generally,

> It was unwritten for a while that you don't want to touch [on religion] directly . . . Within that [commercial broadcast] world if it was front and center, that could be alienating to some people, let alone being controversial . . . Drama is driven by conflict and characters' journeys. Arcs are driven

by vulnerabilities, so if you're going to do something around religion, but you didn't want to risk offending people to the point that advertisers dropped out and stations would drop out, what kind of stories are you going to tell? They end up being incredibly *preachy* and the characters would be very one note. So if you really wanted to dig in [to religion], inherently you knew [that] was going to create these obstacles.[60]

Levin suggests that dependence on advertisers and affiliates led religion to be reduced to being presented in a "preachy" fashion. Preachiness is antithetical to what creatives want to present and be known for, and it also adversely affects channel brands, such as the WB, that depend on differentiating themselves from the undesirable middlebrow audience. Both of these assumptions still hold water in later decades but find their solidification in the 1990s. Levin did not connect this observation to *7th Heaven* directly, and in fact didn't even seem to realize that he could have been talking about the show.

The case of *7th Heaven* illustrates how industrial and cultural factors can figure into a show's development in politically loaded ways. In its initial development, executives and producers thought they were creating a show that used religion to distinguish itself from the risk of producing a family drama without dysfunction. What it became during its eleven years on the air in the public discourse about it was what the creatives and executives had initially tried to avoid: an "uncool," middlebrow, and preachy show.[61] My analysis of *7th Heaven* and its industrial positioning underscores the unwritten rule enacted by creatives and executives within the 1990s neo-network-era: religion is not a subject that can be employed to give a show edge. Levin's observation of this unwritten rule in commercial broadcast reinforces the idea that, in the period before the post-network boom, religious programming rarely appeared unless it was articulated through an inoffensive and somewhat moralizing approach. Thus, in the 1990s, we see established the connection between Christian religiousness and middlebrow appeal within television industrial discourses; subsequently, that connection increasingly ossified as undesirable in terms of both audience targeting and creatives' cultural ideology.

A pattern that I discovered throughout my interviews with individuals involved in producing series in the post-network era was that religion can be known mainly by its abnegation. Writers and executives know what they mean by describing their shows as not religious but they imply undesirable overt Christianity as the connotation of "religious." The belief of these writers and executives in the neo-network era that religious cannot also mean good or quality has persisted and indeed reached the status of industry lore. This lore is so strong and so wedded to shows like *Touched by an Angel* and *7th Heaven* that creatives need not—and likely did not—even watch the shows to react against them. The paratextual discourse around these shows was strong enough to solidify connections among religion, bland moralizing, and middlebrow audiences and tastes.

CONCLUSION

Touched by an Angel and *7th Heaven* were two successful religious dramas that aired in the years immediately preceding the 2003–2016 boom in religious dramas. These shows, and the biblical adaptations produced in the 2010s discussed in the next chapter, exemplify the characteristics of Christian dramas and illustrate how a pejorative sensibility came to construct religion as something to be avoided among creatives. The negative connotations included having a religious message that appeals to middlebrow/mass taste cultures and audiences and being defined in opposition to quality television with its cinematic aesthetics, distinct stylistic traits, complex serialized narratives, and multidimensional, often antiheroic, characters. Since 2003, writers, producers, executives, and marketers of dramas featuring religion have regularly used the idea of overt Christian messaging as a means of understanding and communicating what they are *not* doing. Religious has come to be considered antithetical to their creative ambitions and to what constitutes good television.

Because these middlebrow Christian shows were the most prominent representations of religion prior to the post-network-era boom, among creatives, middlebrow had become deeply tied to the meaning of religious when referring to television dramas. The negative associations created an environment in which it was difficult to imagine religious without the negative, middlebrow, moralizing connotations it gained in the 1990s. In mainstream production culture, even during the boom of religious representation, a show that featured religious representation was assumed to be blandly Christian and moralizing and therefore not good or commercially viable in the post-network era and its reliance on upscale audiences. This legacy of neo-network-era production cultures' understanding of religious representations on mainstream television has been kept alive in the post-network era. Such an understanding is visible, for example, through shows that can be seen as part of *Touched by an Angel*'s legacy: namely, biblical adaptations spearheaded by Roma Downey and her husband's production companies: One Three Media and LightWorkers Media. These biblical miniseries attempted to revive the mass, middlebrow appeal *Touched by an Angel* found in the 1990s but even broadcast television interests had shifted by the time they aired, perpetuating an idea of these shows being out of touch with the desired upscale audiences. The shift from successful religious dramas in the neo-network context to their incongruity in the post-network era is the focus of the next chapter.

2

Biblical Miniseries in the 2010s

Mark Burnett, Roma Downey, and Faithful Christian Representation

Although avoided by much of the Hollywood creative community, the lineage of *Touched by an Angel* and *7th Heaven* continued (as did the shows), albeit more sporadically, in the post-network era with Christian moralizing dramas such as *The Secret Life of the American Teenager* (ABC Family, 2008–2013) and *Heartland* (UP, 2007–). Particularly notable was a cycle of biblical adaptations in the early 2010s, starting with *The Bible* (History, 2013). In a 2013 NPR interview about the success of *The Bible* miniseries, *Time*'s television critic, James Poniewozik, stated the following about representing religion on American television, "There may be elements of controversy that attach to how you adapt the Bible, but the characters have been created . . . It's easier to please a large group of people, I think, when you're dealing with relatively safe material like Bible stories that have been around for thousands of years."[1] Poniewozik's analysis of the *The Bible*'s success applies to assumptions about appeal and economic viability that had been shifting toward more emphasis on such "safe" representations of Christianity in the decade after *Touched by an Angel* ended its run. Most of the biblical miniseries that appeared in the early 2010s were developed through Roma Downey's production company, LightWorkers Media, and in conjunction with her husband, *Survivor* (CBS, 2000–) and *The Apprentice* (NBC, 2004–2017) producer Mark Burnett. LightWorkers and its productions are framed as Christian by both explicit discussions of Burnett and Downey as such and as a general byproduct of their high-profile status as Christians in the television industry. This chapter looks at three of these biblical miniseries as extensions of the *Touched by an Angel* approach to religious serial dramas and how the idea of the audience that made *Touched by an Angel* a hit is no longer able to be mobilized as a mass audience in the increasingly niched television landscape of the post-network era. The series in this chapter use

Divine Programming. Charlotte E. Howell, Oxford University Press (2020).
© Oxford University Press.
DOI: 10.1093/oso/9780190054373.001.0001

Christianity as explicit religion, portraying stories and characters of the Bible as a means of spreading the gospel, or at least Christian-leaning inspiration and messaging. But they are also not solely evangelical in their audience targeting, for all three also tried to appeal to a broad audience, such as the one that watched *Touched by an Angel*. Ironically, success was achieved on a cable scale but not broadcast scale, despite the majority of Americans still identifying as Christian, indicating that the mass audience for dramas won't be found in the Christian-tinged middlebrow appeal that helped shows like *Touched by an Angel* succeed in the 1990s.

The three miniseries that will serve as case studies in this chapter were produced by Downey and Burnett and targeted to both a Christian audience and a more general audience. Following the success of *The Bible* (History, 2013), its sequel, *A.D.: The Bible Continues* (NBC, 2015), and Downey's adaptation of *The Dovekeepers* (CBS, 2015) tested the extent of the previously successful middlebrow approach to overt Christianity on prime-time television in the era of the fractured audience. On the basis of the discourses of failure surrounding both *A.D.: The Bible Continues* and *The Dovekeepers*' ratings and critical reception, the insurgent era of Peak TV proved inhospitable to the method of representation that had rocketed Downey to stardom in the neonetwork era. Thus, this chapter serves as both a continuation of Chapter 1's analysis of the 1990s Christian dramas and the example of how religion-qua-religion without othering or distancing has become incompatible with the television industry's changes since those 1990s dramas succeeded.

TOUCHED BY AN ANGEL AS MODEL: ROMA DOWNEY AND MARK BURNETT'S PURSUIT OF FAITHFUL TV IN AN INCREASINGLY UPSCALE-ORIENTED INDUSTRY

In 2013, Downey and Burnett launched a miniseries adaptation of the Bible (both the Old and New Testaments), securing the History Channel as distributor. *The Bible* miniseries began with Noah (David Rintoul) on the Arc, recounting the creation story, and each episode features dramatic adaptations of a handful of biblical stories. The miniseries was Burnett's first foray into scripted television and would serve as the jewel in LightWorkers Media's crown as well as proof that there was a place for explicitly Christian dramas in the 2010s. According to producer Brian Edwards, *The Bible* was pitched as a good fit for that cable network because of its "measure of historicity . . . That these people [in the Bible] actually existed."[2] Moreover, by explicitly positioning it as an adaptation of the Bible as historical narrative, the miniseries could operate in the liminal space between evangelizing and downplaying its religiosity. Such a line was straddled by Downey and Burnett, who are both evangelical Christians and savvy television producers. They know the pitfalls that Heather Hendershot described in *Shaking the World for Jesus*: "For nonevangelicals, Christian media are uncanny: both distant and intimate, familiar and unfamiliar in their references . . . The seams are showing. And then a message about God—but rarely Jesus—suddenly pops up. While the producers think they have casually slipped in a 'true message,' many of us feel like we've been bonked on the head by a biblical mallet."[3] Where evangelical media often tries to negotiate the secular media landscape by downplaying its religiosity, these biblical miniseries can be both overtly Christian and historical epics, ostensibly appealing to both religious and secular audiences in the tradition of biblical epics.

The biblical-epic film genre popular in the 1950s is perhaps the most useful antecedent for studying the biblical miniseries of the 2010s, at least regarding storytelling and marketing. At the same time, a resurgence in biblical-epic blockbusters in the 2010s illustrates the stark separation of Christian media and its audience and the more general Hollywood media and its audience. In the 1950s, films such as *The Robe* (Koster, 1953), *The Ten Commandments* (DeMille, 1956), and *Ben-Hur* (Wyler, 1959) assumed Christian audiences within a dominant Christian culture. The epics were produced and distributed within the context of a presumed vast but relatively homogenous mass audience, the same mass audience that television was luring away from movie theaters. Biblical epics in the 1950s often employed the new technologies of Technicolor and CinemaScope to provide an audiovisual experience that television could not.[4] The spectacle of these epics distinguished them from the quotidian programming of television. In the post-network era television has taken up the spectacular characteristics of the film epics and translated them to the spectacular events of miniseries and limited series scheduled around Christian holidays, primarily produced by LightWorkers Media for cable and broadcast in the 2010s.

The flexibility of the biblical epic as a genre for the faith-and-family crossover appeal has become the core of LightWorkers Media as well as occasionally influencing Burnett's powerful roles in United Artist Media group and MGM, which bought Burnet and Downey's One Three Media company (including the LightWorkers Media banner) in 2015.[5] Since Burnett and Downey established the LightWorkers Media production company in 2009 through 2016, they produced *The Bible, Son of God* (Spencer, 2014), a Lifetime TV movie called *Women of the Bible* (2014), *A.D.: The Bible Continues,* and *The Dovekeepers.*[6]

In addition to these television productions and the small-scale film *Son of God*, Downey and Burnett's work under the purview of MGM also allowed them to work on the blockbuster biblical epic *Ben-Hur* (Bekmambetov, 2016) as executive producer and producer, respectively.[7] Downey and Burnett were brought onto the film in 2014, which was also the year in which an inter-industry kerfuffle arose around the marketing, reception, and reporting on Darren Aronofsky's big-budget biblical epic, *Noah* (2014). Following the release and somewhat tepid reception and box office revenue of the Paramount-produced film, *Variety* reported on focus groups of Christians who were dissatisfied with *Noah* and Hollywood films' approach to religion more generally, a report that spurred Paramount to release its own internal research that showed support and interest among Christians for the film ahead of its release.[8] Although the story devolved into a Paramount-versus-*Variety* debate and gained little traction outside of trade publications, the move to assure that Christian producers would have a hand in the development of a subsequent big-budget epic can be understood as a reaction to the *Noah* controversy. Although it did not eventually help *Ben-Hur,* which *The Atlantic* called "Hollywood's epic $100m mistake," it signaled Downey and Burnett as go-to Christian producers within mainstream Hollywood production.[9]

That marriage of faith and industry knowledge has been cultivated by Burnett and Downey through their promotional press, usually centering on Downey's history with *Touched by an Angel*. In a feature interview for *Variety* in 2016, Burnett attributed the success of LightWorkers to Downey's knowledge and empathy within "the faith and family community in the United states . . . [which is] greatly underserved . . . This provided an opportunity to [produce] several projects over the last few years . . . Everything we have worked on has had to have an appeal to our personal sensibilities."[10] In a 2013 *Variety* cover story, journalist Cynthia Littleton wrote, "Friends also cite Downey as a steadying influence on her husband . . . Downey's experience as an actress and producer has been important in guiding Burnett's move into scripted programming. The two shepherded 'Bible' hand in hand as co-writers and producers, on top of Downey's onscreen role as Mary. She's maintaining the same active role in the shaping of the follow-up mini[series] for NBC."[11] In the same issue, as part of the spate of articles tying into the cover story, Downey is placed at the center of LightWorkers Media, which is characterized as "her" banner "separate from Burnett's One Three Media."[12] Downey is the force behind LightWorkers and the spiritual heart of her work with Burnett. They are repeatedly portrayed as—and marketed as—a partnership whose shared sensibility is more legibly attached to Downey as the visible former star of a hit Christian show than behind-the-scenes Burnett.

Moreover, Downey has less to lose within the context of mainstream Hollywood television production because she's already associated with Christian content. Burnett, however, faced backlash to his evangelizing, seen most clearly in a *Variety* editorial directed to Burnett. In 2014 Peter Bart wrote in an open letter, "The problem, Mark, is that when you encourage pastors, among others, to buy out multiplexes for *Son of God* in their communities, some would accuse you of a form of spiritual bullying . . . So while you may take pride in 'evangelizing' your film's message, as you put it, you should also be aware that you are politicizing the Mark Burnett brand."[13] Although Bart was premature in his warning, the potential for politically aligning Burnett's Christianity as expressed via his media productions came to a head during the election of 2016 and the 2017 Presidential inauguration, which Burnett produced for television and for which he garnered a great deal of criticism.[14]

THE BIBLE MINISERIES: THE REWARDS OF RISK FOR THE HISTORY CHANNEL

The Bible was a huge ratings success for the History Channel and its emergent twenty-first-century brand, averaging 13.1 million viewers.[15] In the early 2010s, History Channel was second only to ESPN in cable rankings of male viewers, a brand it built on reality shows like *American Pickers* (2010–) and miniseries such as *Hatfields and McCoys* (2012).[16] *The Bible's* success expanded History's appeal to a religious audience while maintaining the male demographic it targeted before. *The Bible* was a gritty historical drama in look and tone, much like *Hatfields and McCoys,* but with an overtly religious story. In many ways the positioning of *The Bible* on the History Channel and in the miniseries format grounded the religious stories in the familiar mode of secular historical miniseries. From the late 1970s through the 1980s, American miniseries skewed toward historical topics and characters in order to elevate the form's melodramatic mode.[17] According to Malgorzata J. Rymsza-Pawlowska, the American miniseries form drew on the emotional lives of its characters similarly to soap operas but achieved greater legitimation by "foreground[ing] particular characteristics of the novel: narrative immersion, character development, and change over time, all of which were becoming increasingly present in serialized television [in the 1970s], but which were intensified" in the miniseries.[18] The secular approach to *The Bible* focuses on the book as—if not a novel—then at least storytelling, or as Andrew Romano argued in a column for *The Daily Beast*, "The Bible, meanwhile, has chapter after chapter and verse after verse of (to put it crassly) action-packed material—Moses, David, Job, Jesus, Revelation, and so on— plus a 'fanbase' that's even larger and more avid than Marvel Comics."[19] But *The Bible* is not just secular, historical storytelling. Acknowledging that and working from a faithful perspective was, according to the producers of *The Bible*, key to the miniseries' success. Burnett expressed as much after the fact and in the context of the spate of media projects that followed *The Bible*'s success: "This is not a subject like doing a western or sci-fi. You can't just make it and hope for the best. There's a way to get a massive audience if you're faithful, and there's also a potential backlash if you're not."[20]

Brian Edwards was an executive producer on *The Bible* and, at the time of my interview with him, was Chief Operating Officer of United Artist Media Group, which was formed in 2014 from the partnership of Mark Burnett's One Three Media (co-owned by Hearst Group until 2016) and MGM and which includes Downey's faith-based LightWorkers Media.[21] Edwards argued that the success of *The Bible* resulted from the following production choices: (1) the decision to do what they called an "unvarnished adaptation [of the Old and New Testaments] . . . [Like] a modern version of a stained-glass window" with "authenticity and quality" that would separate it from others that had sanitized or dramatized biblical stories; (2) the decision to include Christian leaders at the script stage to ensure the faith foundation was strong; and (3) the decision to target the appeal of the miniseries in a "coherent and direct line of sight to a large audience" of heartland viewers.[22] Burnett and Downey are Christians of strong faith, committed to making media with a faith-based agenda (and publicizing that agenda). They present themselves as identifying directly with their audience and speaking to people they know feel underserved by most television series. Burnett has said, "A lot of people said to us, 'Nobody's going to watch *The Bible* in primetime TV. You guys are crazy' . . . But Roma and I said, 'We think you're completely underestimating this faith-based, Christian audience.' And we proved that it was enormous, and that it makes sense to create something in that world."[23] There is no attempt within these adaptations to contain religion geographically, generically, or within the culture of Hollywood—all key traits of post-network-era boom programming to be discussed in subsequent chapters. *The Bible* is a religious miniseries, targeting—at least partially—a religious audience, drawing from a Christian text, and created by Christian producers for evangelical as well as artistic and economic purposes. Even Nancy Dubuc, president of A+E Networks (the parent company of the History Channel), acknowledged and utilized Downey and Burnett's Christian focus as part of History's promotion of the miniseries, telling *Variety*'s Cynthia Littleton, "When Mark and Roma speak about this project, their passion is so evident, it lends authenticity and meaning to the whole effort . . . The marketing they're doing [promoting to Christian groups] punctuates the size and scope of what we've done."[24] For Dubuc and executives at History, Burnett and Downey's faith was a feature of working with them as producers on the project, not something to be avoided.

Of the ten-hour miniseries, the first five hours were devoted to the Old Testament and the last five hours adapted the New Testament. But the stories selected from the Old Testament often follow the Christian theological practice of prefiguration, casting the stories of the Old Testament in the service of telling the story of Jesus. For example, where other Abrahamic religions may focus on the story of the sacrifice of Isaac by Abraham to be one of faith in God, prefiguration reconfigures the story as foreshadowing God's sacrifice of his son, Jesus, for the salvation of humanity. Thus, adaptations of the stories of the Old Testament gain specifically Christian meaning with the addition of the New Testament as Christian context. A prime example of this dual meaning for Old Testament stories is the televising of DeMille's *The Ten Commandments* Easter weekend, which also coincides with the Jewish holiday of Passover.[25] The latter explicitly celebrates the story of Exodus, which is the foundation for the movie, but the scheduling for Easter weekend on broadcast television in a majority-Christian country asserts it as a Christian story, too, if not more so. This televisual spectacle and contextualizing the Old Testament in a Christian context inspired the idea of making *The Bible* miniseries. According to Burnett, while he was watching *The Ten Commandments* with his children, they found the mid-century special effects alienating. He said, "People's first memories of the Bible are usually either a movie or a piece of art. So we thought an updated version could be really powerful."[26] *The Ten*

Commandments' yearly airing acted as inspiration for both production and scheduling of *The Bible*, precedent for the potential success of a biblical epic on television, and a model for presenting Old Testament stories in a way that would resonate with Christian audiences, all factors that would be key to *The Bible*'s success and influence, at least in the story of its success told by its producers.

The Bible launched as a five-week event on March 3, 2013 and scheduled two episodes for each Sunday of the month, culminating on Easter with the two episodes covering the crucifixion and resurrection of Jesus. The event airings attracted over ten million viewers for its early episodes, with relatively little drop-off throughout the month, and *The Bible* would eventually become one of the fastest selling DVDs in years.[27] Its success was attributed to Burnett and Downey's savvy targeting Christian audiences while still attracting more general viewers. The married producers sat for numerous interviews with trade press and major periodicals like *The New York Times* to promote *The Bible*.[28] This is a familiar route of publicity for a television series, especially an event series with few recognizable stars on camera. The emphasis on the miniseries' broad appeal beyond religious audiences was highlighted by Nancy Dubuc, who framed it as such to the press. She told Cynthia Littleton as part of the promotional tour, "It is not an overly religious story, and you don't need to be religious to understand the influence of this book [the Bible] . . . there's a curiosity about the stories and characters that have shaped so many things."[29] Dubuc's description of *The Bible*'s appeal aligns with the normal Hollywood approach to Christianity and the Bible in particular: as cultural mythology that can be separated from religion. Chapters 5 and 6 cover the variations on this approach across prime time, but to frame *The Bible* as such alongside Burnett and Downey's deliberately faithful approach highlights the rarity of the latter.

In addition to the *de rigeur* secular framing of the series, Burnett and Downey also personally extended their promotional tour to churches and faith communities, holding screenings and discussions, as well as "working with a Christian marketing firm to promote their take on the greatest story ever told."[30] They also turned to YouTube and Christian media outlets to ask Christian audiences to "keep this special project in your prayers."[31] Certainly, as Burnett, Downey, and Edwards have said in the interviews analyzed above, the miniseries was a labor of (Christian) love, and one embraced by Christian viewers and thought leaders like celebrity megachurch pastor Rick Warren.[32] Burnett stated his explicitly evangelical motive behind the work, telling Cynthia Littleton that he wanted *The Bible* to "change people's lives . . . This can reach a whole generation of people who have never been to church."[33] Although he did not say that he wants the show to convert people or bring people to the church, such a desire and design for the miniseries indicates that he wanted people to let the teachings of the Bible and the story of Jesus Christ therein shape their lives. However, such an effort was somewhat contained by the compacted schedule of *The Bible's* airing. The use of the miniseries format also worked to structurally mitigate the risk based in the overtly Christian content for the series by containing it to a one-month window that was primed for biblical epics through both religious holidays and the repeated spectacle of the televised *Ten Commandments* and presenting the story as one complete, if limited, narrative experience.

The miniseries format on American television has evolved since its heyday in the 1980s. The decline of "event" live viewing for scripted series with the advent of the VCR, then the DVR, has been attributed to that decline, but recent successes like *Hatfields and McCoys* on History were used to justify the resurgence of the format in the 2010s, especially on cable networks looking to make noise within the industry.[34] Brad Adgate, senior vice president of research at Horizon Media, one of the companies that promoted *Hatfields and McCoys* in 2012, explained in an *AdAge* article that the rewards for the—admittedly expensive—miniseries format lie in their potential as "a valuable venue for brands to introduce new creative campaigns or build an event."[35] In that same article, an advertiser described the benefits from his perspective, "These [miniseries] are tentpole events that lend themselves to a lot of promotion on the side of the networks with big-name stars attached . . . it's a safer bet for advertisers than even traditional programming because you know networks are investing heavily in them."[36] Certainly the event-based promotion and airing of *The Bible* helped it to overcome its lack of star power relative to *Hatfields and McCoys*, which starred Kevin Costner, and helped to establish a model for miniseries success on ad-supported cable channels. The fact that History followed *Hatfields and McCoys* with the heavily promoted *The Bible* foregrounded how the miniseries format could be used, as Adgate said, to set a new creative brand for the History Channel, one that included edgy, history-based scripted dramas. The brand was further highlighted by the premiere of *Vikings* (History, 2013–2020) in the same month as *The Bible*. Where the latter was a tentpole event, an experiment in promoting through both traditional means and Christian audience targeting, and a possible risk as an overtly religious television drama, *Vikings* presented a more familiar series that reflected the cultural obsession with *Game of Thrones* (HBO, 2011–2019) and mitigated risk through its Irish-Canadian co-production. *The Bible* was an event, but History had *Vikings* as a backup in case the event did not go as planned. But it did, and *The Bible* cemented the viability of biblical media in the 2010s.

The Bible was the first in a cycle of historically oriented shows dealing overtly with Jesus or biblical stories and acknowledging their religiousness. This cycle features shows that are religious in much the same way *Touched by an Angel* was perceived: Christian moralizing from evangelical creatives. "One success begets another in relatively quick succession," Edwards claimed by way of explaining what followed *The Bible*. For example, the National Geographic Channel decided to follow up their well-rated nonfiction specials (not affiliated with UAMG), *Killing Kennedy* and *Killing Lincoln* with *Killing Jesus*, which was aggressively marketed ahead of its airing on Palm Sunday of 2015.[37] But the project most directly inspired by *The Bible* would test such a project's viability with the larger broadcast audience that many assumed would be an even better fit for broad Christian audience appeal: *The Bible*'s miniseries sequel, *A.D.: The Bible Continues*.

A.D.: THE BIBLE CONTINUES AND *THE DOVEKEEPERS*: FAILURES OF FAITH ON NETWORK TELEVISION

Following *The Bible*'s success, LightWorkers began developing their own slate of biblically adjacent dramas and miniseries, including *A.D.: The Bible Continues*, an adaptation of early Christian history and the establishment of the Church following Jesus's death and ascension, and a female-focused miniseries for CBS, *The Dovekeepers*, based on the Alice Hoffman bestseller of the same name about the siege of Masada in the first century C.E.[38] Both dramas were promoted heavily in the spring of 2015, but neither garnered the audience or critical response that NBC and CBS had hoped for. Despite having Bible in the title and the recognition garnered from adapting a bestseller, respectively, they didn't have the immediate cultural understanding that *The Bible* did. Viewers of faith or not knew immediately what *The Bible* was as a narrative series; the original text was well known as scripture or history. It could be viewed as either allowing for a dual audience appeal that was further enforced by Downey and Burnett's role extending beyond the series' traditional marketing and into direct address to the Christian community. The success of *The Bible* simply did not translate to the scale of broadcast television in the 2010s. For as much as Roma Downey shaped these series (and their promotion), they were not *Touched by an Angel*.

A.D. was billed as a sequel to *The Bible,* but it appeared on broadcaster NBC. It was meant to appeal to that "direct line of sight to a large audience" that Edwards and others attributed to *The Bible*'s success, and yet *A.D.* was on a broadcast network and the miniseries still had to appeal to a broad audience, including those who might be nonreligious. NBC developed the series and began airing it on Easter Sunday of 2015 in a clear nod to its potential religious audience and effort to recreate the event-based success of *The Bible*.[39] However, *A.D.* did not attract or sustain the anticipated mass audience, even the audience that watched *The Bible* on cable.[40] *A.D.*'s disappointing ratings suggest that the mass Christian audience that made *Touched by an Angel* a success in the neo-network era really might no longer exist—or at least be harder to reach—in the post-network era, especially within the parameters of broadcast television.

A.D. begins its first two episodes by rehashing the final two episodes of *The Bible* that presented the crucifixion and resurrection of Jesus. With a new, more racially diverse cast (both John [Babou Ceesay] and Mary Magdalene [Chipo Chung] are black in *A.D.* but not in *The Bible*), *A.D.: The Bible Continues* explores the political world in which the apostles first started preaching the gospel of Christianity. The inclusion of black characters— and more people of color generally—emphasizes the historical accuracy of the miniseries in a way that further solidifies its mainstream targeting.[41] However, Burnett also explicitly used the diverse casting to target black church audiences.[42] Each element of distinction or uniqueness relative to other broadcast shows and/or *The Bible* that was used to frame and promote the NBC series reflects the show's attempt to balance historical drama for secular viewers and biblical messages for Christian viewers. However, that tension often led to a series that, in its moments with Jesus, the Holy Spirit, and the most central Christian tenets, stumbled in a way that many media products from evangelical producers do, according to Heather Hendershot: "[they] attempted but, for the most part, failed, to be ambiguous" in their Christian messaging.[43] For example, in the second episode, "The Tomb Is Open," scenes among the apostles and the recently resurrected Jesus rarely stray from scripture, but in a scene of merely the apostles fishing in Galilee, the men rib one another for their unsuccessful fishing techniques and for whining about those techniques. The former scenes feel like Sunday school, and the latter is a rare example of a loose, friendly dynamic more familiar to general television viewers.

The other side of this difficult balance between secular dramatic norms and Burnett and Downey's evangelical approach is apparent in the violence and morally compromised political machinations between Roman governor of Judea, Pontius Pilate (Vincent Regan) and Jewish head priest, Caiaphas (Richard Coyle). Pilate is dastardly, killing with impunity and little to no remorse, even when he kills his own Roman guards. His only goal is to use any means necessary to quash Jesus's influence in order to leave what is in Pilate's mind a horrible, barbarous place. Caiaphas, perhaps as an attempt to mitigate centuries of anti-Semitism enflamed by stories of the Crucifixion, is conflicted and occasionally repentant of his complicity in Jesus's death. While the apostles move throughout the land, preaching the gospel, evading persecution, and amassing follower of Jesus's teachings, Pilate and Caiaphas are fighting for dominances in the structure of life in Jerusalem through fear and strategic machinations, respectively. Less stilted and careful than the scripture-influenced scenes of the apostles, the ancient political schemes, despite being drenched in blood and violence, often read as trying too hard to be edgy in the mode of prestige dramas like *Game of Thrones* but still within the restraints of telling a fundamentally Christian religious story. Despite both Downey and Burnett's familiarity and success within mainstream television, and the violence *A.D.* does show, the political stories still suffer from a problem of evangelical media that was identified by Hendershot in her study of that industry, *Shaking the World for Jesus*: "Depicting evil (indeed, depicting *life*) in a convincing-yet-wholesome manner remains a major challenge for evangelicals."[44] Outside of the scenes with Jesus, little of *A.D.* could be described as wholesome, but the drive to appeal to a broad audience and to potentially inspire that broad audience to Christian teachings that is at the core of Burnett and Downey's avowed goals for their production contributes to an oddly staid and "paint-by-numbers" representation of an oppressive regime in the first century A.D.[45]

A.D.: The Bible Continues was not a miniseries by design. It was meant to be a scripted drama that could earn a second season and beyond, but the decision to air the entire series in a concentrated time frame from Easter Sunday in April through June instead of the original standard series premier in September helped to reframe the show as an event series—NBC's "twelve-hour *A.D.: The Bible Continues*" and a "limited drama," for example—like *The*

Bible.[46] *A.D.* emphasized its dual secular and religious appeals even more than *The Bible* had, continuing and expanding on Downey and Burnett's strategy to straddle that line in their promotion of the series. But because the series was on network television instead of a risk-limiting cable channel, Downey and Burnett publicly emphasized the historical, secular appeal in trade press and touted their religious promotion less than they did for *The Bible.* Where the earlier series often was promoted with a foundation in its host of religious experts who shaped the production, Burnett said of *A.D.,* "This is mainstream programming . . . it's like taking *House of Cards* and dropping it into the first-century Jerusalem."[47] As discussed in the earlier section on *The Bible,* historical miniseries have a long legacy of using history and condensed serialized storytelling to elevate melodramatic stories, a method of legitimation echoed in Burnett's citing of a critical darling (at the time), *House of Cards* (Netflix, 2014–2018).[48] Although *A.D.* did not garner the kind of critical plaudits that perhaps Burnett was hoping for, it at least fared better than the much-derided *The Dovekeepers.*

While not as overtly Christian and not even based in a biblical story, *The Dovekeepers* aired in its entirety during the Christian Holy Week leading up to Easter (and the premiere of *A.D.*) in 2015. The scheduling proximity of the two LightWorkers productions and the framing of *The Dovekeepers* as event programming for Holy Week discursively categorized *The Dovekeepers* as part of the resurgence of biblical epics on television in 2015. In an article for *Variety* entitled "Easter Week Is Hopping with High-Profile TV Premieres: *Killing Jesus, The Dovekeepers, A.D.,*" Cynthia Littleton wrote, "The heightened activity during the Easter period reflects the tilt toward year-round programming strategies. Miniseries and limited series like *The Dovekeepers* and *A.D.* will help CBS and NBC cut down on the need for in-season repeats. At the same time, Easter is a natural marketing opportunity for programs with biblical themes."[49] Further framing *The Dovekeepers* as a biblical miniseries, Kelly Kahl, a scheduling executive for CBS told Littleton, "There are probably several places we could have put *Dovekeepers* on the schedule throughout the spring . . . As we sat down and looked at the calendar, the timing during Holy Week just made sense. When you can take advantage of what's going out in the wider world, it helps you piggyback on getting attention for your project."[50] Unsaid but hinted at in the idea that Holy Week "just made sense" is the idea that the miniseries was hoping for a Christian audience, those for whom Holy Week would mean something and draw them to the biblically adjacent project made even more implicitly

Christian in the use of Downey and LightWorkers as part of its promotion. At the Television Critics Association, Downey was present to promote the miniseries and emphasized how moved and inspired she was by Alice Hoffman's book about the Jews who faced the siege at Masada and still stood up for their beliefs, which lead to the show the *Los Angeles Times* called a "religious miniseries."[51]

Despite not acting in the series (as she did with *The Bible*), Downey was key in the promotional tour for the miniseries, appearing at the Television Critics Association tour and on talk shows to promote the series while also providing interviews for press articles to use. Downey's star presence and her association with both *Touched by an Angel* and *The Bible* can activate biblical Christian associations even when not discussed overtly. Downey's mainstream press appearances and interviews often discussed the miniseries as an "inspiration" and a "moving story" of "religious persecution." On an appearance on *CBS This Morning*, the interviewers asked Downey two questions in quick succession that reveal the underlying assumptions of religion that they didn't discuss overtly. When asked, "You produced *The Bible* which has been seen by more than a hundred million people. Why do you think there's still this fascination with this period of time?" Downey discussed Masada as the retreat following the fall of Jerusalem, which, for many Christians, is key to dating both the Gospels and the Crucifixion because Jesus is said to have predicted the event.[52] Although the question and Downey's answer ostensibly focused on history and not religion, the next question belied that assumption: "You've met the Pope?"[53] From first-century history to the God-ordained leader of the Catholic Church is somewhat of a turn unless there is an assumption that the former line of questioning was also informed by Christian faith. Instead of turning to the actress, Rachel Brosnahan, who starred in *The Dovekeepers,* after Downey's first answer, Downey—and her Christianity—remained the focus.

However, for as much as Downey worked to promote the miniseries and frame it in the best light, the series gained jeers instead of plaudits when it aired, even making Brian Lowry's worst television of 2015 list for *Variety,* appearing just under the reality show *Sex Box* (WE, 2015).[54] Lowry especially did not like the miniseries, comparing it negatively to the more feminist, less interested in faith, and more "handsome melodrama," *The Red Tent* (Lifetime, 2014), which focused on the Bible from the perspective of Jacob's four wives.[55] Other critics similarly derided the miniseries. Mary McNamara touched on the earnestness of the series, emphasized by Downey's production, as a problem, writing, "It is so bad it's *almost* good—who knew there was so much adulterous kissing in the days leading up to the mass suicide at Masada? But as *The Dovekeepers* is produced by Roma Downey and Mark Burnett, I think we can rule out intentional camp."[56] Neil Genzlinger for *The New York Times* also drew on the Burnett-Downey production as key extra-textual shaping of the miniseries, writing, "As in that miniseries [*The Bible*], the version of the ancient world they give us here is full of clichéd dialogue served in overwrought fashion."[57] For as much as earnest clichés and overwrought storytelling can work for *The Bible* because it is obviously a religious text with clichés and earnestness at its core, critical reception to *The Dovekeepers* highlights the difficulty of approaching a Bible-adjacent story from a similar position of faith. Such storytelling issues are taken much more seriously because the series was framed as a secular story with Christian undertones instead of a Christian story with potentially broad appeal.

Burnett and Downey did so well when producing and promoting *The Bible* to straddle the line between Christian content and more general appeal that the slight variations on their strategy for their 2015 miniseries underlines how difficult a position that is. Burnett's answer when asked what LightWorkers learned from *The Dovekeepers'* failure invoked *The Bible* as the model that didn't quite fit with *The Dovekeepers*. He said, "It was up against tough competition. It was a subject when you look at Masada, not enough people know about it. The Bible was much better known, obviously. But *The Dovekeepers* was one of my favorite books and we really enjoyed making it. Not everything becomes the biggest hit and it probably was a little bit sexy."[58] *The Dovekeepers* was too earnest for the general, secular audience, but possibly too "sexy" for a Christian audience. *A.D.,* too, could not find the balance—at least on the broadcast scale of what could be considered success for an event series—between Christian storytelling and secular appeal.

As a potential series order, however little discussed as such, *A.D.* was officially canceled in July 2015, although Burnett and Downey did not rule out the possibility of continuing the series on a future digital streaming channel of their own.[59] Nevertheless, the cancellation of *A.D.* on NBC is revealing as a direct point of contrast to *Touched by an Angel's* earlier success. Both were series dealing overtly with religion and faith of a decidedly Christian perspective. Both appeared on broadcast networks and were targeted to broad family appeal via their slight containment of evangelizing within supernatural or historical contexts. And *A.D.* earned substantial ratings for its premiere, enough that it might have become a success had it not had low ratings in target demographic groups and experienced a precipitous decline in its overall viewership. The audiences that advertisers cared about were not watching and gradually even the general audience ceased paying attention. Both deficient viewerships, moreover, fed directly into the assumed logic that overt religion, especially white Christianity, alienated those viewers within target demographics and the secular audience more generally.

THE PERSISTENT PERCEPTION OF ANTAGONISM
BETWEEN FAITH AND MAINSTREAM TELEVISION

Producers at UAMG and its LightWorkers banner embraced the religious aspects of both *The Bible* and *A.D.* because they saw the religious audience as vast and underserved, just as they had been in the 1990s when *Touched by an Angel* and PAX-TV sought to capitalize on them. Edwards told me that the network partner for each show, History and NBC, respectively, took the overall responsibility of marketing the shows to a general audience, but that, led by Mark Burnett and Downey, UAMG did supplemental marketing to Christian groups with their in-house team. As discussed earlier, for both *The Bible* and *A.D.*, Burnett and Downey traveled to a variety of faith communities and met with faith leaders across the United States to build the Christian audience of their series. Burnett explained his business strategy with these shows in a *Hollywood Reporter* op-ed around the time of the launch of *A.D.* The op-ed made an industrial argument informed by religious belief. He maintained that the Christian audience is a mass audience that will watch religious content if it is respectful. His tone was both imploring and a little defensive. He wrote, "Content that tries to disprove Christianity tends to fail, content that alters what Christians believe is 'God's story' tends to fall short, but content that honors that story tends to be well-received. It's just that simple."[60] It is worth noting that on the basis of Burnett's evangelism and his company's work to appeal directly to religious audiences, he believes the mass Christian audience can supplant (or even convert some of) the confederation of secular demographics that form the audience norm in post-network industry practices. He said as much in 2014: "When we looked at it we saw that around about 50 million Americans sit in a church each week . . . On a monthly basis that's almost 150 million, because not everybody goes every Sunday. And that community is tightly knit. The last thing Jesus said to his disciples was to go out and spread the word."[61] On the basis of the limited sample of mainstream faithful programming available, *A.D.* and *The Dovekeepers*' relative failures seem to belie Burnett's contention.

Burnett's op-ed and his biblical adaptations represent an extreme example of support for overtly Christian dramas in such a way that fortifies the connection between religious and middlebrow and the latter's connotation of religious messaging from religious producers. He and Roma Downey tried resurrecting the *Touched by an Angel* legacy in a contemporary industry context in which most creative figures and executives had internalized that legacy as in conflict with their creative and business goals. The potential Christian audience is broad, not narrow, as Burnett rightly points out. However, that breadth follows a mass audience mentality that is now seen as antiquated or out of sync with contemporary industry imperatives. Burnett, in effect, is basically trying to target a heartland audience in an era when that audience has lost focus and favor within the industry because it is constructed as anathema to upscale audiences that are increasingly desirable, even on broadcast networks. Without the demographic narrowness that allows for upscale audience targeting, such an audience is less and less valuable within the television industry.

For as broad as the potential Christian audience is, it has become a niche audience in some respects, but one that further disassociates it from mainstream television and its practices. Moreover, the Christian audience of the imagined heartland of America is by its foundational construction as an identity anathema to nichification, such that nichification becomes seen as oppression. In her study of CBS and PAX's branding as heartland networks in the late 1990s, Victoria E. Johnson argues, "even though ideals of heartland life are largely imaginary, they are central to the national common sense . . . [and] CBS and PAX tap[ped] into a suspicion or anxiety that a core American identity has been lost."[62] The core heartland identity is positioned in opposition to niche, boutique, or fringe identities and programming: that is, counter to the pursuit of upscale demographics that had begun to move to dominance in the late 1990s. Johnson goes on to argue, "The Heartland is, thus, representative of a shared *national* common sense wherein, it is presumed, anyone who values family, home community, and optimistic narrative will, necessarily, ally with the spiritual, explicitly localized, middle-American message" of *Touched by an Angel* and PAX's weekly schedule more generally.[63]

The Christian heartland audience has at various points since 1996 been pointed to as a vast, underserved audience when it comes to mainstream

Hollywood output. Examples of successful media products that do appeal to that audience segment are touted by believers as "'sending a message to Hollywood' about the profitability of Christian films" and television.[64] Attempts to assert the profitability of overtly Christian media undergirds Burnett's op-ed and much of his and Downey's approach to scripted productions under their LightWorkers banner, but it also acknowledges the persecution complex key to understanding how the decentralization of the mass, middle-brow, presumed-white-and-Christian audience could see the use of Christian stories without religiousness as an empirical and widely influential expression of their cultural displacement. Instead of having broadcast networks built around their identity as common sense as they had in the late 1990s, the twenty-first century has consistently provided evidence that Hollywood doesn't care about them. *The Bible* was an exception to the rule that was proven by the failures of *A.D.* and *The Dovekeepers* and cemented the heartland audience as on the outside looking in, no matter how many "messages" the audience members seem to send to Hollywood with their modest approval of works like *The Bible* or *Son of God*.

CONCLUSION

Although Burnett and Downey's biblical adaptations represent one way in which a middlebrow Christian approach has continued into the twenty-first century, their attempts to turn programs with explicit religious agendas into mainstream commercial successes have failed for the most part and been discussed as failures within industry discourse.[65] That failure has helped to strengthen the stigma associated with overtly Christian and moralizing drama and perpetuates the legacy of religious dramas as undesirable creative and industrial endeavors. The success of *The Bible* is forgotten in the wake of the inability to translate that niche history-oriented success into a program with wider appeal on network television.

PART II

DISTANCING CHRISTIANITY THROUGH PLACE AND RACE

The majority of dramas discussed in this book belong to fantastic genres: horror, science fiction, or fantasy. The prevalence of fantastic genres will be discussed in depth in Part III. Religion is central to the dramas that are the focus of Part II but they are realistic rather than fantastic. Realist dramas *Friday Night Lights* (NBC, 2006–2011) and *Rectify* (SundanceTV, 2013–2016) made religion a focal point in their storytelling: Southern Christianity is the foundation for their small-town settings and the families that live there. These two shows span the length of the post-network-era boom, from *Friday Night Lights* in the mid-2000s to *Rectify* in the 2010s. By virtue of their shared realist genre, these shows throw the reaction against middlebrow Christian dramas into stark relief. *Friday Night Lights* began airing a full decade after *7th Heaven*'s premier, but their runs overlapped for one year. As discussed in Chapter 1, *7th Heaven* anchored the association of middlebrow appeal with a religious realist drama even in 2006. This positioning meant that shows that had religious narratives and were aiming for quality, such as *Friday Night Lights,* needed to differentiate their use of religion from the types of overtly Christian dramas discussed in Part I. This need was answered in the containment pattern of geographical distancing of Christianity onto the American South and its culture, seen as "other." This emphasis on religion as a Southern cultural marker became a successful strategy for distinguishing the dramas as quality programming.

Similarly, Christianity can be understood and represented by creatives within the television industry *as a religion* via distancing through another type of otherness: racial difference. Black and Latinx Christianity can represent—and have represented on *Greenleaf* (OWN, 2016–) and *Jane the Virgin* (The CW, 2014–2019)—avenues for in-depth and explicit exploration of institutional Christianity in ways that most of the examples of white

Christianity over the twenty-year period of this study do not. Both chapters in this section explore how Christianity on prime-time dramas can maintain its religiousness through containment discourses of distance of place and difference of race. Both modes of representing Christianity in Part II assume Christianity as a culturally embedded and thus specific element of a milieu distinct from the assumed background of the desirable upscale audiences. Ironically, such reductive thinking enables for much more nuanced engagement with Christianity as a religion in these serial dramatic programs.

3

Southern Realism

Christianity in *Friday Night Lights* and *Rectify*

CHRISTIANITY IN QUALITY REPRESENTATIONS
OF THE AMERICAN SOUTH

Both *Friday Night Lights* (NBC, 2006–2011) and *Rectify* (SundanceTV, 2013–2016) use a Southern American setting to tell the story of characters responding to the presence and impact of Christianity. These shows present a spectrum of belief from atheism to born-again devotion but always within the imagined Southern Christian culture. This Southern setting also provides a way to differentiate them from the aforementioned middlebrow shows in Chapter 1, *7th Heaven* and *Touched by an Angel,* which featured faith-based representations of Christianity. Thus, this chapter follows from Part I's exploration of white Christianity's middlebrow associations to the practices of ideologically distancing religious representation and the creatives who use it in their work to contain those undesirable tastes. Unlike the case studies in Part III, this chapter's case studies and writers acknowledge the religiousness and Christian specificity of religion as it is represented in their work, but the writers nonetheless distance themselves from that religion by pushing it wholly onto Southern culture. Religion is acknowledged, but only as an attribute of a particular, even peculiar culture within the setting of an "authentic" vision of the South to invoke notions of quality television.

Displacing religion onto the South enabled the writers of *Friday Night Lights* and *Rectify* to engage with religion as part of a cultural other, protecting creatives from being thought of as religious. Significantly, the background of the majority of the imagined quality TV audience as well as the background of the writers and producers of the shows under consideration differed substantially from the imagined Southern populace, although each show had at least one Southern writer to act as the arbiter of authenticity. The target

Divine Programming. Charlotte E. Howell, Oxford University Press (2020).
© Oxford University Press.
DOI: 10.1093/oso/9780190054373.001.0001

audience as well as the majority of creatives involved with the two shows that are the subject of this chapter tended to be coastal, affluent, educated, and not particularly religious (or imagined themselves in this manner). As such, the rural, middle-class and working-poor, Christian South was outside their experience. The claim of Southern authenticity provided that displacement within realist genre expectations and quality aesthetics. Both realism and authenticity, it should be noted, are constructions within the realm of fictional television, used to legitimate certain dramatic stories and brand particular shows as quality.

Friday Night Lights and *Rectify* are two of the best examples of the alignment of quality realism with Southern authenticity in the post-network era. This alignment uses Christianity as a cultural anchor for the characters and as a marker of regional difference for the writers, producers, and assumed audience. Through case studies of these two shows, this chapter investigates the representation of religion within the aesthetic of what I call Southern realism, which draws from both the Southern gothic tradition and the indie film culture tradition.[1] I explicate this aesthetic in greater detail later, but in broad strokes, Southern realism appropriates quality production techniques— such as dynamic camera work, naturalistic lighting, on-location shooting, and realistic dialogue—to signify authenticity, and it draws on the Southern gothic for content and tone. Such representational practices at once target quality audiences, contain religion, and keep the writers operating safely within conventions of quality television and the attendant cultural capital it affords them.

Southern realism, as I define it, requires the claim of authenticity and the various connotations of quality that accompany it. Thus, shows that are set in the American South but are not framed as prestigious do not fit this definition. For example, while *Hart of Dixie* (The CW, 2011–2015) or *GCB* (ABC, 2012) both mobilize Southern culture as their milieu, neither employs quality production or marketing techniques to claim an authentic representation of the South. The mode of Southern realism allows writers, executives, producers, and marketers to discuss their work with religion without fearing that they will be perceived as necessarily religious by their industry peers. The fear of being seen as religious that dominates mainstream Hollywood industry culture and production practices is mitigated when it is displaced onto the geographically other American South. This particular containment practice of distancing creates a paradox in which authentically representing the American South necessitates representing Christianity overtly as belief and practice, while writers, producers, executives, and marketers working on these shows discursively downplay or dismiss the religiousness of their show.

SOUTHERN REALISM AND AUTHENTICITY CLAIMS IN THE POST-NETWORK ERA

Southern realism, as I articulate it, is an evolution of the earlier Southern gothic, a mode seen in William Faulkner's novels, Flannery O'Connor's short stories, and myriad media texts such as *To Kill a Mockingbird* (Mulligan, 1962), *Midnight in the Garden of Good and Evil* (Eastwood, 1997), *The Gift* (Raimi, 2000), and *True Blood* (HBO, 2008–2014). In both Southern realism and Southern gothic—particularly the latter's literary expression—there is a preoccupation with Southern Christianity; the gothic's excess has given way to an understated mode of storytelling in the new Southern realist television programs. Many of Southern gothic's narrative foci, such as religion, class, and race, remain present in Southern realism, but they are represented quite differently. Although Southern realism as I construct it is not necessarily television specific, television's ability to approach these foci over many hours of a season or series and its resulting ongoing relationship with its audience allows for extensive and subtle explorations of religion, class, and race. The mode and medium combine to produce "classic American realism . . . the painstaking, almost literal examination of middle- and working-class lives."[2]

Whereas the Southern gothic mode was influenced by horror, Southern realism draws its emphasis on authenticity from indie film culture. As Michael Z. Newman articulates indie, it is a cultural construct formed in opposition to the mainstream, "a form of cinema that is constantly being distinguished from another one which is more popular and commercially significant, but less culturally legitimate."[3] Newman goes on to describe

[t]he ideal of independent cinema . . . as an authentic, autonomous alternative. Authentic, insofar as a film is recognized to be the sincere production of an artist or group of artists. Autonomous, to the extent that the artist or group of artists is free to pursue their personal agenda and not constrained by business demands. And alternative, as the authenticity and autonomy of the film and its production is regarded as a contrast to the dominant process for making movies, which is the Hollywood studio way.[4]

The emphasis on authenticity and alterity are the two guiding principles defining quality television as that idea has evolved in the twenty-first century, using those two principles to legitimate the form in much the same way indie film has done. Moreover, both indie film and quality television share whiteness at the center of their taste cultures, even if it's not often acknowledged as such. Thus, the idea of "authenticity" arises out of a white perspective in Southern realism, contrasting with the way Southernness is used in black-cast drams like *Queen Sugar* (OWN, 2016–) or *Greenleaf* (OWN, 2016–); the latter will be discussed in the next chapter.

As Sarah Banet-Weiser theorizes in her book *AuthenticTM*, authenticity is both a "cultural space defined by branding and a relationship between consumers and branders."[5] For some shows and networks, autonomy of the production culture in relationship to the network becomes a way to build a distinct authentic brand. SundanceTV, in particular, builds its brand by emphasizing its willingness to cede control to its showrunners. SundanceTV brands itself as a channel for television auteurs, a claim that draws directly from indie cinema culture and the film festival with which it shares its name. Whereas film situates the mainstream with the major Hollywood studios, television legitimation situates broadcast television and its construction as middlebrow in opposition to quality.[6] The confluence of claims of authenticity, alterity, and occasionally autonomy informs the quality designation of Southern realism in television programs, which in turn enables the representation of religion within these shows. As David Hudgins, a writer and producer on *Friday Night Lights* characterized its production culture, "We were always conscious to be true to Texas," including its religious culture.[7] The truth of Texas required a realist approach that shaped its representation of Christianity.

Scholars and critics consider both *Friday Night Lights* and *Rectify* to be quality dramas.[8] As Victoria Johnson notes, at first *Friday Night Lights* was discursively constructed as having mass—or, as she puts it, "heartland"—appeal. Its stories of football, family, and the struggles of small-town life seemed custom fit for such. Only after the show failed to attract the heartland (and teen) audiences it was initially targeted toward did programmers and marketers shift to discursively categorizing it as quality.[9] This construction of regional identity/geographic myth undergirds one way that the American television industry imagines its audience: the quality audience and the heartland audience are assumed to be mutually exclusive. Johnson writes,

Indeed, in spite of the broadly "purple" realities of American history—thrown into stark relief in the Obama era—demographic market definitions, industry promotions, and journalistic critical discourses remain characterized by a cultural and conceptual lag that imagine the American consumer, viewer, and polity as divided according to red state versus blue state identifications and their corresponding imagined capital relations.[10]

Johnson's work within the field of media studies has made great inroads with regard to her stated goal of bringing regional identity into consideration, and this chapter aids in that endeavor by critically engaging with the ways that religion is used to construct the geographical myth of the South, while simultaneously fetishizing it for the idea of a quality audience for whom Southern culture, including religion, is believed to be other.

Friday Night Lights set the model of Southern realism that other quality realist shows like *Rectify* follow. These two shows qualify as case studies or religious dramas because of their overt representation of normative Southern Christianity. Other shows that could be considered Southern realist but would not qualify as case studies include *Justified* (FX, 2010–2015) and *True Detective* (HBO, 2014–). While these two shows have represented the American South as Christian, when religious representation has appeared it is as non-normative modes of Christianity such as snake handling and Christianity-based cults. Such religious representation is othering to such an extreme that it no longer is perceived as ideologically threatening; it is outside the realm of the Christian norm that is the foundation for understanding religious as middlebrow.

In this chapter, unlike the 1990s Christian dramas and the biblical miniseries of the 2010s, the creatives and marketers of Southern realist shows are in fact *not* trying to appeal to a Southern or heartland audience. Rather, the heartland audience is largely subsumed within the imaginary of the middlebrow audience and the attendant non-quality textual strategies. The American South and its attendant characters and culture are the objects of these shows but not the target audience, in contrast to Johnson's study. While the Southern realist shows *Friday Night Lights* and *Rectify* represent subjects such as religion associated with the heartland audience, their writers' and executives' geographic displacement of those subjects within quality notions of authenticity help ensure these shows and their creatives are not considered middlebrow despite their overt Christianity.

HEARTLAND SUBJECTS, QUALITY AUDIENCE: *FRIDAY NIGHT LIGHTS*

Friday Night Lights pioneered Southern realism, particularly as a marker of quality. Beyond its use of quality aesthetics, it was considered exceptional by critics, scholars, and its own writers because it featured heartland subjects.[11] This evaluation was especially true because it aired on broadcast television at a time when broadcast television was increasingly considered a site for non-quality programming. *Friday Night Lights* was based on a nonfiction book by H. G. Bissinger and a film by the same name (Berg, 2004). Developed for television by Peter Berg, the show's narrative focused on the small-town stakes and the encompassing culture of high school football in the fictional Texas town of Dillon. The series' main characters included the Taylor family—football coach Eric (Kyle Chandler), guidance counselor Tami (Connie Britton), and their daughter Julie (Aimee Teegarden)—and the various football players and their families who cycled through and around the football teams, the Dillon Panthers and the East Dillon Lions. These players included town tomcat Tim Riggins (Taylor Kitsch); artist, quarterback, and Julie's love interest, Matt Saracen (Zach Gilford); talented and driven Brian "Smash" Williams (Gaius Charles); paraplegic former quarterback Jason Street (Scott Porter); and Christian rocker and eventual kicker, Landry Clark (Jesse Plemons). All the characters struggled with the gravitational pull of small-town, working-class life in Dillon despite their on-field prowess that is the usual ticket out of Dillon to the wider world. And they all attended church. Christianity was foundational for the small-town culture the show presented, filtering into everything from prayers before football games to the driving force in a love triangle. Christianity was portrayed as a natural part of the town culture even if it is a culture that was largely assumed by the creative and executives involved to be alien to the *Friday Night Lights* target quality audience.

Friday Night Lights' industrial context for television was unique as a transitional show. It began its run on NBC and was initially marketed to the middlebrow mass audience. Johnson notes, "Almost all of the original television advertisements for the series were placed in NBC's fall football telecasts. Specifically, by linking *Friday Night Lights* with NBC's *Football Night in America* . . . NBC explicitly promoted *Friday Night Lights* as red state, heartland TV."[12] When it failed to attract that target audience and instead critics began hailing the show as an exceptional-for-broadcast quality drama, NBC repositioned it as such.[13] Throughout, the mode of representation and the production culture behind it remained within the legacy practices of quality television designations, so its repositioning as quality did not affect the show's representational logics. For the show's final two years, NBC and satellite television company DirecTV partnered to ensure that the show stayed on the air, even if its episodes initially aired on DirecTV's niche subscriber-only channel. This change was likely viable due to the removal of the FCC's financial and syndication (fin/syn) rules, granting NBC more aftermarket value for the show as its financer. *Friday Night Lights* ultimately ran for five seasons on broadcast television, where its creatives used its quality television designations to contain its middle-brow subjects, including religion.

Key to the notion of Southern realism is that those who praise it in popular media criticism and within the industry often do so as outsiders looking into that culture. There is an assumed degree of distance for most of those in the quality audience, which is constructed as liberal, coastal elites. Thus, Southern realism is conferred through authorial branding and the judgment of outsiders. Realism, like quality, is not an objective term. Those who deem a fiction presented as realistic must have the cultural power to do so, and that power is not necessarily tied to experience within the represented culture. Within the context of the Southern realist shows, the majority of creatives working on those shows are not Southern. The few who are fill the role of token, although likely unconsciously done. As *Friday Night Lights* executive producer and writer David Hudgins told me, he was often called on as the authority on the South because he grew up in Texas. However, he said his descriptions of the South—such as the practice of weekly church attendance— were often met with incredulity by the other writers.[14] Examples like his illustrate a degree of othering and a fascination with Southern culture among the Hollywood television industry's writers and producers. The regionalism in *Southern* realism must be emphasized to enable the use of its othered nature in containment strategies. The target audience, or at least the assumed target audience, for these shows is in fact not the inhabitants of the milieu it presents. But in order to harness that appeal, the Southernness represented by the show must seem "authentic." Such authenticity, however, was deemed so by writers and by the target quality audience that was constructed as outside the culture. Jason Katims, *Friday Night Lights*' showrunner, described as "a Brooklyn native with little interest in football" by critic Alan Sepinwall, told that critic,

The thing that stood out about the pilot [of *Friday Night Lights*] is what I hear that people generally responded to in the show: how authentic it felt. It felt like I was in this town. It was as if somebody dropped you into this town and you were there. That's what was so exciting about it. The sense of place was so specific, and the sense of this community felt so real, and the people that were in it felt so real.[15]

Katims claimed authenticity as the foundation of the show's appeal, not necessarily claiming it as an outsider but instead letting viewers do that work for him. However, as discussed above, *Friday Night Lights* had a difficult time appealing to the heartland and Southern viewers who might have the authority to claim authenticity. Instead, these claims were made mostly by critics like Sepinwall, with *The New York Times* critic Ginia Bellafante going so far as to call the show "an exquisite bit of anthropology."[16] The appeal of authenticity in Southern realist dramas is an appeal across difference and distance. Quality audiences, imagined in contrast to Southern audiences, like to be transported to a "real" South, but only through their television screens.

During its run from 2006 to 2011, *Friday Night Lights* was constructed by many critics as a show that's "not really about football." Even with that strategic repositioning by NBC and the show's creatives, as Johnson argues, *Friday Night Lights* had difficulty appealing to either heartland or quality target audiences. She writes, "*Friday Night Lights* seemed so counterintuitive to prevailing mythologies of rural, working-class, flyover life as to force the network and television critics to actively agonize over their love for the show and to explicitly redeem their own cultural capital in the face of a heartland text with football as its milieu."[17]

Johnson traces *Friday Night Lights'* transition from its initial marketing alongside mass-appeal NFL football "to its re-valuation as a premium-appeal, subscriber-based, quality TV series by the fall of 2008," as part of an argument about geographical myth, but I think the change also relates to the mode of representing religion throughout the series.[18] Despite its low ratings, it was a critical success and a surprisingly long-running series, primarily because of its quality aesthetics and appeal.[19] Those quality aesthetics and the subsequent targeting of the quality audience established the representation of religion as available to realist genre television because it cultivated quality markers through difference in its representation of an authentic American South.

The churches in small-town Dillon are also sites for exploring the intersection of class, gender, and race within the Southern context. From the earliest episodes, viewers were cued to the centrality of the two town churches: one white and one black. Intercutting between scenes of the two churches and their communities in the series' third episode, "Wind Sprints," was designed to establish both churches as centers around which the communities rotate. Such intercutting simultaneously visually explored their similarities and differences. The black church doesn't appear to have air conditioning; the white church does. The white church is a larger church, both in terms of building and congregation. But both churches share the function of community gathering and provide a nexus for the town's culture. Both feature preachers talking about Jesus and football in equal measure. The black church continues to appear throughout the series' run, but the white church and its community figure more prominently in the narrative by virtue of being the congregation the central characters, the Taylor family, attend. White Christianity is dominant in these Southern realist shows. The next chapter explores nonwhite Christianity as it gains centrality of expression in majority nonwhite cast dramas.

Although Dillon's churches of both races were places where characters network, flirt, seek strength, and so on, the clear connections and slight differences between the two raced congregations are rarely represented as starkly as in that early episode. This episode lays the representational groundwork for establishing Dillon as "authentically" Southern in its overtly, devoutly Christian culture as well as that culture's racial divide. Although not all main characters go to church—notably, Tyra Colette (Adrianne Palicki) and her family of women positioned as outsiders to the dominant powers of the town do not attend—non-Christian and non-churchgoing characters are few and far between. Further, they are usually still positioned within a culture in which Christianity is dominant.

Although the church acts as a shaper of life in Dillon throughout the series run, with many characters being obviously devout, it is not until the fourth season that the series delves into what it means to attend church as an institution beyond the community structuring and normalized behaviors. In the season-four episode, "In the Skin of a Lion," Julie Taylor is preparing to leave for college and reveals to her mother that she probably won't go to church on her own. Church for her had become something she did with her family but not as a representation of her own beliefs. As the episode progresses, her mother, Tami, discusses her fears and difficulty with reconciling Julie's changing beliefs. Eventually they reach an agreement that Julie will continue to go to church with the family but that they will respect her religious choices. This is one of the many examples in *Friday Night Lights* in which the women of the series occupy the main religious space. They discuss religion, are the forces that bring their families to church, and struggle with the conflicts that arise from religious beliefs operating in a complicated lived existence. Moreover, Julie's act of going to church despite her loss of faith reinforces the representation of the authentic South as a place in which Christianity structures culture beyond belief and devotion.

At the other end of the spectrum of belief, the show also represented born-again Christianity. In the second season of *Friday Night Lights*, Lyla Garrity (Minka Kelly) begins to express herself as a born-again Christian after the end of her relationship with injured quarterback Jason Street. Her evangelism is portrayed as true for her—it gives her some stability and peace of mind at a time during which she is obviously unmoored—but also as another instance of Lyla orienting herself around a young man/romantic interest. First, she was the head cheerleader to Jason's star quarterback, then she acted as devoted girlfriend and nursemaid to her now paraplegic boyfriend while also having an affair with Tim, his best friend. Throughout the first season, she often turned to her faith to try to find comfort, but in the first episode of the second season, she was baptized and born again after re-devoting herself to her Christianity over the summer.[20] This decision leads to her main second-season storyline centering around her work at a Christian radio station and her relationship with a radio host there who is also a member of her church, Chris (Matt Czuchry). Like a few other storylines in season two, Lyla's renewed faith and her relationship with Chris were mostly ignored in subsequent seasons. She's still portrayed as Christian and churchgoing, but not with the same fervor and extracurricular activities, and thus without a related ongoing storyline.

Lyla's disappearing evangelism is mostly the result of a storyline that didn't work narratively: creating a new space in the Christian radio station took Lyla out of the orbit of the other main characters and placed her in a mostly separate narrative space, with the only linkage her love triangle with Chris and Tim that wasn't even much of a triangle. But the radio station and Lyla's place there also necessitated a lot of diegetic discussion of a very particular approach to faith: a born-again, evangelical Protestant Christianity that can be off putting for viewers not of that faith. It's culturally associated with televangelist preachers like Jerry Falwell and Pat Robertson, who by the

mid-2000s had become mostly offensive, outdated figures who blamed natural disasters and terrorist acts on homosexuality, feminism, and abortion.[21]
Despite its brief appearance, the turn toward a nonjudgmental portrayal of
being born-again and acknowledging the power that devout faith can have
in people's lives is a characteristic of Southern realism that sets it apart from
other realistic modes. The Southern realist mode can represent born-again
Christianity because it is safely ensconced within the containment strategy
of representing an authentic other: it is assumed that within a portrayal of
the "real" South, there will be some born-again evangelical Christianity because it is part of the cultural myth of the American South. In *Friday Night
Lights*, the Southern realist mode includes representations of Christian faith
and practice by membership and attendance at church as the norm. Yet
representations of nonbelief and evangelism are included within this mode
as well, as long as they remain in relation to the norm of Christian culture.

Friday Night Lights was often praised by both religious audiences and popular critics for its approach to Christianity that allowed the representation of
religion to have weight, to be considered a significant part of people's lived
experiences, and as something that people talk about and rely on.[22] This approach manifested clearly in a few smaller character arcs over the course of
the series. The most notorious was the measured treatment of a story in the
show's fourth season in which high school student, Becky (Madison Burge),
goes to Tami Taylor for guidance as she is considering an abortion. Tami
responds to her question "Do you think I'm going to hell if I had an abortion?" with a sensitive but definitive "No, honey, I don't."[23] This storyline is
informed by the Christian context in which Dillon is set, but it doesn't discuss religion's role in the decision for Becky more than that line (though the
father's parents do use a turn to religion in their attempts to convince the
teenagers to keep the baby). The contrast between Tami Taylor—a devout
Christian woman who personally opposes abortion but sets aside her own
moral choices in order to support a young woman who needs her guidance—
and the similarly Christian parents of the father—who use their religion to
justify pressuring Becky to keep the baby—presents nuanced assumptions
about the Southern Christian context. The representation beyond Southern
stereotype as well as representing the stereotype helps to enforce claims
of authenticity while also enabling the assumed liberal quality audiences
to identify with a main character, Tami. Within the writers' room for the
show, as they worked through this storyline, David Hudgins revealed the
need to claim authenticity when he told me, "Our mantra was: what would

really happen in this situation? . . . [this led to] defaulting to me [as the lone Southerner in the room]."[24] In this case and others, Hudgins's Southern tokenism helped the production culture to write and claim authenticity of Southern culture regarding religion.

For five seasons, *Friday Night Lights* represented specifically Christian religion within the Southern realist context of a small-town community. Its characters prayed often and visibly enacted Christian culture, organized around both football and church. The show's mode of representing Christianity is less abstracted than most of the case studies in this book. Yet, when talking about the religious storyline, Hudgins used the term "spirituality" instead of Christianity or religion. Even as he explained that it was "true to Texas, true to the characters, and true to [his] experience" as the support for his claim that the representation of "spirituality" on *Friday Night Lights* was "authentic," the claim of authenticity was not enough to contain the risk of religion within the ideology of contemporary Hollywood television. Although I used the term religion in the question, Hudgins responded by using spirituality. As with most of the writers I spoke to, religion remains risky and to be avoided regardless of how complex and explicit religious representations appear on the shows they work on. His avoidance implies that the legacy practices used in response to the linking religion with nonquality designations like religious and thus middlebrow, as ossified in the 1990s and perpetuated into the twenty-first century, continues to shape the ideology within the industry to a greater extent than the representation of religion on television indicates. Hudgins's hesitation in relation to *Friday Night Lights*' textual representations of religion exemplifies the paradox my study is analyzing: religious representation as seen on television seems to have little bearing on the ongoing hesitation of creatives who work in that realm to acknowledge religion. Better for them to abstract, displace, or deny religion than be potentially seen as religious or working on religious television.

AUTHENTIC ARTISTIC VISION, QUALITY CHANNEL: *RECTIFY*

Rectify was the first original dramatic series produced for SundanceTV. The channel started in 1996 as the Sundance Channel, a subscription-based premium channel that focused on art-house, international, and independent cinema, much like the film festival with which it shares its name.[25] Bought by AMC networks in 2008, the channel transitioned from subscription-based revenue to limited sponsorship and finally fully ad-supported in 2013, the same year that *Rectify* premiered.[26] Alongside this transition to an ad-supported model, SundanceTV began moving toward more miniseries (e.g., *Carlos* [2010]) and unscripted series (e.g., *Push Girls* [2012–2013]) before launching *Rectify* as its first original scripted series in 2013.[27] *Rectify* was originally developed for SundanceTV's sister channel, AMC, but as *The Walking Dead* shifted AMC's programming toward action, network executives thought it would be a better fit for the SundanceTV, with its history as a place for sometimes quieter indie fare.[28] Following *Rectify*, SundanceTV found critical success with the internationally produced miniseries *The Honorable Woman* (2014) and produced new scripted series like *The Red Road* (2014–2015) and *Hap and Leonard* (2016–2018). *Rectify* also proved a model for series that fit with Sundance's indie history and brand: short, six- to ten-episode seasons, as a natural extension of Sundance's previous focus on film and continued miniseries programming. With *Rectify* as its programming anchor, SundanceTV marketers and programmers have branded the channel as a place where the independent spirit of the Sundance Film Festival still shapes what viewers can watch on the channel; only now it includes television series.

The show focuses on members of the Holden family in the small town of Paulie, Georgia (a fictional town created from locations outside of Atlanta) as they react to the release of Daniel Holden (Aden Young) from death row after nineteen years. Daniel entered jail a teenager and emerges a man, floundering for his place in a family that has changed drastically and a town that still largely considers him a murderer despite his exoneration. While Daniel was in jail, his father died; his mother, Janet (J. Smith-Cameron) remarried; and she and her new husband had a son, a younger brother, Jared (Jake Austin Walker) whom Daniel had never known. In addition, Daniel's classmate Teddy (Clayne Crawford) became his stepbrother, a relationship that brought Teddy's devout wife, Tawney (Adelaide Clemens), into this new family configuration as well. The story moves slowly, with few plot developments taking place in an individual episode. This structure allows the Southern small-town setting and the complex inner workings of the main characters to occupy the majority of the narrative. Within the show's focus on setting and psychology, a central narrative concern of the first season involves the push-and-pull of Christianity within this small Southern town. The show poses the possibility that religion can serve as a path for salvation.

For *Rectify*'s producer, Melissa Bernstein, the religious elements on the show are displaced onto Georgia-born showrunner Ray McKinnon's artistic vision and his desire to represent an authentic South. When asked in an interview about the overt religion on display by the character of Tawney, as well as the first season's overall preoccupation with Christian-framed tenets of penance, redemption, and grace, she deflected, displacing religion's presentation within McKinnon's authentic artistic vision. When I asked about the show's religious elements, she replied,

> I don't think that was Ray's goal from the outset to tell a particularly religious or spiritual story. I will say I think that one of his goals was to . . . you know he's a Southerner and I think that's the world he knows well and the characters he knows well, and I think he wanted to authentically put those stories out there. I think Ray wouldn't even say that; I think he'd just say, "I just wanted to tell a story about real people, about flawed people, about people who are out there." I think he is very interested in man's search for meaning, that is the place that he comes from. So I think it's less about God, or faith, or religion and more about meaning and how do we fit into this crazy universe, how do we make sense of our lives, and how do we choose who we're going to be.[29]

Within the span of her answer, Bernstein moved from acknowledging religion as part of Southern culture to saying the story is not even religious, and ultimately she abstracted the show's religious representation to basic existential questions with no sense of religiosity. Meanwhile, she used Ray McKinnon's authorial goal to authentically tell stories about the South to help distance her from any role within the production of religious representation. Authenticity is a mode of appeal to the quality audience, a mode that is even more pronounced in *Rectify* than in *Friday Night Lights* because of the shows' different distribution outlets and later timeslot. The leeway granted to *Rectify* because of its presence on a quality niche-oriented cable channel contrasts with *Friday Night Lights*' need for broadcast appeal early in its run.

Despite these differences, for both of these Southern realist dramas, the place of religion becomes not just a distinguishing element of the story but also one that is discussed as such in many reviews. This prominence in the critical reception eventually shaped the marketing of the shows, if only via certain proscribed means. According to the Senior Vice President of

Marketing for SundanceTV, Monica Bloom, the network's marketers did not focus their publicity on the religious elements of *Rectify*; however, when online writing about or reviews of the show highlight those features, marketers did like to link, retweet, or post those outside sources to their official social media and the show's website.[30] Thus, while foregrounding religion may not have been an objective of its internal publicity strategy, SundanceTV's marketing department recognized the sales potential of this thread of discourse about the show. The marketers fostered the conversation about the representation of religion as a way to make noise, or at least boost the signal, of the show's distinct characteristics within an ever more competitive and cluttered field of quality cable dramas.

SundanceTV built its cable channel brand and initial programming strategy on movies that fit the indie appeal of the eponymous film festival. Only in 2013 did it move into airing original television series. In the same year, SundanceTV became ad-supported, as discussed above. This move to original series was due to the availability of *Rectify* through the corporate AMC Networks family, the changing media landscape that valued quality television series to establish cable brand, and the rising price of being carried by cable systems.[31] The basic-cable channel's definition of a quality audience prioritizes taste foremost and demographics later. Monica Bloom described *Rectify* as "the first Sundance [original dramatic] series" and addressed how that novelty affected the company's approach to marketing and its identification of its target audience:

> Typically, as we're developing a marketing plan we start with kind of an internal discussion, identifying key attributes of the program itself, what we feel might have some appeal to our audience. We create a positioning statement [from that]. Sometimes we will go into market research in order to test ideas. We did so specifically around the launch of season one of *Rectify* since it was our first scripted drama. We wanted to get a sense of the people who were familiar with Sundance and would this appeal to them as well as to the people who are not familiar with Sundance's brand of storytelling. . . . Part of the reason we [engaged the showrunner Ray McKinnon in this process] is the way that SundanceTV approaches the creation of our programming. We really want to give voice to the creative out there who may not be broadcast-ready. We—much like the heritage of Sundance Institute and the Sundance Film Festival—we're looking for those new and upcoming voices who aren't necessarily heard in other areas [of television],

and we give them a chance. We really want to make sure their vision is seen in an accurate, holistic way.[32]

In this description of her department's work in marketing, Bloom highlighted the significant differences between her work at that small cable channel with a very specific brand identity and the marketing goals of the broadcast networks. She added, "From what I understand of the broadcast networks, they will dictate what direction [the show] will go from a messaging standpoint and the creators don't necessarily have a lot of input."[33]

The direct contrast drawn to the broadcast networks here becomes a way of cultivating cultural capital and identifying SundanceTV's quality audience in contrast to the presumably less discerning broadcast audience. The difference between marketing for a smaller cable channel versus a much more mass-oriented broadcast channel is twofold, according to Bloom: not only is it about targeting a more discerning audience but also about greater input from creatives. Broadcast marketers don't have the same amount of time to confer with the creatives behind their shows, according to Bloom. SundanceTV builds its niche quality brand by ensuring that so-called authentic artistic voices of the channel's showrunners are heard and incorporated during the entire creative process, from development to marketing. This emphasis on an auteurist mode of production helps to build the channel's quality brand and resulting target audience.

SundanceTV's quality brand and audience targeting were further explained in my conversation with Senior Vice President of Scripted Programming at SundanceTV, Christian Vesper. He described the channel's transition from pay-cable service and film-based outlet to one focused on television dramas that appealed to the channel's still-boutique audience. He told me, "[When SundanceTV started] we really focused on—unlike the other networks—art films and European cinema or Asian cinema. . . . We weren't rated [by Nielsen] for most of our history so I have no sense of how many people were watching, but we have a sense that we were reaching a niche audience who cared about film."[34]

For both the marketing and programming executives I interviewed, the history of SundanceTV's appeal to a niche taste culture remains the strongest element of the brand, past and present. This philosophy carries over into the channel's original television dramas, beginning with *Rectify* and carrying through to the era of Peak TV. Without saying so explicitly, Vesper acknowledged the commercial necessity involved in creating quality programming arising out of a premium-channel identity and the imperative of adapting to an ad-supported system. Difference and distinction in terms of channel brand and programming must be amplified while also being high profile enough to appeal to a wider quality audience than perhaps those looking for a Kurosawa film on cable.

Basing notions of quality on the assumed upscale tastes of a channel or network's target audience is fairly prevalent among marketers and executives for niche outlets that require subscription fees for their viewers—either through cable or streaming platforms. The taste-based notion of quality is especially notable in the latter and will be a focus of Chapter 7. But it is worth addressing here with regard to Southern realism and notions of television quality more generally. The demarcation of certain taste cultures (e.g., people who like indie movies) as markers of the quality audience serves as a way of adding a qualitative sense of value for programming that often lacks successful quantitative audience ratings. Part of the determination of quality in the post-network era is that it is rarified. It produces a specific and small in-group of those who have the cultural, and often literal, capital to appreciate them. For *Rectify*, part of that quality appeal rested in its slow, meditative narrative pacing and its approach to religious representation within the Southern realist mode.

Rectify was often described as a slow drama in that its focus is on the internal and interpersonal psychology of its characters while the plot is secondary and elliptical.[35] Although many critics of the show found the characters and their development to be more important to the narrative than the show's premise, its premise did shape the narrative in key ways.[36] *Rectify* was not merely a slice of Southern life narrative. It was also a crime drama. The criminal justice plot was the sub rosa driving force of the series, creating the conditions in which the exploration of the characters' personal and interpersonal development and relationships can develop. It operated similarly to the football in *Friday Night Lights* in that it acted as the narrative glue for the characters, providing the context and foundation for ongoing narrative arcs and conflicts. The show began with the release of Daniel Holden from death row, where he had resided for almost two decades after he was convicted of murder at the age of seventeen. This premise established Daniel's character as a man out of touch with his world. He re-enters his small-town life with a changed family makeup and to a largely alien social and technological world. While he was in prison, Daniel's father died, and his mother remarried, so Daniel must live with his new stepfather and be in the same family with his stepbrother, Teddy, who had moved into the primary filial role when Daniel was in jail. Daniel and Teddy knew each other in high school and did not get along, nor do they connect once Teddy is forced to adjust to being one of two grown sons in the family. The tension between the two remains high as Teddy worries over the connection his wife, Tawney, feels with Daniel and rails against being part of a freed murderer's family life. In the first seasons, Teddy continues to believe that Daniel is guilty of the murder for which he was convicted, despite new DNA evidence implicating Daniel's innocence and setting him free. Daniel's closest ties to the outside world, both in prison and once he has re-entered life outside, are his mother, Janet, and his sister, Amantha (Abigail Spencer), who has worked tirelessly all of her adult life to get him released. Amantha even moved back to Paulie, Georgia, their hometown, from Atlanta to help him adjust.

Rectify was filmed and located in a small town in Georgia, providing a specifically situated Southern milieu. There was a spectrum of character ideologies on display in the show, but they all existed within an imagined Southern mentality in which Christianity, conservatism, and whiteness are the dominant characteristics. All the characters react to or within this paradigm. Tawney is a true believer in Christianity; it guides her and uplifts her and provides her with a support system that her family does not. Through her Christianity, she connects with Daniel in a way that supersedes her relationship with her husband. As a victim of the system, Daniel is both insider and outsider of the hegemony of their culture, as is Tawney regarding her approach to Christianity. Tawney truly believes and applies Christian principles of love and forgiveness to her personal reactions and relationships. However, on the basis of Teddy's occasional reactions to her credulity and the reactions of other supposed churchgoers we see in the series, she is unique in that. Tawney's devotion was not portrayed as naive or negative, but it did seem distinct from a general sense of hypocrisy attached to superficial Christian culture, especially as it is embodied by her husband, Teddy.

Other than Tawney, the dominant expression of Christian belief in *Rectify* is cultural—and often superficial. Teddy, in particular, represents a kind of cultural Christianity that functions for people like him to use as a justification to judge others from that perspective. Part of representing an authentic South involves representing hypocritical and flawed Christians like Teddy, who is cruel to Daniel yet asserts his own moral authority as a proper Christian Southern white man. In *Rectify* the slow drama of character development occurs around a variety of touchstones, including religion and the array of its manifestations in an authentic vision of the South. Similarly to *Friday Night Lights, Rectify* presents a spectrum of belief contained within a Christian culture, a spectrum that can contribute to claims of authenticity through its diversity even within a Southern culture imagined as dominantly Christian.

Tawney's devotion to Christian ideals informs not only her response to Daniel and her empathy toward him but also Daniel's pursuit of stability. In Daniel's mind, Tawney is his rock and his redeemer. She is the only one in the family who didn't know him before his imprisonment and is therefore the only one not constantly comparing him to his earlier self. She sees Daniel for the new, damaged person he is after spending more than half of his life on death row. She is also the object of Daniel's romantic attention because she treats him as a human individual, not a shadow of his teenaged self. Moreover, through her support, Daniel begins to find some spiritual peace through Tawney's religiousness. In the fifth and penultimate episode of the first season, "Drip, Drip," Daniel's most peaceful moment occurs after he joins a congregation community outreach tent to be baptized. He enters the rows of people in white outfits after a night of wandering and struggling with his unstable emotions, seemingly seeking rebirth. As he is baptized, Tawney appears in the tent, and when their eyes meet, it's clear that Daniel needs her connection to Christianity to stabilize his own religious efforts. He resists going under the water until he meets her gaze across the tent; she cries as he is baptized. He then meets her and they share a long hug. Their relationship is strengthened by their now shared faith, and Daniel's apparently improved mental state.

However, as Tawney pulls away to distance herself not only from Daniel's violent tendencies and instability but also from her potential romantic relationship with him, Daniel's Christian faith seems to disappear. We don't see him again attending church, nor do we see him as peaceful as he was post-baptism again for the rest of the season and beyond. In the second season, it becomes clear why religion disappeared from his life when Tawney did: for him, Tawney was his faith. He tells her that she was his salvation in the episode "The Great Destroyer," using Christian faith language and admitting to his conflation of Christian salvation and human salvation through his love of Tawney.

As Tawney moves out of Daniel's storylines in season two, religion, in the form of Christianity, became a more marginal part of the show's narrative. Although there are hints of broader spiritual and mythological symbols and stories, religion as part of the show's Southern realism and representative authenticity disappeared. Instead, there appeared a continued yearning for salvation by Daniel: through Tawney herself, through escape to Atlanta at one point, and through notable scenes in a pecan tree grove that Daniel's father used to take him to as a child. In the first episode of the second season, "Running with the Bull," Daniel dreams as he is in a coma in the hospital after being beaten by the brother and friends of the girl Daniel was accused of killing. In the grove, he encounters both a man who seems to represent divine temptation—Devil or otherwise—a decrepit statue of a satyr that Daniel focuses on, and the spirit of (or representation of) Daniel's one friend from death row, Kerwin (Johnny Ray Gill). This friend is a young man convicted and imprisoned similarly to Daniel but is not depicted as an overtly bad man. Kerwin was not granted a reprieve and thus was executed, but he appears to Daniel as a guiding, possibly divine, force to coax him back to wakefulness and life. Even as religion itself takes a backseat to other stories in *Rectify*'s second season, the show maintains the foundation of metaphysical seeking developed earlier. In addition, the fleeting sense of peace Daniel finds after his baptism indicates the inability of Christianity to fully provide the framework for processing and rectifying the complicated human systems and relationships required of these characters in this story. Christianity is one avenue, Tawney's main avenue, for comfort and meaning, as well as the culturally assumed and prescribed avenue for dealing with such family and community trauma as having a family member returned from death row. But it is clearly not a fulfilling one for any of the characters. Tawney represents the devout Christian end of the spectrum of belief presented within the Southern realist mode, and, as noted above, Amantha represents the nonreligious polar opposite. But both are reactive to the centrality of Christianity.

Like in *Friday Night Lights*, representing a spectrum of Christian belief within a Southern culture structured around Christianity acts as a way that religion can be contained within quality television demarcations. Christianity and religious belief in *Rectify* become ways in which to present the psychologies of characters within a meditative mode of Southern realist drama. Here it is worth returning to executive producer Melissa Bernstein's explanation of religion's place within the production culture and marketing of *Rectify*. She reveals that despite the use of religion in *Rectify*, there remain clear incentives to distance creatives (and for creatives to distance themselves) from religion as a term and concept. She characterized *Rectify*'s use of religion as happenstance to representing "real people" in the American

South, "real" as Ray McKinnon's authorial vision dictates. Moreover, the Senior Vice President of Marketing at SundanceTV made clear that the marketing of the show includes McKinnon's perspective. Thus, its lack of an overt display of religion—aside from in SundanceTV's Publicity social media feeds reposting and retweeting praise from viewers—supports Bernstein's claim that McKinnon would avoid highlighting the religious aspects. In an interview with *The Christian Post*, McKinnon avoided talking about religion, taking a question about redemption and answering it with regard to forgiveness in a relationship.[37] Even within the containment provided by quality aesthetics, audience targeting, and channel brand, religion requires minimizing within its production culture even when it is geographically displaced from the American South.

CONCLUSION

Both *Friday Night Lights* and *Rectify* depict Christianity as a dominant part of white Southern culture, enabling a broad and occasionally deep exploration of religion within the storyworld of their shows. Christianity is a key component of the "real" American South, a heartland value and subject that must be included if a show is to claim it is representing the authentic South. The representation of an authentic South is the guiding principle of Southern realism as an aesthetic mode that targets quality audiences. Southern realism evolved from the Southern gothic mode, maintaining the latter's Southern representational foci on race, class, and religion but translating horrific excess into realist understatement that could be branded as quality. Within Southern realism, religion, specifically Christianity, is of central concern. Thus, Southern realist shows, exemplified by *Friday Night Lights* and *Rectify* but also visible in such shows as *Justified* and *True Detective*, represent Christianity as a dominant cultural structure that shapes the full spectrum of belief represented. From evangelists to atheists, the characters in Southern realist dramas are influenced by the cultural norm of Christianity.

Creatives and executives, outside of that culture, can claim to represent the authentic South of Southern realism, targeting viewers who are also outside of that culture. Southern realist dramas are not perceived as middlebrow like predecessors *Touched by an Angel* and *7th Heaven* were; they're *real*. The Christian content is an authentic part of Southern reality, not a vehicle for religious messaging. Unlike the middlebrow religious dramas discussed in

Part I, the writers, producers, executives, and marketers who create "real" Southern stories such as *Friday Night Lights* and *Rectify*—and position them within the quality brand—use the artistic claims of authenticity to protect themselves from the risk of being seen as religious or blandly inoffensive themselves. The combination of regional realness and otherness enables religion to be displaced and thus distanced from the Hollywood hesitation regarding religion.

Southern realist dramas illustrate a paradox of post-network-era religious representation. Like the other categories of dramas in this study, they are part of a boom in the number and type of religious subjects in nonreligious, mainstream television. But within the industry, there is little corresponding promotion of the presence of religion on television. In fact, from 2003 to 2016 we saw the opposite dominate: a variety of strategies are employed by industry practitioners to disavow, minimize, abstract, and displace religion. These strategies of containment take place within the context of writers' rooms and executive offices and function to make religion ideologically safe to work with in the television industry. As part of those containment strategies for religion, creatives must deal with the legacy of religion as middlebrow. The displacement and distance displayed in discussions with writers, producers, executives, and marketers for the shows in this chapter, *Friday Night Lights* and *Rectify*, illustrate the disconnect between what we see on screen in terms of religion and how creatives discuss their work and their understanding of it with regard to religious representation. For the dramas addressed in this chapter, authenticity and Southern realism are the tools of geographic containment strategies employed. In the next chapter, similar strategies of distancing use nonwhite racial representation instead of place to achieve similar ends.

4

Nonwhite Christian Dramas

Exploration through Otherness in *Jane the Virgin* and
Greenleaf

While this book is primarily concerned with examining white Christianity
as it is represented in television dramas and understood by those who work
on those shows, the analysis of this normative form of religion necessitates
analysis of that which has not been normalized. Thus, this chapter exists to
explore nonwhite representations of Christianity. Admittedly, it is problem-
atic to analyze nonwhite representation as a point of contrast for whiteness,
but such an approach follows the logics of the television industry. As Herman
Gray noted in 1995,

> It is my contention that television representations of blackness operate
> squarely within the boundaries of middle-class patriarchal discourses about
> "whiteness" as well as the historic racialization of the social order. These
> dominant social and cultural discourses maintain normative universes
> within which all other representations and marginalization of difference—
> race, class, ethnic, gender, sexual—are constructed and positioned.[1]

Gray's reasoning certainly was true in the 1980s and early 1990s, the time
period he focuses on in his study. Gray's argument was based in the still-
dominant realm of broadcast television of that time. Since then, the television industry has shifted dramatically, as discussed in the Introduction
and Chapters 1–3. However, outside of the few marginal-identity-focused
outlets, such as BET (black audiences), Univision (Latinx audiences), or Logo
(queer audiences), whiteness remains the normative logic of the television
industry and whom it considers to be the primary and principle audience
for television as a whole. Even as representations of nonwhite characters and
storylines have increased, the persistence of othering through stereotyping
and market positioning persists. As Arlene Dávila argues in the introduction

Divine Programming. Charlotte E. Howell, Oxford University Press (2020).
© Oxford University Press.
DOI: 10.1093/oso/9780190054373.001.0001

to *Contemporary Latina/o Media*, "Liberal racial thinking would tell us that racially based stereotypes would lessen, as racial 'minorities' are everywhere present. But the continued othering of Latin@s in the media suggest that their racialization continues apace."[2]

This assumption of racial disparity between the upscale audiences and the characters on these nonwhite dramas, however, allows for more specific, nuanced, and in-depth engagement with Christianity. *Jane the Virgin* (The CW, 2014–2019) couches its premise and ongoing narratives within the belief system of the Catholic Church and its strictures as related to believers' lived experiences. Jane Villanueva (Gina Rodriguez) begins the series with its narrative premise: because of her Catholicism and the influence of her devout grandmother Alba (Ivonne Coll), Jane decided to remain a virgin until marriage, even after she was accidentally artificially inseminated to become a pregnant virgin. The parallels to the Virgin Mary are an ongoing subplot of the first season, and both Alba and Jane's persistent return to the teachings of Catholicism throughout the series: they attend church regularly, discuss religious primary school for Jane's son Mateo, and struggle with God in times of grief. Their Catholicism is, for both characters, defining. Moreover, it is treated respectfully as religion with nuance while acknowledging the tension between religious tenets and living those tenets.

Contrasting with the personal experience within a greater traditional religious system portrayed in *Jane the Virgin*, *Greenleaf* (OWN, 2016–) is the most recent in a long line of representations of black Christianity on TV via the workings of a specific church. The show tells the story of the Greenleaf family of preachers at the center of Calvary Fellowship World Ministries, a black megachurch in Memphis, Tennessee, and their various traumas and struggles. Grace Greenleaf (Merle Dandridge) returns to Memphis in order to minister to the community and root out the corruption in her family and church. The family drama includes examples that are particularly couched in black church culture: down-low homosexuality, sexual assault and molestation, and political and economic manipulation to accumulate significant wealth for church leaders.

Both *Jane the Virgin* and *Greenleaf* represent departures from the overall trend of the 1996–2016 time period despite many similarities with the other shows discussed throughout this book. Like other case studies, their serialized storylines allow for week-to-week and year-to-year engagement with these overtly Christian characters and storylines. Their target audiences include upscale niches that are further articulated through critical praise.[3]

However, these shows gain a significant amount of leeway in their representation of Christianity by the mere fact that their representation of Christianity is not normalized and hegemonic as white Christianity is. Because it is separate from the dominant whiteness of television and the industry's imagined upscale audiences, nonwhite Christianity becomes another way of "authentically" representing another culture—other relative to normative white culture. These two shows act as case studies that complement and extend the distancing analyzed in the previous chapter, and taken together, the distancing based on place and race illuminates the construction of the imagined upscale audiences as coastal, urban, and white, unperturbed by the representation of religion-cum-religion as long as it does not resemble that which has been normalized as part of (white) American culture.

LATINX CATHOLICISM ON TV

Jane the Virgin is not the first or the only representation of Latinx Catholicism in dramatic television, but its approach to religion is both more pronounced and more sustained than its predecessors (and contemporaries). In the realm of American sitcoms, there have been a handful of shows featuring Latinx lead characters, from *Chico and the Man* (NBC, 1974–1978), which featured Puerto Rican Freddie Prinze as the Chicano character Chico, to *George Lopez* (ABC, 2002–2007) and *Cristela* (ABC, 2014–2015), which featured the titular Latinx comedians within multi-camera family sitcoms. Most recently, the Netflix adaptation of Norman Lear's *One Day at a Time* (2017–) recast the sitcom's family as Cuban-Americans. These sitcoms have not shied away from the main characters' Latinx culture and often explored the specificity of their race and ethnicity within the American context, but there have been relatively fewer serial dramas that similarly addressed Latinx specificity.

The first prime-time broadcast serial drama to feature a Latinx cast and character focus was PBS's *American Family* (2002–2004) about the Gonzalez family of Los Angeles. As Johnny Diaz wrote for the periodical *Hispanic* in anticipation of the show's first season, "Billed as the first Hispanic-themed weekly drama to air on American broadcast television, the show was initially going to air on CBS, which financed the pilot episode two years ago. But CBS didn't find a place for the show on its 2000–2001 schedule and rejected it—leaving the show homeless. In a bold programming move, PBS adopted the show . . . albeit with a smaller budget and a fraction of the projected audience the show would have garnered on CBS."[4] The tale of *American Family's* origin, that it was passed over for mainstream audiences and instead found a home on a more niche and upscale outlet, is echoed by the other early-2000s prime-time drama featuring Latinx characters, *Resurrection Blvd* (Showtime, 2000–2002). That show focused on a multigenerational family of boxers navigating their masculine identity within East Los Angeles' Chicano community and within their family.[5] In the mid-2000s, another Latinx-focused serial hour-long show began airing on network television: *Ugly Betty* (ABC, 2006–2010).

Because both *Ugly Betty* and *Jane the Virgin* were adapted from telenovelas that first aired in Latin America and were then Americanized for US broadcast TV, *Ugly Betty* is the show to which *Jane the Virgin* is often compared.[6] In fact, a *Hollywood Reporter* preview of the show opened with the comparison as *de rigueur*, writing, "[c]omparisons to *Ugly Betty* are inevitable for *Jane the Virgin*. Not only is it one of the few American telenovela adaptations to make it to the air, it's the second Latino family dramedy to come from executive producer Ben Silverman."[7] Additionally, the showrunner for *Jane the Virgin*, Jennie Snyder Urman, promoted the show "as *Ugly Betty* meets *Gilmore Girls*."[8] Most points of comparison were made to promote The CW and/or the show as an evolution of *Ugly Betty*, one that embraced its Latinx telenovela roots, promising more character depth within the adapted format.[9]

Although *Ugly Betty* occasionally engaged with Latinx Catholicism, it was often done at a distance. Betty and her immediate family didn't foreground churchgoing or religious culture outside of the celebration of major holidays such as Christmas. There are images of Catholicism in the Suarez home, such as votive candles, images of saints, and crucifixes/crosses as wall decorations, but the few examples in which the show turns toward spirituality are not overtly Christian. For example, in the penultimate episode of season one, "A Tree Grows in Guadalajara," Betty is led by visions and coincidence to meet the grandmother she thought was dead and ultimately find a degree of absolution for her father. Such a confluence of circumstances might be discussed as a miracle or a blessing by characters deeply engaged in faith, but Betty does not pray for the meeting; she instead allows her personal determination to achieve her goal to be aided by vague spiritual "signs" such as seeing a vision of a mustachioed version of her paramour leading her to her maternal grandmother. *Ugly Betty* and its characters may have exhibited some of the superficial symbols of Latinx Catholicism, but such symbols mostly emphasized the Latinx via the Catholicism instead of exploring the latter as a faith and lived religion. Thus, *Ugly Betty* exemplifies a mode of representing Latinx identity in which Catholicism is a default element of the cultural representation instead of an active foundation of the culture. This mode aligns with demographic trends—in 2010 Pew Research "found that fully two-thirds of Hispanics [in the U.S.] were Catholic"—as well as patterns of representation.[10] Catholicism is key to Latin American stereotypes; according to Antonio V. Menéndez Alarcón, "Catholicism is indeed the most widespread religion in Latin America, but it is not as omnipresent as is often represented in US literature and culture."[11] Within the limited range of Latinx televisual representation, a visually Catholic approach is the most prevalent. In many ways, it acts as an extension of the use of white Christianity as a cultural norm instead of a religion that has become prevalent in the twenty-first century. However, unlike of the tropes of white Christianity becoming unmoored from their religiousness through their transition to pure narrative, the tropes of Latinx Catholicism remain specific, and specifically Catholic, as a way to further identify the otherness of Latinx characters.

Jane the Virgin, in contrast with its antecedents, continually uses the symbols of otherness—both religious and not—to delve deeply into the distinct culture of its Latinx characters and their relationship to American culture. I will be focusing on how *Jane the Virgin* represents its characters' Catholicism relative to other case studies and the logics and legacies of broadcast television production, but the show also foregrounds its otherness from the norm in its formalist choices. First, there is a third-person-omniscient narrator who both frames the narrative of the show and provides commentary on the events as they unfold. The narrator functions to emphasize the telenovela elements, by providing reminders of important background or narrative information that contextualizes the scene, commenting on the interpersonal drama, foreshadowing major narrative twists (such as the repeated promise in seasons one through three that Jane's boyfriend Michael [Brett Dier] would love Jane until the day he died, which he did in season three), and occasionally reflecting on the telenovela genre elements, such as when a shocking revelation occurs, and he says, "I know! Straight out of a telenovela, right?"[12] The self-awareness of the show and its distinctly Latinx genre, going so far as to label it as "telenovela" often, aids in marketplace distinction while also refusing to diminish its Latinx identity. Second, Jane's *abuela* Alba rarely speaks English. Alba knows English; like many immigrants, she understands the language but does not feel confident speaking it regularly. While other characters speak English to her, she responds in Spanish with subtitles conveying her meaning to the viewing audience. Subtitles are rare on American broadcast television; consistent subtitles across all the seasons of a show are even rarer. But Alba's subtitles and use of Spanish cement the show as starkly different and specifically Latinx. Such characteristics are only further emphasized by the show's approach to Catholicism.

THE TELE-NOVELTY OF *JANE THE VIRGIN*'S CATHOLICISM

Jane the Virgin began in 2014 on The CW network, as part of a group of new shows premiering in the 2014–2015 season that balanced the darker, masculine, and supernatural shows that had characterized the network in recent years, such as *Supernatural* (the WB/CW, 2005–2020), *The Vampire Diaries* (The CW, 2009–2017), its spin-off *The Originals* (The CW, 2013–2018), and *Arrow* (The CW, 2012–2020). Along with *Jane the Virgin*, The CW premiered *The Flash* (The CW, 2014–) in the fall of 2014 as its bright and fun DC superhero show, spinning off from the dark-and-gritty *Arrow*. At midseason, *iZombie* (The CW, 2015–2019) premiered as a darkly comedic adaptation of the Vertigo comic of the same name. President of The CW, Mark Pedowitz, said of the network's direction for that season, "We've set out over the last few years to broaden out the 18–34 audience . . . This year, we hope *The Flash* and *Jane the Virgin* broaden out the audience base. I'm just happy to have viewers, in all honesty."[13] In 2015, he described the 2014–2015 season as "pivotal" and emphasized the critical attention to *Jane the Virgin* as key to The CW's strategy of expanding its target audience through "quality programming."[14] Pedowitz and other CW executives further underscored *Jane the Virgin*'s significance to the network because its star, Gina Rodriguez, won the Golden Globe for best actress in a comedy or musical in 2015, bringing both an unprecedented award for the young network and increased attention for the niche show.[15]

Arising from its telenovela origin, *Jane the Virgin* is drama with a high-concept premise that is both underlined by its title and reiterated through exposition throughout the series. The titular Jane chose to wait until marriage to have sex, but through a mix-up at the gynecologist, Jane was accidentally inseminated with the last sperm sample of her former crush, Rafael Solano (Justin Baldoni). Jane; Rafael; his wife, Petra (Yael Grobglas); Jane's boyfriend, Michael; her mother, Xiomara (Andrea Navedo); and grandmother

Alba all navigate the telenovela-worthy trials, tribulations, and complicated love life of Jane as a virgin mother.

Like *Ugly Betty* a decade earlier, *Jane the Virgin* adapted the telenovela format into an amalgam of prime-time soap opera and dramedy familiar for American audiences. Both shows consistently submitted to comedy awards categories and are discussed as comedies or dramedies but carry the serial storytelling and excessive drama of soap operas as their main narrative form. The comedy elements often arise from embracing—if occasionally ironically—the excessive telenovela elements of the shows. In their analyses of prime-time melodramas of the 1980s, both Jane Feuer and Lynn Joyrich, in separate essays, defined and analyzed the genre in terms of excess.[16] Joyrich goes further than most, arguing that melodrama had become "an ideal form for postmodern culture and for television—a form which arises from a fragmented network of space and time yet still seems to offer a sense of wholeness, reality, and living history."[17] For Joyrich, that shared whole is the excess of "consumer overpresence."[18] In the incorporation of melodrama into American television more generally through this emphasis on the viewer as interpellated consumer, Joyrich examined possible counter-readings to the maligned melodramatic form. Feuer, similarly, found the potential for challenging the status quo through prime-time melodrama. Discussing *Dallas* (CBS, 1972–1991) and *Dynasty* (ABC, 1981–1989), Feuer argued,

> Moments of melodramatic excess relate to the serial structure of these dramas and occur as a form of temporary closure within and between episodes and even entire seasons . . . Since serials offer only temporary resolutions, it could be argued that the teleological metaphysics of classical narrative structure have been subverted. The moral universe of the prime-time serials is one in which the good can never ultimately receive their just rewards, yet evil can never wholly triumph.[19]

Feuer's point about narrative excess and endlessly deferred narrative is adapted from daytime soap operas, many of which had been airing in one form or another for half a century by the 1980s. The extended, ongoing, intricate storylines of both daytime and prime-time soap operas gained prominence in the 1980s and have persisted as the popularity of serial dramatic television has increased in subsequent decades. The form of storytelling is familiar, and even somewhat normal, for American prime-time dramas in the twenty-first century.

The familiar form of the prime-time soap opera finds its Latin American echo in telenovelas, but with some key differences. Telenovelas, like American daytime soap operas, air daily, instead of weekly as with a prime-time melodramatic serial. However, as Carolina Acosta-Alzuru argues, telenovelas differ from even daytime American soap operas in a number of ways:

> (a) Telenovelas have a finite number of episodes (120–200); therefore, viewers expect a definitive conclusion to the story; (b) they are financed by television networks and broadcast both in prime time and in the afternoon block; (c) telenovelas determine the stardom system for Latin American actors; and (d) because they perform in various telenovelas, the identities of actors are not tied to the characters they portray.[20]

Jane the Virgin uses in-narrative telenovelas, *The Passions of Santos, Tiago a Través del Tiempo,* and *Los Viajes de Guillermo,* starring Jane's father, Rogelio de la Vega (Jamie Camil), to emphasize both convergence and distinction between the show and the telenovela format. The diegetic telenovelas exemplify even more fraught premises—backstabbing political intrigue, time travel, and a *Gulliver's Travels* adaptation, respectively— than a virgin mother. And often the ridiculousness of these telenovelas is used to both contrast with the grounded stories of Jane and her family and provide more flexibility for *Jane the Virgin's* forays into visual fancy. As Juan Piñón writes in his review of the show for *ReVista,* "Although *Jane* is not a telenovela format, the narrative strategy appears to resemble one, by underscoring some melodramatic properties of the story, but also by underscoring campy and magically oriented over-the-top scenes full of romance or by creating new unexpected twists on the plot."[21] Expanding on Piñón's point, the including of diegetic telenovelas and their production allows for the "over-the-top scenes" and plots to weigh against the exaggerated examples of Rogelio's telenovelas. Where Rogelio must free his costar from a giant sandwich in *Los Viajes de Guillermo,* Jane can be confronted by devotees who believe her a holy virgin in her daily life. Such a storyline appears extreme in comparison with American prime-time soap operas but tame relative to telenovelas. It is within this betwixt-and-between generic space that Jane negotiates the religious elements of its premise and characters within the still-hesitant industrial approach to religion. It does so more thoroughly than previous American series focusing on Latinx characters.

Jane the Virgin's premise is suffused by the Catholic faith, and in particular the devotion to *La Virgen*, Mary, and virginity more generally. The show
begins with the narrator introducing the titular character, her epithet, and
her family through a "prologue": "Our story begins thirteen and a half years
ago, when Jane Gloriana Villanueva was a mere ten years old. It should be
noted that as a mere ten years old, Jane's passions included, in no particular
order: her family, God, and grilled cheese sandwiches. This is Jane's grandmother, Alba Gloriana Villanueva, her passions include God and Jane in that
particular order."[22] While the narrator explains the family of characters, Alba
has Jane crumple a white rose then try to make it look as it did before. Alba
tells Jane that the flower, wilted and wrinkled, is like her virginity: once gone
it can never go back. She asks Jane to never forget that, and the narrator tells
the audience, "And Jane never did."[23] Young Jane is portrayed as frightened
by the threat of lost purity, and very clearly is shaped by it. Piñón focuses
on the specifically Latinx articulation of virginity, writing that Alba "dwell[s]
on longstanding Latin American representations of womanhood informed
by the 'virgin/whore' dichotomy. . . nurtured by Marianismo [female gender
roles based in virginal purity] that reinforces patriarchal norms."[24] The
metaphor of the flower becomes an embodied symbol of purity and the
consequences of losing that purity, which is presented in relation to God
and constructed along the longstanding tropes of Latina representation. The
image of the freshly spoiled flower then transitions to the same crumpled
flower, dried, preserved, and framed on Jane's wall. It serves as a reminder of
Alba's lesson, even as twenty-three-year-old Jane is making out with her boyfriend under it.

The title, the premise, and the introduction of the character all center
around the purity of virginity and a young Catholic woman's choice to wait
to have sex until she is married. The choice is explicitly and irrevocably
connected to Alba's and Jane's shared Catholic faith through the explanation
that both are passionate about God. Moreover, throughout the scene, Alba's
cross necklace is subtly but clearly displayed, codifying her as Christian.
Alba's faith is the foundation of the discussion and a key shaping moment for
young Jane as well as the show's premise. The Catholic beliefs informing the
decision to wait is often discussed alongside Jane's relationship to her grandmother, who remains the show's continued bastion of Catholicism even
when Jane doubts after Michael's death.

After Jane is mistakenly inseminated and she finds out she's pregnant, she
contemplates having an abortion, but alongside her own faith's role in that

choice, Jane wrestles with Alba's reaction should she decide to terminate the pregnancy. Over the course of that first episode, it is revealed that Alba suggested Xiomara abort Jane, and Xiomara, who is not devout, decided to keep her baby even if that made her a mother at sixteen. The revelation is couched in Alba's guilt at her suggestion, as it represented a failing of her devotion to her faith. As Diana Martinez argues briefly in her review for *The Atlantic*, "Morality and religion play a big role in telenovelas, much like they do in the everyday lives of many Latinos and Latin Americans. In *Jane the Virgin*, Catholicism is deployed to test the women's views on sex and motherhood, as seen in the abortion storyline of the first episode."[25] Alba's initial reaction to Jane's pregnancy is even more informed by her religion, as she "wants to embrace [it] as a sign from God," evoking the immaculate conception.[26] From virginity to abortion and virgin pregnancy, *Jane the Virgin*'s plot imbues its premise with Catholic meanings, perhaps none so clearly as when the show uses imagery of *La Virgen de Guadalupe* and connections to the Virgin Mary more broadly.

Jane the Virgin's (and Jane the Virgin's) ties to the other famous virgin mother are not just implied or used as shorthand referents. As mentioned above, Alba thinks of the Virgin Mary when Jane tells her she is pregnant, but in the first season, the parallels become explicit when a group of devoted Catholics begin following Jane as a modern-day Mary. At the Catholic high school where Jane works in that first season, adherents show up with signs depicting Jane as a Holy Mother and ask for her benediction and help with fertility.[27] This plotline acts primarily as a joke; there was nothing necessarily divine about Jane's insemination despite her maintained "purity." However, the believers are not treated as *only* jokes. They are an extreme reaction to the story of Jane's pregnancy, but one that emphasizes that the writers of the show know that a pregnant Catholic virgin would attract attention and would have religious ramifications.

Moreover, the connection to the Virgin Mary reaffirms tropes of Latinx representation that often center around *La Virgen de Guadalupe*, an icon and signal of Mexican Catholicism. Although *La Virgen de Guadalupe* is a syncretic depiction of the Catholic Holy Mother with some visual symbolism particular to indigenous Mexican religions, her status as an iconic representation of Latinx Catholicism flattens both *La Virgen*'s cultural specificity and her dualistic symbolism: indigenous and imperial; potentially feminist and patriarchal; "caring and destructive; spiritual and physical; motherly and independent."[28] Like many representations of difference on television,

Latinidad often deals with erasure as much as presence. In particular, the differences among particular cultures (Mexican, Cuban, indigenous, Central American, South American, etc.) are eroded for a more general Latinx representation. Because of proximity and population, Mexican and Mexican-American culture often overlays these differences, standing for Latinx culture on the whole. Thus, *La Virgen de Guadalupe*, a specifically Mexican religious icon, signifies Latinx Catholicism more generally, especially when the icon is used in *Jane the Virgin's* imagery.

In a recurring trope of the series' promotional art, Jane appears in front of a bright, colorful backdrop with a corona of light around her head. The lightening around her face highlights her expression and draws attention to Jane as the star of the show, but it also evokes the halo of light surrounding images of the Virgin May. Although Jane does not adopt the submissive pose associated with depictions of the Holy Mother, the corona of light implies the connection to well-known Catholic imagery (Figure 4.1).

The trope of the corona is a subtler variation on some of the first key art for the series' initial promotion in 2014. In the image, Jane's halo is brighter and more detailed: not merely a soft fading into a colored background. The corona even echoes the lines of emphasis around the title to the left of the image. Moreover, Jane's hands—holding a pregnancy test—appear to be in a loose prayer formation (Figure 4.2).

Like other religiously themed promotional images discussed in this book, the religiousness is understood mainly if one is looking for it instead of seeing a familiar trope of a particular Latinx Catholic culture.

In later seasons, after Jane has gotten married and is no longer a virgin, Jane's Catholicism continues to evolve both in relation to and outside of her relationship with Alba. No longer the virginal mother and dealing with grief over the death of her husband, Jane explicitly grapples with her faith and expresses doubt in season four. Aside from that instance, much of Jane's faith continues as an established aspect of her character, one that is settled and thus not as often discussed or explicitly depicted as in earlier seasons.

CHRISTIANITY AND BLACK TV IDENTITY

In contrast to *Jane the Virgin*, which is part of a relatively sparse genealogy of Latinx representation on mainstream American television, *Greenleaf* benefits from a longer history of both black and, specifically, black Christian

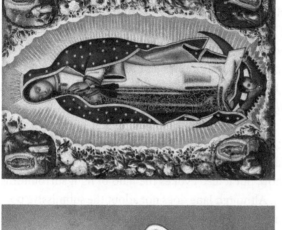

Figure 4.1 Left to right: *Jane the Virgin* promotional art, season two; *Jane the Virgin* promotional art, season three; *La Virgen de Guadalupe* (public domain, courtesy of LACMA)

Figure 4.2 *Jane the Virgin* promotional image, season one

representation on American television. In previous chapters, I discussed two examples: Della Reese and her role in *Touched by an Angel* and the depiction of the black church in Dillon in *Friday Night Lights*. Moreover, portrayals of black Christians pepper television history almost as much as black characters do. From Amos interpreting the Lord's Prayer for his daughter in the 1952 Christmas episode of *Amos 'n Andy* (CBS, 1951–1953) to Florida Evans's devotion to Jesus in *Good Times* (CBS, 1974–1979). But perhaps the most notable historical example of black Christianity is the black-church set sitcom, *Amen* (NBC, 1986–1991).

When *Amen* premiered in the fall of 1986, Aldore D. Collier described the show for *Jet* magazine:

> The Black church has been parodied in numerous movies and television shows. But rarely has Hollywood's look gone beyond the choir and the minister. In "Amen," NBC's new sitcom starring Sherman Hemsley and Clifton Davis, audiences are finally seeing the political as well as humorous side of a centuries-old institution. In the series, which has recorded impressive ratings for its initial episodes, Davis plays the new, straight [sic]-laced minister of a Philadelphia church. He is sometimes called to match wits with Hemsley, who plays a feisty, deviously zealous and extremely funny deacon.[29]

The description—and the positive review—emphasizes the rarity of deeply engaged portrayals of black Christianity while also addressing a readership that it assumes knows the reality of the black church. The article goes on to quote Hemsley, who said, "[B]ut it is not like just going to church rejoicing. We show the board of the church."[30] There are no explanations about the sometimes tense relationships between ministers and deacons or how hilarity might arise from the board of a church. This *Jet* article implies the lived reality of regular attendance, or at least knowledge, of the culture of black churches. Hemsley would later say of the show, "Everything that happened really happened in church . . . I used to see things like that [example from the show] in my church. . . . I never mentioned it; they already had all that covered."[31] The recognizable religious aspects were key to both differentiating the show and providing the foundation for its comedy, a strategy that is still rare.

Moreover, discourse surrounding the show emphasized the respectfulness of religion as part of how the show operated. Hemsley discussed in an interview with the Television Academy Foundation the presence of religious consultants to make sure the show didn't cross the line.[32] And even at the time, Clifton Davis's real-life faith and his calling as a minister were emphasized to ground the show in respect for the church. Davis told *Jet* that he had left Hollywood after his youthful career so as not to compromise his faith and that "he had some initial reservations about the way the Black church would be shown. 'There are no buffoons. It's not like "Amos 'n Andy." Sherman does some foolish things, but that's comedy. It works.'"[33] Although *Amen* fits both historically and generically outside of the purview of this book, it provides a useful example for a pattern of presenting the black church that both echoed predominant representations of white Christianity on dramas (emphasis on respect for faith and avoiding stereotypes) and explored how black Christianity has a deeper history of garnering nuanced and specific portrayals of faith than white Christianity. Where *Amen* leveraged Davis's real-life work as a minister to provide a foundation of respect in the 1980s, in 2016, the creator of *Greenleaf*, Craig Wright, used the fact that he was a former minister to leverage the show as knowing, edgy critique of Christianity. Time, outlet, genre, and audience all play a hand in this key difference, but it is worth noting the parallels up to the point of divergence: respect and nuance for comedy or for dramatic critique.[34]

In recent years, black Christianity has appeared as part of individual character arcs or one-off episodes. The ABC sitcom *Black-ish* (2014–) devoted an entire episode to mining the history of the black church, its differences from white churches, and its place within the family's life.[35] The Fox hit prime-time soap opera, *Empire* (2015–2020), for a drama example, featured a multiple-episode arc in which Andre (Trai Byers), the bipolar eldest son of the Lyon family, finds his faith in God and Jesus following a suicide attempt.[36] Although Andre's arc takes his faith seriously for both the character and how his being born-again affects his semi-criminal, music-producing family, the arc and Andre's faith was often a sidetrack for the overarching, juicier elements of the soap-opera narrative.

Across this brief historical constellation of representations of black Christianity on prime-time television, there exist a few commonalities. The black church is a locus of community identity, but a safe one that is non-threatening to white viewers. Black Christianity is not portrayed as a place for radical politics, and when politics arise, it is mostly in-church politics regarding church power structures. Key to these representations is that, like with Latinx Catholicism, there is an assumed otherness that is exploited to make the representation presumably acceptable to white audiences for whom the culture of the black church is distant from their own experience. There are still constraints placed on what is represented and how—the umbrella of respect still operates—but even the brief discussions of the above examples illustrate more specificity about black Christianity than is often seen in portrayals of white Christianity until (and even during) the era of Peak TV. Whereas *Amen* looked at the black church through the safety of the sitcom genre, and shows like *Empire* used the black church to contrast with its edgier, melodramatic narrative, *Greenleaf* united a nuanced portrayal of a black church with the prime-time soap-opera narrative.

OPRAH'S SOAP OPERA ON THE MEGACHURCH PULPIT: *GREENLEAF*

Greenleaf premiered in the summer of 2016 on the Oprah Winfrey Network (OWN). The series marked a key transition at OWN toward prestige-oriented drama series when its success was followed by *Queen Sugar*'s well-regarded first season in the fall of 2016. This transition toward upscale dramas makes sense in the context of Peak TV and its dwindling audiences sizes, but for OWN, the path toward this transition was far from clear. OWN launched in 2011, the same year *The Oprah Winfrey Show* (syndication,

1986–2011) ended. OWN began as a partnership between Oprah Winfrey's Harpo Films production company and Discovery Communications, with a "goal to remake a forgotten, high-numbered cable channel into Oprah-branded gold."[37] However, the channel struggled in its early years despite "reporting more than 1 million viewers for its first prime-time shows" upon its launch, in part because of Oprah and her staff's focus elsewhere and the lack of Oprah's on-air persona to draw viewers.[38] One of the strategies to turn the channel into a success included a turn toward scripted original programming in 2013. The first scripted original programs developed for OWN were bolstered by a deal with Tyler Perry in October 2012 to produce shows exclusively for OWN. The year 2013 saw the first two of Perry's series developed for OWN (*The Have and the Have Nots* [2013–], a drama, and the sitcom *Love Thy Neighbor* [2013–2017]) as well as two other scripted shows, reported in early 2013: " 'Dogfellas' is the working title for a new show about a former mobster who goes into the dog-grooming and -rescue business; and 'Golden Sisters' is a comedy about three senior-citizen sisters who run a salon."[39]

The foray into scripted programming, specifically the boost from Tyler Perry's productions, and a strong lineup of black, female-oriented unscripted series began to provide ratings and demographic success for the channel in 2013, especially among black women, the core audience for OWN at the time.[40] The unscripted series *Iyanla: Fix My Life* (2012–), *Houston Beauty* (2013), *Six Little McGhees* (2012–2014), *Welcome to Sweetie Pie's* (2011–2018), *Raising Whitley* (2013–2016), and *Life with LaToya* (2013–2014) were "the top six original series for black women ages 25 to 54."[41] In an interview with *Broadcasting & Cable* in May 2013, the president of OWN, Tyler Logan, discussed the evolving relationship between OWN's core demo of black women and the economic viability of the network:

> Clearly the announcement [of the partnership with Tyler Perry] has increased the demand for the network . . . Our launch partners bought into the vision that Oprah was building over the long-term. When we do show up with Tyler Perry, they see it's part of the validation of the dream that they have signed up for, because our launch partners have not gone down since launch, they've gone up . . . We clearly have embraced the adoption that happened early in our growth with the African-American presence, which you clearly see on Saturdays [with their original unscripted block], Tyler's going the help bolster that.[42]

With that black, female audience as the base driving viewership increases and helping the network move into the economic black, the push toward scripted shows continued in part because of Oprah's desires. Logan said, "Oprah is a big fan of scripted. We always felt that scripted was a way for Oprah to continue to tell stories in a different way."[43] However, because of the years of legitimating discourses around quality television up to that point (discussed in Chapter 3), serial dramas seeking recognition implicitly evoke white upscale taste cultures and thus potentially expanding or even shifting OWN's target audience.

Despite the implications of this discourse that OWN was fully embracing its black brand, toward the end of the interview, Logan hedges to seemingly avoid letting the network be pigeonholed as a "black" channel (and thus presumably inaccessible to upscale white audiences). He said, "We do know that the Oprah brand is a very, very wide lane . . . At the same time [as the Saturday night schedule and Tyler Perry productions' popularity], when you look at the drama, you do see us making sure that that wide-lane approach that we have in terms of the big picture for our network is continuing to be built."[44] The "wide lane" of Oprah's brand was key to the growth of OWN in the mid-2010s when Oprah reappeared in front of the camera for some high-profile, in-depth interviews with Lance Armstrong, Lindsay Lohan, and others exclusively for OWN starting in 2013.[45] Logan's 2013 quotation illustrates the seeds of a strategy that would take root at the network in 2015 and be on display by 2016: Using Oprah's personal brand to broaden the channel's appeal beyond its core black audience, particularly trying to attract an upscale audience that would appreciate the complex storytelling and high production values.

OWN's brand is inextricably tied to Oprah herself and her role as a tastemaker. Part of the transition toward upscale serial dramas in 2016 was the creation of discursive knowledge within the industry that Oprah in 2016 "is more involved in hearing pitches for TV shows, reviewing scripts and sending 'notes' on how to improve programming."[46] Using her talk show as a springboard, Oprah created her own culture industry of products: both her own and those she deems worthy of her by giving them a platform in her media empire. Kimberly Springer identified Oprah's industry in 2010:

> Oprah Winfrey's embodiment, her cultural productions, her actions, and her ideology constitute *The Oprah Culture Industry* (TOCI). The sheer number of productions and enterprises indicates TOCI's extensive reach

into American lives, media, and culture. TOCI ranges across a variety of media forms and uses tactics from the psychological to the material to gain a following in the millions and garner consensus for her projects.[47]

With Oprah's widespread reach, particularly across the media industries, her brand as arbiter of American taste became incontrovertible. As Springer points out, "Oprah was named one of *Time Magazine's* 100 Most Influential People in the World for four consecutive years in a row. This influence is often measured in terms of economic impact."[48] Not only were Oprah and her media empire worth billions, but anecdotes also abounded about the impact of her branded approval on a book, movie, or guru's sales figures. Taken together, this has been called the "Oprah effect," as shorthand to describe her ability to sell almost anything by granting it her stamp of approval.[49]

Much of Oprah's impact stems from her accessible spirituality, part of her brand that crosses over to mid-2010s OWN programming. Oprah characterized her own brand of spirituality as a "transition to New Age spirituality from the traditional black Baptist church where she grew up as a transition from the oppressive to the liberatory" and, as Karlyn Crowley identified, this is key to Oprah's spiritual appeal to women, "her ability to filter white, New Age ideas in gendered terms that are legitimized through race."[50] After turning her attention on her talk show and within her media empire to a spiritual, aspirational endeavor to change one's life for the better in the late 1990s, Oprah "widened her hold on the national imagination from a daily hour of convivial girl talk to a full-scale spiritual occupation."[51] In her study of Oprah's monetized spiritual empire, Kathryn Lofton argues, "Every product of Winfrey's empire combines spiritual counsel with practical encouragement, inner awakening with capitalist pragmatism."[52]

OWN's programming continued this spiritual-pragmatic mode of Oprah's brand, starting with the partnership with Tyler Perry. Perry remains connected with religious, particularly black Christian, media, as it was in this arena that he honed his most profitable character, Madea, and developed his media empire. When traditional Hollywood modes of financing and ownership did not align with his target audience of "churchgoing black women" or his desire for control, Perry took his show on the road, literally: he toured the American Southern theater circuit and used that as a way to build his base audience.[53] His work still appeals to "his religious media audience," with films and television shows, particularly any within the Madea transmedia universe, evoking Christian morality.[54] In some ways, Perry's bypassing

traditional media to focus on appealing directly to black Christian audiences
echoes some of the publicity Mark Burnett and Roma Downey engaged in
for their miniseries, discussed in Chapter 2. However, where Burnett and
Downey were trying to appeal to an audience that had been understood as
the norm and majority, Perry worked to make a large but ignored niche visible to the media industries. In addition to Perry's shows for OWN, Oprah
self-financed a seven-part documentary miniseries, *Belief,* which aired in
2015 and explored faith worldwide.[55] With Perry's involvement, *Belief,* and
uplifting unscripted programming like *Ilaya: Fix My Life* and *Super Soul
Sunday* (OWN, 2011–), OWN has continued to earn ratings and attention
from Oprah's spiritual brand and set the foundation for its launch into prestige drama production that would also focus on spirituality, but within the
context of a traditional black Christianity: *Greenleaf.*

Greenleaf was not just an extension of Oprah's brand because it was an
original production for her channel. It also marked Oprah's return to acting
and was heralded as such to distinguish the show in the era of Peak TV and
further tie it to Oprah's particular brand. Oprah's return to acting via the
show was highlighted by a *Wall Street Journal* headline, "Oprah Is Back on
TV," and in articles reviewing or previewing the premiere in which Oprah
"hasn't lost her ability to pitch her performance to the project's level . . . as
engaging as any other Winfrey performance;" she has a "modest but effec-
tive recurring guest role . . . and no doubt her A-list profile will help create
some buzz for the show."[56] In addition to the emphasis on Oprah's acting role,
each review discusses Oprah as an executive producer of the show, implying
her particular skill for selecting meaningful and popular media objects with
which to attach her name.

And Oprah's tastemaking ability is borne out in the mostly positive
reviews that particularly highlight the unique use of religion. Maureen Ryan
follows the lede of her review by describing the show as "a classic nighttime
soap, so all the staples of the genre are there: infidelity, substance abuse, a
love triangle or two, greed, resentment, and vengeance. And yet this capable
drama . . . treats themes of faith and redemption with earnest intelligence."[57]
Cynthia Littleton used *Greenleaf* to explore television shows "finally ready
to have a serious talk about religion," when she wrote that *Greenleaf* "bores
deep into the dark side of the family behind a prosperous Christian mega
church in Tennessee."[58] A review in *Time* is less positive, but still emphasizes
the religious aspect only in stating the show is "unapologetic as a tent-revival
sermonizer about playing things big and broad . . . [but with] little moments

worth delighting over."[59] These reviews cannot avoid the religious aspects of the show that are the result of the premise and setting of a family mega-church, but the writers also exhibit a somewhat blasé and unworried approach to such a premise. Ryan's review goes the most in depth, stating, "The drama treats divine callings and the devoutness of church employees with respect while questioning whether it makes sense for a religious institution to more or less operate by its own rules."[60] And even then, Ryan and Littleton are only implying the uniqueness of this approach to religion. In Littleton's article, she spends the majority of her page-long article by analyzing Hulu's *The Path* (2016–2018). Where Littleton focuses on *Greenleaf* for only one paragraph after it is introduced, she discusses *The Path* in relation to its creator/executive producer, Jessica Goldberg's personal relationship with faith, teasing out why this show about a religious cult could arise out of the mind of a nonpracticing Jewish writer who describes her approach as "intellectual agnosticism."[61] The result, likely more to do with access than intentionality, is an article that, although it never labels the Greenleaf family as black, seems far more interested in understanding why a white creator of a mostly white show on Hulu would seek to engage with religion than would a show on a black-targeted channel that actually deals with issues of Christianity.

For *Greenleaf*, the assumption of soap-opera genre proved no barrier for the power of Oprah's benefaction. According to OWN's press release, *Greenleaf* was the highest rated "new series of 2016 on ad-supported cable for women" and was in the top six for total viewers on ad-supported cable, helping make 2016 OWN's most-watched year.[62] Part of *Greenleaf*'s positioning for its premier was certainly tied to Oprah's brand, but it all fed through the Christian church at the heart of the show. Interviews and press events with Oprah, Wright, cast, and producers usually included at least passing reference to how the show approached its representation of a specifically black megachurch. In an extensive interview with *Fast Company*, Wright described how he, a white man, developed a show about a black church, "I had always wanted to do a show about a church and had never been able to really find a right way to do it. I've come to see dramatizing white privileged spirituality is kind of a dead end—it tends to devolve into either satire or sanctimony."[63] He framed this struggle in contrast with the all-encompassing social nature of a black church with the latter as a better foundation for character and drama. Wright articulated the restrictions placed on representations of white Christianity even in 2016. Yet he implies that there aren't such patterns of constraint on representations of black Christianity. He discussed the writers' room of the show as a place to go more deeply into points of religious discomfort instead of shying away from them in order to not offend: "We had writers who had grown up in the black church and who are still members of the black church going every Sunday. If we came up with a story that rubbed too many people on the team the wrong way, we're like, let's look at why they're upset, and let's find a way to tell what's valuable about it."[64] This approach to religion reflects *Greenleaf*'s both unique and successful approach to creating television dramas that acknowledge their use of religion-qua-religion. This is not the message-heavy Christian moralizing of the 1990s dramas or 2010s biblical miniseries, nor is it the anthropological distance of writing Southern realist white Christianity. Instead, it is an earnest, specific, layered, lived-in faith within a recognizable Christian institution that is represented as central to the characters' lives and relationships; on *Greenleaf* Christian religion is both respected and as deeply flawed as the characters who practice it.

The first season of *Greenleaf* focuses on Grace (nicknamed Gigi) seeking justice for her sister Faith's mistreatment by the church that eventually led to her suicide. The show's most obvious and odious villain is Grace's uncle, Robert "Mac" McCready (Gregory Alan Williams), who has sexually abused many young women and girls over the decades that he has been in positions of power with Calvary. Grace's parents, Bishop James (Keith David) and Lady Mae (Lynn Whitfield), have orchestrated to keep his pattern of abuse hidden so as not to tarnish the prosperous church. And yet all of these characters believe in Jesus Christ and Christian teachings wholeheartedly. Their faith is both what sustains them and what has led them into corruption. In the penultimate episode of the first season, Grace's aunt, Mavis (Oprah Winfrey), tells her as much in conversation: "The church did that to them [Bishop James and Lady Mae]. I know you love your daddy, but Gigi, that church, I mean, just keeping the doors open turned him into some two-bit hustler and my sister some preening swan. And they go on and on about the Lord this and Jesus but it's really just all about the money. Money, money, money."[65] Hypocrisy and putting the church's fate above their family is the cardinal sin of the Greenleaf parents, not faithlessness.

The truth of the Greenleafs' belief is key to several scenes of both Bishop James and Grace preaching from the pulpit. The first episode showcases James's efficacy and sincerity when he articulates the faithful approach the show takes to religion (implicitly calling out the kinds of approaches so popular in shows analyzed in Part III). He tells the audience and his congregation, "The Bible is not a rule book. The Bible is not a bunch of myths. It's not even a work of literature. And it certainly isn't something to be banging people over the head with. The Bible, praise God, is like a bunch of emails from the best friend you ever had saying, 'I love you. I miss you. Come home.' "[66] The homily is delivered with true gratitude, and many subsequent scenes throughout the series reinforce that all the members of the Greenleaf family find strength and peace through the love of God. When Grace preaches after she believes Mac will be in jail for the rest of his life—he later cuts a deal and returns to the sprawling mansion where the whole family lives—she asks for a moment of silence for all those who have been abused, but she says, sincerely and with righteous joy, "Even in the silence, God is here . . . [and] the silence [of complicity] ends today." Throughout the show, the family's actions or inactions are always filtered through their religious faith.

Even the most obviously sinful character still seeks understanding through Christianity. Mac calls James from prison to ask if there is a hell, to which James responds, "I think when we die, Mac, we go immediately and completely into the presence of a pure, loving God. And for some of us, depending on what we've done, to discern in that moment how much damage we did and how much better it could have been—that's going to feel like hell. . . There's always a way out. You just have to confess."[67] To the man who sexually assaulted his daughter Faith and traumatized her to the point of suicide, Bishop James still ministers. He uses both Christian understanding of God and sin and his own personal articulation of his faith to present Mac with a way out, a path out of pain. And yet the fact that Mac is this melodramatic evil, pitiful in jail, and the Bishop is still hiding some dark secret of his own is not forgotten in the context of the scene's religiosity. Instead, as Greenleaf's writers often do, the soap-opera elements and the religious elements balance and heighten one another. Religion is another way of articulating the emotional excess that the characters navigate within the soap-opera genre, but it is one that has rarely been used in such a way. Even among Peak TV dramas that do bring "edge" to Christian representation, Greenleaf is perhaps the most successful in its breadth and depth as well as the length of its run.

Such edgy use of religion is possible only because the black church is understood as other to the normal patterns of representing (white) Christianity: satire or sanctimony, as Wright described it. Instead, the difference of black Christianity within both general conceptions of American culture and especially within the mainstream television industry not associated with Oprah allows for an increased specificity of Christianity. The Greenleafs literally preach from the television screen, yet the show was not generally described—or feared being described as—preachy or religious. Instead, it was positioned by production discourse as unique and respectful while still being critical and edgy. Wright said of the show, "*Greenleaf* doesn't want to destroy anything about the church. In contrast, we're trying to tell stories that, by encouraging thoughtful, clear-eyed critique, can actually burnish the value of the church."[68] Similarly, Oprah shared her conversation with black pastor T. D. Jakes in which she said, "From my lips to your ears, 'I, Oprah Winfrey, am not going to do anything that disrespects the church.'"[69] Respect, for Winfrey and Wright as the front-facing creatives working on the show, however, is not about positive representation but instead about honest, faithful representation even within the soap-opera genre conventions. Wright said that he was grateful to be able to "dramatize religion in a way that doesn't devalue it."[70] The anxiety that is assumed around such representations of religion—that it will be disrespectful, that it will devalue religion, or that it will be toothless or boring—implies the industrial logics that have for decades still placed restraints on Christianity's portrayal on television. But it is through Wright and Winfrey's public discussions and promotional paratexts positioning the show in relation to those anxieties that most clearly articulate the continued power of those industrial understandings and how degrees of difference and the othering of race can limit them but not eliminate them.

CONCLUSION

Both *Jane the Virgin* and *Greenleaf* use the lived Christianity of their characters to propel their narratives with far fewer restrictions on how they use Christianity than do shows that focus on white Christianity. There is less witnessing and inoffensive Christian messaging than in those dramas produced by evangelizing white creatives like Martha Williamson and Mark Burnett, and there is also less hesitation evident through couching Christianity in a distant regional culture like the American South. Instead, because these shows that focus on nonwhite families and the drama of their relationships do not have to worry about offending the vast white mass audience with their portrayals of religion, their racial difference allows for far greater nuance and specificity in their representations of Christianity.

PART III
DISPLACING CHRISTIANITY IN FANTASTIC GENRES

During the post-network era, there has been a steady growth in the number of religious dramas that can be categorized in the fantastic genres: fantasy (e.g., *Lost* [ABC, 2004–2011], *Dominion* [Syfy, 2014–2015], *Constantine* [NBC, 2014–2015], *The Leftovers* [HBO, 2014–2017]), science fiction (e.g., *Battlestar Galactica* [SciFi, 2003–2009]), and horror (e.g., *Supernatural* [the WB/CW, 2005–], *Preacher* [AMC, 2016–2019]), or their combinations (e.g., *Sleepy Hollow* [Fox, 2013–2017], *Lucifer* [Fox/Netflix, 2016–2020]). This generic grouping is by far the greatest source of post-network-era dramas featuring religious narratives with many more serial dramas melding religious and fantastic elements, such as *Joan of Arcadia* (CBS, 2003–2005), *Wonderfalls* (Fox, 2004), *Eli Stone* (ABC, 2007–2008), *Carnivàle* (HBO, 2003–2005), and *Saving Grace* (TNT, 2007–2010) also fitting this mode but not acting as case studies in this book. By definition, the characters and events in shows of the fantastic genres are not bound to conform to realistic conventions, and therefore the shows within the fantastic genres have a wider array of representational possibilities than realist dramas, especially as each represents religion. Representing controversial topics, in particular, is made safe through the unreality of the fantastic. This is the case because audiences can more easily dismiss these representations as fantasy or unreal instead of coming to terms with their implications to their lived religious experiences.[1] In these examples, the displacement occurs by virtue of the unreality of the genre.

Importantly, fantastic dramas also appeal to another segment of upscale audiences in addition to the quality target audience discussed in the prior chapter: fan audiences. Scholar Matt Hills posits that fans, such as those pursued by fantastic series, "are no longer an elite fraction of a coalition audience, but instead make up the entirety of a niche audience" with cultural power.[2]

Fan audiences, like the quality audiences discussed in Chapter 3, are powerful target audiences pursued by television marketers. They may (aim to) overlap with a presumed quality audience, as they do for the shows discussed in Chapter 5, but fans are constructed with different taste profiles outside of the presumptive quality designation associated with realism. Despite these differences, both audiences are presumed by marketers, executives, and creators to be oppositional to middlebrow religious representation.

The generic displacement of Christianity through fantastic genre containment is by far the most powerful and prominent discursive approach to using Christian elements in a serial dramatic series. Each of the chapters in Part III thus contains more case studies than in chapters of the other parts, and abundance that reflects both the overlap between quality and fan audiences as well as the power of fantastic genre to contain religion so effectively that it can turn even the Bible into nonreligious mythology. In Chapter 6, fantastic dramas centered on Christian eschatology form a grouping of shows whose narratives draw upon the biblical apocalypse from the New Testament's Book of Revelation. However, within a post-Christian production context, their biblical literalism is classified as nonreligious, an unacknowledged pastiche of its religious origins. Religion becomes merely "supernatural," a word often used by industry practitioners to designate the full range of fantastic elements from monsters and magic to angels and the Devil himself. The characters and narratives from Revelation are identified as mythology by the creatives working on these shows. This post-Christian denial of religion—while still using Christian motifs such as the Devil raising hell on earth, warring angels, and the biblical end of the world—allows for high-stakes plots and a clear narrative endgame, namely, the end of the world. *Supernatural*, *Dominion*, and *Constantine* are examples of prime-time dramas that are clearly biblical, but contain Christian theological texts and tropes as nonreligious "mythology" through their fantastic genre elements.

Taken together, the two chapters in this section represent two key variations on how fantastic genres are used to contain Christianity. When overlapping with quality discourses, Christian tropes become generalizable and abstracted so as not to alienate the supposedly secular upscale audiences that quality fantastic shows target. In this way, genre, in addition to place and race in the previous section, operates as a basis for containment. But the unreality presented by the fantastic genre allows for a more thorough displacement of Christianity's religiousness, moving even the specificity of biblical literalism, archangels, and the Christian apocalypse to the same unreality of monsters, vampires, and magic. Such range and flexibility in successfully containing the perceived risk of middlebrow religiousness illustrates both how and why fantastic genres are the most popular strategy for containment in the post-network era. Moreover, the prevalence of this approach in the twenty-first century has thus far allowed for more shows that use religion to appear—and often enough succeed—on American prime-time television that by 2015–2016, the logic of containment itself began to be tested.

5

Religion as Unreality

Fantastic TV's Generic Displacement of Christianity

Within quality fantastic series, quality and genre interact, particularly as the former works to legitimate the latter's historically low status. This chapter will focus on fantastic dramas that have gained distinction or been framed as quality dramas, demonstrating some of the strategies of containment from Chapter 3's realist dramas while also analyzing how creatives' discussions of religious representation change when they can use fantastic displacement as a distancing strategy. Chapter 6 examines dramas within the fantastic genres that have not garnered the quality label, requiring different strategies for distancing creatives from religion (including outright denial). The quality designation for the shows in this chapter allows for more acknowledgment of religion-as-religion—an acknowledgment familiar to the realist quality dramas of Chapter 3—while also using fantastic generic conventions of un-reality to abstract religion to the point of spirituality. For creatives' discourse about their work, spirituality avoids the connotations with 1990s middle-brow religious representations while also not requiring complete denial of their work's metaphysical concerns and religious influences (denial being the pattern for the non-quality fantastic dramas in Chapter 6).

Fantastic genres have long histories of approaching the profound questions of culture and humanity through a displaced representational reality. This displacement, in turn, enables a suspension of disbelief in audiences.[1] Fantastic genres represent reality through displacement; they facilitate the abstraction of religion into spirituality. As Heather Hendershot notes in her study of abortion and religion on *Battlestar Galactica*, as a science fiction show, "*Galactica* consistently grapples with religious issues and allows for the possibility that God (or gods) exist . . . [Uniquely, it] is able to break free of the dominant TV formula . . . whereby religious sentiment is inevitably as-sociated with conservative values."[2] In stories that pit monotheism against polytheism or good against evil in a post-Christian framework, creatives

Divine Programming. Charlotte E. Howell, Oxford University Press (2020).
© Oxford University Press.
DOI: 10.1093/oso/9780190054373.001.0001

can use vocabularies that appear spiritual, not religious, with greater alacrity. Spirituality can be seen as the discursive middle ground between religion and mythology, allowing for the seeking of profound or metaphysical meaning without the connotations associated with religion on television.[3]

The overt representation of religious tropes remains central to all the fantastic dramas studied herein. However, for the shows in this chapter, the addition of quality markers allows for the representation of religion's impact on characters' lived experiences, similar to the quality realist dramas of Chapter 3. For *Battlestar Galactica, Lost, The Leftovers,* and *Preacher* the combination of genre and quality allows for religious representation and creatives' discussions of it to thrive without employing the middlebrow content and audience associations that the term religion acquired in the 1990s within the prime-time television industry. Writers on these three quality fantastic shows frequently explore God or gods, divine prophecy, metaphysical purpose, and existential meaning, without fear of alienating their upscale target audiences or appearing religious themselves, because religion is easily discursively contained by genre. The textual tropes and narratives are informed by and reflect traditional religions, particularly Christianity. Thus, I will often refer to the representations as religious even as the creatives working on these shows discuss them as spiritual. The gap between what is represented and how creatives discuss it is at the core of this study and is particularly necessary to highlight for this chapter what bridges realist quality strategies and fantastic generic strategies of containing the industrial risk of religion. For quality fantastic series, religion is contained through abstractions, but these abstractions maintain connection to metaphysical meaning. Even in the abstraction to spirituality, the function of religion remains in place. With this spiritual frame, the writers in these series can explore divine possibility without the risky ideology associated with religion.

The creatives working on these quality fantastic dramas were granted two levels of protection from the ideological risk, both of which also allowed for greater religious representation: generic displacement and quality distinction. For *Battlestar Galactica,* that combination as well as its niche cable outlet allowed for overt religious representation from the beginning. For *Lost,* its slower build toward both its fantastic generic elements and its quality designation meant that its religious representation remained vague until the final season. *The Leftovers* deemphasizes its fantastic generic traits in favor of quality (in keeping with HBO's brand) and thus displaces religious representation onto cults, general spiritual weirdness, or, in the second season, the American South. *Preacher*, as the Peak TV example and with the added protection of adaptation from a comic series known for its religious story, moves between abstracting religion and acknowledging it through its story of a reformed preacher possessed by a heavenly being and on a search for an absentee God.

The discourse generated by the creatives I spoke with as well as critics surrounding theses shows strongly emphasizes the sociocultural verisimilitude and the groundedness of the writing, characters, and narrative to amplify their quality bona fides and bridge the gap between the fantastic genres and quality's assumed default to realism.[4] Catherine Johnson, in her study of the fantastic genres and their industrial discursive construction, argues that the displacement of "the norms, rules and laws of everyday knowledge . . . ask questions that push the boundaries of socio-cultural verisimilitude" and thus often engage with the most pressing questions of our culture.[5] Therefore, the fantastic genres have a great potential for subversive representation.[6] Indeed, each quality fantastic drama in this chapter gains notions of quality through its sociocultural verisimilitude: that is, its ability to represent realistic relationships, tensions, questions, and events. *Battlestar Galactica* engages with the War on Terror culture of mid-2000s America while it also questions predestination and divine purpose. By its final seasons, *Lost* makes it clear that it is exploring the fundamental question of inherent human good and evil while equally focusing on the reality of complex human relationships in the wake of trauma. *The Leftovers* elliptically explores loss and family through the aftermath of a Rapture-like event. *Preacher* features a reverend on a literal search for God while evading (and sometimes joining) agents of both heaven and hell. Each of these series' writers and producers talk about the shows as creative visions and personal writings, helping to further build quality status without dismissing their fantastic natures.

CONTAINMENT THROUGH DISPLACEMENT: *BATTLESTAR GALACTICA*

Battlestar Galactica was a remake of the1970s cult sci-fi show of the same name (ABC, 1978–1979) that Glen A. Larson (*Magnum, P.I.* [CBS, 1980–1988], *Knight Rider* [NBC, 1982–1986]) created. The 2003 remake adapted characters as well as the original premise of a war between humans and robotic cylons. Although the twenty-first-century version shares a deep connection to spiritual stories evident in the original series, in the 1970s version, spirituality was primarily expressed by drawing inspiration from Mormon cosmology. It did so by naming the planets among which the characters navigated with variations on Mormon names, like Kobol referencing the Mormon paradise star/planet Kolob. These expressions of cosmology in name variations seem minor, but they were, however, overt in the context of 1970s television models. In the early 2000s version, *Battlestar Galactica* maintained some of the Mormon-inflected names but also moved into deeper and more explicit engagement with religion and spirituality. The show gained the label of quality among critics and within the industry by virtue of its incredibly complex plot, rich character relationships, and layered religious representations.[7]

The series premise began with the nuclear annihilation of the human home world, Caprica, through the machinations of the cylons. This destruction left the human government in the hands of the Secretary of Education, Laura Roslin (Mary McDonnell), and the Commander of the battlestar spaceship *Galactica*, William Adama (Edward James Olmos). *Galactica* housed the majority of the surviving humans. Adama's crew formed the basis of the series' main characters, including: Kara "Starbuck" Thrace (Katee Sackhoff), Karl "Helo" Agathon (Tamoh Penikett), and Sharon "Boomer" Valerii (Grace Park), who is revealed during the first season to be a cylon. A main departure of the 2000s series from the 1970s version is that the robot-looking cylons still exist, but they have also evolved to include a ruling class of human-looking cylons. These eight human-looking models of cylons (practically seven, since one model is defunct) replicate as much as needed. Replication results in multiple Sharon/Number Eight models, for example. There are two different Sharons who serve as main characters throughout the series: Sharon "Boomer" Valerii, who is a sleeper agent who believes she is human at the beginning of the series, and Sharon "Athena" Agathon née Valerii, who knows she is a cylon from the beginning, but falls in love with Helo, a human, as she seduces him to try to create a human-cylon hybrid that is prophesized in the cylon religion.

The cylons and humans have disparate religions that guide them: the cylons believe in a monotheistic god that draws heavily from Abrahamic religion, while the humans worship polytheistic gods with Hellenic names such as Athena and Artemis. The characters' beliefs in these religions guide much of the action in the series. Their beliefs function to determine who is a real prophet for the future of humanity, how the fleet will find their new home world (Earth, according to prophecy), and the meaning of the tag line "all of this has happened before and all of it will happen again." Their beliefs guide both the overarching narrative of the series and many of the interpersonal conflicts and tensions that motivate the series ongoing dramatic urgency over five seasons. Religious beliefs are used to justify attempts at genocide, creation of internment camps, suicide missions, and a war of terror (and a war on terror). These beliefs act as televisual reflections of much of the wider cultural post-9/11 context.

According to Ronald D. Moore, the creator and showrunner of *Battlestar Galactica* who wrote the miniseries-cum-pilot, the religious narrative was built into the series from the beginning. However, Moore's ideological inculcation of religious risk within industry culture shaped the creative team's initial approach to religion. When developing the project, Moore assumed that religion was something that had to be sneaked into the script rather than dealt with head on. Only by going undetected by network executives could religion be featured within the show, at least initially. Moore said that he added the line "God is love" to the dialogue of cylon Caprica Six (Tricia Helfer) in the miniseries as a way to test the waters for the kind of "spirituality" he wanted to explore later in the show. He said, "I didn't want to play it strongly in the pilot [but] an executive at SciFi seized on it [and wanted more]."[8] The executive's reaction countered Moore's internalized assumption going into production that religion was undesirable for a cable show targeting upscale audiences. This moment of surprise on his part is significant. On the one hand, it manifests the influence of the powerful legacy practices of self-policing that by the early 2000s had become internalized within the industry with regard to religion. Moore's training as a staff writer for *Star Trek: The Next Generation* (syndication, 1987–1994) and *Star Trek: Deep Space Nine* (syndication, 1993–1999) ingrained in him the idea that religion was risky and unavailable to use for storylines unless hidden, sneaked in, or contained within the show. On the other hand, this encounter reveals a moment of rupture in the consistent narrative of religious avoidance within the post-network-era television industry that made this ideology of religion-as-risky more visible *as an ideology,* not a fact. In disrupting what was assumed to be common sense and natural—that religion is to be avoided—the moment of surprise revealed to Moore that what he thought was rigid logic was in fact subject to change, if not abandonment, with regard to religious representation.

This moment of surprise allowed Moore and the writers' room he helmed to represent religion more thoroughly and diversely than what had previously appeared on television. Nevertheless, the ideology of "religious television is middlebrow television" persisted enough to lead Moore and other *Battlestar Galactica* writers to avoid the religious label in their discussions of the show, instead opting for the more abstract and acceptable "spiritual" adjective in describing their work and the show. Even as religious representational barriers fell for *Battlestar Galactica*'s showrunner, the ideology ossified in the 1990s that made creatives avoid association with religion (if only by calling it spirituality) remained a powerful shaper of industrial discourses about religious representation.

Battlestar Galactica's first years on SciFi also coincided with significant industrial shifts at the niche cable outlet. In the time between *Battlestar Galactica*'s miniseries in December 2003 and its first full season of episodes, which appeared in October 2004, SciFi, which was owned by Universal, became part of the newly formed NBC/Universal media conglomerate. This shift in ownership came with attendant corporate pressures to broaden the channel's target audience from niche sci-fi genre fans.[9] NBC/Universal wanted SciFi to extend beyond its core male-skewing genre audience, but "at the same time SciFi worked to establish itself as the destination spot for high-quality sf [science fiction] television."[10] The desire to establish a cable channel brand with high-end original programming for added value was not SciFi's alone. FX, USA, and other cable outlets were beginning to produce original content to distinguish themselves in the crowded cable marketplace. It is within this context that *Battlestar Galactica* appeared, supported by a channel striving for genre quality within the decision-making volatility of an industry in transition.

Battlestar Galactica benefitted from a number of factors that helped mitigate the writers' sense of risk around representing religion and reinforce the potential for reward.[11] One way that the show circumvented risk was through its placement in the science fiction genre. Bradley Thompson was a writer who had worked on a number of fantastic shows both before and since *Battlestar Galactica*, including *Star Trek: Deep Space Nine* (syndication, 1993–1999), *Falling Skies* (TNT, 2011–2015), and *The Strain* (FX, 2014–2017). When asked if anything surprised him about the production of *Battlestar Galactica* and its religious storylines, he stated that he was surprised that "we got away with it at all." He further explained that the network was very supportive and even liked the religious stories.[12] This reaction corroborates the aforementioned discussion that SciFi was not worried about the show's use of religion, which Moore's encounter with the SciFi executive who wanted to know more about "God is Love" illustrates. SciFi executives' comfort with the show's religious content was another fortuitous factor enabling the show to explore religion in its representation, themes, and content. But hesitation when discussing religion persisted among the show's creatives. Though they informed the creative context within which the show was developed, the writers maintained that direct references to the September 11th terrorist attacks and the resulting "War on Terror" were avoided.[13] Such a claim is made possible by the science fiction genre, and the discourse of displacement that operated to avoid seeming too reactive and reductive for a show that was praised for its moral ambiguity. *Battlestar Galactica*'s genre was fortuitously situated on a niche cable outlet that both supported the science fiction genre and enabled the greater embrace of religious content because of its network's shifting corporate context. Prior cultural and industrial perceptions of risk regarding the representation of religion could be violated in part because of a corporate restructuring process that demanded a greater flexibility and openness among management seeking branding and distinction.

During interviews, the *Battlestar* writers I spoke with remembered that the channel was in a state of transition during the early run of the show due to the 2004 NBC-Universal merger. This moment of transition occasionally allowed *Battlestar Galactica* to slip through the cracks of executive overreach. In later seasons, when management power at the channel stabilized, the show had become enough of a phenomenon with critics and journalists that the executives were not inclined to step in as much as they might have been before or after the company's period of transition.[14] To support his claim that SciFi was surprisingly unconcerned by the religious storylines, writer Bradley Thompson shared a small sampling of the network notes he received for one of his and his writing partner David Weddle's scripts, "The Hand of God," the tenth episode of the first season. Significantly, the notes focused almost entirely on plot legibility and clarity, not on religious content, even though the episode dealt explicitly with religious prophecy.

Battlestar Galactica helped place SciFi within the budding nexus of basic-cable channels producing quality programming. The mid-2000s saw a number of basic-cable channels beginning to air original programming that sought to attract quality audiences. FX's *The Shield* (2002–2008) used its edgy approach to law enforcement to gain critical attention, including a Peabody Award in 2005.[15] USA Network aired its own upscale science fiction dramas *The Dead Zone* (2002–2007) and *The 4400* (2004–2007) before establishing its 2000s original programming brand as a home for quirky mystery dramas with *Monk* (2002–2009) and *Psych* (2006–2014). And AMC began airing the British series *Hustle* (2004–2012) before establishing itself as the "quality" basic-cable channel with *Mad Men* (2007–2014) and *Breaking Bad* (2008–2013).[16] The quality designation briefly granted SciFi and *Battlestar Galactica*'s creative team cultural capital within the industry. The specific transition of power that SciFi experienced as *Battlestar Galactica* began airing was part of the much wider industry transition in the early twenty-first century addressed in the Introduction of this book. The channel's position in the emerging televisual landscape and its science fiction generic brand identity mitigated risk for *Battlestar Galactica*.

SciFi was arguably the cable channel best suited to provide the most intense focus on religion in a show not aiming for a religious audience *because* it was dedicated to the genre most associated with tackling controversial issues through allegory. While the fact that a SciFi executive favored the religious element in the miniseries is surprising, it is not surprising that a science fiction show would be and—along with fantasy and horror series—remains the most likely genre to feature religious storylines on television. SciFi's specific industrial position in 2003–2004, in the wake of its rebranding and becoming part of the NBC/Universal conglomerate, was unique. This status allowed the network to engage in a more sustained focus on religion and spirituality than other programming did on television either before or since. *Battlestar Galactica* is both a vanguard and one of the most pronounced exemplars of the 2003–2016 boom in religious programming.

In contrast to *Battlestar Galactica*'s early exploration of religion in its narrative, *Lost*'s writers bided their time, waiting until well into the show's run before revealing its religious focus. *Lost* slowly, and with apparent calculation, shifted from broader supernatural representation to more pointed spiritual stories. Indeed, it was only in *Lost*'s last season that the ongoing spiritual discussion and representation on the show approached the level *Battlestar Galactica* consistently displayed throughout the course of its run. Such variation in representation can be seen to be a function of the different creative and industrial contexts within which *Lost* developed and evolved.

ABSTRACTION TO SUPERNATURAL SPIRITUALITY: *LOST*

Lost's premise was relatively simple: a group of plane crash survivors must figure out how to live on and someday escape from a mysterious island.

The show was notable at the time of its premiere for its sprawling and diverse ensemble cast of characters: Jack Shepherd (Matthew Fox), a doctor transporting his dead father home; Sawyer (Josh Holloway), a smooth con man; Kate (Evangeline Lilly), a criminal; Jin (Daniel Dae Kim) and Sun (Yunjin Kim), a Korean couple struggling with their marriage roles; Hurley (Jorge Garcia), an affable lottery winner; Sayid (Naveen Andrews), an Iraqi intelligence officer; Charlie (Dominic Monaghan), a drug-addicted British rock star; Claire (Emilie de Ravin), a near-to-term pregnant woman; and John Locke (Terry O'Quinn), a former paraplegic. These are just the characters introduced in the first few episodes of the series who remained main characters throughout the series' run. Many more characters were added over the show's six seasons, as the castaways discovered survivors from the tail end of the plane, found people left over from the pseudo-scientific Dharma Initiative on the island, left the island and came back, and encountered the two powerful archetypal entities who used the island as their grand experiment about the nature of humanity. For many scholars and critics, *Lost* represented the pinnacle of the emergent trend of narrative complexity; it provided a key example of a new mode of storytelling in which upscale fan audiences could view shows repeatedly and analyze and discuss the intricacies of their stories in online spaces.[17] Less discussed than these narrative and reception-oriented characteristics, however, was how the show's story structure incentivized ambiguous religious representation.

Lost's first seasons are populated by storylines that had little to do with religion or even abstract spirituality. While some characters like Mr. Eko (Adewale Akinnuoye-Agbaje), a relatively short-lived addition to the castaways, were religious, the religious or spiritual elements were largely relegated to appearing among the small clues to the series' bigger mystery, such as the statuettes of the Virgin Mary being used to distribute heroin. These clues appeared sporadically throughout the show, and their purpose and relationship to the larger mystery and character arcs were largely unknown until later seasons. In an interview, co-showrunner Damon Lindelof said that neither the network nor the writers were ever hesitant to represent spiritual storylines. Instead he remembers the writers' desire to establish the characters in the first two seasons—adding in and exploring the implications of the presence of the tail side of the plane in the second season—as the necessary foundation for getting the audience to care about the wider mysteries and spiritual themes to be addressed later in the show's run. Lindelof explained that it wasn't until the end of the first season that he; his co-showrunner, Carlton Cuse; and the rest of the writers had the opportunity to discuss the "big questions," but he said that he "always knew the concept for the island . . . as a place where God and the Devil could test the hypothesis: are humans naturally good or naturally bad."[18] From the beginning, he planned for the island's smoke monster to behave like the Devil, tempting the castaways with their deepest desires. Christian culture strongly informed his discussion of this premise, particularly in terms of its focus on temptation as the mode of exploring evil. Lindelof, throughout his interview, implied that his vision was more assertively religious and that "ambiguity and spirituality are where we migrated toward eventually."[19] He made it clear that this was not a directive from ABC, but he also said that ABC was pleased with the series' ambiguity, pushing them to "keep it going [and] don't answer too much."[20] The push for narrative ambiguity, and the suggestion that Lindelof backed off from some of his more explicit exploration of the "big questions," implies a continuing perceived risk attached to religious storylines, even for a phenomenally popular drama within the purportedly safe genre of fantasy.

Because the spiritual elements that would eventually be a major part of the show's overarching storyline and conclusion were not necessarily evident in the early seasons (and therefore not necessarily evident in early network meetings and decisions about the show), *Lost* had a lot of leeway to establish itself and its mysterious island-based storyworld early on. As the show progressed, spiritual and religious questions and answers began to make their way into the story of the island, particularly with the introduction of the character Jacob (Mark Pellegrino) in the last episodes of season five. Jacob is a somewhat divine personification of goodness who is revealed to have appeared at key moments of decision for the major characters. Lindelof, when answering questions about the show's spiritual storyline, focused on the battle between Jacob, as the fiduciary for God, and the Man in Black/Smoke Monster (Titus Welliver), who was the essence of the worst of humanity. The Man in Black represented chaos and immorality and was confined to the island until he and Jacob could resolve their grand experiment testing the nature of humankind: is it good or bad? While the Man in Black was trapped on the island, Jacob was not. Jacob, as is revealed through flashbacks in later seasons, was there to offer comfort, gentle guidance, and sympathy to many of the characters in moments of great choice and great sadness. He was there to remind them of hope and of their connection to other people. He appears to have some powers of omniscience and is able to transport himself between locations. The Man in Black focuses on temptation; Jacob focuses on love.

They both fit into archetypes that align closely with the Devil and God (or even with God in the Old versus the New Testament). According to Lindelof, the team eventually shifted away from the idea of Jacob and the Man in Black as literal constructs of these big ideas, and instead had them serve "more as fiduciaries" of those entities who could carry out the work of setting up their experiment and interact with the other characters.[21] The mere abstraction of the traditional religious beings—God and the Devil—allows for these characters to occupy the middle ground between religion and supernatural mythology. They can function *as if* without gaining the risky weight of being called by religious titles. Such abstraction both appeases the network desire for continued ambiguity and allows Lindelof to tell spiritual stories without the fear of either concluding narrative threads too soon or being associated with religion as a middlebrow taste marker. The persistent mystery and ambiguity were being encouraged by ABC for their appeal to upscale target audiences.

The final season, and particularly the final episode, of *Lost*, however, more directly and dramatically revealed the centrality of the spiritual storyline that had shaped the series in subtle ways up to that point. The show's narrative concludes by explaining that the island that served as mysterious setting for the series housed a mystical light that connects all of humanity. The desire for this light and its power is what pits Jacob and the Man in Black against each other and brings various cycles of humans to the island. Moreover, the series ends by ambiguously revealing that the characters have all been waiting for one another after their individual deaths, so that they could all pass to the afterlife together. They have been waiting in a church—even if the church contains a variety of symbols for other religions and beliefs. They exit to the afterlife out the church doors, past two baptismal founts, and into a bright white light. Although the representational bricolage window housed in the church (Figure 5.1) and the vaguely spiritual "light" of the island both nod to Lindelof's claims of spirituality, the fact that the bricolage is contained in a church and the view of the afterlife is mostly Christian illustrate the post-Christian sensibility and its influence. Lindelof can claim spirituality and use the postmodern combination of beliefs to support that narrative claim, but the influence of Christian culture on American culture—with the church contributing to the legibility of the afterlife—remains strong even as it is denied by creatives.

Lost's approach of waiting to represent religion until later seasons preserved the ambiguity of its spiritual story. This practice of delay has since

Figure 5.1 The conclusion of *Lost* occurs in a church with a religious bricolage window

become a legacy strategy of containment that can be contrasted to *Battlestar Galactica*'s early-on approach of containing religion through displacement into a fantastically unreal world. (Shows such as *Supernatural* and *Daredevil*, discussed in later chapters, share this affinity for hesitation.) Lindelof said that the hesitation and postponement were about establishing the show's quality characteristics through character development. Nonetheless, his team's approach aligns with the pervasive sense by creatives and executives of religion as risky, something especially pronounced during the early years of the religious narrative boom. Hints of religious abstractions arise within the show, so that religion is not antithetical to a targeted audience's enjoyment of the show. As long as those abstractions do not disrupt the verisimilitude that the show's containment practices effect, new content becomes accessible to the writers, producers, and executives, the representational field of the text, and the marketing strategies of the show.

Such hesitation to represent overtly traditional religious concepts is indicative of the self-policing that Ronald D. Moore illustrated in his "God is Love" anecdote. The legacy structures of the television industry regarding representation changed dramatically in the post-network era in that religion was now a usable representational element in quality and fantastic modes of dramatic programming. Religious representation broke out of the middlebrow silo with *Battlestar Galactica*. The practices of ideologically containing religion for the writers and producers working on these shows, however, remained shaped by the idea of religion as risk. These showrunners' stories about executives openly embracing religious representations in personal cases of boundary testing illustrate the textual transformation and its persistent ideological limitations for creatives. Writers frequently still self-police and hold back from inserting or acknowledging religious narratives—at least until they feel safe within the structures of containment that allow audiences to tolerate, if not embrace, religion. This paradox, in which incipient constraints on religious content dissipate as the target audience accepts and engages with the religious representation of a show, is essential to understanding the post-network boom in religious representation. This paradox must be viewed in relation to the simultaneous persistent perceived risk within the mainstream television industry of engaging with or explicitly acknowledging an engagement with religion among industry peers as well as the wider public. Significantly, in 2003 and 2004, *Lost* and *Battlestar Galactica* presented this modality of progressive introduction of religion into a show as the avant-garde. Yet despite new channels and platforms, greater demographic targeting, and emerging distribution outlets in the intervening dozen years, little has changed in terms of dominant ideologies of executives and creative regarding religion.

Lost's surprising success among a coalition of upscale viewer niches, in true post-network style, helped to reinforce ABC as a broadcast channel in which quality could be found and fostered.[22] ABC executives' willingness to take risks with both *Lost* and its network peer, *Desperate Housewives* (ABC, 2004–2012), marked ABC and its 2004 dramas in contrast to the new shows of the previous broadcast season, including *Las Vegas* (NBC, 2003–2008), *NCIS* (CBS, 2003–), and *The Lyon's Den* (NBC, 2003), which were seen as largely redundant, formulaic, and without interesting ideas.[23] This coalition of upscale audiences included quality audiences, fan audiences, "critics, bloggers, and even some television researchers [who] credited its popularity to its character-driven storylines and, most importantly, to the fact that no one could easily explain the answers to the many questions the program raised."[24] *Lost*'s supernatural mysteries and its popularity among upscale audiences helped to contain the risk of the show's eventual reveal of its spiritual premise and framing.

The spiritual elements on *Lost* were not the most radical and risky parts of the show when it began. As Gregg Nations, a writer for *Lost*, remembers,

ABC took a big risk in supporting the show because its serialization and fantastic genre elements were rare on broadcast at the time. He states in an interview that his memory of the show's legacy was that "genre television wasn't really a thing yet [on broadcast, and] the science fiction stuff was unknown and risky," as was the serialized storytelling.[25] This is part of Lost's ongoing appeal with viewers and critics as well as its categorization as a quality fantastic show: it provided a template and high-risk high-reward transmedia franchise model for post-network-era television. In his recounting of the mid-2000s genre landscape, Nations omitted cable science fiction series like Battlestar Galactica and netlet fantasy programming like Supernatural (see the next chapter), as well as subtler supernatural dramas like Alias (ABC, 2001–2006) and Joan of Arcadia (CBS, 2003–2005). In doing so, he implies that the creativity displayed by Lost was unique. According to Nations, ABC was dubious about the show because the genre was still considered niche, and ABC wanted "as big an audience as they could get."[26] He said that ABC also wanted a character-driven drama, which the network believed could draw a "big hit" type of ratings, Lost did in fact provide ABC with a character-driven drama, along with the added element of an ongoing mystery designed to get the big audience ABC wanted. At the time ABC bought that there was an audience for a show that married the idea of a plane crash (a cultural preoccupation in a post 9/11 world) with the idea of castaways on an island making do à la Survivor.[27] ABC executives told Lindelof and Cuse not to serialize the show and not to "make it weird"; they did it anyway, according to Lindelof, although they did initially balance it with some more episodic storytelling.[28] ABC went along with Lindelof and Cuse, because the show succeeded from the outset, becoming a cultural phenomenon that was a great success for the network.[29] Eventually, as the show began to delve more deeply into spiritual concerns, network executives did not care, or at least they did not care enough to voice any substantive concerns to the showrunners.[30] The show had already proven its worth and established its brand. To make its spirituality more overt was not a business risk anymore, merely a narrative one and a cultural one within the writers' room and the larger ideology of Hollywood.

Both Lindelof and Nations said they knew that the viewer reaction to the final season's spiritual turn would be mixed. Lindelof in particular cited the increased permeability between audience and writers as the show went on, indicating that as a forerunner in new media interactivity between producers and viewers, the creative team was aware of audience expectations and reactions.[31] Lindelof and Cuse were cognizant of fan expectations, or at least had an understanding of how fans actively engaged via forums like Lostpedia and Twitter. Those expectations and fan constructions generally were not in support of receiving spiritual answers. The perceived resistance of viewers on the part of the creatives supports one of the many assumptions that has guided the development of spiritual and religious storylines on television dramas: that fan audiences, like quality audiences, are inherently oppositional to religious stories.[32]

Fear and hesitancy have shaped the beliefs by those involved in television productions with regard to storylines that utilize religious themes and concepts. To the writers on these fantastic shows, such fear and hesitancy would be a hindrance to their project and vision because they were trying to represent unreality that necessitates wider imaginations. Yet before *Lost* and *Battlestar Galactica*, that mode was the only way they had seen to represent religious storylines. Reacting to this dominant—and constraining— ideology, writers assumed that their shows' upscale viewers would not necessarily react well to an overtly religious story. Among many writers whom I interviewed for this chapter and others, the fear of being seen as "preachy," a fear articulated in the 1990s by Jordan Levin as being understood as antithetical to quality, persisted. For *Lost*, in particular, this belief resulted in a slow-burn revelation of the show's narrative focus on religious and spiritual themes through the exploration of God, the Devil, and human nature. In contrast, *Battlestar Galactica,* and later, *The Leftovers,* placed their religious stories front and center—even though they also displaced or minimized the presence of religion through the shows' fantastic genre characteristics.

MINIMIZING GENRE, MAXIMIZING QUALITY: *THE LEFTOVERS*

The Leftovers began airing three years after the conclusion of *Lost*, and involved one of its two showrunners, Damon Lindelof, in its creation. Notably, *The Leftovers* carried similar traits of quality fantastic approaches to religion that appeared in the mid-2000s. Yet *The Leftovers* as a program featured on pay-cable network HBO was not beholden to particular genre branding, as was *Battlestar Galactica* on SciFi, or to the necessities of broadcast television, as was *Lost*. HBO had established its brand of quality television in the 1990s with comedies like *The Larry Sanders Show* (1992–1998) and reinforced this branding with late 1990s–early 2000s shows like *The Sopranos* (1999–2007) and *The Wire* (2002–2008).[33] However, in the late 2000s and early 2010s, with its tent-pole quality series ended, HBO had lost its dominance as a place for consistent quality.[34] The HBO channel at the time that *The Leftovers* was developed and began airing was one that continued to brand itself as a quality outlet but had fewer successful examples to show for it as cable channels like FX and AMC became known for their quality dramas.[35] Moreover, HBO's subscription base was in decline, perhaps due to the rise in streaming platforms like Netflix.[36] In 2014, HBO was struggling to revise its strategy and rebuild its brand in an emergent streaming universe with more fractured audiences, a struggle that perhaps aided *The Leftovers'* development.

The Leftovers ostensibly was provided more space for the exploration of religion through fantastic spiritual abstraction. Its appearance on pay-cable outlet HBO and the quality aspects inherent in its status as a literary adaptation contributed to creating a production culture and textual strategies focused on quality characteristics that largely downplayed generic aspects of *The Leftovers* while still utilizing the hesitation granted by a supernatural premise. Despite ten years separating *The Leftovers* from *Lost* or even the realist *Friday Night Lights*, its creatives remain inculcated by the pervasive sense of religion as risk. *The Leftovers*, like *Rectify* in Chapter 3, illustrates the persistence of ideological risk associated with working with religious representation across the span of the boom in religious programming.

The Leftovers is an adaptation of a novel (St. Martin's Press, 2011) by Tom Perrotta, one that is considered "literary" in that it comes from a lauded author whose work has been adapted to the big screen with Academy Award–nominated film adaptations, such as *Little Children* (Field, 2006).[37] When we spoke, Lindelof identified the quality elements of *The Leftovers* through the show's connection with realist literary adaptation. He observed, "*Lost* was more pulpy. JJ [Abrams] said we were doing a B-genre story with an A-level treatment . . . *The Leftovers* takes a fantastic concept and treats it with a grounded, realistic approach."[38] In direct contrast to *Lost*, Lindelof's description of *The Leftovers'* frame for religious containment implies maximizing its quality elements while simultaneously minimizing its fantastic genre elements. A decade after *Lost*, this mode of containment resulted in a program that, while under the creative auspices of the same showrunner as *Lost*, represents religion with less abstraction and more displacement (e.g., religion is placed onto the source text and the cults presented in *The Leftovers*).

The religiously framed premise is a central part of the source text of *The Leftovers*. Damon Lindelof discussed his love of the book, *The Leftovers*, and his appreciation of Tom Perrotta as a writer as part of his account of how he came to adapt the book as an HBO series. He inherently emphasized the double quality aspects of the program as both a literary adaptation and a prestige drama for HBO.[39] When asked about the religious narrative and how his team handled it in translating it from the book to the show, Lindelof said that he always feels strange talking about the show's premise, because it is so much derived from Perrotta. In his mind, "it's Perrotta's baby"; Lindelof considers himself "just the caretaker."[40] Reliance on source text as the origin of the show's religious concepts is a strategy that creatives often use to distance themselves from the ideologically dangerous idea that they are religious or invested in religious messaging. For similar examples, Melissa Bernstein did it with regard to Ray McKinnon's vision for *Rectify*, described in Chapter 3, and producers of *Constantine* did so with regard to religious "gimmes" based on the source text that will be discussed in Chapter 6. In answer to my query regarding *The Leftovers*' development of its religious narrative, Lindelof did say that one of the questions driving his writing that he viewed as a takeaway from the book was "the human reaction to this mass experience that doesn't fit into any religious box; it blows up all religions, even atheism. When that happens, do you double down or abandon it in search of a new system?"[41]

The premise of *The Leftovers* is that at one point in recent history, ten percent of the human population disappeared, with no clear reason as to why it happened, how it happened, and why those who were taken were chosen. It is called the Sudden Departure but borrows strongly from Christian notions of the Rapture. In both the book and the series, the characters strongly assert that this is not the Rapture that many Christian denominations believe in. The Pope was taken, yes, but so was Gary Busey.[42] What actually happened is a mystery, completely open to interpretation and promising no answers. This open question is part of the conceit of the show and part of its appeal to quality audiences: naturalistic and grounded character reactions to a worldwide, unavoidable supernatural event and a subsequent sense of fantastic possibilities for more supernatural effects. In response to this event, a number of cults arise. Lindelof's described the wake of the Sudden Departure as a time with "pockets of religions forming . . . in an age of prophets."[43] The fact that the Sudden Departure is never explained is also central to the show's source material. It serves as a direct rebuke of the criticisms levied against Lindelof on the conclusion of *Lost* that evoked demands for further answers. The narrative of *The Leftovers* and popular discourse around the show indicates that *Lost* taught Lindelof never to promise answers and that the move from broadcast to premium cable provided him a place on television where the audience more willingly accepts elliptical storytelling.[44] Moreover, the promise of no answer to the Rapture-like event allows the show's writers to avoid making any religious claims and to remain securely in the ambiguity that this mystery provides. The context of ambiguity allows for religious explanations, but it does not require them.

The adaptation of Perrotta's source text as well as the support of the pay-cable distributor HBO granted Lindelof a great deal of freedom to explore religion less abstractly than he could on *Lost*. This freedom was evidenced by his more open, explicit discussion of religion on *The Leftovers* versus his more careful manner when discussing the "spirituality" on *Lost*. However, the burden of religious representation in the first season of *The Leftovers* is largely placed on the "pockets of religions" that are diegetically classified as cults. The supposed absence of faith following the Sudden Departure dominates, while religious functions (aside from one exception in the form of Reverend Matt Jamison [Christopher Eccleston]) are taken over by cults such as the Guilty Remnant or followers of "Holy" Wayne Gilchrest (Paterson Joseph).

The decidedly unresolved mystery of the event results in a narrative world that must dynamically grapple with notions of faith, belief, and religion. The narrative explores how flawed human characters understand their world, a theme that is an established modality of quality dramas such as *Rectify* and *Lost*.[45] The first season follows the Garvey family of Mapleton, New York: Kevin (Justin Theroux), the father, taking care of his daughter, Jill (Margaret Qualley); Laurie (Amy Brenneman), the mother who left the family following the Sudden Departure; and her son Tom (Chris Zylka), a young man who is supposed to be at college but has become a follower of a supposed holy man, Wayne Gilchrest (Paterson Joseph). In the context of a world after the Departure, traditional religions like Christianity are rocked into instability and a variety of new religions like cults arise. These cults represent the "age of prophets" about which Lindelof spoke. They act to displace religious thinking safely onto "othered" groups, specifically cults that are positioned as outside of familiar, traditional religious traditions.

In both the source material and the television show, the main focus of this displacement of religion is a cult called the Guilty Remnant. The Guilty Remnant is categorized as a cult both by cultural and by the diegetic government. They require all their adherents to conform to a collective identity of silence, smoking, and wearing all white. They believe themselves to be the necessary reminders of the disappearance and the nihilism that resulted. In an extreme example, the Guilty Remnant stage a stoning, actually killing one of their own, to force the community of Mapleton to acknowledge them. The stoning practice and its visual representation is meant to align them with a traditionally Christian motif.[46] Despite the fact that there are more adherents to the Guilty Remnant in Mapleton than to the Church by an order of magnitude, the Guilty Remnant is always characterized as a cult, and the only cult in this one town, even though an array of cults are now crossing the country and presumably the world. There is such a plethora of cults that the Department of Alcohol, Tobacco, Firearms, and Explosives has added Cults to its title and directive in this post-Disappearance America.

The Guilty Remnant provide a structure and a reasoning to life after the Sudden Disappearance and thus they gain followers. But by the end of the first season, Wayne Gilchrist, the leader of another cult, has supposed powers that are presented as less smoke-and-mirrors and more as potentially real. In the first-season finale, Kevin Garvey encounters a dying Wayne in a diner's restroom.[47] Wayne entreats Kevin to make a wish, the granting of which, Wayne says, ". . . will mean I was real," revealing a chink in his egomania. It implies that even Wayne was unsure of his powers and wants to prove his chosenness as his last act on earth, hoping that proof of his power will outweigh his misdeeds and manipulations. Wayne looks to Kevin, who does not say his wish aloud, and then Wayne says, "Granted," and dies. The viewer does not know precisely what Kevin wishes for, but on the basis of his arc throughout the season, one presumes it is that he have his family made whole again. The final scenes of the episode feature a version of that with Kevin and Jill returning home to find his girlfriend, Nora (Carrie Coon), kept from leaving him by finding a baby—Wayne's child—on the Garvey front porch. It is not exactly what we presume Kevin wished for, but his disbelieving smile hints that it is close.

The question of Wayne's powers and his role as a potential prophet are one of many instances of supernatural occurrences on *The Leftovers* that could be truly marvelous or divine or might just be the result of delusions, psychological manipulation, or coincidence. The displacement of religion largely onto cults and the abstraction of religious representation into these few vaguely supernatural events (in the context of a massive supernatural event) follow containment strategies associated with ensuring such religious representation does not alienate the supposedly nonreligious quality audience. Instead of using fantastic genre expectations to help contain these moments of the potentially divine (as the shows such as *Supernatural* studied in the next chapter do), *The Leftovers* largely ignores fantastic genre elements in favor of employing quality strategies such as focusing on interpersonal relationships but not excess emotionalism; representing a full range of human experiences, including addiction, sex, and graphic violence; and presenting high production values and resulting "cinematic" aesthetics. Aside from Wayne's "granting" of Kevin Garvey's wish, the clearest instance of this fantastic hesitancy between divine and worldly explanations is Reverend Matt Jamison's endeavor to get enough money to keep his church from being bought by the Guilty Remnant in the third episode of season one, "Two Boats and a Helicopter."[48] Reverend Jamison is largely the nexus, especially in the first season, of traditional religious representation. However, the focus of that representation on one character allows it to be marginalized in a wider world of cults.

Traditional Christian representation centers on Reverend Matt Jamison, beginning in the first season. In the first-season episode, "Two Boats and a Helicopter," Matt gains then loses the $135,000 needed to keep ownership of his church but eventually loses his church to the Guilty Remnant. Matt's faith was tested with this experience but not broken. After the loss of the church, he continues to act as he feels his vocation requires: he is spiritual guide to the handful of residents who still turn to Christianity to provide solace and a sense of purpose in a world that has seemingly turned to nihilism. Even more than that, Matt focuses even more on trying to help—as he sees it—the Guilty Remnant. His optimism is represented as antithetical to reality. Similarly, religious representation in a show without containment is constructed as oppositional to quality realist representation and prevailing industry ideologies.

The second season, which many critics praised as a leap in quality from the first, moved the Garveys from Mapleton, New York to Miracle, Texas.[49] As the town's name implies, the small community is deeply imbued with religious faith, as it is heralded as the only town not to experience any departures. Matt Jamison moved there, the Garveys follow, and a new family, the Murphys, are added to the character roll as natives of Miracle (formerly Jarden), Texas. The season's marked rise in attributions of quality results from a variety of causes, including moving beyond the weighty world-building of the first season as well as displaying a clearer idea of characters. These elements infused new life into the series along with adding the new family and presenting a new mystery. The show also has placed questions of faith more explicitly at the center of the series. Miracle is a town of religions, mostly Christianity; residents attribute the eponymous miracle to this circumstance. Thus, the town markets itself as miraculous. It's a national park, a tourist trap, and a place where broken people arrive to seek healing. The way Christianity is portrayed in this second season as something unique and interesting, but not necessarily normal, mirrors the show's move to Texas; it is borrowing from the Southern realist mode of religious representation and its geographical displacement of religion onto Southern culture. This motif develops even as the exploration of the Sudden Departure and the subsequent possible departure of three girls from Miracle become more and more mystical and fantastic. Subsequent seasons amplified the weird, the spiritual, and the interpersonally marvelous that the progression from seasons one to two displayed. The first season established *The Leftovers'* quality containment strategies—strategies that the show implemented further by using the second season's incorporation of Southern realism. That process of containment, in turn, allowed the show to pay more attention to religious representation beyond its displacement onto cults or naive believers (i.e., Matt). This increased attention to religion included using its fantastic genre elements to explore religion representationally as mystical and metaphysical, not "realistically" atavistic.

ADAPTING EDGINESS AND THE PURSUIT OF GOD: *PREACHER*

Preacher is the most recent example of the trend of representing religion in mainstream television to appear and potentially among the first in a turning point in representation as well as industrial discourses of religion on television. On the basis of the source material, early promotional materials (see Figure 5.2), and an interview with the creator of the original series, Garth Ennis, *Preacher* was positioned to be among the edgiest, most envelope-pushing examples in this study—possibly even more challenging than Amazon's *Hand of God* (2015–2017), which will be explored in the final chapter. *Preacher* had the benefit of airing on AMC, a cable channel known for depicting extreme violence and explicit thematic content in its shows, such as *Breaking Bad* and *The Walking Dead*. However, the comic book source for the television adaptation is a stretch in terms of violence, sexuality, and language even for AMC. As Jordan Smith, a reporter for Hollywood.com, described after the pilot development was announced, "[E]veryone is a target

Figure 5.2 *Preacher*, first promotional poster

for its warpath of satire: the South, the North, Heaven, Hell, and even God himself don't escape without a good lashing . . . It will be tough to do the series justice while remaining within the parameters of basic cable propriety."[50]

Preacher makes a fine pairing with *The Walking Dead* in relation to AMC's ongoing development of its brand in relation to the hit zombie show. *Preacher* debuted following the mid-season finale of the spinoff, *Fear the Walking Dead* (2015–), on May 22, 2016 and took over *Fear the Walking Dead*'s timeslot in subsequent weeks.[51] The first attempt at adapting *Preacher* to television had failed in the development stages at HBO because it was, according to Mark Steven Johnson, the director working on the adaptation, "just too dark and too violent and too controversial."[52] That *Preacher* was too dark and controversial for HBO in 2008 but wasn't for AMC, a basic-cable channel, in 2016 illustrates the great deal of change that the television landscape underwent in just a few years as well as the latitude granted by a runaway success like *The Walking Dead*.

Both *Preacher* and *The Walking Dead* are adaptations of violent, graphic, and thematically challenging horror comic book series. However, whereas *The Walking Dead* battles with questions of humanity's resilience or weakness in the face of inhumanity, in *Preacher* the threat comes from the living, not the undead. In *Preacher*, the villains and the violence most often originate from more worldly threats: greed, pride, toxic masculinity, xenophobia, and a general inability to accept new perspectives and ideas. The cable channel's boundaries of acceptable content are likely to be challenged more by the religious narrative than they will be by the graphic content. In potentially fresh and challenging ways, the show was poised to confront—or dismiss as no longer necessary and ignore—the largely unwritten industry codes and production norms regarding when, how, and in what contexts religion can or cannot be integrated into television narratives—as well as how such textual presentations are addressed via industry discourse. However, in execution, *Preacher*'s unevenness and its incredible slowdown of the narrative—the first season explores the story from approximately ten pages from the original comic—stymied this potential as well as undermining some of its quality framing.

In the series, the role of Jesse Custer (Dominic Cooper) as a preacher is treated respectfully, but that his path to, struggle with, and spiritual value gained from his vocation becomes mostly a platform for his negotiation of personal relationships with his girlfriend, Tulip (Ruth Negga), and Cassidy (Joseph Gilgun) and Arse-face (Ian Colletti). The use of "supernatural" in industry discourse around the show suggests that there is still a hesitancy around discussing religion as presented in dramas on television. This hesitancy in is evident *even* in a show called *Preacher*, which is based on a comic book series that has long ago crossed those boundaries and thus mitigated the risk associated with controversially depicting religion.

Preceding the premiere of the show, the industry discourse around the television adaptation was very clearly oriented toward fans of the comic book and an engagement with claims of fidelity, including the religious themes. In an interview conducted during the 2014 South by Southwest festival, Eric Vespe of *Ain't It Cool News* (AICN), an Austin-based genre-focused fan and news website, interviewed producers Evan Goldberg and Seth Rogen and asked about *Preacher*. Rogen proclaimed, "It seems like the language is going to be the most restrictive thing, but that I'm not worried about . . . the religious stuff, they're [AMC executives] totally cool with. The violence, they're totally cool with. The nudity is hard, but we can find ways around that. Overall, it was one of the best meetings I've ever had, honestly."[53] Although Rogen said that AMC was "totally cool" with the religious elements, when I asked Garth Ennis about his sense of how *Preacher*'s religious storyline would evolve for television based on his initial meetings, sitting in on some writing sessions and the first season outline, he responded,

> I think they're leading up to some of the religious elements rather than stating them plainly from the get-go, but that may be as much to do with the overall plan as it is to do with anyone getting nervous. They apparently want to get 5–6 seasons out of this, and if they went with what they've got in the comic [the first volume of 7 issues, of 75 total] they'd barely manage one and a half. So one way to lengthen the story is to spend more time on the little Texas town where Jesse starts the story, rather than being done with it in four issues as I was. I think they'll take a bit longer defining Jesse's mission before sending him out on it.[54]

Ennis' perspective added some nuance to Rogen's somewhat blasé response to the role of religion in the show, but it did not necessarily contradict Rogen's sense of AMC's content standards and "coolness" with the religious narrative. Moreover, AMC's attitude corresponded with the reaction Ennis remembered with regard to the religious themes in the comic book, which he characterized thus: "After the initial outcry, people quickly figured out whether they liked the book or not, and anyone who didn't pretty much left us alone. We had the occasional kerfuffle, but nothing major—stuff like, 'My daddy's a Preacher and I bought him this book, and he was horrified,' but even those you could count on the fingers of one hand. No one ever had a serious go at us, tried to start any kind of movement to ban the book."[55] *Preacher* is assumed to be boundary pushing in terms of both general content and especially religious content, but no actual protest arose. The positioning of *Preacher* as edgy quality fare within AMC's brand has not yet used religion much in its positioning as such, but neither has it dismissed it as a potential avenue for distinction. Aside from the first promotion poster with the inverted church, *Preacher's* marketing has mostly emphasized the weirdness, irreverence, and action of the show. The search for God, undertaken at the end of the first season and forming the narrative foundation of the second season, was used more to connect the road-trip narrative to the beloved *Blues Brothers* (Landis, 1980) and their "mission from God" road trip than to explore Jesse's religious powers or the implications of a real-but-absentee God. By the end of the series, the heavenly bureaucracy, Hell, God, and the apocalypse have all become part of the show but through emphasized weirdness instead of emphasized religion.

This agnostic framing of religion indicates the risk incurred for AMC remains high despite the network's branding as an outlet for upscale horror. The potential ratings for AMC shows, at least on the basis of ratings for *The Walking Dead*, are in line with successful broadcast television series.[56] As Goldberg said of AMC in one of the March 2014 interviews, "They've implied they want us to go on a *Walking Dead*–type path. That seems to be their strategy."[57] While these comments were all made quite early in the development process, they set the stage for how *Preacher* would continue to be constructed via marketing and journalistic materials. Namely, it was presented as a serialized horror drama in the vein of *Walking Dead*. Early discourses pointed to a show that would be incredibly violent but cautious about language and sex—the two content elements that most often have caused controversy and mobilized a conservative backlash.[58]

Significantly, *Preacher's* creatives and AMC's executives expressed little concern about the show's presentation of religious themes and narratives. Although this is not the first instance of executives being portrayed as surprisingly sanguine regarding religion (remember Ronald D. Moore's *Battlestar Galactica* anecdote), it is still fairly rare within this study. Garth Ennis, who sat in on some of the initial meetings and offered feedback on an early outline of the show's first season, reiterated via personal correspondence that the *The*

Walking Dead was a vital influence on *Preacher*'s development: "I'm told that AMC are doing this at the optimum moment, as comic book adaptations are flourishing and the particular success of *The Walking Dead* has indicated an acceptance of non-superhero comics. So when HBO had a go with *Preacher* about eight years ago, the time wasn't right, but now the groundwork's been laid and we've got a better shot."[59] What Ennis didn't discuss about "the time being right" now is the much lower stakes in terms of ratings numbers. Even though *The Walking Dead*'s ratings often beat broadcast ratings numbers in the early 2010s, because of AMC's different business model—as well as its ownership stake in *Preacher*—such ratings are not imperative.[60] *Preacher* fit AMC's brand at the moment and seemed a clear extension of its most successful show, but it also aired at a time in the post-network era when a small, devoted, and affluent audience niche can sustain a show as controversial and weird as *Preacher* is. But that weirdness, like its approach to religion, is understood as part of the text because of its comic book source that already exorcised much of the religious controversy around the story and characters. And within the vestiges of quality-audience appeal that AMC employed in its framing of the show, the religious elements can use religion without being religious.

CONCLUSION

Battlestar Galactica, Lost, The Leftovers, and *Preacher* represent a spectrum of how religion has been presented and discussed in post-network-era quality fantastic television. Even if depicted only as abstracted spirituality, these shows work in such a way as to maintain religion's function, rather than reducing it to areligious mythology, the latter being a strategy explored in the next chapter. This spectrum of religious representation can be summarized as follows. *Lost* illustrates how religious representation in quality fantastic dramas can be vaguely spiritual—but that takes a few seasons to realize. *Battlestar Galactica* showed that it can clearly be explored—but within the benefits of more niche-oriented cable outlets, during moments of transition in executive oversight, or through highly unreal premises. Or, as *The Leftovers* did, Christian representation might combine elements of these two strategies, while minimizing its fantastic elements in favor of quality notions. Finally, if enough levels of generic and industrial containment are in place, *Preacher* exemplifies how creatives and executives might frame the religious elements as superficially religious but with the abstraction or religiousness already assumed and thus little discussed. In spite of these variations, all of these shows share the protection of quality discursive designations and fantastic genre conventions. Such conventions help make religion be deemed acceptable to their target upscale and fan audiences. Additionally, these genre expectations and quality designations aid in sustaining legacy practices of containment among the writers of the shows. Religion was and remains displaced, abstracted, or minimized in creatives' discussion of it throughout the span of these series, from 2003 to 2016, to ensure that the writers and creatives working on these shows aren't assumed to be religious themselves. The creatives working on these shows, even in the context of the shift toward more open discussions of religion and edgy presentations of it in 2015, remained in their interviews with me hugely influenced by the legacies that shaped much of the boom's discourse. They can discuss religion as spirituality, one non-institutional way to tackle the "big questions" within the safety of fantastic generic displacement of the real. Without these protections for texts and creatives, religion loses its religiousness; it is no longer even an avenue to tackle the "big questions," as will be explored in the next chapter.

6

The Biblical Book of Revelation as Mythology

Apocalyptic TV

THE POST-CHRISTIAN END OF THE WORLD AND APOCALYPTIC TELEVISION

Eschatological fantastic dramas simultaneously literally represent stories and characters from the Bible while their writers deny that such stories or characters are religious. Representationally, they are among the most overtly religious, but among writers and producers involved with them, that religion is characterized as nonreligious mythology—in other words, emptied of religious meanings. These shows exemplify the postmodern, post-Christian sensibility within mainstream, prime-time dramas that use representations of religion as blank parody or pastiche removed from their religious meanings, discussed as mythology. *Supernatural* (the WB/CW, 2005–2020), *Dominion* (SyFy, 2014–2015), and *Constantine* (NBC, 2014–2015) are exemplars of this category. There are few examples of series that fit this grouping beyond these three case studies; examples include *Sleepy Hollow* (Fox, 2013–2017), *The Messengers* (The CW, 2015) and (vaguely, with more focus on the antichrist than Revelation) *Damien* (A&E, 2016). Eschatological fantastic shows contrast with the fantastic shows analyzed in the previous chapter because these series are generally not considered quality dramas by viewers, critics, creatives, or scholars; rather, they are positioned by industry stakeholders, critics, and viewers as genre shows, cult hits, or guilty pleasures. They represent a different kind of upscale audience imaginary than quality series such as *Lost* and *The Leftovers*, but they and their target audiences are also constructed as secular.[1] As a result, these three shows and their grouping within the category of eschatological fantasy lead their writers to be even less inclined to acknowledge their work as religious. They may use the Christian

Divine Programming. Charlotte E. Howell, Oxford University Press (2020).
© Oxford University Press.
DOI: 10.1093/oso/9780190054373.001.0001

Bible as a source, but they don't consider the work created from it as necessarily Christian or religious. Instead, eschatological fantastic shows contain Christianity by reframing the Book of Revelation as mythology.

Christian visions of the end of the world as presented in the Book of Revelation long have been primary scripture of Christian theology and of interest to religious studies scholarship.[2] Eschatology is a term abiding in theology and in the academy. It is not used much in the wider culture, unlike "apocalypse," which has become shorthand for catastrophe, as, for example, in non-eschatological fantastic series like *Buffy the Vampire Slayer* (the WB/UPN 1997–2003) and its spinoff *Angel* (the WB, 1999–2004).[3] In his study of apocalyptic themes in film, Jon R. Stone notes the conundrum of using a language that still invokes the particularly religious aspects of apocalypse when it has generally lost its specific and powerful religious meanings. He writes,

> It has become commonplace to speak of any cataclysmic event as an "apocalypse" or as "apocalyptic." Such collegial misuse of these potent terms, though widespread, stems from a conceptual and definitional misunderstanding. By definition, apocalypses are revelatory texts whose sources of knowledge are otherworldly or divine. As such, an apocalypse reveals a reality not previously known to the prophet, the recipient of the revelation, or to its intended audience. As a literary genre, an apocalypse has two common elements: its revelatory narrative framework and its eschatological orientation, an orientation that anticipates final judgment and punishment of the wicked.[4]

In general, the series in this chapter do not center around the revelatory framework; even other shows such as *The Messengers,* which focused on delivering the message of the apocalypse, did not focus on the element of prophecy. They may have prophets—*Supernatural* has had four since its fourth season—but their stories are not primarily about the prophecy or about those who hear it and repeat it. Instead, the focus of the series examined in this chapter is the eschatological battle itself, the war between good (the hero-protagonists of the series) and evil (the Devil; high-ranking demons and the legions of Hell; resentful angels abandoned by God and looking to destroy the world in a kind of pseudo-tantrum for attention).

Eschatological fantastic dramas use an abstracted version of the biblical apocalypse presented in Revelation, culturally familiar beyond Christian adherents. In their study of the apocalypse on film, scholars

Karen A. Ritzenhoff and Angela Krewani explain the basics of the biblical apocalypse and its reduction in popular understanding: "In the course of the narrative and due to secularization, the narrative of the apocalypse has changed from being a threefold story [including the final building of a New Jerusalem] to a twofold story: the sinful mankind and its destruction as God's punishment."[5] In eschatological fantastic dramas, the end of the world is structured around this basic interpretation of the Book of Revelation from the New Testament. However, they avoid any sense of judgment at the end of the world. Judgment is the overarching narrative threat; the tribulations that precede it are the foundation of these shows' premises. The characters in eschatological fantastic dramas are in the middle of the fight and do not care about the possibility of justice or punishment in the afterlife. Even in series that do represent Heaven and/or Hell as real locations where characters have gone, the focus remains on the terrestrial battle and the active experience of trying to stop the end from actually occurring, or at least delay it a few more millennia. In theological terms, these shows follow a premillennial view of Christian eschatology that expresses the view that the world is getting worse as it progresses toward the ultimate apocalyptic end that heralds Christ's return and defeat of Satan.[6] What is distinctive about these shows, however, is that they take that story foundation and then claim it as nonreligious mythology. This post-Christian eschatological context further asserts that the angels fighting in these apocalyptic tribulations are not religious figures.

For many eschatological fantastic dramas, angels are central agents of this eschatological battle, and in secular iterations of the Book of Revelation, the same is true. Religious scholar Peter Gardella writes, "In apocalyptic writing, angels often take on strange and possibly symbolic forms . . . No book of the Bible contains more angelic activity and more angels acting on a cosmic scale than the twenty-two chapters of Revelation."[7] Gardella studies angels both in their theological context and in their American mytho-cultural context, theorizing contemporary understanding of angels as "transtheistic." [8] Gardella uses this term to situate angels within a culture beyond Christianity alone without losing their religious significance. His study of angels, however, is strongly tied to American Christian culture even if it extends beyond it. Gardella's study of angels helps to situate eschatological fantastic dramas in relationship to apocalyptic literature and studies of angels within that context. Because of their nonreligious mythological characterization among prime-time television writers, in the post-network era, angels are flexible character types in religious apocalyptic fantasy stories, frequently becoming supernatural heroes and villains. Obviously, the Bible is the urtext for stories of angels, but the discourses around these shows situate such stories and characters outside of the Christianity in which they originate. They have become a postmodern pastiche of their religious iteration. Gone are the benign, inherently good angels like those in *Touched by an Angel*. The angels of the post-network era are as complex and flawed as their human counterparts. They may fight on either side of the apocalyptic war, although they often are antagonists for the human characters rather than "guardian" angels. The reinterpretation of angels as antagonists helps to further dissociate these programs from *Touched by an Angel* as the paragon of religious dramas.

CONTAINMENT THROUGH PASTICHE: *SUPERNATURAL*

Supernatural is a drama about two brothers fighting monsters, angels, and demons to prevent the apocalypse and keep humanity safe. It began airing on the WB in 2005, at the same time that both *Lost* and *Battlestar Galactica* were significant cultural and industry successes. It continued on the netlet after the WB merged with UPN to form The CW in 2006 and finished its run there in 2020. However, *Supernatural*'s place in the cultural and industrial landscape was much smaller; perhaps its more marginal cultural status at a low-culture, teen-oriented channel, the WB/CW, protected it from religious backlash and scrutiny. Notably, *Supernatural*'s early seasons overlapped briefly with the final seasons of *7th Heaven*, setting the fantastic drama's religious representation in stark contrast to that of its middlebrow network sibling. The former got a pass because it was of the fantastic genres and thus about mythology, not religion; the latter persisted among creatives as an example of why to avoid religion.

   Supernatural, despite its low but consistent ratings in its first seasons, added value to the WB and The CW as a vertically integrated product of Warner Bros. Television. *Supernatural*'s ratings could be low or average, but their consistency and the show's strong youth and female audiences helped it survive.[9] This was the case even as it was often paired with the relatively male-skewing Superman drama, *Smallville* (the WB/CW 2001–2011) for much of the late 2000s. This pairing represented the netlet's effort to attract more male viewers to its heavily female-skewing network.[10] Eventually, *Supernatural* became the anchor of The CW's programming and Warner Bros.' alternative revenue strategies, exemplified by its 2011 (relatively early for streaming)

Netflix licensing agreement.[11] In terms of genre and brand, it helped push the network toward more supernatural and fantastic genre-based programming like *The Vampire Diaries* (CW, 2009–2017) and its mid-2010s lead-in, *Arrow* (CW, 2012–2020). *Supernatural* is by far the longest-running series among the case studies in this book. Its marginal status in the mid-2000s kept its potentially groundbreaking/blasphemous approach to religious representation largely under the radar outside of its fan audience, which included many critics and scholars. *Supernatural's* perpetual position "on the cancelation bubble" of even a small netlet allowed for it to take a chance on more risky and overt religious representation because each season could be its last. And instead of isolating its target audience of upscale fantastic genre fans, *Supernatural's* religious narrative was embraced by its consistent viewer base. Moreover, it serves as the paragon of what I call eschatological fantastic dramas for how it uses its fantastic genre to claim the Bible as a source for nonreligious mythology.

Supernatural began with a fairly simple premise: two brothers travel the country by car and fight monsters and demons. The Winchester brothers, Sam (Jared Padalecki) and Dean (Jensen Ackles), grew up knowing that the things that go bump in the night were real. Their mother was killed by a demon in Sam's nursery when Sam was still a baby and Dean only four years old. After that, their father (Jeffrey Dean Morgan) became nomadic in his quest for vengeance, traveling across the country in his classic Chevrolet Impala with his two sons, learning how to hunt the monsters that he knew were responsible for his wife's death. This background is established in the first five minutes of the pilot before jumping to Dean and Sam in their twenties and establishing their disparate approaches to their family tradition of hunting monsters: Dean continues to hunt with their father, seeking to emulate him, and Sam seeks to leave both hunting and his family behind. When Sam's girlfriend is killed in the same way his mother was, Sam joins Dean on the hunt. Although the basic premise of brothers hunting evil things is the basis of the show, the overarching religious narrative first appeared in the fourth episode of the series, "Phantom Traveler." That episode marks the first demon that the brothers must fight, and it hints at a wider world of the hunt that includes heavenly and infernal players.

Over the first five seasons of *Supernatural*, the narrative is that Sam and Dean are part of a larger biblical story that includes the two men discovering the following: that their exploits, in the form of the "Winchester Gospel," have been recorded by a prophet as a novel series; that God is absent; that

angels are real and as amoral as demons; and that the brothers are prophe-
sied to be the vessels for Lucifer (Mark Pellegrino) and the archangel Michael
in the final apocalyptic battle that will destroy the earth. All of these eschatological discoveries flow from one essential plot revelation in the fourth-
season episode "Sympathy for the Devil": Mary Winchester made a deal with
a demon that allowed him to establish an influence on Sam in order to pre-
pare Sam to be Lucifer's vessel.[12]

Within this five-season biblical apocalypse narrative on *Supernatural*,
the main characters call angels "dicks," find Heaven to be emotionally tor-
turous, and say "screw him" when they find God absent. Eschatological
fantastic shows such as *Supernatural*, as well as *Dominion*, operate in a post-
Christian sensibility in which Christian elements such as angels, God, and
the Devil are subservient to the storytelling in a way that removes their religiousness. These religious representational elements have become mere
pastiche versions of religious figures, stories, and tropes: blank parodies
emptied of their meaning.[13] Eric Kripke, the creator and showrunner during
Supernatural's first five seasons, often described the show's Christian elements as "mythology" in this mode.[14] For example, in an interview with television critic Maureen Ryan, he said.

> Religion and gods and beliefs—for me, it all comes down to your
> brother. . . . it's about human connections. What you'll find as the my-
> thology of [Season 5] unveils, it's this massive, Byzantine mythology of
> angels and demons and what they want and their destinies for the world.
> But it's basically about two red-blooded, human brothers giving them all
> the middle finger.[15]

This explanation articulates the propensity of creatives on non-quality fantastic shows to diminish the religious power of religious characters and
stories. In doing so, writers of fantastic dramas can use them freely for their
own purposes without fear of being perceived as religious, let alone blas-
phemous. "Religion and gods and beliefs" become "Byzantine mythology"
even during the course of a single interview quotation. The containment of
religion in the term mythology further illustrates the potential for cultural
critique, if only at an angle, that such post-Christian religious representation and production practices of containment can allow because creatives
and executives have disavowed their shows' religiousness. Kripke explicitly
framed the Christian tropes and figures in his show as hollow mythology in

this quotation and other interviews, including an oral history of the show in honor of its 200th episode.[16] However, the overall religious narrative can be read as largely anti-religious.[17] The series questions—and often challenges—a host of theologies, and as Kripke says, "gives them the middle finger." Such blatant criticism of religion is possible only when the religiousness of such figures and the systems they arise out of has been contained both within the show and among its writers and producers, in effect transformed to the point of pastiche. When these fantastic eschatological shows no longer represent religion, critique becomes blank parody instead of blasphemy.

Supernatural is a model of eschatological fantastic dramas via its denial of its overt religious representation. In many ways it set the pattern for religious representations in this category—by virtue of being the first and most successful in cultivating its fan audience—and utilized strategies that other shows' creatives repeated in order to distance its mythology from any sense of religiousness. Its representation of explicitly Christian figures, tropes, and narratives was unparalleled in its biblical literalism by the fifth season. Moreover, Supernatural's fantastic generic context, its industrial position within the marginal netlet, its cult fan audience, and its creators' insistence that the show was not religious allowed its religious representation to be accepted as mythology, not necessarily tied to Christianity as a religion. However, the show did not make this biblical apocalyptic arc explicit in the first two seasons. Like Lost, in its early seasons, Supernatural hesitated in revealing its central religious narrative as central to a season- or seasons-long plot; instead, it hinted at it through the acknowledgment of demons and hell through one-off episodic stories.

Supernatural did feature monsters and foes of explicitly non-Christian origin, especially in the first two seasons. In addition to traditional horror monsters like ghosts and vampires, the first season featured episodes with Native American skinwalker and wendigo antagonists. Supernatural writers used this strategy to mitigate the Christian representational frame created by the focus on demons and the eventual eschatological narrative. Writers point to the use of other belief systems for one-episode adversaries as proof that their shows aren't religious and to buttress their claims of Christian tropes as merely part of a tapestry of American mythology.[18] But monsters from other belief systems do not minimize a five-season-long Christian apocalyptic narrative.

Despite building the show's ongoing narrative around a patently Christian frame, the producers and writers on Supernatural still distance themselves from religiousness in their discussions of the work. As one writer for *Supernatural* who joined the room in the show's later seasons told me, "It does seem that there was an organic process [to writing] that resulted in deeper explorations of religious subject matter—that it wasn't necessarily part of the original plan for the show but the deeper they got into demonology the more appealing and/or necessary it became to introduce demons' opposites."[19] This writer is one of the few throughout this study who used the term religious when referring to Christian representation, acknowledging the religious grounding of demons and angels. This openness may be because the writer was granted anonymity or more likely because of not being involved in that "organic process," having only joined the writing staff in the later seasons. The "it does seem" provides distancing from the sense of religiousness that the discursive denial of religion does for other creatives. Although this writer says angels were introduced as demons' opposites, *Supernatural* is notable for being the first among these shows to configure angels as equally complicit in a plan to end the world. Furthermore, the writer's positioning of religious subject matter as an eventual necessity once again illustrates the hesitation on display. Creatives engaged in the type of self-policing discussed in the previous chapter. The slow burn toward the religious narrative arc, by, for example, introducing angels only in the fourth season highlights the continued sense of potential regarding religious narratives, especially those that feature angels because of their association with the overtly religious *Touched by an Angel*, even as the show made very clear that angels, demons, and other religious supernatural beings existed within the same nonreligious representational field as vampires, ghosts, and Native American skinwalkers.

Despite the increase in religious representation in television dramas since 2003 for which *Supernatural* stands as an explicit example, the logic of risk within writers' rooms persists, even when religious representation is couched in post-Christian characterization of religion as mythology and pastiche. This cautiousness is built on years of ideological learning as writers honed their skills both by watching television and working in writers' rooms and at networks where religion was understood as risky. Until *Battlestar Galactica,* there was no well-known, let alone well-regarded, series that used religion as one of its key thematic and narrative concerns without being considered de facto middlebrow. Thus, it became imperative within the ideology that shaped *Supernatural,* as well as so many other shows of this time period, that creatives frame Christian narrative tropes through post-Christian denial.

CONTAINMENT THROUGH DENIAL: *DOMINION* AND
CONSTANTINE

Dominion aired for two seasons on Syfy (formerly the Sci-Fi Channel then SciFi) from 2014 to 2015. Syfy at the time was undergoing a brand identity crisis, its second since 2009 as the channel tried to navigate its post–*Battlestar Galactica* landscape. The first brand identity crisis occurred in 2009—the same year that early 2000s tent-pole *Battlestar Galactica* ended—when SciFi announced that it was changing its name to Syfy in an effort to expand its output (and hopefully its viewer base) beyond the genre of science fiction.[20] Whereas throughout the 2000s, SciFi focused on shows such as *Battlestar Galactica*, *Andromeda* (2000–2005) and *Stargate: Atlantis* (2004–2009) that were overtly science fictional and niche, the rebranded Syfy found success by emphasizing lighter, more broadly fantastic programming such as *Warehouse 13* (2009–2014), *Eureka* (2006–2012), and the reality show *Ghost Hunters* (2004–2016). The movement away from science fiction and toward more fantasy, horror, and broadly fantastic programming underlined the name change in ways that alienated the science fiction fan audience that had supported SciFi and *Battlestar Galactica*.[21] Unfortunately, none of these newer shows recreated the critical success of *Battlestar Galactica* (2003–2009).[22] In 2014, Syfy began a new public relations campaign, called by some a de-rebranding, to court the "quality" science fiction audience the network had lost when it had shifted to more lighthearted series from 2009 to 2014.[23] In a 2014 article, *Entertainment Weekly* reporter Bill Hibbard explained Syfy's latest brand shift with shows such as *The Expanse* (2015–), *Ascension* (2014), and *12 Monkeys* (2015–2018): "Largely in the last year, Syfy has shifted its course. [Syfy president David] Howe hired new programming chief [Bill McGoldrick] . . . obtained a larger programming budget from parent company Comcast, and has amassed a truly impressive development slate . . . Howe said[,] 'We want to be the destination for the smartest, most provocative [genre dramas].'"[24] While *Dominion* had already aired its first season by the time Howe made this statement, it still was discussed along with this new programming slate. However, *Dominion* was not configured as a quality science fiction like *Battlestar Galactica*. Instead, it was provided as an example of Syfy's willingness to tell stories that include "rough stuff," particularly graphic violence.[25] Although *Dominion*'s "rough" content and dark tone aligned it with the brand shift at Syfy, the series gained neither the buzz nor ratings desired by Syfy, and as such, it was canceled in 2015.[26]

Dominion was a continuation of the 2010 film *Legion* (Stewart), which focused on the archangel Michael (in the film, Paul Bettany; on television, Tom Wisdom) battling the heavenly host in order to protect one human child, a chosen one. *Dominion's* plot starts more than twenty years after the film's plot, jumping to when that child, Alex Lannen (Christopher Egan), is an adult, and his destiny is beginning to be realized. The series focuses on the city of Vega, a human stronghold in a world in which angels, led by Gabriel (Carl Beukes), have taken over. Vega survives in part because Michael acts as its protector. Alex's destiny is slowly revealed to him over the course of the first season; during this season, he is shown reconciling his role and responsibility as the prophesized savior of mankind. Meanwhile, Alex must also bide his time among the humans in which certain powerful elites battle for dominance. Concurrent with Alex's struggles, Michael must negotiate his place within the world. Michael protects humanity, and particularly Alex, but he struggles to do so while still considering the other angels his family. Like *Supernatural, Dominion* humanizes its angels by rewriting their religious vocations as familial obligations; for example, the angels Michael, Gabriel, and Uriel (Katrina De Candole) are portrayed as siblings dealing with an absent father (God).

In the plot of *Dominion,* the angel war already has raged, bringing about the apocalypse, albeit one that might be mitigated and reversed with the presence of a new savior of mankind, prophesized to be Alex. Whereas *Supernatural, Sleepy Hollow,* and *The Messengers* focused on preventing the biblical apocalypse, on *Dominion* the apocalypse in effect already has occurred. It's not a direct Revelation-based version of the apocalypse with Lucifer playing a key role, but it does feature chosen ones who must fight the end of days as well as the angel Gabriel fulfilling Lucifer's standard role as an angel jealous of humanity's place among God's creations and reacting to this supposed slight. Gabriel on *Dominion* is not the light bringer or tempter, but he is the show's adversary and acts in the fallen-angel-seeking-dominion-over-humanity role often occupied elsewhere by Lucifer.

The post-Christian elision of Christian culture and American cultural myths was apparent when *Dominion* writers Brusta Brown and John Mitchell Todd explained in an interview that they don't consider *Dominion* to be a religious show.[27] On the one hand, in stating this, they were in line with almost every other writer for these eschatological fantastic shows that I interviewed. No writer I spoke with characterized these shows—shows featuring battling archangels and the Four Horsemen of the Apocalypse, which are characters and tropes taken directly from the Bible and decades of evangelical culture—as religious. To them, as was the case with the quality fantasy series addressed in the previous chapter, religious meant middlebrow, though they did not explicitly use that term. For most of these writers, the framework for understanding religious television was still stuck in the 1990s era I discuss in Chapter 1. From the interview with Brown and Todd, I speculated about their attitude toward religious representation, based on how they reacted to the idea that a show such as *Dominion* might be described as religious: they said there was "no religious source" for the show even as Todd said he had spent years before he began working on the show and studying angels.[28] The writers' contradictions underscore the complicated negotiation of what "religious" means among many post-network-era shows' creatives. For Brown and Todd, their distinction between a "religious source" and angels implies the latter has moved discursively into nonreligious categorization, at least within the fantastic genres. Writers in the fantasy and science fiction genres on contemporary television appear much more comfortable discussing their shows' use of mythology than they do discussing religion or even spirituality. This inclination remains the norm, even for these 2014 dramas, especially those like *Dominion* that are faced with less studio and network support and an increased sense of precarity within the writing process. The reliance on these old discursive strategies of distancing was becoming less the norm as the influence of streaming television accelerated change in 2015–2016.

Since the 1990s, mythology has increasingly become an accepted term among television writers, used with regard to both multi-season narrative arcs and the presence of cultural stories featuring supernatural elements.[29] The term mythology can carry religious or spiritual connotations, and it often, but not always, carries such connotations when used in relation to eschatological fantastic dramas. The slipperiness of the term is not new or wholly reserved for television: Joseph Campbell's *The Hero with a Thousand Faces* has a long arm of influence in contemporary entertainment, and it examines familiar mythology—Hellenic and occasionally other oral storytelling traditions—both as a component of spiritual life and as a key storytelling structure of Western culture. Thus, the use of the term mythology both for crafting an ongoing serial narrative and using supernatural elements to create a set of rules for a show's fantastic world is not unusual for television writers to use. However, folding Christianity into either or both functions belies the cultural presence and impact that Christianity holds in America. For many writers' rooms of contemporary American prime-time dramas,

Christianity might be just as far from the staff's cultural milieu as Indigenous American beliefs. This is the case because, as many of the writers I talked to acknowledged, television writers were and remain majority atheist, agnostic, or Jewish. However, because these creatives' writing was also inscribed within an industrial system that must anticipate an audience wider than the makeup of the writers' rooms—even if that audience is no longer mass audience—the fear of alienation remains. Therefore, it is far less risky for writers to cordon off the religious elements—whether consciously or not—than it is for them to acknowledge their role in telling religiously themed stories.

Although ideologically, as well as in terms of industry acceptability, it makes sense that the writers for *Dominion* might not consider the show to be religious and may be due to other factors. More specifically, such elusiveness could be the result of a somewhat difficult production schedule. As *Dominion* writers Brusta Brown and John Mitchell Todd told me, they were faced with notable logistical and creative challenges during the process of writing the first season of the series. These included a condensed time frame for writing the series' episodes from pilot to finale, minimizing the length of time in which to organize the writers' room, break the episodes, and write the scripts; locational difficulties because the writers' room was in Los Angeles but shooting and production occurred in South Africa, making it difficult for the writing staff to clearly communicate with the production team across such time and distance; and struggles during the first season to find the appropriate tone of the show and voices for the characters.[30] With the room facing such challenges, the writers' decision to characterize the writing as nonreligious had some significant practical advantages. For one, dealing with angels-qua-religious figures would very likely require research that they simply didn't have the time to conduct. For another, any spiritually contentious themes or scripts might force the network's executives to step in, adding another layer to a writing process that was already significantly compressed.

Thus, very likely for pragmatic reasons, the *Dominion* writers' room was described to me as "religiously sterile," trying to stay away from religious "button words."[31] However, at the same time, they said that there were "no hard rules" about religion, a position that they explained meant that there was no religious "source" to their writing; that is, they didn't knowingly draw from the Bible.[32] The primary source they had to engage with was the film on which the series was loosely based; they also drew from their own cultural knowledge of angels and of the dramatic television writing process. Of course, to say that there were "no rules" about religion within the writers' room mere moments after they discussed their desire to stay away from religious "button words" demonstrates the deep ambivalences felt by those on the creative side of the television industry in terms of dealing with religion. On the one hand, Brown and Todd said that the show was "meant to reach everyone" and that they were "trying not to alienate any audience," but on the other, they were writing a show about warring angels that opens with the archangel Michael participating in an orgy. The writers "took all the stuff humanity deal[s] with and put it on the angels," allowing them to "study humanity through angels." This projection was conceived of as a part of their creative responsibility as television writers: to write relatable stories.[33] However, positioning angels as nonreligious figures in a nonreligious show aided in these claims of crafting relatable stories. This denial of religion was a pragmatic construction of an industrial discourse that maximized the risk-reward balance of a high-concept fantastic premise on Syfy, a niche cable outlet trying to regain the industry position it had when it aired a fantastic quality drama that happened to also represent religion, *Battlestar Galactica*. *Dominion*'s writers could protect their work and position within Hollywood television culture by characterizing religious tropes as mere cultural mythology.

Contrasting with *Dominion*'s niche cable context, *Constantine* was a broadcast adaptation of Vertigo/DC's *Hellblazer* comics that ran from the 1980s on and off into the present and was adapted into a widely panned film starring Keanu Reeves in 2005.[34] The most popular run of the series was written by Garth Ennis. Ennis also created and wrote the *Preacher* series for Vertigo/DC that was adapted into AMC's *Preacher*. In an interview, Ennis said he was invited into the writers' room for *Preacher* but not for *Constantine*.[35] Such a different set of experiences points to the varied approaches to both properties, based on their respective outlets. In the case of NBC's *Constantine*, the marginalization of one of the creative forces from the source property foreshadows the chain of poor executive decisions that led to the show's failure. *Hellblazer*'s history as a challenging adult-oriented comic within the mature Vertigo imprint brand and the show *Constantine*'s approach to religious representation through adaptation were appropriate for a show targeting upscale niche audiences such as comic book and fantastic genre fans. Such a confederation of upscale niches fits within the post-network-era industry structures. However, according to producer Mark Verheiden, from the outset, NBC wanted the show to appeal to a broader network audience. The network's desired audience clashed with the show's genre, its writers' intentions, and its mode of religious representation.

Constantine aired on NBC for only one thirteen-episode season in 2014 and early 2015. It was paired on Friday nights with NBC's relatively long-running fantasy procedural, *Grimm* (2011–2017). Friday was NBC's slightly more niche-oriented programming slot, anchored by *Grimm*, in which the network had, immediately prior to *Constantine,* placed upscale fantastic dramas such as *Dracula* (2014–2015) and *Hannibal* (2013–2015), both European co-productions to which *Constantine*'s attempt at broadness seemed a corrective despite its Christian overtones.[36] *Grimm* had proven that Friday nights didn't have to be a television graveyard, but the network bar for ratings success—even on Friday nights and even with live plus DVR ratings numbers—was too high for *Constantine* to achieve.[37] Additionally, the show lost some of its comic book fans and credibility early on when it departed from its comic book origins to become more of a procedural along the lines of *Grimm*.[38] In my conversation with Verheiden, he confirmed the network's desire to broaden the show's appeal.[39] While he appreciated that NBC made a big marketing push for the show early on, their desire for the "broadest possible audience" was difficult to reconcile with the show's main character and narrative premise, a similar tension to what the writers for *Dominion* discussed above; Christian representation wasn't discussed as a detriment. He said, "If we had issues creatively on *Constantine*, they were more about 'What is the show?' and 'What are we trying to accomplish with it?' Is the show procedural? . . . Or is it more serialized? NBC wanted more of the former."[40]

The push for procedural structure was born out in NBC's targeting of the audience for *Constantine*, which according to Verheiden was seeking slightly ludicrous multi-quadrant appeal. He told me, "So for [*Constantine*] we'd be . . . hoping the housewives would like it, and that the dockworker could like it, and that the sophisticated comic book fan would like it. It really is a broad brush, and it's a thing that makes it difficult to do that show because you're trying to hit so many audience segments."[41] This aim at coalition (but not necessarily upscale) audience appeal for a semi-serialized, comic-book-based story about a morally ambivalent man who accidentally sent an innocent girl to hell and battles demons, seemed bound to fail. It is surprising that NBC tried to simultaneously appeal to such disparate—and generally thought of as genre averse—target audiences as stay-at-home moms and their teenaged sons.[42] Writers working today largely reject the desire for broad appeal and stigmatize it as trying to appeal to too many types of (middlebrow) audiences, especially if the genre and content for the show are at odds with what is assumed to be middlebrow style and narrative conventions. Thus *Constantine*, a horror-fantasy show adapted from an adult-oriented imprint cult comic book, became a site of challenging Christian representations drawn from its comic book source while network considerations tried to (unsuccessfully) push it in content and marketing toward middlebrow, multi-quadrant audience appeal.

Constantine presented overt religious representations such as occult magic drawn directly from its comic book source material. The occult magic used by John Constantine (Matt Ryan) used mystical elements of a variety of world religions, but mainly Christianity. The representation of Christianity as one path of occult magic is a continuation of fantastic genre strategies used in the eschatological fantastic dramas discussed so far. And like those dramas, the specificity of religious representation is pronounced while its religiousness is denied among the writers and producers. For *Constantine*, Christian representation was made safe due to its status as what Mark Verheiden called "gimmes," drawn from the source text.[43]

The specific Christian elements inoculated as mythological "gimmes" of the adaptation and genre is displayed in a two-episode arc in which Constantine and his cohorts visit an old friend, Anna Marie (Claire van der Boom) at a nunnery in Mexico. Anna Marie was an occultist who was present the night that John Constantine lost a girl's soul to Hell. She subsequently retreated to the sisterhood to try to atone for her role in that failed exorcism. At the nunnery, she encountered a Mesopotamian demon, Lamashtu (Paloma Guzmán), disguised as a nun, who is taking newborns to a dastardly but vague end (consumption is implied, but broadcast standards kept the babies' fate unclear). Despite this female demon being Mesopotamian in origin, she is discussed within the show as related to the apocryphal Bible story of Lilith, Adam's demonic first wife. Moreover, when an exorcism is performed in the episode in question, "Saint of Last Resorts," the practice adheres to the cultural knowledge we have of Catholic exorcisms, indicating Christianity's power as a signifier that carries beyond its own book of stories and characters.[44]

As Mark Verheiden explained, the use of Catholic nuns as a front for a baby-stealing demon was not a problem for NBC. Indeed, he noted that most of the potentially controversial religious elements are considered givens as enabled by the source material.[45] He said that he "was actually surprised about what *didn't* push buttons on the network side . . . I wrote the episode where Constantine underwent an exorcism . . . But no one brought up that a non-ordained female nun was performing the exorcism . . . I suspect there is a group of viewers [who might have a problem with that but] who would not be interested in *Constantine* based on the subject matter like literal demons."[46] The acceptability of this deviant exorcism may be because Catholic church organizations have a long history on television, particularly on procedural television series like *Law and Order* (NBC, 1990–2010), for serving as useful visual and narrative shorthand for insular, suspicious, and outside-the-law sites where dreadful, ritualistic activities take place.[47] Catholic otherness, along with knowledge of the source material's known use of various religions' dogma, mysticism, and supernatural elements, set the boundaries of representation available for the program. *Constantine*'s use of religion is within these boundaries of its genre expectations even as it is contained by the ideology of the show's creatives and NBC's untroubled approach, due to that containment, to Christian representation.

CONCLUSION

In this chapter, I've argued that creatives working on eschatological fantastic dramas consider their shows' religious representations as not religious in any way they can claim discursively. In fact, they don't even consider their shows to be spiritual in the sense that creatives for quality fantastic dramas in the previous chapter claimed. For eschatological fantastic dramas, religion has become a pastiche of itself in the form of mythology. This strategy of containment manifests in slightly different ways across the three shows considered as case studies for this chapter, *Supernatural, Dominion,* and *Constantine*. *Supernatural,* as the earliest and longest-running series of this group, hesitated to overtly represent the biblical apocalypse in its first seasons, only hinting at the religious narrative that was the show's guiding premise. When the religious narrative became central during season four, *Supernatural*'s writers and showrunner asserted that their use of the biblical apocalypse, angels, Lucifer, and God were not religious, but rather functioned merely as mythology to be used to tell a humanistic story. *Dominion*'s writers too maintained that their show about angels and the apocalypse was not religious. Their assertion, couched in contradictions and practical limitations on the writing process, illustrated the ways that Christian representation and writers' understanding of it is unstable. *Constantine*'s executive producer denied religiousness of the broadcast show while acknowledging the religious tropes of its comic book source.

Despite the different ways they discussed their respective shows' religious representations, all of the showrunners, staff writers, and producers I spoke with uniformly maintained that—as used in their shows—the Bible was mythology, not religion. Such abstraction, to the point of pastiche, indicates the longevity of the network-era ideology that religion is alienating for both creatives and the upscale audiences their shows target. This decades-old perspective largely remained in place even with fantastic genres that provided the safety of displaced reality. The fantastic genres' allowance of the "reality" of monsters, magic, and myth creates a safe space for representing Christianity—that is, as long as the creatives working in that genre group biblical elements with the unreal.

PART IV

ACKNOWLEDGING CHRISTIANITY IN THE ERA OF PEAK TV

Parts I through III have explored the paradox that Christian representation on television dramas in the post-network era has increased and diversified while simultaneously the reluctance and hesitancy about acknowledging Christianity among creatives working on those shows have persisted through a range of forms, eras, and outlets. Part IV turns to the newest iteration of television, streaming platforms, to determine whether or not the emergence of new technologies, shifting modes of consumption, and ongoing transformations in business models changed this paradoxical pattern. Since the advent of cable in the 1980s, one of the greatest changes the television industry has undergone is the rise of streaming platforms in the twenty-first century. Like cable outlets before them, streaming television such as Amazon, Netflix, and Hulu represented a change in how content was consumed. They initially focused on licensing evergreen content rather than financing or distributing original programming.[1] But as their economic foundation solidified through licensing, these streaming outlets eventually began producing original scripted programming, an expensive progression in their business model.

As competition for old content became more intense, prices continued to rise for such content, and as these streaming platforms sought to differentiate themselves from their competitors, they began to adapt certain legacy television models and practices to their own purposes. Beginning in 2012, services such as Amazon and Netflix began commissioning original content to compete with established outlets such as HBO, Showtime, and AMC. In the 2010s, content for these platforms generally has been considered equal to broadcast, cable, and premium content in terms of production quality.[2]

Streaming television mixed old approaches to television (e.g., targeting upscale quality and fan audiences, using established properties to gain viewers, positioning themselves as not-TV by representing violence, sex, language, etc. as well as high-end stylistics) with newer strategies such as intense serialization to promote binge watching and, significantly, in the case of Amazon's *Hand of God* (2015–2017) used edgy representation of religion to distinguish itself. The pursuit of quality audiences through controversy and branding content as "not-TV" were two of key legacy practices to be translated and revised for streaming platforms.[3]

For as much as the streaming outlets perpetuate a discourse of newness—and for as much as such newness does in fact bear out in some aspects of their productions, including with religious representations—and despite the espousal of freedom and newness, the ideology that shapes the writers on these streaming dramas has changed very little from 2003. Religion remains perceived as ideologically risky for writers, much as it was with *Battlestar Galactica, Supernatural,* and other case studies discussed earlier. However, on streaming platforms, the discourse of newness has granted them enough symbolic capital that it has been possible to push through that ideology by 2015–2016. Part IV analyzes the dramas *Daredevil* and *Hand of God* to demonstrate that streaming television's approach to Christianity is not new; it is an intensification of the nichification of television audiences and programming that has been described throughout this book. Thus, this final section analyzes the mid-2010s more as a culmination of that industrial shift during which the industrial logics of containment that still operate, demonstrating considerable staying power even if somewhat mitigated by the discourses of newness and freedom offered by Peak TV's preponderance of offerings.

7

Streaming Religion

Netflix's *Daredevil* and Amazon's *Hand of God*

PEAK TV IS STILL TV: NEW TELEVISION, OLD IDEOLOGIES

Streaming services often established themselves by trying to make noise, that is, gain attention in the industry, with the press, and with potential viewers by highlighting their novelty, innovation, and originality. Amazon and Netflix made noise in 2014 and 2015, for example, with a range of programming (from award winners like *Transparent* [Amazon, 2014–2019] and *Orange Is the New Black* [Netflix, 2013–2019] to less well-received programs like *Marco Polo* [Netflix, 2014–2016] and *Mad Dogs* [Amazon, 2015–2016]). Two particular streaming programs provided unique approaches to religion, approaches that expanded on early modes of representation and tested the boundaries of religion's containment both in representation and creatives' discourse.[1] For Amazon, the most prominent show to do so was *Hand of God* (2015–2017), about a recently born-again judge who has potentially divine visions guiding him to find and exact revenge on the people who had hurt his son. *Hand of God* is unique in terms of religion: it is the only show in my study that has made it through a season and to public consumption and been able to address white Christianity in an edgy fashion. For Netflix, the show to engage most directly with religion by the mid-2010s is *Daredevil* (2015–2018), which portrayed the origin and evolution of blind lawyer (and superhero vigilante) Matt Murdock (Charlie Cox), aka Daredevil. *Daredevil* gained attention from journalists after its release for representing religion as a positive force in Matt Murdock's life.[2] Religion serves a guiding principle in the development of the series, though it was not evident in the show's initial marketing.

Despite being framed by journalistic and industrial discourses of technological, narrative, and industrial newness, these streaming dramas and,

Divine Programming. Charlotte E. Howell, Oxford University Press (2020).
© Oxford University Press.
DOI: 10.1093/oso/9780190054373.001.0001

in particular, *Daredevil*, remain shaped in the writers' rooms by the legacy ideologies and practices of self-policing regarding religious representation. However, the borderlines formed in the 1990s have become more flexible and permeable in the mid-2010s, particularly for shows on these new outlets. The practices of containment on these two streaming dramas have not proven to be as limiting as they have in the case studies discussed in prior chapters. The writers for these shows have tested and expanded the boundaries for discussing white Christianity and representing it on television because they felt they had more room to experiment within their distinctive industrial context. The sense that television itself was changing in light of streaming platforms' influence on the industry aided in the potential for 2015–2016 to mark a shift in both religious representation (with *Hand of God* and *Preacher* [AMC, 2016–2019] potentially serving as examples) and how creatives understand that work in the context of the television industry's ideology and culture. For example, writers for *Daredevil* told me they had expected Netflix and Marvel to push back on an overtly Christian scene they wrote. They were surprised at the lack of executive problems with religion in much the same way Ronald D. Moore was in 2003 when his assumption of the undesirability of religious representation was contradicted by an executive at SciFi.

Many of the strategies for navigating use and representation of religion in television discussed in earlier chapters are evident in shows created for streaming platforms. Despite streaming platforms' collective reputation as innovative television makers and risk takers, similar in kind but greater in degree to some linear television outlets like AMC and HBO, the writers and producers of *Hand of God* and *Daredevil* remained wary of executives' reaction to their use of Christianity in the shows' narratives. These writers adhered to the unwritten norms of television that religion, particularly the specifics of belief, remains a dangerous topic if you want to appeal to any kind of audience demographic. However, the hesitation that these writers discussed appeared during the shows' development and then was overcome, as was the writers' hesitation in discussing their work as religious. The writers for both the shows that comprise the case studies for this chapter discussed the hesitation and fear they felt even as they wrote their religious stories and ultimately as their shows gained notice for their religious narratives. Such hesitation was consistent with that expressed to me by writers for linear outlets. But such hesitation began to wane when the shows appeared on their platforms and gained recognition and praise for their religious representation, among other narrative and stylistic elements. *Daredevil* eventually embraced the praise it had garnered for uniquely representing religion; in fact, Netflix employed a marketing strategy for its second season that emphasized religious framing via a trailer recapping the first season through church frescoes and a promotional poster mimicking Michelangelo's *The Last Judgment* in the Sistine Chapel (see Figure 7.1).[3] Amazon, meanwhile, used *Hand of God* to buttress its brand as a "conversation starter;" the retailer-cum-streaming service aggressively highlighted its religious representations as edgy, becoming the only outlet to employ such a strategy in this study.

Although both shows increasingly embraced a reliance on religion in their marketing materials, there are notable differences industrially between the two platforms. When it comes to religion, the creative ideology driving Netflix's *Daredevil* was far less new than the service on which it appeared. Amazon, in contrast, has mined religion for whatever dramatic stories it offers without fear of offending people or courting controversy. It has done so in order to help the company build a brand and distinguish itself from Netflix. Amazon's strategy *is* unique but only in terms of its application within the framework of presenting religion on American dramas. The strategy of positioning shows as edgy is not new: this long has been a containment strategy for nonreligious objectionable material, such as sex and violence, used by broadcast networks in the 1980s and early 1990s.[4] Much as their broadcast and cable predecessors did with violent and sexually explicit content, the creatives and executives working on *Hand of God* consciously have used religion to cultivate edge.

The following sections provide the context for understanding original programming on streaming television. Included are overviews of the three main original content producers as of 2016: Netflix, Amazon, and Hulu. Within this survey, I discuss Netflix and Amazon's respective target audiences and examine how they build on the models of quality and fan audiences that have been employed by those involved with the shows discussed in previous chapters. The streaming outlets' imagining of their audiences as upscale—or their pursuit of an upscale demographic—both informs the ways in which legacy practices of containment still operate on *Daredevil* and *Hand of God*'s writers, producers, and executives and works to legitimate streaming sites as television outlets worthy of quality praise. Once achieved, as Netflix has done, the strategy turns more fully to efforts (which had been ongoing simultaneously with but with less discussion than legitimated programming) to diversify rapidly into other forms of content. The legitimation of their brands through original programming is key to understanding how

Figure 7.1 *Daredevil* poster, season two

streaming dramas navigate the risk—both textually and among creatives—in representing Christianity. This negotiation is especially fraught for Netflix, given its dominance within the streaming sector of the television industry.

NETFLIX AND AMAZON: HISTORY, BRANDING, AND MODELS OF SUCCESS IN A CHANGING INDUSTRY

Although original scripted streaming content has been a part of the entertainment media landscape for more than a decade, with prominent examples including *The Guild* (YouTube/XBox, 2007–2013) and *Doctor Horrible's Sing-Along Blog* (Whedon, 2008), it is only in the 2010s that web-first content gained enough traction to approach the status and production values of broadcast and cable television content. As noted above, the three main competitors for streaming television dominance in the twenty-first century, at least through 2016, were Netflix, Amazon, and Hulu. All are streaming services (including websites and apps) that offer subscription-based access both to their original content and to their massive libraries of licensed television shows and movies.

Netflix began as a DVD-by-mail rental service in the late 1990s, transitioned to a subscription-based DVD rental model in the 2000s, added streaming video as an option in 2007, and began licensing original content in 2012.[5] Although the technology of streaming was new as of the late 2000s, there are precedents to it in terms of licensing, acquisitions, distribution, and consumption. In tracing the history of Netflix, Chuck Tryon points out that the model for Netflix's self-positioning within the market replicates what HBO has been doing since the 1990s. He argues, "Netflix, like HBO, has sought to attract new subscribers and to retain current users through a strategy in which it promoted itself as a superior form of entertainment to a version of standard, or linear, television that really hasn't existed for some time."[6] Regarding Netflix's claims of quality within its industrial history, Tryon concludes, "Netflix increasingly casts itself as participating in the reinvention of television and in the cultivation of new modes of TV storytelling."[7] Like HBO, Netflix aligns its brand identity, at least in part, with quality television and quality TV's textual possibilities. Not surprisingly, this alignment also means that Netflix perpetuates the legacy production practices of containment for religious representation that have been affecting television distribution channels across the television landscape since 1996. Moreover,

Netflix competes with HBO, Showtime, and other linear platforms in bidding for content from the same suppliers of creatives, but it gains the advantage in its relative newness, enabling those creatives to navigate what Netflix—along with other financiers of the programming—will allow.

More recently, Netflix's debt to older television models has become explicit as it has named itself a "global Internet TV network." At the 2016 International Consumer Electronics Show, for example, Netflix co-founder Reed Hastings described what being a global TV network meant to Netflix: "With this launch, consumers around the world . . . will be able to enjoy TV shows and movies simultaneously—no more waiting. With the help of the Internet, we are putting power in consumers' hands to watch whenever, wherever and on whatever device."[8] While simultaneity of consumption was also the claim of the first television networks in America and the reasoning behind the network-affiliate technological and industrial model of television, Hastings was describing something different here: *simultaneous access*. This access was Netflix's promise—made possible primarily through its original productions, not its library content. The rebranding of Netflix as a global network was an effort to grow their subscriber base globally. The lure for new subscribers is based on the value added by original content, which makes their original programming's ability to gain buzz central to their business model. This approach is not unlike HBO's long-standing business model, made even more so by HBO's 2015 launch of their own stand-alone streaming platform: HBO Now.

In the 2010s, Amazon Prime Instant Video (henceforth, Prime Video) borrowed heavily from Netflix's successful acquisitions and licensing practices. However, Amazon's origins were in video sales rather than rental. Prime Video's streaming service started with the online retailer's shift into video-on-demand downloads (like Apple's iTunes store) in 2008. The service shortly thereafter added streaming video on demand for purchase (similar to cable's on-demand services). In 2011, Amazon Video on Demand changed its name to Amazon Instant Video and offered its Prime subscribers access to a limited amount of content from its streaming video library, Prime Video.[9] Prime Video acquires its original content from Amazon Studios, which was founded in 2010, but didn't produce original television series for Prime Video until 2013.[10] Unlike Netflix, which offers access to its full library to subscribers but provides no options for streaming rental or purchase beyond that library, Prime Video has created a tiered system. For example, Prime subscribers can buy a DVD and get it shipped to them for free within two days; they can rent or purchase a film, television episode, or complete season and have it instantly available for streaming on their devices; or they can watch any of the Prime video library instantly for "free" (with their $99/year subscription to Prime). Additionally, Amazon Prime Video works to add value to Amazon's business model by drawing subscribers to their multiple services (digital books, streaming music, free two-day shipping) and to multiple purchases, including those beyond digital media.[11] As Karen Petruska described, "All of Amazon's Prime benefits [including streaming] serve one end: to situate customers within its corporate ecosystem more fully, firmly, and inescapably."[12] This abundance of options makes unlimited entertainment available to consumers, advertised through a discourse of openness intended to rival Netflix. However, Amazon occupies a secondary place in the market, far behind Netflix in terms of number of subscribers.[13] Amazon Studios differentiated itself initially from Netflix and Hulu, both of which had the advantage of having entertainment media as their primary product since their beginnings, by focusing on crowdsourcing content from creators outside of the established television system.[14] Although that strategy changed after viewers and critics largely overlooked the first "season" of original programming, the focus on "visionary creators" continued as a way for Prime Video to differentiate its programming.[15] The incentive to take risks and cultivate edge in Amazon Studios' original programming is a strategy developed to counter Netflix's market dominance as well as incentivize Amazon Prime subscriptions.

Hulu is the third of the big three streaming but is unique in its origination from a partnership among the television networks of media conglomerates, NBC Universal and Fox (and later Disney and Warner Media), to have more control over their own content and access.[16] Hulu, like Netflix and Amazon, offers movies that it has licensed as well as television streaming reruns from its partnerships. Hulu's mid-2010s brand focus was on providing an online streaming platform for currently airing shows from its corporate co-owners, only in 2017 gaining industry attention for its original dramas.[17] Hulu also differs from Netflix and Amazon in that it still clings to the legacy television distribution practice of releasing episodes week to week instead of a season at a time, likely because of its closer partnership with the broadcast networks. Despite (or perhaps because of) Hulu's connection with legacy television production, Hulu's *The Handmaid's Tale* (2017–) marks a breakthrough in streaming platforms' legitimacy because of its status as the first streaming show to win an Emmy for outstanding drama series.[18] Although

The Handmaid's Tale could fit into this book thematically, it began airing after the end of the period of this study. Thus, Hulu must be discussed but only in this brief section outlining how streaming television shaped the television industry in the early 2010s, as Netflix, Hulu, and Amazon began producing their own original dramatic series.

All three of the major SVOD platforms, as Amanda Lotz argues, "derive the most value from content that is exclusive to their libraries. Exclusivity—although long a tool of television scheduling—achieves even greater strategic use in the context of subscriber-funded portals."[19] Original productions exemplify exclusive content in their libraries, even more so when those original productions also garner critical attention.

Both Netflix and Amazon's original programming brands rely heavily on a handful of shows that have won notable awards and gained critical acclaim: most notably *Transparent, House of Cards,* and *Orange Is the New Black.* All three shows were critical and awards darlings within the industry. Moreover, their nominations and wins at traditional industry awards ceremonies such as the Emmys serve to legitimate streaming services as sites for quality television, posed in contrast to the more "mass appeal" broadcast networks. In 2013, *House of Cards* not only won Netflix its first Emmy for best directing in a drama series but was also nominated for an Emmy for Outstanding Drama Series. As many a feature news article noted, none of the five broadcast networks earned a nomination in that category that year.[20] News stories about the nomination explicitly tied *House of Cards*—and Netflix—to HBO and its history as a home for quality, award-winning series. For example, Jon Weisman at *Variety* compared the nomination to the first-ever cable series nomination twenty years previously: HBO's *The Larry Sanders Show.*[21] After the awards show, T. C. Stock for *The Verge* drew yet another HBO comparison, writing, "The Emmy nods, coming nearly 15 years after *The Sopranos* became the first cable series to earn an Emmy nomination for best television drama, signal an important validation of the internet streaming model and the company's aggressive push into original programming. . . . Netflix has said that 'the goal is to become HBO faster than HBO can become us.'"[22] For all that Netflix and Amazon, as HBO before them, built their brands as avenues for quality television by being not-TV, the accolades garnered from their television industry peers establish their services as tied to quality television's history. Their target audiences and how they are constructed—intelligent, connected, affluent—only reinforce that these audiences are not new. Often the same labels have been revitalized to describe the same quality and fan audiences as a way to brand an outlet as up-scale, as HBO did in the 1990s. What is distinct for these streaming platforms is the addition of the notion of connectedness, which implies a certain level of technological access and engagement.

With the rise of these services and their affordances as well as the shifting fragmentation of viewers and new business models across the television landscape and influenced by their rise, new variations on the old ideologies of religion as risk and its resulting industrial and representational contain-ment strategies gain viability. This is not to say that production discourses have openly and fully embraced religion-as-edge or even in overt ways. Fear still dominates creatives' discussions of religious representation, but *Hand of God* and *Daredevil* to a lesser extent represent shows that can arise once creatives have overcome that ideological fear and its resulting self-policing.

RELIGION IN THE CONTEXT OF MARVEL'S BRAND: *DAREDEVIL*

In April 2015, *Daredevil* became the first of five series to be made avail-able to consumers via Netflix's exclusive partnership with Disney's Marvel Entertainment division (*Jessica Jones* [2015–2019], *Luke Cage* [2016–2018], and *Iron Fist* [2017–2018] follow). *Daredevil* represented one of the most explicit appeals made to a fan audience via Netflix's Original Productions slate. As noted earlier, *Daredevil* tells the comic book origin story of Matt Murdock, the blind lawyer and vigilante who patrols New York City's Hell's Kitchen neighborhood while he is using his heightened senses to compen-sate for his lack of sight. *Daredevil* and other Netflix comic book adaptations such as *Jessica Jones* and *Luke Cage* target the fan audience that the Marvel Cinematic Universe has carefully cultivated since 2008's *Iron Man* (Favreau). As with Marvel's broadcast productions for ABC (also owned by Disney), *Agents of S.H.I.E.L.D.* (ABC, 2013–2020) and *Agent Carter* (ABC, 2015–2016), these shows provide a means for extending the Marvel universe and provide a richer storyworld for existing fans and potentially new entry points for new viewers as well.

Netflix and Marvel's television partnership effectively merged the fan and quality audiences. The Marvel-Netflix productions take Matt Hills's declara-tion that "fans are always already consumers" and amend that to the Netflix-perpetuated quality discourse: Netflix viewers are always already hailed as quality consumers.[23] This position discounts the variety of other target audiences that Netflix appeals to—children (with their Kids Only profile/section), older adults (evidenced by their licensing of *Longmire* [A&E/Netflix, 2012–2017]), and middlebrow audiences (*Fuller House* [Netflix, 2016–]). Building on the HBO model as "not-TV"—meaning not "ordinary" or middlebrow fare as a discursive positioning more than business model—much of Netflix's original programming assumes the Netflix audience is a quality audience. Not only does this contingent of the audience pay to subscribe, but they also pride themselves as being different from the viewers of regular television. They see themselves as coming to this quality programming because of its high production values and complex stories and characters, as well as critical acclaim and awards. The assumptions about the quality fan audiences discussed in Chapter 5 with regard *to Battlestar Galactica* (SciFi, 2003–2009) and *Lost* (ABC, 2004–2011) persist with the *Daredevil* writers. More specifically, at least with regard to the Daredevil writers with whom I spoke, there was a perpetuation of the belief that the fan audience would be oppositional to religious representation unless these representations are contained within the genre. Only a vague spirituality would be acceptable, much as is the case with *Lost* and *Battlestar Galactica* in Chapter 5. These perspectives continue in part because the writers anticipate how Netflix and Marvel executives would react to religion. They preemptively contain their representations as protection against anticipated executive responses, a practice consistent with broadcast and cable post-network-era practices. But this self-policing occurs only within the writers' disclosed thinking about their religious writing. How *Daredevil* as a case study and Netflix as an outlet differ is that their industrial positioning as new and innovative invites writers to push past the boundaries of their self-policing and try for different, slightly less contained religious representations.

With its dark cinematography, its brutal violence, and its heightened serialization, *Daredevil* ticks many edgy boxes, especially for a superhero show. Yet, consistently with the shows discussed in previous chapters, both Marvel and Netflix executives initially hesitated about the use of religion on the show.[24] Writers for the show told me that the executives worried about the potential of religion to hinder the show's success in international markets, and they worried about being seen as "disrespectful." This fear of being disrespectful is an inherent acknowledgment that television writers' rooms are seen as being dominated by nonreligious creatives. Even as of 2015, these creatives still didn't know how to represent religion for religious audiences (i.e., those who might feel disrespected), in part because such audiences were not seen as being among TV's coveted target audiences and in part because religious representations have been ideologically contained and avoided, and thus not directly presented to mainstream audiences, since the early 2000s.[25] This hesitancy is rooted in ongoing corporate assumptions (and skittishness) about depicting religion in mainstream entertainment media. This attitude persists in *Daredevil* despite the fact that religion is a key element of the show's comic book source text as well as an acknowledged and assumed element of the main character's motivation.

As writers for *Daredevil*, Ruth Fletcher Gage and Christos Gage, told me, original showrunner Drew Goddard (*Lost, Cabin in the Woods* [Whedon, 2012]), developed the show's approach to religion around the idea that "religion is a positive force" in the lives of many and in particular in the life of their version of Matt Murdock.[26] Goddard developed the series and ran the writers' room for the first few months of a thirteen-month-long writers'-room production. Goddard is Catholic and, the Gages said, felt that Matt's Catholicism, particularly its role as a positive force in his life, was both important to the character and something that is rarely explored on television.[27] This thinking about religion in relation to television representation aligned Goddard's thinking with the assumptions and logics that have generally guided writers and producers since the early 2000s: that representation of religion *as religion* is rare and therefore unique. Goddard was in a position of power as the show's initial showrunner and had the personal experience with religion to supersede the implicit ideology of religion as risky. Goddard's acknowledged religiousness inoculated him to the fear of being considered religious. Goddard's religiousness, however well known in the writers' room and during the development process, wasn't publicly disclosed as part of the marketing and positioning of the show, nor was it an element discussed in press about the show. It operates within the production and affects that culture's ideology and work regarding Christian representation, possibly paving the way for pushing through self-policing.

According to the Gages, the decisions that led to highlighting Matt's Catholicism in the show—not only as a character trait but also as a dominant influencer in how he views, acts in, and finds purpose in the world— were unexpected in their resonance.[28] Although the use of Catholicism in the show came from Drew Goddard's vision of the show, the presentation of religion was further developed because of the presence of Ruth Fletcher Gage and Christos Gage in the writers' room. Both Gages admit that they, while not religious, come from religious backgrounds that inform their writing. Ruth Gage's family history involves historical persecution of her Protestant ancestors and eventual settling in western North Carolina, in a rural Southern context in which Christianity is a normalized part of the culture. Christos Gage's family is Greek Orthodox, and both say that their backgrounds gave them a particular understanding of the place of religion in Matt's dramatic story arc. Additionally, Ruth Gage pursued graduate studies in comparative religion and theology, so her particular personal history includes curiosity about and desire for knowledge of religion. While having a religious background doesn't necessarily impact one's ability to write religious or spiritual storylines, it can act as a buttress against worries of offense and disrespect when one is writing about religion. This was certainly the case for the Gages on *Daredevil*.[29]

As they explained in an interview with me, the Gages were assigned episode nine of thirteen, "Speak of the Devil," which was the episode of the series in which Matt Murdock has a long and deep discussion about ethics, morality, and personal responsibility with his Catholic priest, Father Lantom (Peter McRobbie). Up until their episode, Father Lantom's presence within the story had been light, and he had appeared minimally in only a few episodes.[30] Father Lantom's main contribution up to that point had been taking Matt's confession in a scene that was used to structure the show's promotional trailers. However, in "Speak of the Devil," the episode written by the Gages, the discussion between Lantom and Matt is the centerpiece of the episode and a "pivotal moral scene" for the series from their perspective.[31] The scene focuses on a discussion of what has become a well-worn superhero question: Is it ever worth the moral price the hero must pay to kill the villain? In this scene, Matt and Lantom move through the church, discussing the nature of the Devil and performing exegesis on some Bible passages that Father Lantom feels are pertinent. Within their religious discussion, the question of the Devil's existence and role in humanity is not just theological debate. For Father Lantom as well as for Matt, this discussion is grounded in the world they experience. Their conversation is not just about the Devil but also about evil and adversity and whether they exist in the form of a person causing such harm to humanity that killing them is necessary.

Father Lantom applies biblical exegesis to Matt's moral conundrum, considering a quotation from the Bible that the Gages chose specifically for its relatively unknown status as well as its openness to interpretation.[32] Father Lantom says to Matt,

There is a wide gulf between inaction and murder, Matthew. . . . "Like a muddied spring or a polluted fountain is the righteous man who gives way before the wicked." Proverbs 25-something, I never can remember. Meaning righteous men have a duty to stand up to evil. One interpretation. Another is that when the righteous succumb to sin, it is as harmful as if the public well were poisoned. Because the darkness of such an act . . . of taking a life . . . will spread to friends, neighbors . . . the entire community.[33]

The Gages deliberately chose the quotation from Proverbs so that they could have the characters perform exegesis on it in the scene and allow the characters to discuss the possible meanings in a serious way. Interestingly, even in the context of the supposedly vast array of textual possibilities granted to streaming television productions, the Gages were surprised that the scenes between Lantom and Matt survived at length throughout the editing process and through both Netflix's and Marvel's supervision of the series' production. They attributed the scene's survival to the first season's showrunner, Steven DeKnight, who came on board as showrunner midway through the show's thirteen-month development and writing period. DeKnight said he'd fight for them and their episode.[34] The fear of the scene being cut and the idea that the showrunner had to be prepared to intercede indicate the still-risky position of such blatant engagement with religion. But the fact that the scene made its way into the final cut suggests a shift in what industry practitioners were willing and able to provide to their viewership in this stage of the post-network era.

The above scene is one of the best examples in this study of the sometimes stark differences between religious representation provided in a television text and the writers' discussion of that religious representation. The Gages' episode, and especially the scene described above, not only represents religion-qua-religion within a specifically Christian (not post-Christian) paradigm, but it also represents how a belief system functions within the character's life. It is explicitly Catholic and religious in a way rarely seen in post-network-era prime-time dramas. And yet, the creatives working on the show, writing this representation, and presenting the narrative to the executive decision-makers confessed that at the time they wrote it, they considered the scene a textual impossibility. In their discussion of the fear in writing it, the internalized norms of television production can be seen as on full display. Both Gages had not worked much within the television industry before becoming staff writers for *Daredevil*, yet they too were subject to the legacy practices and attendant ideologies of mainstream television that consider religion risky.

The scene ultimately served multiple purposes for the series. It allowed for an explicit discussion of the morality of the superhero within an interpretive frame that was well known to many American viewers, making what could have been an unnatural discussion flow easily in terms of character and narrative. This pivotal scene also reasserts and reaffirms Matt's Catholicism as a defining characteristic, which, in turn, gives more weight to his decision to try to kill his adversary, Wilson Fisk (Vincent D'Onofrio), at episode's end. And, as many reviews of the series highlight, the scene distinguished the show for its approach to religion.[35] The praise of religion in the scene and episode, gained after the series was released to the public, emphasizes the view that a lot of writers have and that the Gages explicitly articulated: that expectations are low among viewers and critics for representing religion on television. If such representations make their way onto the screen—and these representations can somehow present religion as "part of a complex lived experience"—they have cleared a very low bar.[36] Both Gages were surprised by the overwhelmingly positive reviews of their episode and the series as a whole.[37] Ruth Fletcher Gage was particularly surprised by the breadth of religious outlets that praised the show, noting a Mormon reviewer's praise as particularly surprising.[38] Their surprise supports my claim throughout this study that the religious audience is not a consideration for the television industry, so much so that each time religious viewers enjoy a show not targeted at them, it surprises those creatives working on the shows (see also the view expressed by SundanceTV/*Rectify*'s marketer in Chapter 3).

Matt's Catholicism, particularly as expressed through that scene, also struck a chord with critics who saw the approach to religion as unique for a television show. This presentation of religion, in turn, was seen as helping to elevate superhero genre as a whole. On the entertainment news website *Collider*, Evan Valentine's review of "Speak of the Devil" argued that the use of Catholic theology breathed new life into the recurring superhero conflict of whether or not to kill the villain. He wrote, "Here however, it's considered with a fresh take in that the answer to this question is linked primarily to Matt Murdock's religious background in Catholicism. This is an area (a superhero's religion) that *isn't* explored as much."[39] Valentine's review places *Daredevil* in conversation with contemporaneous superhero media to highlight its difference: that religion serves as a central place both within the narrative and for the character's development.

This assessment was not unique. For many reviewers—both popular press and trade—Matt Murdock's Catholicism was so distinctive to the show that it became a defining characteristic of both the superhero *and* the story. For *Slate*, Charles Moss wrote, "To really understand Daredevil—both the comic book and the new show—you have to understand his Catholicism."[40] And even before the series became available, the *Hollywood Reporter* titled its interview with the titular star, "*Daredevil*'s Charlie Cox on Becoming a Religious Superhero," despite the fact that they ask only one question (out of nine) about that topic.[41] Because the approach to religion is singular for Daredevil and the show, it becomes more significant than just serving as a mere character trait. Instead, it becomes defining for the show as a whole and the season's narrative arc.

Such reviews indicate that Goddard and the Gages' approach was taken as it was intended. They wanted to portray religion as "part of a complex lived experience" and a "positive force" in Matt Murdock's life, the foundation to which he turns to when in need of guidance. As such, religion became in many ways a foundation for the narrative arc of Daredevil's origin story in the first season. Moreover, the praise for the religious representation in the series led to a shift in how Netflix positioned its representation of religion in its marketing for *Daredevil*'s second season. *Daredevil* having been accepted (or at least not visibly panned) by Netflix's target audiences—and thereby disproving long-standing assumptions about quality and fan audiences' negative reactions to religious representation—the first trailer for *Daredevil*'s second season recaps the first season through its representation as a series of fresco paintings on the walls and ceiling of a Catholic church. As this presentation via the trailer shows, once the show's religious representation had been proven safe—and even desirable among both audience and industry— Netflix's marketing department subsequently literally re-inscribed the first season into a religious representational frame (see Figure 7.1 above). Such a marketing strategy recalls the paratextual use of *The Last Supper* in marketing *Lost* and *Battlestar Galactica* (Figures I.1 and I.2 in the Introduction) in the mid-2000s and similarly indicates no particular religious influence on the plot, merely the use of arresting and familiar visuals to help market the show. The second season actually had far less religious representation than the first, possibly because writers such as the Gages and Drew Goddard were no longer involved. The vicissitudes of the industry and its season-by-season labor practices can sometimes lead to variations of representational approach and industrial discourse season to season as well.

RELIGION TO CULTIVATE EDGE: AMAZON'S *HAND OF GOD*

Despite the many similarities between Amazon and older models of television production, the former distinguishes itself through its conception of its audience. According to an executive in charge of dramas at Amazon Studios, Carolyn Newman, Amazon considers its Prime members, who comprise the viewer pool for its productions, to be "intelligent viewers, binge watchers interested in conversation."[42] In an interview with me, she further explained that Amazon productions are meant to appeal to either the Comic-Con (Comic Convention) audience or the NPR (National Public Radio) audience.[43] Of course, these are not necessarily mutually exclusive categories in practice (*Hand of God* was positioned for crossover appeal based largely on its star, Ron Perlman, and his history in genre fare), but Amazon Studios envisions them as two clear niches that they wish to target with different types of programs. *Transparent* targets the NPR audience, and *The Man in the High Castle* (2015–2019), a Phillip K. Dick adaptation, was positioned as more for the Comic-Con audience. These two target audiences align with more commonly used descriptions of the engaged fan audience and the affluent quality audience. As Amazon's use of Comic-Con and NPR to describe their target audience indicates, they are targeting a niche within a niche.

The Comic-Con audience, on the basis of my extrapolation from Amazon executive Newman's discussion of it, is affluent enough to attend a convention, engaged enough to wait hours in line for a panel or screening, often promiscuous in their adoration within a genre, and knowledgeable enough to use social media to perform publicity for the media object as a mode of reciprocity. The Comic-Con audience is an audience comprised of fans, but fans who are overtly affluent consumers. That is the key implication of describing these viewers in terms of Comic-Con: Popular culture conventions, particularly San Diego Comic-Con, require (often hefty) payment to get into the gates. In the twenty-first century, they have rapidly become a key site of publicity for major media properties by major media conglomerates. Fans must buy their way in and are then expected to both figuratively and literally buy media products. As Matt Hills argues, "Fandom has been curiously emptied of the dimensions which, I would suggest, most clearly define it: dimensions of affect, attachment, and even passion, as well as, crucially, the dimensions of commodification through which these processes are enabled and constrained."[44] Describing Prime Video's viewers as Comic-Con viewers similarly empties, or at least minimizes, the affective elements of fandom in

STREAMING RELIGION   189

favor of the fan activity that can be commodified or methodically tracked and surveilled. Many of the same assumptions made about (the affluent fan's) audience content with shows like *Supernatural* and *Preacher* are made about Prime Video's "Comic-Con audience" as well.

Meanwhile, Amazon's so-called NPR audience—again extrapolated from Newman's use of the term—is based on older industry imaginings of the quality audience. The NPR audience invokes ideas of liberal, affluent, coastal elites, or, in the words that National Public Media uses to describe its radio branch's audience: "cultural, connected, intellectual and influential . . . affluent and curious."[45] Judging by the series that Amazon Studios creates that are meant to appeal to an upscale, liberal, niche audience (e.g., *Transparent, Mozart in the Jungle* [2014–2018], *Mad Dogs* [2015–2016]), the company is using progressive ideology to prominently appeal to a certain contingent of viewers in addition to their less visible children's programming. Amazon's first breakout success, at least in terms of entering into the cultural discussion of quality television, was *Transparent*, a family drama centering around a parent transitioning genders later in her life. With this show, Amazon leveraged its progressive content to gain the attention of a small niche of elite viewers (or at least viewers who perceived themselves as such). Like Netflix, Amazon does not release its audience data. Nonetheless, a cursory survey of the responses of television critics, journalists, public intellectuals, and activists on social media displays much discussion, lauding, and even evangelizing about the show in its early seasons.[46] The NPR audience is imagined to be connected by social media; more specifically, they are connected to like-minded people. In 2011, a study by Duke scholars used the connected social networks of journalists to determine political ideologies of a variety of news journalists and websites. The researchers concluded, on the basis of the public social networks of those working there, that NPR did indeed have a slight liberal bias, confirming what conservatives have decried about the partially publicly funded NPR for decades. Such a discovery reinforces the idea of NPR as a site around which affluent liberals can be identified.[47]

This connection made between the NPR audience and the quality audience updates how affluent liberals have been seen by scholars and industry practitioners as engaging with certain types of TV since the early 1970s. In her study of MTM sitcoms in the 1970s and the construction of their quality designation, Jane Feuer concludes, "Quality TV is liberal TV."[48] This simple linkage has continued for decades, even though the specific genres, styles, and narrative forms associated with quality TV have evolved during that time. There have been changes and alterations as American culture and the television industry have changed, but there remains an articulation between affluence and progressivism in the quality-audience configuration. While this linkage persists with Amazon's construction of an NPR audience, this niche, unlike the quality audience, is not imagined for the purposes of selling audiences to more high-end or elite advertisers. The business model is different, and so the viewers and the shows they consume are valued differently as well. Amazon uses NPR as shorthand for affluence and liberalism, yes, but also for connectedness and influence. The retailer-streaming service is looking to appeal to those elites who will go on Twitter and Facebook and do the publicity work for the show through either their praise or their conversations about the show's controversial subject matter. They seek brand missionaries to help sell—and help buy—what Amazon is selling.[49]

Each streaming service establishes its brand through PR, advertising, and content licensing deals. The particular licensed (i.e., evergreen) shows vaunted as exclusive to the particular streaming service help Amazon to refine its target audience(s) and brand identity. Original programming from Amazon Studios, in turn, provides another means by which Amazon can refine its brand and differentiate itself in the marketplace, much as was the case when cable networks such as HBO, FX, and TNT moved into producing originals in the 1990s and early 2000s. Such practices of distinction and differentiation are especially important to pursue for Prime Video, which functions as a small division within a larger mega-company broadly perceived to be the world's largest retailer.

As noted above, Amazon, in particular, has used its exclusive deals to differentiate its service from the well-established Netflix. For Amazon, this task included an exclusive, long-term licensing deal of HBO's older content like *The Sopranos* (1999–2007), *The Wire* (2002–2008), and *The Comeback* (2005, 2014) in May 2014.[50] This deal with HBO was finalized less than a month after Amazon greenlit *Transparent* for a ten-episode series.[51] The "pilot season" during which *Transparent* was ordered to series also included series that were marked by many quality television characteristics: antihero protagonists (*Bosch* [2014–]), established television auteurs such as Chris Carter at the helm (*The After* [2014]), and a comedy about the backstage dynamics of a symphony (*Mozart in the Jungle* [2014–2018]). This wave of original series represented a stark departure from Amazon's earlier original content, *Alpha House* (2013–2014) and *Betas* (2013–2014), which were broader comedies. While Netflix often has been accused of trying to mimic

HBO's brand, Amazon literally established itself as a quality service by exclusively licensing programming that established HBO's quality television brand in the first place. Amazon's HBO Collection was promoted similarly to Prime Video's original series within both the website and app. Prime Video uses both library and original series to mutually build its identity.

One thing that Amazon Studios sees its "two audiences" as sharing is an interest in media forms that evoke conversation. Amazon executive Carolyn Newman said as much and went on to apply that perspective to the *Hand of God* pilot: "The pilot did exactly what we intended: there were people who loved it and others who hated it . . . We expected some people feeling attacked."[52] The idea of provoking conversation by presenting a subject or topic that is underrepresented in the current television spectrum aligns with long-standing television industrial practices of cultivating an edgy brand for a show or outlet. One need only look to Prime Video's tent-pole quality series, *Transparent*, and the industrial and critical discourses about its representations of transgender identities. At the center of *Transparent*'s marketing, critical praise, claims to uniqueness in content and style, awards, and, most importantly for this study, discourses about its production culture (before the accusations of harassment in 2018) is its fresh, distinctive representation of transgendered identity.[53] The conversation about *Transparent* as something new to television is largely driven by its representation of transgender individuals, an edgy subject that makes noise in the post-network-era landscape. *Hand of God* similarly was positioned by Amazon Studios as edgy in order to create conversation. However, even though in this project *Hand of God* represents the example of a show that comes closest to using religious representation to explicitly cultivate edginess, its creatives were far less direct in how they spoke about religion with the press, and the marketing of the show was far less explicit about its treatment of religion than *Transparent* was in its treatment of transgender representation.

Hand of God and *Transparent* both illustrate Amazon's desire to spur conversation, even controversy, by representing themes and stories perceived to be polarizing. Shows tailored for the so-called NPR audience of Prime Video were not the only ones treated in such a fashion. For example, in early 2015, Amazon greenlit *The Man in the High Castle* to series. Based on a Philip K. Dick story, *High Castle* presents an alternate history in which the Axis powers won World War II and succeed in world domination.[54] While the threat of Nazi takeover (situated in a safely historical context) is less controversial than transgender issues or exploring religious corruption, the neo-Nazi trappings of the show are not necessarily safe, made even less so by its marketing that replicated Nazi symbols on wrapped subway cars and in Amtrak ticket wallets.[55] This is the kind of show likely to cause the type of conversation desired among its Amazon's Comic-Con audience. It illustrates Prime Video's general strategy with its original programming: courting controversial conversations—both within particular niches and beyond them—in order to cultivate edge.

Building on its use of *Transparent* and other dramas such as *Mad Dogs* and *Mozart in the Jungle* to cast itself as the place to go for television that could not appear anywhere else, Amazon Studios picked up *Hand of God* following its appearance in Amazon's August 2014 pilot season (the season following *Transparent*'s pickup). The series began in September 2015 and includes a number of examples of "edgy" content: the main plot of the pilot features a corrupt judge, Pernell Harris (Ron Perlman), who becomes a born-again Christian following the brutal beating of his son and the rape of his daughter-in-law (Alona Tal) by an assailant. The reason for this attack and the responsible parties behind it are revealed to Pernell through divine visions over the course of the first season. The show explores religion as a major factor of American culture, one not exempt from the corruption that many quality television dramas have explored in such areas as governance, law enforcement, business, families. Ben Watkins, the creator or *Hand of God*, described the show as one "where the main character thinks that God is talking to him and another main character is a preacher, but the show itself is not actually about religion."[56] As this statement indicates, even *Hand of God*, which takes a deliberately edgy approach to religious representation, is not immune from being presented by its one of its key creative figures as "not actually about religion." In other words, here again we see the general sense of risk in Hollywood and the television industry about religious television in effect. But Watkins' denial was an exception to a largely more engaged public discourse about religion as a subject of television drama.

Before *Hand of God* even premiered in Amazon's fall 2014 pilot season, *IndieWire* journalist Jai Tiggett asked showrunner Watkins about creating a show with such an overt religious narrative. *Hand of God* was the first series created and overseen by Watkins, who had previously written and acted on *Burn Notice* (USA, 2007–2013). Tiggett asked, "Spirituality and religion can be controversial topics, especially for TV. Did you have any pushback or hesitation about tackling it in the show?"[57] The framing of this question suggests a perception that the show would receive negative reactions. However, Watkins answered with surprising candor:

> When we went out to pitch it, people would be frightened to death about the idea of a show with the word "God" in the title, and I actually got approached about changing the title and I said no. Even as a writer I hesitated a little bit to go down that road, knowing that it would scare a lot of people. But when I decided to write it I felt like, "I have to write this, and even if I don't ever make it I'll never regret writing it." And then I just pushed forward. Every time my rational self would say, "You should pull back a little bit on that," I just had to remember what the purpose was and try to do what scared me.[58]

The use of words like "frightened" and "scared" indicate the high stakes of trying to sell this kind of project, even as streaming platforms were beginning to take the lead in exceeding the usual standards of acceptable content. Such a response in light of Watkins's denial discussed above indicates the ambivalence of creatives working within the persistent cultural hesitation regarding religion while also in a platform that foregrounds distinction, with an ultimate willingness to engage in a public discourse about religious representation on television dramas.

Notably, Watkins's framing of his treatment of religion—including a description of the hesitation and danger of pitching and writing the show, followed by his acceptance of the fear and his willingness to keep going—calls attention to his courage as a writer. He presents a heroic authorial persona of himself, an image of someone who pursues art despite what the arbiters of the market or the managers of culture might say. Such a persona is further supported in Watkins' minimal social media presence. On Twitter during the show's run, he mostly retweeted the social media of his cast and crew or fans who were talking positively about *Hand of God*. Occasionally, his retweets were political, especially in cases of nationwide attention to racial injustices. However, he rarely presented his own voice on Twitter.[59] The image thus created is of an iconoclast who doesn't care about offending people in his pursuit of what he perceives as truth or art. As the shooting of the first season of *Hand of God* ended in late May 2015, Watkins retweeted an Instagram photo from Ron Perlman *(Beauty and the Beast* [CBS, 1987–1990], *Hellboy* [Del Toro, 2004]), star of the show, in which Watkins is wearing a shirt that, somewhat obscured by fabric folds, reads, "I met God, She's black."[60] This T-shirt choice and its subsequent sharing on social media via Ron Perlman (who had the largest number of followers among the cast) supported both Watkins's persona and his show's narrative premise. Like the T-shirt, the show risked offense in order to elicit conversation. The risk and resulting conversation is precisely the point; they grant the show its "edgy" bona fides.

The content of the show continually reinforced the show as edgy and uniquely folds religion into this industrial positioning. In the pilot, Judge Pernell Harris conscripts a violent disciple to kill in the name of God, even as he explores his spiritual rebirth in a church led by a dubious former child star. *Hand of God* presents religion's corruption in both believers and hypocrites, indicting both as part of its all-over bleak view of corrupt humanity. The characters curse freely, the violence is graphic, and drug use is commonplace. Yet it is not the behavior of the religious characters, but rather corruption in the institution of religion that sets this show apart. *Hand of God*, despite Watkins's inconsistent disavowal of it as a religious show, explores religion in relation to the normalized idea of American religion and the dominant location of religious corruption: white, patriarchal, Protestant Christianity. Importantly, in *Hand of God*, the dimensions of this vision of religion are explored as specifics, not as norms within a post-Christian sensibility, as has been the case with other series in this project, including *Supernatural* and *Dominion*.

The series begins with Pernell speaking in tongues, naked in a local fountain, implying that he has gone through a ritual baptism in order to be born again during a three-day absence from his work and family. The image mirrors scenes of baptism in *Friday Night Lights* and *Rectify*, and it establishes Pernell as probably insane but also invested in his role as a religious figure—and a public one at that. Soon thereafter, the show reveals one of Pernell's visions/hallucinations. He visits his comatose and brain-dead son in the hospital and hears his son's voice speak to him, requiring a covenant of revenge. The son asks Pernell to remember his promise to avenge his death and directs Pernell to take an active role, saying, "You find him . . . You made a promise to me. Keep it." It is an order from something beyond him. Pernell's later encounters with the visions granted him through his son's tragedy continue to build on his idea that he is on a mission from God. Religion is addressed as a specific structuring institution of culture and power. Perhaps this specificity of belief is because Watkins was inspired by a very narrow vision of religious hypocrisy: he has said he was inspired by "these really popular preachers [such as Ted Haggard] with huge mega-churches, and then they'll have a fall from grace." Alternately, perhaps Watkins's presentation of religion stems from his position as a person of color for whom whiteness is not invisible.[61] *Hand of God* is notable for not only its edgy approach to its subject matter but also its conscious exploration of how race and gender shape notions of American Christianity.

Regarding race, *Hand of God* does not overtly comment on the fact that all three characters at the core of the religious story—Pernell, his felonious "disciple" KD (Garret Dillahunt), and Reverend Paul Curtis (Julian Morris), the head of the church that the judge joins by the end of the pilot—are white men. The religious world that *Hand of God* represents is one led by white men, although later in the thirteen-episode first season, the reverend works with an African-American preacher toward the goal of televising his church's proceedings. In contrast to this largely white world, Pernell's friend, Mayor Robert "Bobo" Boston (Andre Royo), who is African-American; Pernell's white wife, Crystal (Dana Delaney); and Pernell's regular prostitute, Tessie (Emayatzy Corinealdi), who is a black woman, all react with explicit skepticism to his claim of being "born again" and called to a higher purpose by God. On display here is not the Southern Christian parity between races as portrayed on *Friday Night Lights*. The women and the people of color who round out the ensemble of *Hand of God* are almost entirely outside of and dubious of the claims of religion. The only exception is Reverend Curtis's own disciple, Alicia (Elizabeth McLaughlin), who uses her beauty and wiles to gain money and power for Reverend Curtis's Hand of God church. She is a believer and an integral part of the eponymous church and religious story. However, that "integral part" is one of ostensible submission—to Reverend Curtis, to Pernell, and to other powerful men to support her cause. Thus, Alicia serves to further highlight the white masculine dominance of religion in America, or at least the religion that is typically represented through television across the mainstream landscape. Alicia is the arrow that points to the all-white, all-male power structure that is normalized in American Christianity and critiqued in the show.

Additionally, Pernell uses his daughter-in-law, Jocelyn, to try to establish his religious power in the pilot. Pernell's visions begin with the voice of his comatose and brain-dead son, who was beaten nearly to death after being forced to watch his wife be raped. Pernell's visions begin as whispers only he can hear from his son, telling him that he has to find the perpetrator of the crime. This demand leads to Pernell believing that God is operating through his son to call Pernell to a higher purpose, and as a result, he fights to keep his son on life support after his wife and daughter had decided to remove it. Beyond merely usurping the female family members' decision regarding life support, Pernell further asserts his power—via his visions—over Jocelyn when he forces her to examine the man he believes to be her rapist in the only way she could recognize the man and in the way that forces her to relive her trauma: by looking at his genitals. It is humiliating and traumatic for her, and it seemingly disputes Pernell's claims of divine vision. She says the suspect is not the man who raped her. However, at the end of the episode, KD beats the suspect until he admits that he is the man who raped Jocelyn, saying that "they" made him. On this enigmatic note, which quashes Jocelyn's power and idea of truth in favor of the men's visions and actions, Pernell's visions are affirmed, as is his role as a prophet. By the end of the season, Pernell's visions have been further proven as they revealed the truth of the conspiracy that led to his son's beating.

For the men in *Hand of God*, religion is tied to fame, class, and power. Reverend Curtis is introduced as a former child star on daytime soap opera *The Young and the Restless* and possibly a con man. Regardless of the truth of his faith, which is presented as dubious, he is interested in the money, fame, and resulting power that being a charismatic, popular religious leader can bring. This personality trait is further explored as his goal to become a tel-evangelist is revealed and almost successfully reached throughout the first season. Subsequently we see Curtis's ultimate broken disappointment when his televangelist hopes are not realized. The final images of Curtis for the season are of him sadly playing the piano, singing the hymn that was the foundation for his dream of his first televised preaching.

All of these aspects of *Hand of God*'s representations of religion are nuanced, complex, and explored as existing within the structuring power systems of American culture. *Hand of God* is looped into the same sense of textual possibilities with which post-network quality dramas approach other controversial subjects, such as drug use, sexuality, and graphic violence. Like *Daredevil*, the content of *Hand of God* illustrates the evolving openness of streaming sites' original programming in tension with the vestiges of the legacy of the risk of directly presenting and critiquing religion via indus-trial discourse. Where *Hand of God* most distinguishes itself from Netflix's *Daredevil* is in its market positioning; from the beginning, Amazon's *Hand of God* uses Christianity—not as mythology or spirituality but as traditional religion—as a strategy of cultivating edge and market differentiation. Despite this overt textual strategy, Watkins's ambivalence but ultimate openness in discussing religious representation indicates the power of the legacy ideology of avoiding religious discourses as well as the potential challenge and change to this ideology's dominance.

Among the programs in this study, *Hand of God* employs the most controversial representation of religion by using it to explore corruption across social institutions, including religion. According to Amazon executive Carolyn Newman, Amazon Studios' metric for success is "about getting conversations going," which is, of course, a rhetorical strategy for a company that, like Netflix, does not disclose viewer numbers.[62] But this claim also sheds light on Prime Video's audience targeting and branding within the discourses of the television industry. Instead of numerical data, Amazon executives construct ideas of success around "conversation," particularly conversation that can be seen and quantified through online spaces like Amazon's customer reviews, IMDb ratings (a site also owned by Amazon), and social media posts. These metrics are similar to audience engagement measurements that are increasingly employed by legacy outlets.[63] For example, Nielsen began measuring Twitter TV ratings in 2014, and engagement ratings since have gained enough prominence in the industry to begin being published regularly in *Variety* at that time as well.[64] But unlike with engagement, which is often discussed as fairly innocuous, Amazon's search for "conversations" implies conflict and explicitly risks alienation on the part of some viewers. Newman said of the *Hand of God* pilot,

> People really responded to the show [because it] tackled the subject matter [of religion], and a lot of people expressed that it was something that they hadn't seen before. And some people hated it who felt like it was religion-bashing. And we accepted that too because obviously it's not. Some people felt that it was attacking their beliefs, and we knew that that was going to be part of the conversation. And that's exactly what we expected. That's what we thought the show would be: a touchstone [to that conversation about belief that] we're still in the early processes [of seeing shows] talk about.[65]

Part of Newman's job as an executive at Amazon Studios is to craft a narrative about their studio and their programming that differentiates it from older forms of television, despite drawing on those older forms. Newman implies that Amazon has sloughed off the fear of audience alienation that has presumably kept truly risky art away from reaching viewers. Part of the cultural and industrial narrative perpetuated by those involved with shows on new streaming platforms is that their shows are the avant-garde of a new wave of content. While this narrative is mostly a marketing strategy, these platforms and their programming do possibly represent a shift in terms of representing religion and how creatives discuss that representation.

Hand of God's marketing reflected its cultivation of edge through subtle (and, at times, not so subtle) references to the show's representation of religion. In addition to the cultivation of Ben Watkins as fearless auteur illustrated most clearly in the *IndieWire* interview analyzed above, *Hand of God*'s first-season marketing push used religious tropes in a way rarely seen in a show's first-season marketing. The posters and billboards for the series featured variations on one image and tagline: Ron Perlman's horizontal face occupying the bottom third of the poster, looking up, past gray space and the tagline "In Sanity We Trust," and toward the top third occupied by origami doves (Figure 7.2). The tagline invites viewers to think about God, since that is the word in the familiar phrase that has been replaced by "Sanity." Concurrently, visible is a man's face seemingly looking to the Heavens for answers. As revealed in the pilot, the white paper doves decorated the Church space in *Hand of God*; a white dove also serves as a long-standing icon for the Holy Spirit of the Christian trinity. While these elements imply religion, they are not overt. *Hand of God* cultivates religion-as-edge more so than any other case study in this book, but it is still far from the strategies of edge by which other controversial subjects are framed, such as transgender identity in its sister program *Transparent*.

CONCLUSION

This chapter began with a detailed overview of the streaming platforms Netflix and Prime Video, their marketing and key target audiences, and the discourses of innovation and quality they have circulated in order to build their respective brands. On the basis of industry discourses about new media and SVOD sites, one might expect Amazon and Netflix to be places for innovation in representing religion on shows and as well as in creative and industrial discourses. Indeed, this chapter presents examples that reflect that innovation: *Daredevil* and *Hand of God*. Yet, to an extent, their representations of religion still belie the persistent sense among their writers that religion is risky. The production of the first season of Marvel's *Daredevil* for Netflix exemplifies this perspective. In marketing and interviews with

Figure 7.2 *Hand of God* promotional art, season one

creatives, it is evident that *Daredevil* faced more scrutiny, hesitancy, and containment of religion than did Amazon's *Hand of God*. The different cultural discourses circulating around these shows is a product of their distinct industry positioning: Certainly Netflix—and Marvel—didn't need to create noise via marketing and industry positioning through their use of religion in their series; as part of the Marvel Cinematic Universe, the show was already well known, highly likely to be successful, and a useful brand extension. As such, *Daredevil* did not need to have edge cultivated through the show's religious representation, nor did Netflix or Marvel feel the need to contain religious representations. However, the writers and producers for *Daredevil* still began their work on the show while believing that such containment was a necessity, despite the supposed openness of Netflix's brand. Only as they became comfortable in the writers' room and in their relationship with Netflix and Marvel did they more directly engage with religion in their stories—and public discourse. The creatives' continued belief that religion would *of course* be contained illustrates how the legacy practices of Hollywood television production have been so internalized and normalized that creatives assume, regardless of outlet, the television industry resists religion across the board. Only in 2016 and beyond, perhaps, can we see some more substantive cracks in this ideological armor, spearheaded by streaming platforms but, as the case of *Preacher* indicates, not necessarily limited to them.

Meanwhile, Amazon's struggle to take on Netflix directly has pushed it to license and support the one show in this study that unhesitatingly tested the boundaries of religious representation and risked blasphemy, backlash, and audience alienation in doing so. *Hand of God* gained some protection in doing so by positioning creator Ben Watkins in the quality auteurist mode, folding the approach to religion into his "brave" artistic vision, and linking the show to edginess via marketing materials. *Hand of God*, then, was perhaps the first show of a new era in which religion is finally treated like any other controversial subject: ready to be exploited—and discussed head on by creatives and executives—within the television industry.

Conclusion

Polarized Culture and Dual Approaches to Christianity on TV

While television's history of representing religion is almost as long as the medium's history itself, the 1990s stand as a turning point in the way writers of prime-time American television understood and used religious representations. That decade within the neo-network era saw the bifurcation of prime-time television into two broad categories. On one hand, there were shows that cultivated edge through style, sex, violence, language, and other means that would very likely offend middlebrow tastes; such programs were most evident on certain cable outlets and on emerging netlets. On the other hand, there were shows that continued to appeal to the imagined middlebrow mass audience of the classic-network era. Where religion appeared on television during this period, it was on shows that epitomized the latter category. *Touched by an Angel* on CBS and *7th Heaven* on the WB were prime examples of 1990s-era middlebrow series. Together, these two shows represented how broadcasting's legacy practices continued to shape new networks' programming.

Both *Touched by an Angel* and *7th Heaven* exemplified certain representations of religion. Religion became associated with specific middlebrow approaches in genre, style, narrative, and iconography. By 1996, when both shows were airing and winning in the ratings, they formed the foundation for what "religious" TV was understood to be, both within the industry and outside of it. The two shows were perceived as visually uninteresting, generically realist, narratively unimaginative and moralistic, and iconographically middle of the road. Middlebrow became associated with blandness, placed in opposition to the edginess depicted in quality dramas of the time, such as *NYPD Blue* (ABC, 1993–2005), *ER* (NBC, 1994–2009), and *Northern Exposure* (CBS,1990–1995). To be overtly Christian was to be middlebrow religious in a way that meant uninspired and conservative in an era of new possibilities, at least according to the dominant nonreligious ideology of mainstream prime-time television practitioners. Furthermore, from the

Divine Programming. Charlotte E. Howell, Oxford University Press (2020).
© Oxford University Press.
DOI: 10.1093/oso/9780190054373.001.0001

executive perspective, to target audiences with middlebrow shows was to target those with less discriminating tastes and presumably less spending power as well.

On the basis of such assumptions, practices developed that were designed to contain religious representations. Through processes of containment, mainstream Hollywood television executives and creatives averted the twin risks of alienating upscale audiences and being perceived as religious. Both *7th Heaven* and *Touched by an Angel*'s reruns, as well as similar family-friendly fare with an overtly Christian sensibility (e.g., *The Guard* [Ion, 2008–2009], *Ties That Bind* [UP, 2015], *The Secret Life of the American Teenager* [ABC Family, 2008–2013]), continued to appear on niche cable outlets that targeted the middlebrow audience (UP, ION, Hallmark, etc.) during this time and into the present, even expanding to heartland-targeting streaming platforms like Dove Channel and LightWorkers' streaming portal. Thus, this middlebrow strand of programming did not come to an end in the 1990s. Instead, it largely moved to distribution channels that explicitly targeted Christian audiences or audiences of faith. Significantly, a decade later, *Touched by an Angel*'s star, Roma Downey, and her husband, Mark Burnett, began producing biblical adaptations such as *The Bible* (History, 2013), *A.D.: The Bible Continues* (NBC, 2015), and *The Dovekeepers* (CBS, 2015) for cable and broadcast networks. Such programs were not explicitly aimed primarily at religious audiences. Nonetheless, in their depiction of religiously framed morality lessons, such shows perpetuated the link between religious and middlebrow into the post-network era. *Touched by an Angel* and *7th Heaven*, along with the post-network-era biblical dramas that succeeded them, were shows that functioned as negative reference points, sustaining certain staid and conservative assumptions and practices regarding religious representation on television.

In the post-network era, outlets expanded and program offerings diversified. More cable channels were producing more diverse original dramatic series, creating space for greater experimentation in terms of form, genre, and storytelling. Antiheroes appeared across the television landscape in series such as *The Sopranos* (HBO, 1999–2007), *The Shield* (FX, 2002–2008), *Mad Men* (AMC, 2007–2015), and *Breaking Bad* (AMC, 2008–2013); their stories featured more sex, violence, nudity, drug use, frank language, and other edgy content than had appeared previously. Starting in 2003, religion was also increasingly represented and was even used to structure narratives and premises. Yet, religion was different from the other topics emerging on television at the time. Religion, unlike sexuality, violence, nudity, drug usage, and so on, was not deployed as a means of cultivating edginess until the mid-2010s. Though religious television dramas largely abandoned their prior middlebrow associations of Christian representation, new creative and industry strategies were employed to contain religion, and thereby make it safe for storytelling purposes.

The containment strategies that emerged in this programming context were not only textual in nature, but also necessarily extended to the writers' rooms and executive offices, evidenced by the ways creatives spoke (or didn't speak) about religious representation. Such containment strategies have not restricted the number or diversity of religious representations present on television. But these strategies facilitated acceptable ways of presenting religion in mainstream hour-long narratives. Certainly, television has a history of containing controversial subjects within quality designations and quality aesthetics or within generic displacement. In the 1960s, new power dynamics of family and gender were explored through fantastic family sitcoms like *Lost in Space* (CBS, 1965–1968) and *Bewitched* (ABC, 1964–1972). Similarly, race and intolerance were portrayed through alien conflicts on *Star Trek* (NBC, 1966–1969).[1] In television programming featuring religious stories and representations, the strategies of containment were more pronounced in terms of the disconnect between the religious concepts presented on television and the ways that creatives working on those shows spoke about their labor on those shows.

As this book illuminates, from 2003 to 2016, a boom in television series featuring religious storylines and representations occurred, although it was not seen as such by people within the industry. This boom was shaped by industrial and cultural changes that also further contributed to the desire to distance these shows from the idea of religious television. The invasion of Iraq in 2003 and the resulting centralizing of religious difference in the culture helps to explain why the boom began in 2003, and the persistent dialogue between politics and Christianity amplified the cultural risk for being seen as religious in liberal enclaves like Hollywood. Meanwhile, the television industry struggled with changing technology and the competition posed by the rise of several new streaming distribution outlets and platforms. All of these forces pushed the boom toward a new level of both diversity of representation and more creative acknowledgment of religion. Yet these forces only truly became evident in and around the 2015–2016 season—and only in a few cases such as *Hand of God, Preacher,* and *Greenleaf.* In observing such a boom from the outside, one should not presume that creatives had free rein to present religion however they saw fit, nor should one presume that creatives would speak openly about how they chose to present religion. Among those working in television during the post-network era, religion has been regularly contained within certain ideological and ritualistic practices of writers, producers, executives, and marketers. Indeed, journalistic accounts and interviews with creatives scarcely discussed the growing presence of religion on TV, attesting to the degree of containment and the tacit denial that content was religious.

The analysis of ongoing and evolving practices of containment reveal that post-network-era television practices maintain certain continuities— legacies traced to practices employed in prior phases of television. Even in the face of vast changes in television as an industry, technology, and cultural object, religion as programming content continues to evoke hesitancy, caution, and compulsive resort to containment tactics and strategies.

During the course of my study, I identified three different prominent strategies of containment that have evolved within the television industry to combat the association between middlebrow tastes and Christian representation cemented in the 1990s:

1. Containment of religion by isolating it geographically in the American South or racially among characters and communities of color as an "other" that can be authentically represented in television dramas. *Friday Night Lights* and *Rectify* served as two case studies that have spanned the boom period and show how Southern realism shaped religious content as it has appeared on both broadcast and cable outlets. *Jane the Virgin* and *Greenleaf* represent the similarly othered approach to nonwhite Christianity wherein race acts to distance the portrayal of Christianity from the common (white) cultural understanding of American religion. This containment strategy has enabled creatives working on these shows to represent religion as real Christian practice, but at a distance—geographically or racially. This distancing ensures Christian representation in the dramas is not milquetoast, middlebrow, or blandly inoffensive.

2. Containment of religion by using both quality television designations and fantastic genre conventions. This approach displaces religion

by using genre conventions that allow creatives to present religion as a vaguer, abstract spirituality. Creatives who worked on *Battlestar Galactica, Lost, The Leftovers,* and *Preacher* acknowledged religion's social function as faith for their characters and within the show's storyworld. These creatives spoke of religion only in terms of spirituality. Spirituality was suggestive of a vague middle ground between how the creatives of Southern realist shows such as *Friday Night Lights* and *Rectify* acknowledged religion-qua-religion and how the creatives of non-quality fantastic series such as *Supernatural, Dominion,* and *Constantine* outright denied religion's role in their work of religious representation.

3. Containment of religion by deploying fantastic genre conventions in order to discursively deny its religiousness. Within this genre, which includes such shows as *Supernatural, Dominion,* and *Constantine,* the religious elements represented do not signify any actual faith or authentic religious practice. To creatives working in this mode, religion becomes mythology—that is, a supernatural narrative structure without religious function. The displacement of religion into mythology coincides with the targeting of the upscale fan audience and to assumptions creatives held that those upscale fans oppose religion. While religion is not safe, mythology is. These strategies of containment create a paradox whereby explicit religious representations take place even as the creatives working on the shows wholly deny religiousness.

The chapters of this book illustrate that despite radical changes in television as a medium and as an industry, these containment strategies and the ideologies on which they are based persist within the writers' rooms and board rooms. The last case-study chapter moved on to explore whether such strategies and self-policing persisted on newer nonlinear platforms such as streaming sites. Writers for *Hand of God* and *Daredevil*, at least initially, still believed that network and studio executives would meet religious representations with hesitation. In this sense, their perspective echoed the point of view held by *7th Heaven*'s Brenda Hampton and *Battlestar Galactica*'s Ronald D. Moore many years earlier. The ideologies that figure religion as risky among creatives within dramatic television persist. But the favored tendencies of containment deployed during the boom period of 2003 to 2016 reached a tipping point in November 2016.

THE TIPPING POINT

Even as new practices, business models, and industrial relationships emerge within the television industry, the persistence of the old patterns of containment reveals religion as one subject that has changed far less quickly in terms of its televisual representation than other controversial subjects. The delay and resulting different strategies of both representation and creatives' discussion of religion reveal certain ways that television as an industry and medium has not changed as totally as some scholars and journalists claim. As Lisa Gitelman articulates in *Always Already New*, "The introduction of new media . . . is never entirely revolutionary: new media are less points of epistemic rupture than they are socially embedded sites for the ongoing negotiation of meaning as such. Comparing and contrasting new media thus stand to offer a view of negotiability in itself—a view, that is, of the contested relations of force that determine the pathways by which new media may eventually become old hat."[2] In the post-network era, television is a technology and a cultural form that is imbued with discourses of newness by industry creatives, pundits, and academics alike. Gitelman offers a corrective to the idea of newness as a break, and a counternarrative is important for television of this moment. The discourses of newness are undermined by the long reach of the past in terms of learned ideology among creatives.

Certainly, there are a few examples of potential ruptures to creatives' assumption of religion as too risky to tackle or acknowledge (such as Ronald D. Moore's "God is Love" anecdote and the Gages' story of the *Daredevil* showrunner being willing to but not needing to fight for their Catholicism-focused episode) within this study of how the post-Christian sensibility emerges in the television writers' rooms and on screens. Yet much of this ideology has remained intact so far, at least where religion is concerned.

When this first iteration of this project was completed in the summer of 2016, I thought that the general practice of containment would continue but ruptures such as those seen in the first half of 2016 would herald an increased dialogue between the two points of negotiation—faithful, Christian middle-brow dramas and edgy, upscale religious dramas that denied their religiousness. I believed shows like *Daredevil*, *Preacher*, and *Greenleaf* marked a new openness of the possibilities of blurring those boundaries between faith and narrative utilitarian approaches to religion. And that might still be possible in the near future, but since the 2016 election, as with so many aspects of American society, instead I have seen a polarization of these two modes of representing religion in prime-time dramas. The long-standing practices of religious inoculation within Hollywood culture have persisted and become exaggerated on most programs and most channels. Christian culture in America is still a large part of how the industry imagines the nation as a heartland-based mass, if only through audience demographics. And that mass culture is not, for the most part, the culture of the television industry headquartered in Hollywood.

In the immediate aftermath of the 2016 election, and Trump's successful mobilization of white, middle-class resentment, particularly in states like Michigan, Wisconsin, and Ohio that geographically represented the heartland, the television industry moved to capitalize on this resuscitated heartland audience. President of ABC Entertainment Channing Dungey said that the election made her rethink ABC's programming, discussing the slate of Shonda Rhimes produced dramas about diverse groups of professionals relative to the economic anxiety narrative of Trump's victory. She said, "We absolutely want to continue to tell those stories because wish-fulfillment is a critical part of what we do as entertainers. But in recent history we haven't paid enough attention to some of the true realities of what life is like for everyday Americans in our dramas."[3] While categorizing upscale characters and their lives as "wish-fulfillment," Dungey echoed the dominant narrative in late 2016 of the Trump victory: that his victory was won by the white working class who felt that they had become culturally invisible. While later analysis of the election data revealed that race more than economics was a deciding factor in Trump's victory, the cultural narrative of upscale audiences as not "real" Americans (read: Trump voters) had attained common-sense status. While the broadcast networks certainly seemed to allow that sensibility to shape at least some of their programming in 2017, the other side of the upscale-middlebrow divide reasserted its presence in January 2017 with the Women's March and subsequent, persistent visibility of "the resistance."[4]

Combined, the election of Trump and the rise of the resistance to him and his policies presented these two warring ideas of America in stark relief. Contributing to and exacerbating the discourse of two Americas and the polarization of those two Americas as oppositional—a discourse with its origins decades earlier, as discussed in the introduction—created an environment for television programming that exaggerated the fracturing of the audience into two taste cultures without much, if any, overlap. Those two taste cultures aligned with the understanding of television audiences that had been fomenting since the 1990s and was apparent in Christian representation.

Instead of 2016 marking a tipping point toward increased flexibility of religious representation, the divisions between faithful, middlebrow fare and edgy, not-religious use of religion became amplified. On broadcast, shows like *Kevin (Probably) Saves the World* (ABC, 2017–2019), *Living Biblically* (CBS, 2018), and *God Friended Me* (CBS, 2018–) are middle-of-the-road, inoffensive, and vaguely inspirational religious shows, not lauded by the elites but appealing, at least enough for a green light, to the middlebrow audience. But even on broadcast, we can see the continued distancing of upscale appeal from religiousness in the late 2010s. From the pitch through the third season, showrunner Mike Schur has been adamant that *The Good Place* (NBC, 2016–2020), his much-lauded but low-rated sitcom about heaven and hell and what it means to be a good person, is not religious.[5] Meanwhile, more edgy dramas like *American Gods* (Starz, 2017–) showed no qualms in portraying Jesus as multiple (and multiracial) somewhat irreverent versions of the Son of God to little fanfare or backlash because it was understood the prone-to-offense Christian audience wouldn't be watching the upscale fantasy drama.[6] *Preacher*'s second season was even more wacky and irreverent regarding Christianity and Jesse's symbiosis with Genesis than the first season, and perhaps no television drama more loudly proclaimed challenge to Christian norms as *The Handmaid's Tale* (Hulu, 2017–) and its portrayal of its Christian fundamentalist dystopia. As the thrust of television dramas featuring Christian narratives has been in the twenty-first century, so it continues even during this period of polarization.

Finally, the imagined linkage between "Trump's America" and the middlebrow approach to religious television will very likely only further solidify the negative associations with "religious" television within the mainstream television production culture. The cultural alignment between that community and the resistance, as well as the latter's increasing marketability as an identifiable and lucrative consumer audience, make avoidance of the middlebrow audience—and the approach to religious representation that for twenty years has been reinforced as theirs—continue to make industry cultural sense. This economic logic is even shaping the production direction of the bastions of that middlebrow appeal: Mark Burnett and Roma Downey. Their next scripted television project is *Messiah*, a drama with mystery and political thriller aspects about a man claiming to be the Messiah in the present-day Middle East. While at first glance, the series seems in line with Downey and Burnett's many attempts to make faithful Christian programming, the show is being produced for Netflix and for simultaneous global distribution in 2019.[7] As discussed in Chapter 7, Netflix has constructed a brand around risk-taking and dynamic shows among its "original productions" label, indicating that perhaps *Messiah* will be an example of flexible Christian representation that seemed so possible in mid-2016: faithful without being message heavy or bland, edgy without dismissing its religiousness, able to explore the complex implications of representing religion in a serial television form, for an audience that could be both middlebrow and upscale. Or it could indicate that the middlebrow approach to representing religion has become so toxic in an industry context due to its association with an audience aligned with Trump voters that even Mark Burnett and Roma Downey have abdicated the potential of the approach and the underlying idea that white Christianity is the common-sense foundation of the American television audience to be treated as such.

In the introduction and over the course of this book, I used the changes from Reverend Camden to Reverend Custer to illustrate how Christian representation and creatives' understandings of it shifted over the twenty-year period of this study. And in this conclusion, I have pointed out a number of more recent shows engaging with Christian representation that echo approaches from ten to fifteen years previous to the new shows. As much as the industry has shifted and the way production cultures discuss Christianity has changed to fit those shifts, there are striking continuities throughout the twenty-year span of this book.

Going forward, the story of two *Good Christian Bitches* may best illustrate a new path forward for Christian representation. In 2012, ABC aired an acerbic hour-long serial dramedy based on Kim Gatlin's book, *Good Christian Bitches*. The series focused on the church community and hypocrisy in an affluent Dallas suburb. After pushback to the initial show title, the same as the source book, ABC ultimately aired the show under the inscrutable title *GCB* (2012).[8] The show was canceled after only ten episodes and was largely forgotten among the glut of programs growing toward Peak TV—that is, until it was announced in November 2018 that a new television adaptation of Gatlin's book, keeping the full title, is in the works at The CW.[9] Early reporting indicates that the major differences between the two versions of *Good Christian Bitches* would rest on the newer version ignoring any potential Christian backlash; the producers of both versions have apparently been assured the title would be preserved.[10] Instead of worrying about offending Christian viewers, which was key to the title change in 2012, the curse word in the title establishes the potential new series as edgy. The only other publicized change as of early 2019 is one of location: from conservative, affluent Dallas suburbs to a hip, urban Austin-based church. It will be fascinating if the new *Good Christian Bitches* makes it to air with these shifts, because the portrayal of a liberal Christianity through serial storytelling that doesn't shy away from the religiousness of that representation has been relatively absent from mainstream television dramas in the twenty-first century. Such a representational shift would be a logical next step beyond the twenty years of containment strategies for Christian narratives in order to appeal to upscale audiences. From these decades of shifting ideologies and industry logics, with enough instances of "getting away with" certain modes of Christian representation, perhaps the start of the 2020s will include Hollywood production cultures discovering a new variation on upscale taste cultures: progressive Christians.

Interviews

Anonymous A, writer
Anonymous B, writer, *Supernatural*
Anonymous C, writer, *Sleepy Hollow*
Melissa Bernstein, producer, *Rectify*
Monica Bloom, Senior Vice President Marketing and Digital Media, SundanceTV
Brusta Brown and John Mitchell Todd, staff writers, *Dominion*
Rio Cyrus, Senior Vice President of Marketing, Fox Home Entertainment
Brian Edwards, Chief Operations Officer, United Artists Media Group; producer, *The Bible*
Ruth Fletcher Gage and Christos Gage, staff writers, *Daredevil*
Marc Guggenheim, co-creator and co-showrunner, *Eli Stone*
David Hudgins, writer and producer, *Friday Night Lights*
Jordan Levin, former CEO of the WB Network
Damon Lindelof, showrunner, *Lost* and *The Leftovers*
Ronald D. Moore, showrunner, *Battlestar Galactica*
Gregg Nations, writer and producer, *Lost*
Carolyn Newman, executive in charge of drama, Amazon Studios
John Rogers, creator and showrunner, *The Librarians*
Bradley Thompson, writer and producer, *Battlestar Galactica*
Mark Verheiden, writer and producer, *Battlestar Galactica* and *Constantine*
Christian Vesper, Senior Vice President Scripted Development, SundanceTV
David Weddle, writer and producer, *Battlestar Galactica*
Aaron Zelman, creator and showrunner, *Resurrection*

Notes

Introduction

1. Peter Sciretta, "HBO Kills Preacher Television Series," *Slashfilm*, August 26, 2008, http://www.slashfilm.com/hbo-kills-preacher-television-series/; Rob Allstetter, "Mark Steven Johnson: No *Preacher* on HBO," *Comics Continuum*, August 25, 2008, http://www.comicscontinuum.com/stories/0808/25/index.htm?loc=interstitialskip.
2. Josef Allstetter, "There Were Over 400 Scripted TV Shows on the Air in 2015," *Vulture*, December 16, 2015, http://www.vulture.com/2015/12/scripted-tv-shows-2015.html
3. Clark Collis, "Why the *Preacher* Producers Trashed Their Original Plans for the Show," *Entertainment Weekly's* EW.com, May 13, 2016, http://www.ew.com/article/2016/05/13/preacher-seth-rogen-trashed-plans.
4. Pew Research Center, " 'No Religion' on the Rise: 19.6% Have No Religious Affiliation," Pew Forum on Religion & Public Life, October 9, 2012, http://www.pewforum.org/Unaffiliated/nones-on-the-rise.aspx.
5. Ibid.
6. Ibid.
7. Jean-Luc Nancy, "The Deconstruction of Christianity," in *Religion and Media*, ed. Hent de Vries and Samuel Weber, trans. Simon Sparks (Stanford, CA: Stanford University Press, 2001), 116–17.
8. Rudolph Binion, *After Christianity: Christian Survivals in Post-Christian Culture* (Durango, CO: Logbridge-Rhodes, 1986), 121.
9. Stig Hjarvard, "The Mediatisation of Religion: Theorising Religion, Media and Social Change," *Culture and Religion* 12, no. 2 (June 2011): 128–29.
10. Timothy Havens, "Towards a Structuration Theory of Media Intermediaries," *Making Media Work: Cultures of Management in the Entertainment Industries*, ed. Derek Johnson, Derek Kompare, and Avi Santo (New York University Press, 2014), 50–51. (emphasis in original)
11. Herman Gray, *Watching Race: Television and the Struggle for "Blackness"* (Minneapolis: University of Minnesota Press, 1995), 9.
12. Ron Becker, *Gay TV and Straight America* (New Brunswick, NJ: Rutgers University Press, 2006), 95.
13. Matthew Hills, *Fan Cultures* (Routledge, 2002), 43.
14. Ibid, 27; Henry Jenkins, *Convergence Culture* (New York: New York University Press, 2006), 12.
15. For examples of the short cycles of religious programming in 2003, 2006, and 2014, all of which present this programming strategy as new, see Pamela McClintock, "Exex Place Faith in Shows," *Variety*, August 25, 2003, sec. Television; Scott Roxborough,

"TV Execs Feel 'Passion' Religious Content Becomes Hot Topic," *Hollywood Reporter*, April 1, 2004; David S. Cohen, "Hollywood Gets Religion," *Variety*, May 29, 2006; Andrew Romano, "Hollywood Declares 2014 the Year of the Bible," Daily Beast, January 9, 2014, http://www.thedailybeast.com/articles/2014/01/09/hollywood-declares-2014-the-year-of-the-bible.html.

16. "*Battlestar Galactica*," Peabody Awards, accessed April 11, 2016, http://www.peabodyawards.com/award-profile/battlestar-galactica; James Hibberd, "Syfy Plans to Lure You Back with These 5 Shows," *Entertainment Weekly*'s EW.com, October 28, 2014, http://www.ew.com/article/2014/10/28/syfy; Richard Vine, "Better Than *The Wire?*," *Guardian*, March 18, 2009, sec. Television & radio, http://www.theguardian.com/culture/2009/mar/19/battlestar-galactica-review.

17. James Fallows, "Bush's Lost Year," *Atlantic*, October 2004, http://www.theatlantic.com/magazine/archive/2004/10/bushs-lost-year/303507/.

18. Ronald D. Moore, telephone interview, March 6, 2015.

19. Tiffany Vogt, "TV Watchtower: Is Religion Killing Good Sci-Fi Shows?" Airlock Alpha, October 19, 2010, http://airlockalpha.com/node/7945/tv-watchtower-is-religion-killing-good-sci-fi-shows.html.

20. Kevin Arceneaux and Stephen P. Nicholson, "Who Wants to Have a Tea Party? The Who, What, and Why of the Tea Party Movement," *PS: Political Science and Politics* 45, no. 4 (2012): 700–10.

21. Ibid.

22. Horace Newcomb, "'This Is Not al Dente': The Sopranos and the New Meaning of 'Television,'" in *Television: The Critical View*, 7th edition, ed. Horace Newcomb, (New York: Oxford University Press, 2006), 575.

23. Amanda D. Lotz, *The Television Will Be Revolutionized* (New York: NYU Press, 2007), 3.

24. Ibid., 5.

25. Philip Napoli, *Audience Evolution: New Technologies and the Transformation of Media Audiences* (New York: Columbia University Press, 2010), 156–57.

26. Newcomb, "This Is Not al Dente," 575.

27. Ibid.

28. Josef Adalian, "There Were Over 400 Scripted TV Shows on the Air in 2015," *Vulture*, December 16, 2015, http://www.vulture.com/2015/12/scripted-tv-shows-2015.html.

29. Ibid.

30. Josef Adalian and Maria Elena Fernandez, "The Business of Too Much TV," *Vulture*, May 18, 2016, http://www.vulture.com/2016/05/peak-tv-business-c-v-r.html.

31. Denise Mann, "It's Not TV, It's Brand Management," in *Production Studies: Cultural Studies of Media Industries*, ed. Vicki Mayer, Miranda J. Banks, and John T. Caldwell (Routledge, 2009); Derek Kompare, "'More 'Moments of Television': Online Cult Television Authorship," in *Flow TV: Television in the Age of Media Convergence*, ed. Michael Kackman et al. (Routledge, 2010); Jason Mittell, "Authorship," *Complex TV*, accessed July 16, 2013, http://mediacommons.futureofthebook.org/mcpress/complextelevision/authorship/.

32. John Thornton Caldwell, *Production Culture: Industrial Reflexivity and Critical Practice in Film and Television* (Durham, NC: Duke University Press, 2008); Catherine Johnson, *Telefantasy* (London: British Film Institute, 2005); Elana Levine, "Toward a Paradigm for Media Production Research: Behind the Scenes at *General Hospital*," *Critical Studies in Media Communication* 18, no. 1 (2001): 66–82; Vicki Mayer, "Studying Up and F**cking Up: Ethnographic Interviewing in Production Studies," *Cinema Journal* 47, no. 2 (2007): 141–48; Laura Grindstaff, *The Money Shot: Trash, Class, and the Making of TV Talk Shows*, 1st edition, (Chicago: University of Chicago Press, 2002); David Hesmondhalgh and Sarah Baker, *Creative Labour: Media Work in Three Cultural Industries*, 1st edition. (Routledge, 2011).

33. Caldwell, *Production Culture*.

34. For genre and ideological analysis, I draw on Mittell, "A Cultural Approach"; Fiske, *Television Culture*; and C. Johnson, *Telefantasy*.

35. Anonymous A, telephone interview, January 18, 2015.

36. Ibid.

37. Ibid.

38. Lotz, *Television Will Be Revolutionized*, 216.

39. Victoria E. Johnson, "Welcome Home? CBS, PAX-TV, and 'Heartland' Values in a Neo-Network Era," *Velvet Light Trap: A Critical Journal of Film & Television*, no. 46 (Fall 2000), 40.

Part I

1. ThomasMallonandPankajMishra,"Highbrow,Lowbrow,Middlebrow—DoTheseKinds ofCulturalCategoriesMeanAnythingAnymore?," *New York Times*, July 29, 2014, http:// www.nytimes.com/2014/08/03/books/review/highbrow-lowbrow-middlebrow- do-these-kinds-of-cultural-categories-mean-anything-anymore.html.

Chapter 1

1. Amanda D. Lotz, *The Television Will Be Revolutionized* (New York: NYU Press, 2007).

2. Jennifer Holt, *Empires of Entertainment: Media Industries and the Politics of Deregulation, 1980–1996* (New Brunswick, NJ: Rutgers University Press, 2011).

3. Michael Curtin, "On Edge: Culture Industries in the Neo Network Era," in *The Media Studies Reader*, first edition, ed. Laurie Ouellette (New York: Routledge, 2013),280.

4. Ibid., 284.

5. Ibid., 279.

6. Ien Ang, *Desperately Seeking the Audience* (London: Routledge, 1991), 88.

7. Joseph Turow, *Breaking Up America: Advertisers and the New Media World* (Chicago: University of Chicago Press, 1998), 59.

8. John Thornton Caldwell, *Televisuality: Style, Crisis, and Authority in American Television* (New Brunswick, NJ: Rutgers University Press, 1995).

9. Jason Mittell, *Complex TV: The Poetics of Contemporary Television Storytelling*, pre-publication edition (MediaCommons Press, 2012–2013), accessed March 25, 2016, http://mcpress.media-commons.org/complextelevision/

10. Caldwell, *Televisuality*; Mittell, *Complex TV*; Steve Neale, *Genre and Hollywood* (New York: Routledge, 2000).

11. I will address prior phases of quality television below in the history section, A Brief History: Establishing the Norms of Representing Christianity on Teleivion.

12. Michael Z. Newman and Elana Levine, *Legitimating Television* (New York: Routledge, 2011), 13.

13. Ron Becker, *Gay TV and Straight America* (New Brunswick, NJ: Rutgers University Press, 2006), 95.

14. Ibid., 108.

15. Julia Himberg, *The New Gay for Pay: The Sexual Politics of American Television Production* (Austin: University of Texas Press, 2018), 13.

16. Ibid., 6–7.

17. Becker, *Gay TV and Straight America*, 106.

18. Heather Hendershot, *Shaking the World for Jesus: Media and Conservative Evangelical Culture* (Chicago: University of Chicago Press, 2010),7.

19. Ibid., 61.

20. Robert Wuthnow, *After Heaven: Spirituality in America since the 1950s*, eBook (Berkeley: University of California Press, 1998), accessed March 3, 2014, 107.

21. Stewart M. Hoover, "Visual Religion in Media Culture," in *The Visual Culture of American Religions*, ed. David Morgan and Sally M. Promey (Berkeley: University of California Press, 2001), 156.

22. Horace Newcomb, "Religion on Television," in *Channels of Belief: Religion and American Commercial Television*, ed. John P. Ferre (Ames: University of Iowa Press, 1990), 41

23. Jennifer Fuller, "Branding Blackness on US Cable Television," *Media, Culture & Society* 32, no. 2 (March 1, 2010): 285–305.

24. Turow, *Breaking up America*, 56.

25. Hendershot, *Shaking the World for Jesus*, 11.

26. Victoria E. Johnson, *Heartland TV: Prime Time Television and the Struggle for U.S. Identity* (New York: NYU Press, 2008), 2.

27. Darrell Y. Hamamoto, *Nervous Laughter: Television Situation Comedy and Liberal Democratic Ideology* (New York: Praeger, 1989), 1.

28. Ibid., 4.

29. Justin Gest and David Lubell, "The New Frontier of Race and Immigration: Middle America," *Los Angeles Times*, August 21, 2017, http://www.latimes.com/opinion/op-ed/la-oe-gest-lubell-immigration-frontiers-20170821-story.html.

30. Johnson, *Heartland TV*, 18.

31. Richard Dyer, *White* (New York: Routledge, 1997), 3.

32. Fuller, "Branding Blackness": 285–305.

33. Dyer, *White*, 17.

34. While the WB straddled mass and niche distinctions as a netlet, it was aimed toward a multigenerational broad audience as a "family drama" (discussed below). It used

mass-appeal broadcast shows such as *Eight is Enough* and *The Andy Griffith Show* as inspiration and was the highest-rated WB show for most of its run. Thus, I situate it as mass-audience-oriented similar to *Touched by an Angel*.

35. Joel Stein and Patrick E. Cole, "The God Squad," *Time* 150, no. 12 (September 22, 1997): 97.

36. It is the case that certain shows did go more narrowly, of course, and the quality TV discourse did start with broadcast.

37. Victoria E. Johnson, "Welcome Home? CBS, PAX-TV, and 'Heartland' Values in a Neo-Network Era," *Velvet Light Trap: A Critical Journal of Film & Television*, no. 46 (Fall 2000).

38. Susanne Daniels and Cynthia Littleton, *Season Finale: The Unexpected Rise and Fall of the WB and UPN* (New York: HarperCollins, 2007),109.

39. Ibid., 94.

40. Ibid., 109.

41. V. Johnson, "Welcome Home?,"40.

42. Ibid., 40.

43. Ibid., 48.

44. Ibid., 45.

45. V. Johnson, "Welcome Home?,"40.

46. Ibid.

47. Ibid., 40.

48. Pierre Bourdieu, *Distinction: A Social Critique of the Judgement of Taste*, trans. Richard Nice (Cambridge, MA: Harvard University Press, 1984), 6.

49. V. Johnson, "Welcome Home?," 41.

50. "Touched by an Angel," Wikipedia, the Free Encyclopedia, June 20, 2016, https://en.wikipedia.org/w/index.php?title=Touched_by_an_Angel&oldid=726176089.

51. Ibid, 42.

52. Ibid., 42

53. Elizabeth Jensen, "WB's *7th Heaven* a Hush-Hush Hit," *Los Angeles Times*, February 22, 1999, http://articles.latimes.com/1999/feb/22/entertainment/ca-10415.

54. Richard Wolff, *The Church on TV* (New York: Continuum, 2010), 185.

55. Jordan Levin, personal interview, October 16, 2014.

56. Ibid.

57. Ibid.

58. It is fascinating that Kellner, according to Levin, had the initial idea to give the show a Christian context and premise. This choice, however, can be seen as compatible with Kellner's history of making high-risk programming decisions. Kellner was an executive at the Fox network during its first seven years (1987–1994) until he left to found the WB in 1994 (Lotz, *Television Will Be Revolutionized*). His transition from Fox to the WB provided a through line in terms of network strategies: there were several similarities in terms of how the WB pursued early viewers and what Fox previously had done. Both initially targeted African-American viewers, only to then transition to appealing to young white adults. Indeed, Kellner even went so far as to bring in Aaron Spelling as a key figure in each network's ascent, with *Beverly Hills,*

90210 in the case of Fox (1990–2000) and *7th Heaven* for the WB. In addition to reproducing the same audience targeting and programming strategies, Kellner's role in the WB's origin story also underscores the high-risk/high-reward consideration of representing religion on a prime-time drama. Such risk taking is available only to someone in as high a position of power as a CEO who need not worry as much as middle executives or writers about job security or ostracization. Even with this as the case for Kellner, the idea of focusing on a pastor was still somewhat contained religious representation. Kellner displayed more flexibility within the ideology of religion-as-risk, but only when his stance was compared to the self-policing and avoidance generally displayed by writers and mid-level executives of the time.

59. Todd Gitlin, "Prime Time Ideology: The Hegemonic Process of Television Entertainment," in *Television: The Critical View*, ed. Horace Newcomb (New York: Oxford University Press, 2000), 531.
60. Levin interview; emphasis added.
61. Jensen, "WB's *7th Heaven* a Hush-Hush Hit."

Chapter 2

1. "*The Bible* Is a Smash, on TV," NPR.org, March 24, 2013, http://www.npr.org/2013/03/24/175173105/the-bible-is-a-smash-on-tv.
2. Brian Edwards, telephone interview, April 21, 2015.
3. Heather Hendershot, *Shaking the World for Jesus: Media and Conservative Evangelical Culture*, 1st edition (Chicago: University of Chicago Press, 2004), 212.
4. David Bordwell, Janet Staiger, and Kristen Thompson, *The Classical Hollywood Cinema: Film Style and Mode of Production to 1960* (New York: Columbia University Press, 1985), 359.
5. Cynthia Littleton, "Proving Herself in the Desert," *Variety*, August 9, 2016, 84.
6. Gaita, Paul. "Close Personal Bonds." *Variety*, August 9, 2016, 102.
7. Littleton, "Proving Herself," 84.
8. Kim Masters, "Rough Seas on *Noah*: Darren Aronofsky Opens Up on the Biblical Battle to Woo Christians (and Everyone Else)," *Hollywood Reporter*, February 12, 2014, https://www.hollywoodreporter.com/news/rough-seas-noah-darren-aronofsky-679315; Alex Stedman, "Survey: Faith-Driven Consumers Dissatisfied with *Noah*, Hollywood Religious Pics," *Variety* (blog), February 17, 2014, http://variety.com/2014/film/news/98-of-faith-driven-consumers-dissatisfied-with-noah-survey-shows-1201109347/.
9. David Sims, "*Ben-Hur, The Passion of the Christ*, and Hollywood's Failed Play for Christian Audiences," *Atlantic*, accessed January 26, 2018, https://www.theatlantic.com/entertainment/archive/2016/08/why-hollywood-thought-remaking-ben-hur-was-a-good-idea/496868/.
10. Gaita, "Close Personal Bonds," 102.
11. Cynthia Littleton, "Mark Burnett and One Three Media Eye Bigger, Bolder Productions," *Variety* (blog), September 17, 2013, http://variety.com/2013/biz/

news/mark-burnett-and-his-one-three-media-eye-bigger-bolder-productions-
1200613995/.

12. Cynthia Littleton, "Accentuating the Positive," *Variety*, September 17, 2013.

13. Peter Bart, "Will the Culture Wars Leave Faith-Based Films Dispirited?," *Variety*,
March 11, 2014.

14. Sara Boboltz, "Mark Burnett Presents: A Donald Trump Inauguration Day,"
Huffington Post, December 9, 2016, sec. Arts & Culture, http://www.huffingtonpost.
com/entry/mark-burnett-presents-a-donald-trump-inauguration-day_us_
58495e9ae4b0f9723d005efc; Cynthia Littleton, "Mark Burnett's Ties to Trump Put
Him in Tricky Situation," *Variety* (blog), January 19, 2017, http://variety.com/2017/
tv/news/mark-burnett-donald-trump-1201963228/.

15. Rick Kissell, "History Scores Big with *The Bible* and *The Vikings*," *Variety*, March 4,
2013, http://variety.com/2013/tv/ratin   gs/history-scores-big-with-the-bible-and-
the-vikings-1200002918/.

16. Carol Memmott, "History Channel Comes Out Shootin'," *USA Today*, accessed March
31, 2016.

17. Malgorzata J. Rymsza-Pawlowska, "Broadcasting the Past: History Television,
'Nostalgia Culture,' and the Emergence of the Miniseries in the 1970s United States,"
Journal of Popular Film & Television 42, no. 2 (April 2014):86.

18. Ibid., 85.

19. Andrew Romano, "Hollywood Declares 2014 the Year of the Bible," *Daily Beast*, January
9, 2014, http://www.thedailybeast.com/articles/2014/01/09/hollywood-declares-
2014-the-year-of-the-bible.html.

20. Ibid.

21. Samantha Highfill, "MGM Is Once Again Launching the United Artists Media
Group," *Entertainment Weekly's* EW.com, September 22, 2014, http://www.ew.com/
article/2014/09/22/mgm-united-artists-media-group.

22. Ibid.

23. Romano, "Hollywood Declares 2014."

24. Cynthia Littleton, "History, Producers Spread Gospel in 10-Hour Mini," *Variety*
(blog), March 1, 2013, http://variety.com/2013/tv/news/history-producers-spread-
gospel-in-10-hour-mini-821007/.

25. Alissa Wilkinson, "The Ten Commandments Has Been a Springtime TV Staple
since 1968, with Good Reason," Vox, April 15, 2017, https://www.vox.com/culture/
2017/4/15/15243480/ten-commandments-movie-of-week-passover-easter;   Vivian
Carol Sobchack, *The Persistence of History: Cinema, Television, and the Modern Event*
(New York: Routledge, 1996), 107.

26. Romano, "Hollywood Declares 2014."

27. Ibid.

28. Cynthia Littleton, "Deep Pockets, Family Feel at Mark Burnett's One Three Media,"
Variety (blog), September 17, 2013, http://variety.com/2013/biz/news/deep-pockets-
family-feel-at-mark-burnetts-one-three-media-1200614004/; Gaita, "Close Personal
Bonds"; Littleton, "Proving Herself in the Desert"; Bill Carter, "Reality-TV Producer
Mark Burnett Tackles the Bible," *New York Times*, May 24, 2011, sec. Television,

https://www.nytimes.com/2011/05/24/arts/television/reality-tv-producer-mark-burnett-tackles-the-bible.html.

29. Littleton, "History, Producers."

30. Cynthia Littleton, "Mark Burnett, Roma Downey Promo *Bible* Mini to Faithful," *Variety* (blog), February 8, 2013, http://variety.com/2013/tv/news/mark-burnett-roma-downey-promo-bible-mini-to-faithful-1118065870/.

31. Ibid.

32. Emma Allen, "Prime-Time Scripture; Swords and Sandals," *New Yorker*, March 18, 2013.

33. Cynthia Littleton, "History, Producers."

34. Jeanine Poggi, "The Miniseries, a Onetime TV Mainstay, Poised for an Encore," *Advertising Age* 83, no. 25 (June 18, 2012): 6.

35. Poggi, "Miniseries," 6.

36. Ibid.

37. Patrick Hipes, "*Killing Jesus* Premiere Date Set for March 29 on Nat Geo—Full Trailer," *Deadline*, February 18, 2015, http://deadline.com/2015/02/killing-jesus-premiere-date-trailer-national-geographic-channel-1201375969/.

38. Cynthia Littleton, "Roma Downey Pursues Passion Projects, *Bible* Sequel with LightWorkers Banner," *Variety*, September 17, 2013, http://variety.com/2013/biz/news/roma-downey-pursues-passion-projects-bible-sequel-with-lightworkers-banner-1200614054/; A. J. Marechal, "LightWorkers Media Options *The Dovekeepers* for Miniseries," *Variety* (blog), September 16, 2013, http://variety.com/2013/tv/news/lightworkers-media-options-the-dovekeepers-for-miniseries-exclusive-1200610855/.

39. Anthony D'Alessandro, "Jerusalem a Dangerous Place after Christ In NBC's *A.D.*—Trailer," *Deadline*, November 29, 2014, http://deadline.com/2014/11/a-d-video-nbc-miniseries-life-after-jesus-christ-death-1201302212/.

40. Rick Kissell, "NBC's *A.D.* Leads Easter Sunday but Can't Match *The Bible*," *Variety* (blog), April 6, 2015, http://variety.com/2015/tv/ratings/nbcs-a-d-the-bible-continues-opens-to-solid-but-unspectacular-ratings-1201466801/.

41. Adrienne Samuels Gibbs, "*A.D. The Bible Continues*: Casting a More Diverse Bible Story," NBC News, April 5, 2015, https://www.nbcnews.com/news/nbcblk/behind-bible-ad-casting-more-diverse-bible-story-n335491.

42. Hamil R. Harris, "TV Producer Talks about Casting Diverse Actors in *A.D. The Bible Continues*," *Washington Post*, February 6, 2015, sec. Local, https://www.washingtonpost.com/news/local/wp/2015/02/06/tv-producer-talks-about-casting-diverse-actors-in-a-d-the-bible-continues/.

43. Hendershot, *Shaking the World for Jesus*, 180.

44. Ibid., 205.

45. Brian Lowry, "TV Review: *A.D. The Bible Continues*," *Variety* (blog), April 3, 2015, http://variety.com/2015/tv/reviews/tv-review-a-d-the-bible-continues-1201461544/
.

46. Cynthia Littleton, "Easter Week Is Hopping with High-Profile TV Premieres: *Killing Jesus, The Dovekeepers, A.D.*," *Variety* (blog), February 18, 2015, http://variety.com/

2015/tv/news/easter-week-high-profile-tv-premieres-killing-jesus-the-dovekeepers-a-d-1201436194/; Natalie Stone, "Mark Burnett, Roma Downey's *A.D. The Bible Continues*: Jesus' Death 'Changed World History,'" *Hollywood Reporter*, April 5, 2015, https://www.hollywoodreporter.com/live-feed/mark-burnett-roma-downeys-ad-786443; Michael O'Connell, "Mark Burnett Talks about 'Mainstreaming' the Bible in *A.D.*—and His Growing Beard," *Hollywood Reporter*, January 16, 2015, https://www.hollywoodreporter.com/live-feed/mark-burnett-talks-mainstreaming-bible-764431.

47. O'Connell, "Mark Burnett Talks about 'Mainstreaming' the Bible in *A.D.*"

48. Rymsza-Pawlowska, 85–86. For further discussion of discursive legitimation of television, see also Michael Z. Newman and Elana Levine, *Legitimating Television* (Routledge, 2011).

49. Littleton, "Easter Week Is Hopping.

50. Ibid.

51. Yvonne Villarreal, "TCA '15: With *Dovekeepers*, Roma Downey Looks to Provide Inspiring TV," *Los Angeles Times*, January 12, 2015, http://www.latimes.com/entertainment/envelope/cotown/la-et-st-tca-15-with-dovekeepers-roma-downey-looks-to-provide-tv-that-inspires-20150112-story.html.

52. CBS News, "Roma Downey and Rachel Brosnahan on *The Dovekeepers*," CBSnews.com, April 1, 2015, accessed February 5, 2018, https://www.cbsnews.com/news/roma-downey-rachel-brosnahan-dovekeepers-cbs-special/; Jimmy Akin, "Jesus' Mysterious Prophecy about the Temple," National Catholic Register, April 27, 2017, http://www.ncregister.com/blog/jimmy-akin/jesus-mysterious-prophecy-about-the-temple.

53. CBS News, "Roma Downey and Rachel Brosnahan."

54. Brian Lowry, "The Worst TV Shows of 2015," *Variety* (blog), December 11, 2015, http://variety.com/2015/tv/columns/worst-tv-shows-2015-true-detective-fear-the-walking-dead-texas-rising-1201658055/.

55. Lowry, "TV Review: *The Dovekeepers*"; Brian Lowry, "*Red Tent* Has Perfect Pitch," *Variety*, December 2, 2014.

56. Mary McNamara, "Masada in CBS' *The Dovekeepers*: Bad Storytelling in Every Way," *Los Angeles Times*, March 31, 2015, http://www.latimes.com/entertainment/tv/la-et-st-cbs-dovekeepers-review-20150331-column.html.

57. Neil Genzlinger, "Review: *The Dovekeepers*, a CBS Mini-Series Starring Cote de Pablo," *New York Times*, March 29, 2015, sec. Television, https://www.nytimes.com/2015/03/30/arts/television/review-the-dovekeepers-a-cbs-mini-series-starring-cote-de-pablo.html.

58. Debra Birnbaum, "Mark Burnett on His New Role at MGM, Faith-Based TV and *Celebrity Apprentice*," *Variety* (blog), December 14, 2015, http://variety.com/2015/tv/news/mark-burnett-mgm-president-celebrity-apprentice-1201661388/.

59. Cynthia Littleton, "NBC Cancels *A.D.* as Producers Plan Digital Revival for Biblical Drama," *Variety* (blog), July 3, 2015, http://variety.com/2015/tv/news/a-d-the-bible-continues-nbc-cancels-mark-burnett-roma-downey-1201533794/.

60. Mark Burnett, "Mark Burnett Op-Ed: *A.D.* Producer on Faith and Hollywood," *Hollywood Reporter*, April 3, 2015, http://www.hollywoodreporter.com/news/mark-burnett-op-ed-ad-786225.

61. Romano, "Hollywood Declares 2014."
62. V. Johnson, "Welcome Home?," 43.
63. Ibid., 49.
64. Hendershot, *Shaking the World for Jesus*, 201.
65. Rick Kissell, "Ratings: *A.D. The Bible Continues* Drops Off, But Still Tops Demos." *Variety*, April 13, 2015, http://variety.com/2015/data/news/a-d-the-bible-continues-ratings-week-2-1201471277/.

Chapter 3

1. Although my use of the term draws on histories of realism in literature and media, and has sometimes been used to refer to mid- to late-nineteenth-century realist novels from Southern writers like Kate Chopin, it is not as a compound term often used, and not with as specific a meaning as I give it here.
2. Charles Mcgrath, "The Triumph of the Prime-Time Novel," *New York Times*, October 22, 1995, sec. Magazine, http://www.nytimes.com/1995/10/22/magazine/the-prime-time-novel-the-triumph-of-the-prime-time-novel.html.
3. Michael Z. Newman, *Indie: An American Film Culture* (New York: Columbia University Press, 2011), 2.
4. Ibid., 226.
5. Sarah Banet-Weiser, *Authentic TM: The Politics and Ambivalence in a Brand Culture* (New York: NYU Press, 2012), 10.
6. Michael Z. Newman and Elana Levine, *Legitimating Television* (New York: Routledge, 2011), 18.
7. David Hudgins, telephone interview, September 11, 2015.
8. Andrew J. Bottomley, "Quality TV and the Branding of U.S. Network Television: Marketing and Promoting *Friday Night Lights*," *Quarterly Review of Film and Video* 32, no. 5 (July 4, 2015): 482–97; Matthew Zoller Seitz, "Sundance's *Rectify*, Perhaps the Most Quiet Drama on TV, Is Truly Christian Art," *Vulture*, June 19, 2014, http://www.vulture.com/2014/06/tv-review-rectify-season-2.html?mid=facebook_vulture; Mary McNamara, "Review: *Rectify* Is a Revelation That Sets a New Standard," *Los Angeles Times*, April 22, 2013, http://articles.latimes.com/2013/apr/22/entertainment/la-et-st-rectify-20130422; Hale, " 'Rectify' on the Sundance Channel."
9. Victoria E. Johnson, "The Persistence of Geographic Myth in a Convergent Media Era," *Journal of Popular Film & Television* 38, no. 2 (June 2010): 59.
10. Ibid.
11. Bottomley, "Quality TV and the Branding of U.S. Network Television"; V. Johnson, "Geographic Myth"; Hudgins interview; Sarah Hughes, "Why *Friday Night Lights* Is One of the Best US Shows of Recent Years," *Guardian*, February 13, 2012, sec. Television & radio, http://www.theguardian.com/tv-and-radio/tvandradioblog/2012/feb/13/friday-night-lights.
12. V. Johnson, "Geographic Myth," 60.

13. For more on NBC's marketing of *Friday Night Lights* as quality, see Bottomley, "Quality TV and the Branding of U.S. Network Television."

14. Hudgins interview.

15. Alan Sepinwall, *The Revolution Was Televised* (New York: Simon & Schuster, 2012), 277–78.

16. Sepinwall, *Revolution Was Televised*; Nancy Franklin, "The Heart of Texas," *New Yorker*, October 8, 2007, http://www.newyorker.com/magazine/2007/10/08/the-heart-of-texas; Ginia Bellafante, "A *Friday Night Lights* Farewell," *ArtsBeat*, July 16, 2011, http://artsbeat.blogs.nytimes.com/2011/07/16/a-friday-night-lights-farewell/; James Poniewozik, "*Friday Night Lights* Watch (Repost): Let's Go Home," *Time*, July 16, 2011, http://entertainment.time.com/2011/07/16/friday-night-lights-watch-repost-lets-go-home/.

17. V. Johnson, "Geographic Myth," 62.

18. Ibid., 62.

19. Ibid., 63.

20. "Last Days of Summer," *Friday Night Lights*, season two.

21. Laurie Goodstein, "After the Attacks: Finding Fault; Falwell's Finger-Pointing Inappropriate, Bush Says," *New York Times*, September 15, 2001, sec. U.S., https://www.nytimes.com/2001/09/15/us/after-attacks-finding-fault-falwell-s-finger-pointing-inappropriate-bush-says.html; Joe Brown, "Religious Conservatives Claim Katrina Was God's Omen, Punishment for the United States," Media Matters for America, October 10, 2007, https://www.mediamatters.org/research/2005/09/13/religious-conservatives-claim-katrina-was-gods/133804.

22. Bellafante, "*Friday Night Lights* Farewell"; Poniewozik, "*Friday Night Lights* Watch (Repost)"; Rebecca Cusey, "Friday Night Gets Religion," *National Review Online*, October 5, 2007, http://www.nationalreview.com/article/222408/friday-night-gets-religion-rebecca-cusey; Brett McCracken, "Saying Farewell to the Best Show on TV," *RELEVANT Magazine*, July 14, 2011, http://www.relevantmagazine.com/culture/tv/features/26184-saying-farewell-to-the-best-show-on-tv.

23. "I Can't," *Friday Night Lights*, season four.

24. Hudgins interview.

25. Christian Vesper, telephone interview, October 31, 2014.

26. Sam Thielman, "This Fall the Sundance Channel Will Begin Airing Ads," *Adweek*, March 24, 2013, http://www.adweek.com/news/television/sundance-channel-goes-ad-supported-148128.

27. Ibid.

28. Melissa Bernstein, telephone interview, September 22, 2014.

29. Ibid.

30. Monica Bloom, telephone interview, October 17, 2014.

31. Vesper interview.

32. Bloom interview.

33. Ibid.

34. Vesper interview.

35. Sundi Rose-Holt, "More Than One Kind of Silence in *Rectify*," *Entertainment Weekly's* EW.com, August 7, 2014, http://community.ew.com/2014/08/07/more-than-one-kind-of-silence-in-rectify/;Seitz, "Sundance's *Rectify*"; Hale, "*Rectify* on the Sundance Channel."

36. Seitz, "Sundance's *Rectify*"; McNamara, "Review: *Rectify* Is a Revelation."

37. Emma Koonse, "*Rectify* Series Creator Ray McKinnon Talks Television, Redemption, and the Future for Daniel Holden," *Christian Post*, July 10, 2014, http://www.christianpost.com/news/rectify-series-creator-ray-mckinnon-talks-television-redemption-and-the-future-for-daniel-holden-123104/.

Chapter 4

1. Herman Gray, *Watching Race: Television and the Struggle for "Blackness"* (Minneapolis: University of Minnesota Press, 1995), 9–10.

2. Arlene Dávila, "Introduction," in *Contemporary Latina/o Media: Production, Circulation, Politics*, ed. Arlene Dávila and Yeidy M. Rivero (New York: NYU Press, 2014), 10.

3. Geoff Berkshire, "*Jane the Virgin*: Golden Globe Afterglow Gives Boost to Show, CW," *Variety* (blog), December 12, 2014, http://variety.com/2014/tv/awards/jane-the-virgin-golden-globe-nominations-cw-1201377695/; Mary McNamara, "Oprah Winfrey's *Greenleaf* Deserves High Praise, but Her Network May Not Receive Its Full Bounty," *Los Angeles Times*, June 21, 2016, http://www.latimes.com/entertainment/tv/la-et-st-greenleaf-review-20160620-snap-story.html.

4. Johnny Diaz, "Meet the Family," *Hispanic*, February 2002, 36.

5. Michelle A. Holling: "El Simpático Boxer: Underpinning Chicano Masculinity with a Rhetoric of Familia in Resurrection Blvd.," *Western Journal of Communication* 70, no. 2 (July 1, 2006): 91–114, https://doi.org/10.1080/10570310600709994.

6. Michael O'Connell, "*Jane the Virgin* Showrunner Wants *Ugly Betty* Meets *Gilmore Girls*," *Hollywood Reporter*, July 18, 2014, https://www.hollywoodreporter.com/live-feed/jane-virgin-showrunner-wants-ugly-719620; Brenda Salinas, "Is America Ready to Fall in Love with the Telenovela?," NPR.org, November 9, 2014, https://www.npr.org/sections/codeswitch/2014/11/09/362401259/is-america-ready-to-fall-in-love-with-the-telenovela; Zayda Rivera, "Gina Rodriguez Talks *Jane the Virgin*, Similarities to Character: 'I Was a Huge Prude,'" *NY Daily News*, October 9, 2014, http://www.nydailynews.com/entertainment/tv/gina-rodriguez-stars-cw-telenovela-adaptation-jane-virgin-article-1.1968944.

7. O'Connell, "*Jane the Virgin* Showrunner."

8. Ibid.

9. Rivera, "Gina Rodriguez Talks *Jane the Virgin*."

10. Jessica Hamar Martinez and Cary Funk, "The Shifting Religious Identity of Latinos in the United States," Pew Research Center's Religion & Public Life Project (blog), May 7, 2014, http://www.pewforum.org/2014/05/07/the-shifting-religious-identity-of-latinos-in-the-united-states/.

11. Antonio V. Menéndez Alarcón, "Latin American Culture: A Deconstruction of Stereotypes," *Studies in Latin American Popular Culture* 32, no. 1 (May 21, 2014): 81.

12. "Chapter Twenty-Two," *Jane the Virgin*. This is a quotation also used occasionally in recaps and "previously on" teasers to explain the abundance of plot that the show has moved through.

13. Yvonne Villarreal, "CW Boss Mark Pedowitz Talks *The Flash* and Broadening Out," *Los Angeles Times*, July 18, 2014, http://www.latimes.com/entertainment/tv/showtracker/la-et-st-cw-boss-mark-pedowitz-talks-broadening-out-genre-sensibility-20140718-story.html.

14. Jonathan Kuperberg, "TCA: CW's Pedowitz Says Last Season 'Pivotal' for Network," Broadcasting & Cable, August 11, 2015, http://www.broadcastingcable.com/news/programming/tca-cw-s-pedowitz-says-last-season-pivotal-network/143303.

15. Villarreal, "CW Boss Mark Pedowitz Talks *The Flash*"; Kuperberg, "TCA: CW's Pedowitz Says Last Season 'Pivotal'; Nellie Andreeva, "Golden Globes TV: The CW, Cinemax & Amazon Arrive to Awards Party," *Deadline* (blog), December 11, 2014, http://deadline.com/2014/12/golden-globes-tv-analysis-jane-the-virgin-transparent-1201320225/; Maureen Ryan, "The Man behind the Heroes: Mark Pedowitz Breaks The CW out of Its Niche," *Variety* (blog), October 14, 2015, http://variety.com/2015/tv/features/mark-pedowitz-the-cw-the-flash-arrow-1201617084/.

16. Jane Feuer, "Melodrama, Serial Form and Television Today," *Screen* 25, no. 1 (1984): 4–17; Lynn Joyrich, "All That Television Allows," *Private Screenings: Television and the Female Consumer*, 1st edition, ed. Lynn Spigel, (Minneapolis: University of Minnesota Press, 1992), 227–51.

17. Joyrich, "All That Television Allows," 246.

18. Ibid., 228.

19. Feuer, "Melodrama, Serial Form and Television Today," 12.

20. Carolina Acosta-Alzuru, "Tackling the Issues: Meaning Making in a Telenovela," *Popular Communication* 1, no. 4 (December 2003): 194.

21. Juan Piñón, "*Jane the Virgin*," *ReVista* 17, no. 1 (Fall 2017): 26.

22. "Chapter One," *Jane the Virgin*.

23. Ibid.

24. Piñón, "*Jane the Virgin*," 23.

25. Diana Martinez, "*Jane the Virgin* Proves Diversity Is More Than Skin Deep," *Atlantic*, October 19, 2015, https://www.theatlantic.com/entertainment/archive/2015/10/jane-the-virgin-telenovelas/409696/.

26. Brian Lowry, "Sudsy *Virgin* Delivers Charm," *Variety*, October 7, 2014.

27. "Chapter Seven," *Jane the Virgin*.

28. Marietta Messmer, "Transformations of the Sacred in Contemporary Chicana Culture," *Theology & Sexuality* 14, no. 3 (January 1, 2008): 268.

29. Aldore D. Collier, "Sherman Hemsley and Clifton Davis Return to TV as Stars of Own Show," *Jet*, October 27, 1986, 58.

30. Ibid., 59.

31. "Amen—Sherman Hemsley on the Religious Consultants on Amen, and His Admiration for Ed. Weinberger," Archive of American Television, accessed January 10, 2018, http://emmytvlegends.org/interviews/shows/amen; FoundationINTERVIEWS, Sherman Hemsley Interview Part 2 of 3, EMMYTVLEGENDS.ORG, n.d., https://www.youtube.com/watch?time_continue=881&v=Eqz2IQcn1MM.

32. "Amen—Sherman Hemsley on the Religious Consultants."

33. Collier, "Sherman Hemsley and Clifton Davis," 59.

34. K. C. Ifeanyi, "How Oprah's New Drama *Greenleaf* Is Built on Faith, Flawed Characters . . . and Tattoos?," *Fast Company*, June 21, 2016, https://www.fastcompany.com/3061105/how-oprahs-new-drama-greenleaf-is-built-on-faith-flawed-charactersand-tattoos.

35. "God," *Black-ish*.

36. Debbie Emery, "*Empire* Goes to Church: Andre Gets Baptized, Cookie Can't Keep Her Mouth Shut," *TheWrap*, October 21, 2015, https://www.thewrap.com/empires-andre-gets-baptized-cookie-curses-in-church-quit-trying-to-turn-us-into-sinners/.

37. Jenna Goudreau, "Will Oprah Winfrey Spin OWN into Network Gold?," *Forbes*, October 10, 2011.

38. Ibid.;Sam Schechner, "Corporate News: Oprah Winfrey's Network Draws Large Opening-Night Audience," *Wall Street Journal*, Eastern edition, January 4, 2011; Verne Gay, "Oprah Winfrey Launching OWN, Her New TV Network," *McClatchy–Tribune Business News*, January 16, 2008, *ProQuest*, https://search-proquest-com.ezproxy.bu.edu/docview/457078504/abstract/B7A6F826D03143F5PQ/1.

39. William Launder, "Corporate News: Winfrey Network to Add Six Series," *Wall Street Journal*, Eastern edition, January 7, 2013.

40. "Black Women Help OWN Achieve Its Second Year of Double-Digit Growth," *Chicago Citizen*, January 15, 2014; Raven S. Maragh, "'Our Struggles Are Unequal': Black Women's Affective Labor between Television and Twitter," *Journal of Communication Inquiry* 40, no. 4 (October 1, 2016): 352.

41. Ibid.

42. Andrea Morabito, "OWN Scripts Growth Strategy with Help From Tyler Perry," *Broadcasting & Cable* 143, no. 21 (May 27, 2013): 17.

43. Ibid.

44. Ibid.

45. Nick Niedzwiadek, "Oprah Steers Cable Turnaround—OWN Network Rises as Rivals Struggle by Shifting Its Lineup toward Dramas," *Wall Street Journal*, Eastern edition, March 21, 2016.

46. Ibid.

47. Kimberly Springer, "Introduction: Delineating the Contours of the Oprah Culture Industry," in *Stories of Oprah: The Oprahfication of American Culture*, ed. Trystan T. Cotten and Kimberly Springer (Oxford, MI: University Press of Mississippi, 2010),xii.

48. Ibid., viii.

49. Peggy Sue Loroz and Bridgette M. Braig, "Consumer Attachments to Human Brands: The 'Oprah Effect,'" *Psychology & Marketing* 32, no. 7 (July 1, 2015): 751.

50. Karlyn Crowley, "New Age Soul: The Gendered Translation of New Age Spirituality on *The Oprah Winfrey Show*," in Stories of Oprah: The Oprahfication of American Culture,

ed. Trystan T. Cotten and Kimberly Springer (Oxford, MI: University Press of Mississippi, 2010), 34.

51. Kathryn Lofton, "Practicing Oprah; or, the Prescriptive Compulsion of a Spiritual Capitalism.," *Journal of Popular Culture* 39, no. 4 (August 2006):605.

52. Ibid., 599.

53. Eithne Quinn, "Black Talent and Conglomerate Hollywood: Will Smith, Tyler Perry, and the Continuing Significance of Race," *Popular Communication* 11, no. 3 (July 2013): 202.

54. Anna Everett, "Black Film, New Media Industries, and BAMMs (Black American Media Moguls) in the Digital Media Ecology," *Cinema Journal* 53, no. 4 (Summer 2014): 132.

55. Debra Birnbaum, "Her OWN Woman," *Variety*, October 6, 2015, 48.

56. John Jurgensen, "Oprah Is Back on TV; Oprah Winfrey Takes a Part in *Greenleaf*, a TV Series about a Memphis Megachurch," *Wall Street Journal* (online), June 16, 2016, sec. Arts; Daniel D'Addario, "*Animal Kingdom* and *Greenleaf* Are Summer Surprises," *Time* 187, no. 24 (June 27, 2016): 51; Maureen Ryan, "*Greenleaf*," *Variety*, June 21, 2016, 111.

57. Ryan, "*Greenleaf*," 111.

58. Cynthia Littleton, "Shows Are Finally Ready to Have a Serious Talk about Religion," *Variety*, May 3, 2016 https://variety.com/2016/voices/columns/tv-series-path-greenleaf-tackle-religion-1201765858/.

59. D'Addario, "*Animal Kingdom* and *Greenleaf*," 51.

60. Ryan, "*Greenleaf*," 111.

61. Littleton, "Shows Are Finally Ready."

62. "Ratings—OWN Set to Deliver Its Highest-Rated and Most-Watched Year in Network History," *Futon Critic*, December 16, 2016, http://www.thefutoncritic.com/ratings/2016/12/16/own-set-to-deliver-its-highest-rated-and-most-watched-year-in-network-history-25510/20161216own01/.

63. Ifeanyi, "How Oprah's New Drama *Greenleaf* Is Built."

64. Ibid.

65. "Veni, Vidi, Vici," *Greenleaf*.

66. "A Time to Heal," *Greenleaf*.

67. "Men Like Trees Walking," *Greenleaf*.

68. Ifeanyi, "How Oprah's New Drama *Greenleaf* Is Built."

69. Mikey Glazer, "Oprah Winfrey Defends Scandalous Church Drama *Greenleaf*, Prepares for Backlash," *TheWrap*, May 26, 2016, https://www.thewrap.com/oprah-winfrey-defends-scandalous-church-drama-greenleaf-prepares-for-backlash/.

70. Meredith Blake, "Oprah Winfrey's Megachurch Series *Greenleaf* 'Takes Faith Really Seriously,'" *Los Angeles Times*, April 21, 2016, http://www.latimes.com/entertainment/tv/showtracker/la-et-st-oprah-winfrey-greenleaf-20160420-story.html.

Part III

1. Catherine Johnson, *Telefantasy* (London: British Film Institute, 2005), 7.

2. Matthew Hills, *Fan Cultures* (New York: Routledge, 2002), 43.

Chapter 5

1. Jan Johnson-Smith, *American Science Fiction* (Middletown, CT: Wesleyan University Press, 2005); M. Keith Booker, *Science Fiction Television* (Westport, CT: Praeger, 2004).

2. Heather Hendershot, "'You Know How It Is with Nuns . . .': Religion and Television's Sacred/Secular Fetuses," in *Small Screen, Big Picture: Television and Lived Religion*, ed. Diane Winston (Waco: TX: Baylor University Press, 2009), 205–6.

3. This "spirituality" is related to Ursula King's feminist use of the term instead of religion as a way of distancing religiousness from the traditional and patriarchal connotations associated with "religion" as a concept, but among creatives it is an unacknowledged and nonpolitical dissociation, unlike with King. For more on feminist use of "spirituality" instead of "religion" see Ursula King, *Women and Spirituality: Voices of Protest and Promise*, 2nd edition (London: Macmillan, 1993).

4. Matt Fowler, "Syfy Looking to Get Back to Battlestar Galactica-Quality Sci-Fi," *IGN*, October 30, 2014, http://www.ign.com/articles/2014/10/30/syfy-looking-to-get-back-to-battlestar-galactica-quality-sci-fi; Michael Kackman, "Flow Favorites: Quality Television, Melodrama, and Cultural Complexity," Flow, 2010, accessed April 5, 2016, http://www.flowjournal.org/2010/03/flow-favorites-quality-television-melodrama-and-cultural-complexity-michael-kackman-university-of-texas-austin/; Jordan Lavender-Smith, "Networking Families: *Battlestar Galactica* and the Values of Quality," *Flow*, 2009, accessed April 5, 2016, http://www.flowjournal.org/2009/12/networking-families-battlestar-galactica-and-the-values-of-quality-jordan-lavender-smith-city-university-of-new-york/; Cory Barker, "Sophomore Jump: How *The Leftovers* Became the Best Show on TV," *TV.com*, December 3, 2015, http://www.tv.com/shows/the-leftovers/community/post/the-leftovers-season-2-improvement-144907112784/.

5. Catherine Johnson, *Telefantasy* (London: British Film Institute, 2005), 4.

6. Ibid., 7.

7. "*Battlestar Galactica*," Peabody Awards, accessed April 11, 2016, http://www.peabodyawards.com/award-profile/battlestar-galactica; James Hibberd, "Syfy Plans to Lure You Back with These 5 Shows," *Entertainment Weekly's* EW.com, October 28, 2014, http://www.ew.com/article/2014/10/28/syfy; Richard Vine, "Better Than *The Wire*?," *Guardian*, March 18, 2009, sec. Television & radio, http://www.theguardian.com/culture/2009/mar/19/battlestar-galactica-review.

8. Ronald D. Moore, telephone interview, March 6, 2015.

9. Ibid.

10. Ibid.

11. For more on firsts and industrial ideological change, see Todd Gitlin, "Prime Time Ideology: The Hegemonic Process of Television Entertainment," in *Television: The Critical View*, ed. Horace Newcomb (New York: Oxford University Press, 2000).

12. Bradley Thompson, telephone interview, January 31, 2015.

13. Moore interview; Thompson interview.

14. Thompson interview.

15. "*The Shield*," Peabody Awards, accessed April 11, 2016, http://www.peabodyawards.com/award-profile/the-shield.

16. Deborah L. Jaramillo, "AMC Stumbling toward a New Television Canon," *Television & New Media* 14, no. 2 (March 1, 2013): 167–83, https://doi:10.1177/1527476412442105.

17. Jason Mittell, "Forensic Fandom and the Drillable Text," *Spreadable Media*, accessed December 6, 2015, http://spreadablemedia.org/essays/mittell/.

18. Damon Lindelof, personal interview, June 7, 2015.

19. Ibid.

20. Ibid.

21. Ibid.

22. It's worth noting that at this time, ABC's executives faced overhaul at the top, and the new president of the network was able to take credit for *Lost* and *Desperate Housewives*, even though they were developed by his predecessor. This factor helped to perpetuate the discourse of ABC as a place for fresh ideas and risks in 2004.

23. Robert Bianco, "A Good Season, with Reason," USAToday.com, April 27, 2005, http://usatoday30.usatoday.com/life/television/news/2005-04-26-tv-lookback_x.htm.

24. Lynn Schofield Clark, "You Lost Me: Mystery, Fandom, and Religion in ABC's *Lost*," in *Small Screen, Big Picture: Television and Lived Religion*, ed. Diane Winston (Waco, TX: Baylor University Press, 2009), 323.

25. Gregg Nations, telephone interview, April 24, 2015.

26. Ibid.

27. Lindelof interview.

28. Ibid.

29. Bianco, "A Good Season."

30. Of course, Lindelof and Nations might have been painting a rosier picture of the network that was reality, since both are still working in the industry, but Lindelof, at least, by virtue of his persona and success with HBO/clout within the industry, seems to have little reason to fear.

31. Lindelof interview.

32. For example: Tiffany Vogt, "TV Watchtower: Is Religion Killing Good Sci-Fi Shows?," Airlock Alpha, October 19, 2010, http://airlockalpha.com/node/7945/tv-watchtower-is-religion-killing-good-sci-fi-shows.html.

33. Deborah L. Jaramillo, "The Family Racket: AOL Time Warner, HBO, *The Sopranos*, and the Construction of a Quality Brand," *Journal of Communication Inquiry* 26, no. 1 (January 1, 2002): 59–75.

34. Marisa Guthrie, "HBO Not 'Hung' Up on Decision-Making," *Broadcasting & Cable* 139, no. 23 (June 8, 2009): 34.

35. Lacey Rose, "FX Chief: 'HBO and FX Absolutely Dominated the Race for Quality in Television,'" *Hollywood Reporter*, January 18, 2015, http://www.hollywoodreporter.com/live-feed/fx-chief-hbo-fx-absolutely-764581; Tim Appelo, "Emmys: How AMC Became HBO's Nightmare," *Hollywood Reporter*, June 18, 2011, http://www.hollywoodreporter.com/news/emmys-how-amc-became-hbos-203084.

36. Todd Spangler, "As Netflix Rises, Subscriptions to HBO, Showtime and Other Premium Nets Shrink as Percentage of U.S. Households: Report," *Variety*, January 20, 2014, http://variety.com/2014/digital/news/as-netflix-rises-more-people-are-canceling-hbo-and-showtime-1201065399/.

37. Mark Shanahan, "Adaptation: Tom Perrotta Is Growing Accustomed to Seeing His Books on the Big Screen," *Boston.com*, October 18, 2006, http://archive.boston.com/news/globe/living/articles/2006/10/18/adaptation/.

38. Damon Lindelof, personal interview, June 7, 2015.

39. Ibid.

40. Ibid.

41. Ibid.

42. "Pilot," *The Leftovers*.

43. Ibid.

44. Joanna Robinson, "How the Emotionally Satisfying *Leftovers* Finale Learned from the Mistakes of *Lost*," *Vanity Fair*, December 7, 2015, http://www.vanityfair.com/hollywood/2015/12/leftovers-finale-damon-lindelof-lost; "From *Lost* to *Leftovers*, Show Creators Embrace Ambiguity and the Unknown," NPR.org, accessed April 12, 2016, http://www.npr.org/2015/12/02/458143133/from-lost-to-leftovers-show-creators-embrace-ambiguity-and-the-unknown.

45. Alan Sepinwall, "Review: *The Leftovers* Is Still TV's Best Drama as Season 2 Begins," *HitFix*, September 30, 2015, http://www.hitfix.com/whats-alan-watching/review-the-leftovers-is-still-tvs-best-drama-as-season-2-begins.

46. Daniel McDermon, "*The Leftovers* Recap: What Happened to Gladys," *ArtsBeat*, 1406541640, http://artsbeat.blogs.nytimes.com/2014/07/28/the-leftovers-recap-what-happened-to-gladys/.

47. "The Prodigal Son Returns," *The Leftovers*.

48. Tsvetan Todorov, "The Fantastic: A Structural Approach to a Literary Genre," in *Fantastic Literature: A Critical Reader* by Tsvetan Todorov. (Westport, CT: Praeger, 2004), 136.

49. Barker, "Sophomore Jump."

50. Jordan Smith, "Our Thoughts, Hopes, and Worries about Seth Rogen's *Preacher* Series," Hollywood.com, February 7, 2014, http://www.hollywood.com/news/tv/56778818/seth-rogen-evan-goldeberg-preacher-amc.

51. Denise Petski, "*Preacher* AMC Drama Series Gets Premiere Date," *Deadline*, March 14, 2016, http://deadline.com/2016/03/preacher-amc-drama-series-premiere-date-1201719886/.

52. Rob Allstetter, "Mark Steven Johnson: No *Preacher* on HBO," *Comics Continuum*, August 25, 2008, http://www.comicscontinuum.com/stories/0808/25/index.htm?loc=interstitialskip; Peter Sciretta, "HBO Kills *Preacher* Television Series." *Slashfilm*, August 26, 2008, http://www.slashfilm.com/hbo-kills-preacher-television-series/.

53. Allstetter.

54. Eric Vespe, "Quint talks *Neighbors, Deleted Scenes and Preacher* with Seth Rogen and Evan Goldberg!", *Ain't It Cool News*, March 12, 2014, http://www.aintitcool.com/node/66516.

55. Ibid.

56. Dominic Patten, "'The Walking Dead' Ratings: More Cable Records In Live+3 Results," *Deadline*, October 17, 2014, http://deadline.com/2014/10/the-walking-dead-premiere-ratings-new-cable-record-season-5-853406/.

57. Garth Ennis, correspondence.

58. Ted Johnson. "New Campaign Addresses Violence in Media." *Variety*, February 27, 2013, http://variety.com/2013/tv/news/new-campaign-addresses-violence-in-media-820084/; "Valenti: TV Reducing Violence." *Variety*, November 8, 1993, http://variety.com/1993/tv/columns/valenti-tv-reducing-violence-115701/.

59. Ennis, personal correspondence, May 1, 2015.

60. Patten, "*The Walking Dead.*"

Chapter 6

1. Matthew Hills, *Fan Cultures* (New York: Routledge, 2004), 43.

2. See Karen A. Ritzenhoff and Angela Krewani, eds., *The Apocalypse in Film: Dystopias, Disasters, and Other Visions about the End of the World* (Lanham, MD: Rowman & Littlefield, 2015); Jeffrey M. Tripp, "Gabriel, Abortion, and Anti-Annunciation in *The Prophecy, Constantine*, and *Legion*," *Journal of Religion and Popular Culture* 27, no. 1 (2015): 57–70.; Maaheen Ahmed and Martin Lund, "Apocalypse Why? The Neutralisation of the Antichrist in Three Comics Adaptations," *Scan: Journal of Media Arts Culture* 9, no. 1 (2012), http://scan.net.au/scn/journal/vol9number1/Maaheen-Ahmed-and-Martin-Lund.html; Torin Monahan, "Marketing the Beast: Left Behind and the Apocalypse Industry," *Media, Culture & Society* 30, no. 6 (November 1, 2008): 813–30, doi:10.1177/0163443708096095; W. Andy Knight, "Eschatology, Religion and World Order," *Religious Studies and Theology* 29, no. 1 (2010): 1–24, doi:10.1558/rsth.v29i1.1.

3. Both shows feature many catastrophes called "the apocalypse" but do not use the biblical version or its characters explicitly. Thus, they are not part of this grouping.

4. Jon R. Stone, "A Fire in the Sky: 'Apocalyptic' Themes on the Silver Screen," in *God in the Details: American Religion in Popular Culture*, 2nd edition, ed. Eric Michael Mazur and Kate McCarthy (New York: Routledge, 2011), 64.

5. Ritzenhoff and Krewani, "Introduction," in *The Apocalypse in Film*, xiii.

6. Lisa McMinn, "Y2K, The Apocalypse, and Evangelical Christianity: The Role of Eschatological Belief in Church Responses," *Sociology of Religion* 62, no. 2 (2001):208, doi:10.2307/3712456.

7. Ibid., 188.

8. Peter Gardella, *American Angels: Useful Spirits in the Material World* (Lawrence: University Press of Kansas, 2007), 2.

9. Laura Prudom, "*Supernatural* at 200: The Road So Far, an Oral History," *Variety*, November 11, 2014, http://variety.com/2014/tv/spotlight/supernatural-oral-history-200-episodes-ackles-padalecki-kripke-1201352537/; "Ratings—*Smallville* and *Supernatural* on the Rise, Performing at or Near Season Highs," *Futon Critic*, October 31, 2008, http://www.thefutoncritic.com/ratings/2008/10/31/smallville-and-supernatural-on-the-rise-performing-at-or-near-season-highs-29378/20081031cw01/.

10. Prudom, "*Supernatural*"; Matt Webb Mitovich, "*Smallville, Supernatural* Returns Delayed a Week," *TVLine*, January 28, 2011, http://tvline.com/2011/01/27/smallville-supernatural-returns-delayed-a-week/; Ken Tucker, "The CW's Identity Crisis: Are *Supernatural* and *Smallville* Better Than *Gossip Girl* and *90210*?," *Entertainment Weekly's* EW.com, February 26, 2010, http://www.ew.com/article/2010/02/26/cw-smallville-supernatural-smallville-gossip-girl-90210.

11. Mike Flacy, "Netflix Cuts Deal for *Supernatural* and Other CW Shows," *Digital Trends*, October 13, 2011, http://www.digitaltrends.com/home-theater/netflix-cuts-deal-for-supernatural-and-other-cw-shows/.

12. I want to note that the iterative mode of storytelling that this plot point exemplifies may connect with Christian theology's artistic trope of prefiguration in which stories, images, and people from before the time of Christ are reconfigured as foreshadowing Jesus's coming.

13. Freidric Jameson, "Postmodernism, or the Cultural Logic of Late Capitalism," in *Media and Cultural Studies: Key Works,* rev. edition, ed. Douglas M. Kellner and Meenakshi Gigi Durham (Malden, MA: Blackwell, 2006), 493.

14. Prudom, "*Supernatural*"; Liana Bekakos, "*Supernatural* Creator Eric Kripke Answers Fan's Questions—Part III," *EclipseMagazine*, accessed April 12, 2016, http://eclipsemagazine.com/supernatural-creator-eric-kripke-answers-fan%E2%80%99s-questions-%E2%80%93-part-iii/

15. Maureen Ryan, "'It's the Fun Apocalypse': Creator Eric Kripke Talks *Supernatural—* The Watcher," *Chicago Tribune*, August 26, 2009, http://featuresblogs.chicagotribune.com/entertainment_tv/2009/08/supernatural-season-5-eric-kripke-cw.html.

16. Prudom, "*Supernatural.*"

17. Elizabeth G. Wolfe, "The Greatest of These: The Theological Virtues and the Problem of an Absent God in *Supernatural*," in *"Supernatural," Humanity, and the Soul*, ed. Susan A. George and Regina M. Hansen (New York: Palgrave Macmillan, 2014), 13–26; Charlotte E. Howell, "God, the Devil, and John Winchester: Failures of Patriarchy in *Supernatural*," in *"Supernatural," Humanity, and the Soul*, ed. Susan A. George and Regina M. Hansen (New York: Palgrave Macmillan, 2014), 13–26; Regina M. Hansen, "Deconstructing the Apocalypse? *Supernatural*'s Postmodern Appropriation of Angelic Hierarchies," in *"Supernatural," Humanity, and the Soul*, ed. Susan A. George and Regina M. Hansen (New York: Palgrave Macmillan, 2014), 13–26; Erika Engstrom and Joseph M. Valenzano, "Demon Hunters and Hegemony: Portrayal of Religion on The CW's *Supernatural*," *Journal of Media and Religion* 9, no. 2 (April 30, 2010): 67–83; Annalee Newitz, "Is *Supernatural* for Atheists?," May 21, 1009, http://io9.com/5265112/is-supernatural-for-atheists.

18. Anonymous writer C, telephone interview, September 16, 2014.

19. Anonymous writer B, personal correspondence, May 20, 2015.

20. Barbara Selznick, "Branding the Future: Syfy in the Post-Network Era," *Science Fiction Film and Television* 2, no. 2 (2009): 177.

21. Marisa Guthrie, "Syfy's Two-Pronged Rebrand Strategy," *Broadcasting & Cable*, June 21, 2009, http://www.broadcastingcable.com/news/programming/syfys-two-pronged-rebrand-strategy/34994.

22. Selznick, "Branding the Future," 196; James Hibberd, "Syfy Plans to Lure You Back with These 5 Shows," *Entertainment Weekly's* EW.com, October 28, 2014, http://www.ew.com/article/2014/10/28/syfy.

23. Rowan Kaiser, "Syfy Is De-Rebranding and It's the Most Compelling Thing on TV," *Inverse*, November 19, 2015, https://www.inverse.com/article/8354-syfy-is-releasing-a-film-de-rebranding-and-becoming-super-interesting.

24. Hibberd, "Syfy Plans to Lure You."

25. Ibid.

26. Ibid; Elizabeth Wagmeister, "Syfy Cancels *Dominion* after Two Seasons," *Variety*, October 13, 2015, http://variety.com/2015/tv/news/dominion-cancelled-syfy-season-two-1201617277/.

27. Brusta Brown and JM Todd, interview, April 23, 2015.

28. Ibid.

29. Mythology has also colloquially become used for the general serial narrative, very likely based on its use in reference to the alien-mystery-based episodes of *The X-Files* (Fox, 1993–2002).

30. Brown and Todd interview.

31. Ibid.

32. Ibid.

33. Ibid.

34. Brian Lowry, "TV Review: *Constantine*," *Variety*, October 22, 2014, http://variety.com/2014/tv/reviews/tv-review-constantine-1201331412/; Steven Schneider, "Why NBC's *Constantine* Will Make You Forget about Keanu Reeves," *Tech Times*, October 24, 2014, http://www.techtimes.com/articles/18659/20141024/why-nbcs-constantine-will-make-you-forget-about-keanu-reeves.htm; Roger Ebert, "*Constantine* Movie Review & Film Summary (2005)," RogerEbert.com, accessed April 16, 2016, http://www.rogerebert.com/reviews/constantine-2005.

35. Garth Ennis, personal correspondence, May 1, 2015.

36. Diane Haithman, "*Grimm* Producers Consider What Makes a 'Breakout Hit' and the Friday Night Curse: TCA," *Deadline*, January 6, 2013, http://deadline.com/2013/01/grimm-nbc-tca-david-greenwalt-jim-kouf-397819/; Lowry, "TV Review: *Constantine*"; Jacob Bryant, "David Goyer Doesn't Think *Constantine* Should Have Ended Up at NBC," *Variety*, October 20, 2015, http://variety.com/2015/tv/news/constantine-david-goyer-nbc-arrow-cameo-1201622606/.

37. Nellie Andreeva, "*Constantine* Cancelled by NBC, Will It Find New Life Elsewhere?," *Deadline*, May 8, 2015, http://deadline.com/2015/05/constantine-cancelled-nbc-life-elsewhere-1201423289/.

38. James Hibberd, "*Constantine* Team on Why NBC Character Isn't Bisexual, Smoking Cigarettes," *Entertainment Weekly's* EW.com, July 13, 2014, http://www.ew.com/article/2014/07/13/constantine-bisexual-smoking.

39. See also Bryant, "David Goyer Doesn't Think *Constantine* Should Have Ended Up at NBC.".

40. Mark Verheiden, telephone interview, February 2, 2015.

41. Ibid.

42. Ibid.
43. Ibid.
44. "The Saint of Last Resorts," *Constantine*.
45. Verheiden interview.
46. Ibid.
47. For more information on how crime procedurals have used religion for spectacle, see Kyra Hunting, "Genre's Disciplining Discourses: Cultural Difference and Contemporary Genre Television, " Order No. 3725306, Madison: University of Wisconsin, 2014, *ProQuest*, http://ezproxy.lib.utexas.edu/login?url=http://search.proquest.com/docview/1722488000?accountid=7118.

Part IV

1. Derek Kompare, "Publishing Flow DVD Box Sets and the Reconception of Television," *Television & New Media* 7, no. 4 (November 1, 2006): 335–60, doi:10.1177/1527476404270609.
2. Chuck Tryon, "TV Got Better: Netflix's Original Programming Strategies and the On-Demand Television Transition," *Media Industries* 2, no. 2 (December 27, 2015), http://www.mediaindustriesjournal.org/index.php/mij/article/view/126; T. C. Sottek, "Netflix Challenges the TV Establishment with Emmy Wins for *House of Cards*," *Verge*, September 22, 2013, http://www.theverge.com/2013/9/22/4759754/netflix-challenges-the-tv-establishment-with-emmy-wins-for-house-of; James Poniewozik, "Streaming TV Isn't Just a New Way to Watch. It's a New Genre," *New York Times*, December 16, 2015, http://www.nytimes.com/2015/12/20/arts/television/streaming-tv-isnt-just-a-new-way-to-watch-its-a-new-genre.html.
3. Jaramillo, Deborah L. "The Family Racket: AOL Time Warner, HBO, *The Sopranos*, and the Construction of a Quality Brand." *Journal of Communication Inquiry* 26, no. 1 (January 1, 2002): 59–75; Tryon, "TV Got Better."

Chapter 7

1. Charles Moss, "Daredevil's Greatest Superpower Is His Catholicism," *Slate*, April 10, 2015, http://www.slate.com/articles/arts/culturebox/2015/04/netflix_s_daredevil_show_understands_that_catholicism_is_the_superhero_s.html; Bilal Mian, "*Daredevil*'s Charlie Cox on Becoming a Religious Superhero," *Hollywood Reporter*, April 10, 2015, http://www.hollywoodreporter.com/live-feed/daredevils-charlie-cox-becoming-a-787809; Jai Tiggett, "Interview: *Hand of God* Creator Ben Watkins Talks Hollywood's Fear of Religion, Creating 360° Portrayals of Black Women, More," *Shadow and Act, IndieWire*, August 27, 2014, http://blogs.indiewire.com/shadowandact/interview-hand-of-god-creator-ben-watkins-talks-hollywoods-fear-of-religion-creating-360-portrayals-of-black-women-more-20140827; Meghan O'Keefe, "Amazon Fall Pilot Season: *Hand of God* Is Disturbing and Ridiculous," *Decider*, August 28, 2014, http://decider.com/2014/08/28/amazon-hand-of-god/.

2. Moss, "Daredevil's Greatest Strength"; Mian, "*Daredevil's* Charlie Cox."

3. Gavia Baker-Whitelaw, "Decoding the Artistic Inspiration behind *Daredevil's* Gorgeous Season 2 Posters," *Daily Dot*, March 15, 2016, http://www.dailydot.com/geek/daredevil-season-2-caravaggio-posters/.

4. Michael Curtin, "On Edge: Culture Industries in the Neo Network Era," in *The Media Studies Reader*, 1st edition, ed. Laurie Ouellette, (New York: Routledge, 2013).

5. See Chuck Tryon, "TV Got Better: Netflix's Original Programming Strategies and the On-Demand Television Transition," *Media Industries* 2, no. 2 (December 27, 2015), http://www.mediaindustriesjournal.org/index.php/mij/article/view/126.

6. Ibid.

7. Ibid.

8. "Netflix Is Now Available around the World," *Netflix Media Center*, January 6, 2016, https://media.netflix.com/en/press-releases/netflix-is-now-available-around-the-world.

9. Christina Warren, "HANDS ON: Amazon's Prime Instant Video," *Mashable*, February 22, 2011, http://mashable.com/2011/02/22/amazon-prime-instant-video/.

10. Sarah Perez, "Amazon Studios Now Funding Original Content Series for Amazon Instant Video Service," *TechCrunch*, May 2, 2012, http://techcrunch.com/2012/05/02/amazon-studios-now-funding-original-content-series-for-amazon-instant-video-service/.

11. Amazon is also in the business of data in order to target potential customers. For more, see Timothy Havens, "Media Programming in an Era of Big Data," *Media Industries* 1, no. 2 (September 15, 2014), http://www.mediaindustriesjournal.org/index.php/mij/article/view/43.

12. Karen Petruska, "Amazon Prime Video: Where Information Is Entertainment," *From Networks to Netflix: A Guide to Changing Channels*, ed. Derek Johnson (New York: Routledge, 2018), 358.

13. Jeff Baumgartner, "Netflix Has Lowest Churn Rate among OTT Services: Study," *Multichannel News*, April 14, 2016, http://www.multichannel.com/news/content/netflix-has-lowest-churn-rate-among-ott-services-study/404142.

14. Ibid.

15. Michael Malone, "TCA: 'Visionary Creators' Wanted, Says Amazon's Price," *Broadcasting & Cable* (January 11, 2016), http://www.broadcastingcable.com/news/programming/tca-visionary-creators-wanted-says-amazon-s-price/146863.

16. Brad Stone, "Testing Over, Hulu.com to Open Its TV and Film Offerings This Week," *New York Times*, March 11, 2008, http://www.nytimes.com/2008/03/11/business/media/11hulu.html.

17. David Lieberman, "Hulu Introduces $11.99 Commercial-Free Option, but Vows to Boost Ad Sales," *Deadline*, September 2, 2015, http://deadline.com/2015/09/hulu-ad-free-service-1201512438/.

18. Brian Stelter, "Hulu Makes History with Emmy Wins," CNNMoney, September 18, 2017, https://money.cnn.com/2017/09/18/media/hulu-emmy-win/index.html.

19. Amanda D. Lotz, *Portals: A Treatise on Internet-Distributed Television* (Ann Arbor, MI: Maize Books, 2017).

20. "EmmyWinnersandNominees2013:TheCompleteList," *HollywoodReporter*, September 22,2013,http://www.hollywoodreporter.com/news/emmy-winners-nominees-2013-complete-633769.

21. Jon Weisman, "Emmy Nominations Announced: *House of Cards* Makes History," *Variety*, July 18, 2013, http://variety.com/2013/tv/awards/emmy-nominees-2013-emmys-awards-nominations-full-list-1200564301/.

22. T. C. Sottek, "Netflix Challenges the TV Establishment with Emmy Wins for *House of Cards*," *Verge*, September 22, 2013, http://www.theverge.com/2013/9/22/4759754/netflix-challenges-the-tv-establishment-with-emmy-wins-for-house-of."

23. Matt Hills, *Fan Cultures* (New York: Routledge, 2002), 27.

24. Interview with Ruth Fletcher Gage and Carlos Gage.

25. Ibid.

26. Ibid.

27. Ibid.

28. Ibid.

29. Ibid.

30. Ibid.

31. Ibid.

32. Ibid.

33. "Speak of the Devil," *Daredevil*.

34. Gage interview.

35. Kate O'Hare, "How Catholic IS *Marvel's Daredevil* on Netflix?," *Patheos*, April 10, 2015, http://www.patheos.com/blogs/kateohare/2015/04/how-catholic-is-marvels-daredevil-on-netflix/; Brad Miner, "Daredevil and the Devil," *Catholic Thing*, May 18, 2015, https://www.thecatholicthing.org/2015/05/18/daredevil-and-the-devil/; Moss, "Daredevil's Greatest Superpower"; Mian, "*Daredevil's* Charlie Cox."

36. Gage interview.

37. O'Hare, "How Catholic IS *Marvel's Daredevil?*"; Miner, "Daredevil and the Devil"; Moss, "Daredevil's Greatest Superpower"; Mian, "*Daredevil's* Charlie Cox."

38. Gage interview; O'Hare, "How Catholic IS *Marvel's Daredevil?*"; Miner, "Daredevil and the Devil."

39. Evan Valentine, "*Daredevil* Season 1 Episode 9 'Speak of the Devil' Recap," *Collider*, May 7, 2015, http://collider.com/daredevil-season-1-episode-9-speak-of-the-devil-recap/.

40. Moss, "Daredevil's Greatest Superpower."

41. Mian, "'*Daredevil's* Charlie Cox .'"

42. Carolyn Newman, telephone interview, January 13, 2015.

43. Ibid.

44. Hills, *Fan Cultures*, 65.

45. "Public Radio Audience Demographics—NPR Profiles," National Public Media, accessed May 18, 2015, http://nationalpublicmedia.com/npr/audience/.

46. James Poniewozik, "Streaming TV Isn't Just a New Way to Watch. It's a New Genre," *New York Times*, December 16, 2015, http://www.nytimes.com/2015/12/20/arts/television/streaming-tv-isnt-just-a-new-way-to-watch-its-a-new-genre.html; Alan

Sepinwall, "Review: Amazon's *Transparent* Clearly the Best New Show of the Fall," *HitFix*, September 24, 2014, http://www.hitfix.com/whats-alan-watching/review-amazons-transparent-clearly-the-best-new-show-of-the-fall; Emily Nussbaum, "Open Secret," *New Yorker*, September 29, 2014, http://www.newyorker.com/magazine/2014/09/29/open-secret; Lori Rackl, "Chicago Native Jill Soloway Creates Season's Best New Show, *Transparent*," *Chicago Sun-Times*, September 25, 2014, http://chicago.suntimes.com/entertainment/chicago-native-jill-soloway-creates-seasons-best-new-show-transparent/; Willa Paskin, "See Me: *Transparent* Is the Fall's Only Great New Show," *Slate*, September 29, 2014, http://www.slate.com/articles/arts/television/2014/09/transparent_on_amazon_prime_reviewed_it_s_the_fall_s_best_new_show.html.

47. Jeff Bercovici, "Science Settles It: NPR's Liberal, but Not Very," *Forbes*, March 22, 2011, http://www.forbes.com/sites/jeffbercovici/2011/03/22/science-settles-it-nprs-liberal-but-not-very/.

48. Jane Feuer, "The MTM Style," *MTM "Quality Television*," ed. Jane Feuer, Paul Kerr, and Tise Vahimagi (London: British Film Institute, 1984), 56.

49. Henry Jenkins, Joshua Benjamin Green, and Sam Ford, *Spreadable Media: Creating Value and Meaning in a Networked Culture* (New York: NYU Press, 2012).

50. Marisa Guthrie, "HBO Inks Exclusive Deal with Amazon Prime," *Hollywood Reporter*, April 23, 2014, http://www.hollywoodreporter.com/news/hbo-inks-deal-amazon-prime-698379.

51. Natalie Jarvey, "Amazon Studios' Roy Price Reveals Series Orders (Q&A)," *Hollywood Reporter*, March 31, 2014, http://www.hollywoodreporter.com/news/amazon-studios-roy-price-reveals-687846.

52. Newman interview.

53. Cael Keegan, "Op-Ed: How *Transparent* Tried and Failed to Represent Trans Men," *Advocate*, October 22, 2014, http://www.advocate.com/commentary/2014/10/22/op-ed-how-transparent-tried-and-failed-represent-trans-men; Margy Rochlin, "In *Transparent*, a Heroine Evolves Further Still," *New York Times*, November 27, 2015, http://www.nytimes.com/2015/11/29/arts/television/in-transparent-a-heroine-evolves-further-still.html; Ryan Gajewski, "Emmys: *Transparent*'s Jeffrey Tambor, Jill Soloway Speak Out about Transgender Issues," *Hollywood Reporter*, September 20, 2015, http://www.hollywoodreporter.com/news/emmys-transparents-jeffrey-tambor-jill-825280; Malina Saval, "Jeffrey Tambor on *Transparent*: 'People's Lives Depend on This,'" *Variety*, March 18, 2016, http://variety.com/2016/scene/vpage/transparent-jeffrey-tambor-j-j-abrams-man-on-the-land-1201733683/.

54. Hilary Lewis, "Amazon Orders 5 New Series Including *Man in the High Castle*," *Hollywood Reporter*, February 18, 2015, http://www.hollywoodreporter.com/news/amazon-orders-5-new-series-774725.

55. Laura Wagner, "New York Subway Pulls Nazi-Themed Ads for New Show, *Man in the High Castle*," NPR.org, November 25, 2015, http://www.npr.org/sections/thetwo-way/2015/11/25/457410075/new-york-subway-pulls-nazi-themed-ads-for-new-show-the-man-in-the-high-castle.

56. Tiggett interview.

57. Ibid.
58. Ibid.
59. Ben Watkins, "How I Wish This Wasn't True. https://twitter.com/mrmilitantnegro/status/600130681620955136 . . . ," microblog, @_Benipedia_(May 18, 2015),https://twitter.com/_Benipedia_/status/600131248426586113.
60. Ron Perlman, "Me Explaining to @_benipedia_ Why I Prefer Acting While Standing on 1 Foot . . . , https://instagram.com/p/3MVRkoonps/." Microblog. @perlmutations, May 27, 2015, accessed May 28, 2015, https://twitter.com/perlmutations/status/603604200321318912.
61. Tiggett interview.
62. Newman interview.
63. Amanda D. Lotz, *The Television Will Be Revolutionized* (New York: NYU Press, 2007).
64. Adam Flomenbaum, "How Nielsen Social Is Measuring the Evolution of Social TV," *AdWeek*, January 26, 2015, http://adweek.it/1yVjb0w; Andrew Wallenstein, "Variety to Publish Weekly TV and Film Fan Engagement Measurement Combining All Major Digital Platforms," *Variety*, September 2, 2014, http://variety.com/2014/digital/news/variety-to-publish-weekly-tv-and-film-fan-engagement-measurement-combining-all-major-digital-platforms-1201294076/.
65. Newman interview.

Conclusion

1. Lynn Spigel, *Welcome to the Dreamhouse: Popular Media and Postwar Suburbs* (Durham, NC: Duke University Press, 2001); Catherine Johnson, *Telefantasy* (London: British Film Institute, 2005).
2. Lisa Gitelman, *Always Already New: Media, History, and the Data of Culture* (Cambridge, MA: MIT Press, 2006), 6.
3. Joe Otterson, "ABC Head Channing Dungey Says Donald Trump Made Her Rethink Programming Strategy," TheWrap, December 2, 2016, https://www.thewrap.com/abc-channing-dungey-donald-trump-programming/; Alex Ritman, "ABC Entertainment Chief: Network Hasn't Paid Enough Attention to 'True Realities' of America," Hollywood Reporter, December 2, 2016, https://www.hollywoodreporter.com/news/abc-entertainment-chief-network-hasnt-paid-attention-true-realities-america-952189.
4. David Canfield, "On CBS during Election Season, Viewers Watched Trump's America in Prime Time," *Slate*, November 29, 2016, http://www.slate.com/blogs/browbeat/2016/11/29/how_cbs_s_2016_shows_catered_to_trump_s_america.html.
5. Joanne Ostrow, "How Will NBC's *The Good Place* Tackle Religion?," *Hollywood Reporter*, September 15, 2016, https://www.hollywoodreporter.com/live-feed/good-place-religion-explained-mike-schur-interview-927402; Jeremy Egner, "Michael Schur on *The Good Place*, Ted Danson and Kantian Ethics," *New York Times*, January 18, 2017, sec. Television, https://www.nytimes.com/2017/01/18/arts/television/michael-schur-on-the-good-place-ted-danson-and-kantian-ethics.html; Nicholas

Carlson and Anna Mazarakis, "*The Good Place* Creator Talks Morality and His Unique Concept of the Afterlife," INSIDER, October 5, 2017, http://www.thisisinsider.com/ good-place-michael-schur-interview-showrunners-2017-10; Anna Menta, "How *The Good Place* Is Revolutionizing the TV Sitcom," *Newsweek*, October 19, 2017, http://www.newsweek.com/good-place-mike-schur-interview-688754.

6. Charles Pulliam-Moore, "*American Gods*' Jesus Shows What Happens When a God Becomes Too Popular," io9, June 20, 2017, https://io9.gizmodo.com/ american-gods-jesus-shows-what-happens-when-a-god-becom-1796255952.

7. Denise Petski, "*Messiah*: Netflix Orders Religious Drama Series from Mark Burnett & Roma Downey," *Deadline* (blog), November 16, 2017, http://deadline.com/2017/ 11/messiah-netflix-orders-drama-series-mark-burnett-roma-downey-james-mcteigue-direct-1202208898/.

8. Nellie Andreeva, "*Good Christian Bitches* Dramedy Based on Book in Works at The CW with Leila Cohan-Miccio, Darren Star & Kapital," *Deadline* (blog), November 29, 2018, https://deadline.com/2018/11/good-christian-bitches-dramedy-based-on-book-the-cw-leila-cohan-micci-darren-star-aaron-kaplan-1202510743/.

9. Ibid.

10. Ibid.

Bibliography

Acosta-Alzuru, Carolina. "Tackling the Issues: Meaning Making in a Telenovela." *Popular Communication* 1, no. 4 (December 2003): 193–215.

Adalian, Josef. "Anatomy of a Hit: Why *Sleepy Hollow* Became Fall TV's Breakout Success." *Vulture*, October 14, 2013. http://www.vulture.com/2013/10/why-fox-sleepy-hollow-breakout-hit.html.

Adalian, Josef. "There Were Over 400 Scripted TV Shows on the Air in 2015." *Vulture*, December 16, 2015. http://www.vulture.com/2015/12/scripted-tv-shows-2015.html.

Adalian, Josef, and Maria Elena Fernandez. "The Business of Too Much TV." *Vulture*, May 18, 2016. http://www.vulture.com/2016/05/peak-tv-business-c-v-r.html.

Ahmed, Maaheen, and Martin Lund. "Apocalypse Why? The Neutralisation of the Antichrist in Three Comics Adaptations." *Scan: Journal of Media Arts Culture* 9, no. 1 (2012). http://scan.net.au/scn/journal/vol9number1/Maaheen-Ahmed-and-Martin-Lund.html.

Akin, Jimmy. "Jesus' Mysterious Prophecy about the Temple." *National Catholic Register*, April 27, 2017. http://www.ncregister.com/blog/jimmy-akin/jesus-mysterious-prophecy-about-the-temple.

Alarcón, Antonio V. Menéndez. "Latin American Culture: A Deconstruction of Stereotypes." *Studies in Latin American Popular Culture* 32, no. 1 (May 21, 2014): 72–96.

Albanesius, Chloe. "Hulu Inks Distribution Deal for Original Shows." *PCMAG*, March 12, 2012. http://www.pcmag.com/article2/0,2817,2401453,00.asp.

Allen, Emma. "Prime-Time Scripture; Swords and Sandals." *New Yorker*, March 18, 2013.

Allstetter, Rob. "Mark Steven Johnson: No *Preacher* on HBO." *Comics Continuum*, August 25, 2008. http://www.comicscontinuum.com/stories/0808/25/index.htm?loc=interstitialskip.

Anders, Charlie Jane. "The Biggest Winners and Losers of Comic-Con 2015!" *io9*, July 13, 2015. http://io9.com/the-biggest-winners-and-losers-of-comic-con-2015-1717547126.

Andersen, Kurt. "I Want My HBO." *NYMag.com*, 2004. http://nymag.com/nymetro/news/columns/imperialcity/12199/.

Andreeva, Nellie. "*Constantine* Cancelled by NBC, Will It Find New Life Elsewhere?" *Deadline*, May 8, 2015. http://deadline.com/2015/05/constantine-cancelled-nbc-life-elsewhere-1201423289/.

Andreeva, Nellie. "Full Series Rankings for the 2009–10 Broadcast Season." *Deadline*, May 28, 2010. http://deadline.com/2010/05/full-series-rankings-for-the-2009-10-broadcast-season-44277/.

Andreeva, Nellie. "Full 2011–2012 TV Season Series Rankings." *Deadline*, May 25, 2012. http://deadline.com/2012/05/full-2011-2012-tv-season-series-rankings-277941/.

Andreeva, Nellie. "Golden Globes TV: The CW, Cinemax & Amazon Arrive to Awards Party." *Deadline* (blog), December 11, 2014. http://deadline.com/2014/12/golden-globes-tv-analysis-jane-the-virgin-transparent-1201320225/.

Andreeva, Nellie. "*Good Christian Bitches* Dramedy Based on Book in Works at The CW with Leila Cohan-Miccio, Darren Star & Kapital." *Deadline* (blog), November 29, 2018. https://deadline.com/2018/11/good-christian-bitches-dramedy-based-on-book-the-cw-leila-cohan-micci-darren-star-aaron-kaplan-1202510743/.

Ang, Ien. *Desperately Seeking the Audience*. London: Routledge, 1991.

Ang, Ien. *Living Room Wars: Rethinking Media Audiences for a Postmodern World*. New York: Routledge, 1996.

Appelo, Tim. "Emmys: How AMC Became HBO's Nightmare." *Hollywood Reporter*, June 18, 2011. http://www.hollywoodreporter.com/news/emmys-how-amc-became-hbos-203084.

Arceneaux, Kevin, and Stephen P. Nicholson. "Who Wants to Have a Tea Party? The Who, What, and Why of the Tea Party Movement." *PS: Political Science and Politics* 45, no. 4 (2012): 700–10.

Baker-Whitelaw, Gavia. "Decoding the Artistic Inspiration behind *Daredevil*'s Gorgeous Season 2 Posters." *Daily Dot*, March 15, 2016. http://www.dailydot.com/geek/daredevil-season-2-caravaggio-posters/.

Balderston, Michael. "SXSW: Seth Rogen and Evan Goldberg on Their Pilots at HBO, AMC and FX (Video)." *TheWrap*, March 10, 2014. http://www.thewrap.com/seth-rogen-evan-goldberg-developing-pilots-hbo-amc-fx/.

Banet-Weiser, Sarah. *Authentic TM: The Politics and Ambivalence in a Brand Culture*. New York: NYU Press, 2012.

Barker, Cory. "Sophomore Jump: How *The Leftovers* Became the Best Show on TV." TV. com, December 3, 2015. http://www.tv.com/shows/the-leftovers/community/post/the-leftovers-season-2-improvement-144907112784/.

Baron, Steve. "Live+7 Ratings: Complete 2014–15 Season *The Big Bang Theory* Leads Adults 18–49 Ratings Increase; *The Messengers* Earns Biggest Percentage Increase, *The Blacklist* Tops Viewership Gains." TV by the Numbers by zap2it.com, June 8, 2015. http://tvbythenumbers.zap2it.com/2015/06/08/live7-dvr-ratings-complete-2014-15-season-the-big-bang-theory-leads-adults-18-49-ratings-increase-raising-hope-earns-biggest-percentage-increase-the-blacklist-tops-viewership-gains/.

Bart, Peter. "A Letter to Mark Burnett: Faith-Based Films vs. Culture Wars." *Variety* (blog), March 13, 2014. http://variety.com/2014/voices/columns/heres-some-advice-for-mark-burnett-as-the-prolific-tv-producer-embarks-on-faith-based-campaign-1201129663/.

"*Battlestar Galactica*." Peabody Awards. Accessed April 11, 2016. http://www.peabodyawards.com/award-profile/battlestar-galactica.

Baumgartner, Jeff. "Netflix Has Lowest Churn Rate among OTT Services: Study." *Multichannel News*, April 14, 2016. http://www.multichannel.com/news/content/netflix-has-lowest-churn-rate-among-ott-services-study/404142.

Becker, Ron. "Prime-Time Television in the Gay Nineties." In *The Television Studies Reader*, edited by Annette Hill and Robert C. Allen, 389–403. New York: Routledge, 2004.

Becker, Ron. *Gay TV and Straight America*. New Brunswick, NJ: Rutgers University Press, 2006.

Bekakos, Liana. "*Supernatural* Creator Eric Kripke Answers Fan's Questions—Part III." *Eclipse Magazine*. Accessed April 12, 2016. http://eclipsemagazine.com/supernatural-creator-eric-kripke-answers-fan%E2%80%99s-questions-%E2%80%93-part-iii/.

Bellafante, Ginia. "A *Friday Night Lights* Farewell." *ArtsBeat*, July 16, 2011. http://artsbeat.blogs.nytimes.com/2011/07/16/a-friday-night-lights-farewell/.

Bercovici, Jeff. "Science Settles It: NPR's Liberal, but Not Very." *Forbes*, March 22, 2011. http://www.forbes.com/sites/jeffbercovici/2011/03/22/science-settles-it-nprs-liberal-but-not-very/.

Berkshire, Geoff. "*Jane the Virgin*: Golden Globe Afterglow Gives Boost to Show, CW." *Variety* (blog), December 12, 2014. http://variety.com/2014/tv/awards/jane-the-virgin-golden-globe-nominations-cw-1201377695/.

Bianco, Robert. "A Good Season, with Reason." *USAToday.com*, April 27, 2005. http://usatoday30.usatoday.com/life/television/news/2005-04-26-tv-lookback_x.htm.

Birnbaum, Debra. "Her OWN Woman." *Variety*, October 6, 2015.

"Black Women Help OWN Achieve Its Second Year of Double-Digit Growth." *Chicago Citizen,* January 15, 2014.

Blake, Meredith. "Oprah Winfrey's Megachurch Series *Greenleaf* 'Takes Faith Really Seriously.'" *Los Angeles Times*, April 21, 2016. http://www.latimes.com/entertainment/tv/showtracker/la-et-st-oprah-winfrey-greenleaf-20160420-story.html.

Blake, Meredith. "Television Puts More Faith in Religious-Themed Projects." *Los Angeles Times*, March 28, 2015. http://www.latimes.com/entertainment/la-et-st-religious-shows-television-killing-jesus-dovekeepers-20150329-story.html#page=1.

Boboltz, Sara. "Mark Burnett Presents: A Donald Trump Inauguration Day." *Huffington Post*, December 9, 2016, sec. Arts & Culture. http://www.huffingtonpost.com/entry/mark-burnett-presents-a-donald-trump-inauguration-day_us_58495e9ae4b0f9723d005efc.

Booker, M. Keith. *Science Fiction Television*. Westport, CT: Praeger, 2004.

Bordwell, David, Janet Staiger and Kristen Thompson. *The Classical Hollywood Cinema: Film Style and Mode of Production to 1960*. New York: Columbia University Press, 1985.

Bottomley, Andrew J. "Quality TV and the Branding of U.S. Network Television: Marketing and Promoting *Friday Night Lights*." *Quarterly Review of Film and Video* 32, no. 5 (July 4, 2015): 482–97. doi:10.1080/10509208.2015.1031624.

Bourdieu, Pierre. *Distinction: A Social Critique of the Judgement of Taste*. Cambridge, MA: Harvard University Press, 1984.

Bourdieu, Pierre. *The Field of Cultural Production: Essays on Art and Literature*. New York: Columbia University Press, 1993.Bradley, Laura. "Why Latin Lover Narrator Is the Best Character on *Jane the Virgin*." *Slate*, May 11, 2015. http://www.slate.com/blogs/browbeat/2015/05/11/jane_the_virgin_s_narrator_is_the_best_thing_about_the_cw_show.html.

Brown, Joe. "Religious Conservatives Claim Katrina Was God's Omen, Punishment for the United States." Media Matters for America, October 10, 2007. https://www.mediamatters.org/research/2005/09/13/religious-conservatives-claim-katrina-was-gods/133804.

Brunsdon, Charlotte. "Problems with Quality." *Screen*, no. 31 (1990): 67–90.

Bryant, Jacob. "David Goyer Doesn't Think *Constantine* Should Have Ended Up at NBC." *Variety*, October 20, 2015. http://variety.com/2015/tv/news/constantine-david-goyer-nbc-arrow-cameo-1201622606/.

Bunting, Sarah D. "On The Sixth Day—*Rectify*." *Previously.TV*, May 21, 2013. http://previously.tv/rectify/on-the-sixth-day/.

Burke, Liam. *The Comic Book Film Adaptation: Exploring Modern Hollywood's Leading Genre*. Jackson: University Press of Mississippi, 2015.

Burnett, Mark. "Mark Burnett Op-Ed: *A.D.* Producer on Faith and Hollywood." *Hollywood Reporter*, April 3, 2015. http://www.hollywoodreporter.com/news/mark-burnett-op-ed-ad-786225.

Caldwell, John T. "Cultures of Production: Studying Industry's Deep Texts, Reflexive Rituals, and Managed Self-Disclosures." In *Media Industries: History, Theory, and Method*, edited by Jennifer Holt and Alisa Perren, 1st edition, 199–212. New York: Wiley-Blackwell, 2009.

Caldwell, John T. *Production Culture: Industrial Reflexivity and Critical Practice in Film and Television*. Durham, NC: Duke University Press, 2008.

Caldwell, John Thornton. *Televisuality: Style, Crisis, and Authority in American Television*. New Brunswick, NJ: Rutgers University Press, 1995.

Callahan, Maureen. "TV Shows Are Going Way Too Far to Attract Viewers." *New York Post*, April 10, 2016. http://nypost.com/2016/04/10/in-a-race-to-outshock-the-viewer-quality-shows-become-ever-more-immoral/.

Canfield, David. "On CBS during Election Season, Viewers Watched Trump's America in Prime Time." *Slate*, November 29, 2016. http://www.slate.com/blogs/browbeat/2016/11/29/how_cbs_s_2016_shows_catered_to_trump_s_america.html.

Carlson, Nicholas, and Anna Mazarakis. "*The Good Place* Creator Talks Morality and His Unique Concept of the Afterlife." INSIDER, October 5, 2017. http://www.thisisinsider.com/good-place-michael-schur-interview-showrunners-2017-10.

Carter, Bill. "Reality-TV Producer Mark Burnett Tackles the Bible." *New York Times*, May 24, 2011, sec. Television. https://www.nytimes.com/2011/05/24/arts/television/reality-tv-producer-mark-burnett-tackles-the-bible.html.

CBS News. "Roma Downey and Rachel Brosnahan on *The Dovekeepers*." CBSnews.com, April 1, 2015. Accessed February 5, 2018. https://www.cbsnews.com/news/roma-downey-rachel-brosnahan-dovekeepers-cbs-special/.

Chitwood, Adam. "Evan Goldberg Talks AMC *PREACHER* TV Series, *THE INTERVIEW*, and *CONSOLE WARS*." *Collider*, March 9, 2014. http://collider.com/preacher-tv-news-evan-goldberg/.

Chow-White, Peter A., Danielle Deveau, and Philippa Adams. "Media Encoding in Science Fiction Television: Battlestar Galactica as a Site of Critical Cultural Production." *Media, Culture & Society*, July 22, 2015, 0163443715594031. doi:10.1177/0163443715594031.

Clark, Lynn Schofield. "You Lost Me: Mystery, Fandom, and Religion in ABC's *Lost*." In *Small Screen, Big Picture: Television and Lived Religion*, edited by Diane Winston, 319–41. Waco, TX: Baylor University Press, 2009.

Clarke, Scott H. "Created in Whose Image? Religious Characters on Network Television." *Journal of Media & Religion* 4, no. 3 (July 2005): 137–53. doi:10.1207/s15328415jmr0403_2.

Collier, Aldore D. "Sherman Hemsley and Clifton Davis Return to TV as Stars of Own Show." *Jet*, October 27, 1986.

Collis, Clark. "Why the *Preacher* Producers Trashed Their Original Plans for the Show." *Entertainment Weekly*'s EW.com, May 13, 2016. http://www.ew.com/article/2016/05/13/preacher-seth-rogen-trashed-plans.

Copeland, Kameron J. "From New Black Realism to Tyler Perry: The Characterizations of Black Masculinity in Tyler Perry's Romantic Storylines." *Journal of Men's Studies* 25, no. 1 (March 1, 2017): 70–91. https://doi.org/10.1177/1060826516641096.

Crowley, Karlyn. "New Age Soul: The Gendered Translation of New Age Spirituality on *The Oprah Winfrey Show*." In *Stories of Oprah: The Oprahfication of American Culture*, edited by Trystan T. Cotten and Kimberly Springer, 33–47. Oxford, MS: University Press of Mississippi, 2010.

Curtin, Michael. "Matrix Media." In *Television Studies after TV : Understanding Television in the Post-Broadcast Era*, 1st edition, edited by Graeme Turner and Jinna Tay, 9–19. Hoboken, NJ: Taylor and Francis, 2009.

Curtin, Michael. "On Edge: Culture Industries in the Neo Network Era." In *The Media Studies Reader*, 1st edition, edited by Laurie Ouellette, 275–87. New York: Routledge, 2013.

Cusey, Rebeccca. "Friday Night Gets Religion." *National Review Online*, October 5, 2007. http://www.nationalreview.com/article/222408/friday-night-gets-religion-rebecca-cusey.

"CW Unveils New Art for *The Flash*, *iZombie*, *The Messengers* and *Jane the Virgin*." *Screener* (blog), May 10, 2014. http://screenertv.com/news-features/cw-unveils-new-art-for-the-flash-izombie-the-messengers-and-jane-the-virgin/.

D'Addario, Daniel. "Animal Kingdom and Greenleaf Are Summer Surprises." *Time* 187, no. 24 (June 27, 2016): 51–51.

D'Amour, Zon. "What Do You Believe?" *Los Angeles Sentinel*, June 16, 2016, sec. ENTERTAINMENT.

Daniels, Susanne, and Cynthia Littleton. *Season Finale: The Unexpected Rise and Fall of the WB and UPN*. New York: HarperCollins, 2007.

Dávila, Arlene. "Introduction." In *Contemporary Latina/o Media: Production, Circulation, Politics*, edited by Arlene Dávila and Yeidy M. Rivero, 1–18. New York: NYU Press, 2014.

"DeBartolo Performing Arts Center's Facebook Page," March 26, 2015. https://www.facebook.com/DeBartoloPerformingArtsCenter/photos/a.144465798913331.26377.137427826283795/1089410527752182/?type=1&theater.

Deuze, Mark. *Media Work*. Digital Media and Society Series. Cambridge: Polity Press, 2007.

Diaz, Johnny. "Meet the Family." *Hispanic*, February 2002.

"Does NPR Have a Liberal Bias?" *Columbia Journalism Review*, March 15, 2011. http://www.cjr.org/news_meeting/does_npr_have_a_liberal_bias.php.

Dony, Christophe. "The Rewriting Ethos of the Vertigo Imprint: Critical Perspectives on Memory-Making and Canon Formation in the American Comics Field." *Comicalités: Études de culture graphique*, April 18, 2014. http://comicalites.revues.org/1918.

Douthat, Ross. "The Changing Culture War." *New York Times*, December 6, 2010. http://www.nytimes.com/2010/12/06/opinion/06douthat.html.

Durkheim, Emile. "The Social as Sacred." In *Introducing Religion: Readings from the Classic Theorists*, edited by Daniel L. Pals, 99–142. New York: Oxford University Press, 2009.

Dyer, Richard. *White*. New York: Routledge, 1997.

Easton, Anne. "*Hand of God* Creator on the Personal Grief That Shaped His Dark Amazon Series." *Observer*, September 3, 2015. http://observer.com/2015/09/hand-to-god-creator-on-the-personal-grief-that-shaped-his-dark-amazon-series/.

Eberl, Jason T., and Jennifer A. Vines. "'I Am an Instrument of God': Religious Belief, Atheism, and Meaning." In *"Battlestar Galactica" and Philosophy*, edited by Jason T. Eberl, 155–68. Blackwell, 2007. http://onlinelibrary.wiley.com/doi/10.1002/9780470696460.ch13/summary.

Ebert, Roger. "*Constantine* Movie Review & Film Summary (2005)." RogerEbert.com. Accessed April 16, 2016. http://www.rogerebert.com/reviews/constantine-2005.

Egner, Jeremy. "Michael Schur on *The Good Place*, Ted Danson and Kantian Ethics." *New York Times*, January 18, 2017, sec. Television. https://www.nytimes.com/2017/01/18/arts/television/michael-schur-on-the-good-place-ted-danson-and-kantian-ethics.html.

Eliade, Mircea. "Religion as Response to the Sacred." In *Introducing Religion: Readings from the Classic Theorists*, edited by Daniel L. Pals, 271–308. New York: Oxford University Press, 2009.

Emery, Debbie. "*Empire* Goes to Church: Andre Gets Baptized, Cookie Can't Keep Her Mouth Shut." TheWrap, October 21, 2015. https://www.thewrap.com/empires-andre-gets-baptized-cookie-curses-in-church-quit-trying-to-turn-us-into-sinners/.

Eskridge, Sara K. "Rural Comedy and the 'Foreign' South." In *Small-Screen Souths: Region, Identity, and the Cultural Politics of Television*, edited by Lisa Hinrichsen, Gina Caison, and Stephanie Rountree, 133–49. Baton Rouge: Louisiana State University Press, 2017.

Esposito, Jennifer. "What Does Race Have to Do with Ugly Betty? An Analysis of Privilege and Postracial(?) Representations on a Television Sitcom." *Television & New Media* 10, no. 6 (November 1, 2009): 521–35. https://doi.org/10.1177/1527476409340906.

Everett, Anna. "Black Film, New Media Industries, and BAMMs (Black American Media Moguls) in the Digital Media Ecology." *Cinema Journal* 53, no. 4 (Summer 2014): 128–33.

Fallows, James. "Bush's Lost Year." *Atlantic*, October 2004. http://www.theatlantic.com/magazine/archive/2004/10/bushs-lost-year/303507/.

Feuer, Jane. "Melodrama, Serial Form and Television Today." *Screen* 25, no. 1 (1984): 4–17.

Feuer, Jane, Paul Kerr, and Tise Vahimagi. *MTM: Quality Television*. London: British Film Institute, 1984.

Fish, Stanley. "One University Under God?" *Chronicle of Higher Education*, January 7, 2005. https://chronicle.com/article/One-University-Under-God-/45077/.

Flacy, Mike. "Netflix Cuts Deal for *Supernatural* and Other CW Shows." *Digital Trends*, October 13, 2011. http://www.digitaltrends.com/home-theater/netflix-cuts-deal-for-supernatural-and-other-cw-shows/.

Flomenbaum, Adam. "How Nielsen Social Is Measuring the Evolution of Social TV," January 26, 2015. http://adweek.it/1yVjb0w.

Ford, Rebecca. "Mark Burnett and Roma Downey: How *The Bible*'s Power Couple Work Together." *Hollywood Reporter*, December 18, 2013. https://www.hollywoodreporter.com/news/bible-mark-burnett-roma-downey-666378.

Forkan, Jim. "Comedy, FX Lead Push to Racy." *Multichannel News* 20 (September 21, 1999): 30A.

FoundationINTERVIEWS. Sherman Hemsley Interview Part 2 of 3—EMMYTVLEGENDS. ORG, n.d. https://www.youtube.com/watch?time_continue=881&v=Eqz2IQcn1MM.

Fowler, Matt. "Syfy Looking to Get Back to *Battlestar Galactica*-Quality Sci-Fi." *IGN*, October 30, 2014. http://www.ign.com/articles/2014/10/30/syfy-looking-to-get-back-to-battlestar-galactica-quality-sci-fi.

Franklin, Nancy. "The Heart of Texas." *New Yorker*, October 8, 2007. http://www.newyorker.com/magazine/2007/10/08/the-heart-of-texas.

"From *Lost* to *Leftovers*, Show Creators Embrace Ambiguity and the Unknown." NPR.org. Accessed April 12, 2016. http://www.npr.org/2015/12/02/458143133/from-lost-to-leftovers-show-creators-embrace-ambiguity-and-the-unknown.

Fuller, Jennifer. "Branding Blackness on US Cable Television." *Media, Culture & Society* 32, no. 2 (March 1, 2010): 285–305. doi:10.1177/0163443709355611.

Gaiman, Neil. "'One Million Moms' Says New Fox TV Series *Lucifer* 'Mocks the Bible,' Starts Petition Urging for Show's Cancellation." Tumblr. Neil-Gaiman. tumblr.com, May 29, 2015. http://neil-gaiman.tumblr.com/post/120223970701/one-million-moms-says-new-fox-tv-series.

Gaita, Paul. "Close Personal Bonds." *Variety*, August 9, 2016.

Gajewski, Ryan. "Emmys: *Transparent*'s Jeffrey Tambor, Jill Soloway Speak Out about Transgender Issues." *Hollywood Reporter*, September 20, 2015. http://www. hollywoodreporter.com/news/emmys-transparents-jeffrey-tambor-jill-825280.

Gardella, Peter. *American Angels: Useful Spirits in the Material World*. Lawrence: University Press of Kansas, 2007.

Gay, Verne. "Oprah Winfrey Launching OWN, Her New TV Network." *McClatchy–Tribune Business News*. January 16, 2008. *ProQuest*, https://search-proquest-com. ezproxy.bu.edu/docview/457078504/abstract/B7A6F826D03143F5PQ/1.

Genzlinger, Neil. "Review: *The Dovekeepers*, a CBS Mini-Series Starring Cote de Pablo." *New York Times*, March 29, 2015, sec. Television. https://www.nytimes.com/2015/03/ 30/arts/television/review-the-dovekeepers-a-cbs-mini-series-starring-cote-de-pablo. html.

Gibbs, Adrienne Samuels. "*A.D. The Bible Continues*: Casting a More Diverse Bible Story." NBC News, April 5, 2015. https://www.nbcnews.com/news/nbcblk/behind-bible-ad-casting-more-diverse-bible-story-n335491.

Gitelman, Lisa. *Always Already New: Media, History, and the Data of Culture*. Cambridge, MA: MIT Press, 2006.

Gitlin, Todd. "Prime Time Ideology: The Hegemonic Process of Television Entertainment." In *Television: The Critical View*, edited by Horace Newcomb, 574–94. New York: Oxford University Press, 2000.

Gitlin, Todd. *Inside Prime Time: With a New Introduction*. 1st edition. Berkeley: University of California Press, 2000.

Glazer, Mikey. "Oprah Winfrey Defends Scandalous Church Drama *Greenleaf*, Prepares for Backlash." *TheWrap*, May 26, 2016. https://www.thewrap.com/oprah-winfrey-defends-scandalous-church-drama-greenleaf-prepares-for-backlash/.

Goldberg, Lesley. "Greg Berlanti Drama *God Friended Me* Lands CBS Pilot Order." *Hollywood Reporter*, January 23, 2018. https://www.hollywoodreporter.com/live-feed/ greg-berlanti-drama-god-friended-me-lands-cbs-pilot-order-1077721.

Goodman, Tim. "Tim Goodman: How to Not Get Canceled in the New World of Television." *Hollywood Reporter*, October 8, 2015. http://www.hollywoodreporter. com/bastard-machine/tim-goodman-how-not-get-830807.

Goodstein, Laurie. "After the Attacks: Finding Fault; Falwell's Finger-Pointing Inappropriate, Bush Says." *New York Times*, September 15, 2001, sec. U.S. https://www. nytimes.com/2001/09/15/us/after-attacks-finding-fault-falwell-s-finger-pointing-inappropriate-bush-says.html.

Gornstein, Leslie. "Is Scorsese's HBO Show the Most Expensive Ever?" *E! Online*, January 19, 2010. http://www.eonline.com/news/162826/is-scorsese-s-hbo-show-the-most-expensive-ever.

Goudreau, Jenna. "Will Oprah Winfrey Spin OWN into Network Gold?" *Forbes*, October 10, 2011.

Gray, Herman. "Television, Black Americans, and the American Dream." *Critical Studies in Mass Communication* 6, no. 4 (December 1989): 376–86.

Gray, Herman. *Watching Race: Television and the Struggle for "Blackness."* Minneapolis: University of Minnesota Press, 1995.

Gray, Jonathan. *Show Sold Separately: Promos, Spoilers, and Other Media Paratexts*. New York: NYU Press, 2010.

Gray, Jonathan, and Amanda D. Lotz. *Television Studies*. Malden, MA: Polity Press, 2012.

Grindstaff, Laura. *The Money Shot: Trash, Class, and the Making of TV Talk Shows.* 1st edition. Chicago: University of Chicago Press, 2002.

Guthrie, Marisa. "HBO Inks Exclusive Deal with Amazon Prime." *Hollywood Reporter,* April 23, 2014. http://www.hollywoodreporter.com/news/hbo-inks-deal-amazon-prime-698379.

Guthrie, Marisa. "HBO Not 'Hung' Up on Decision-Making." *Broadcasting & Cable* 139, no. 23 (June 8, 2009): 34–34.

Guthrie, Marisa. "Syfy's Two-Pronged Rebrand Strategy." *Broadcasting & Cable,* June 21, 2009. http://www.broadcastingcable.com/news/programming/syfys-two-pronged-rebrand-strategy/34994.

Habermas, Jürgen. "Notes on Post-Secular Society." *New Perspectives Quarterly* 25, no. 4 (September 1, 2008): 17–29. doi:10.1111/j.1540-5842.2008.01017.x.

Haithman, Diane. "*Grimm* Producers Consider What Makes a 'Breakout Hit' and the Friday Night Curse: TCA." *Deadline,* January 6, 2013. http://deadline.com/2013/01/grimm-nbc-tca-david-greenwalt-jim-kouf-397819/.

Hale, Mike. "Steven Van Zandt in Norwegian Netflix Series *Lilyhammer.*" *New York Times,* February 5, 2012. http://www.nytimes.com/2012/02/06/arts/television/steven-van-zandt-in-norwegian-netflix-series-lilyhammer.html.

Hall, Sheldon. "Selling Religion: How to Market a Biblical Epic." *Film History* 14, no. 2 (2002): 170–85.

Hamamoto, Darrell Y. *Nervous Laughter: Television Situation Comedy and Liberal Democratic Ideology.* New York: Praeger, 1989.

Hansen, Regina M. "Deconstructing the Apocalypse? Supernatural's Postmodern Appropriation of Angelic Hierarchies." In *Supernatural, Humanity, and the Soul,* edited by Susan A. George and Regina M. Hansen, 13–26. New York: Palgrave Macmillan, 2014.

Harris, Hamil R. "TV Producer Talks about Casting Diverse Actors in *A.D. The Bible Continues.*" *Washington Post,* February 6, 2015, sec. Local. https://www.washingtonpost.com/news/local/wp/2015/02/06/tv-producer-talks-about-casting-diverse-actors-in-a-d-the-bible-continues/.

Havens, Timothy. "Media Programming in an Era of Big Data." *Media Industries* 1, no. 2 (September 15, 2014). http://www.mediaindustriesjournal.org/index.php/mij/article/view/43.

Havens, Timothy. "Towards a Structuration Theory of Media Intermediaries." *Making Media Work: Cultures of Management in the Entertainment Industries.* Edited by Derek Johnson, Derek Kompare, and Avi Santo, 39–62. New York: New York University Press, 2014.

Hendershot, Heather. "'You Know How It Is with Nuns . . .': Religion and Television's Sacred/Secular Fetuses." In *Small Screen, Big Picture: Television and Lived Religion,* edited by Diane Winston, 201–32. Waco, TX: Baylor University Press, 2009.

Hendershot, Heather. *Shaking the World for Jesus: Media and Conservative Evangelical Culture.* Chicago: University of Chicago Press, 2010.

"Here's What the Critics Have to Say about Oprah's New TV Role." *Fortune.* Accessed January 17, 2018. http://fortune.com/2016/06/21/oprah-greenleaf-tv-show-reviews/.

Hesmondhalgh, David. "Bourdieu, the Media and Cultural Production." *Media, Culture & Society* 28, no. 2 (March 1, 2006): 211–31. doi:10.1177/0163443706061682.

Hesmondhalgh, David, and Sarah Baker. *Creative Labour: Media Work in Three Cultural Industries.* 1st edition. New York: Routledge, 2011.

Hibberd, James. "*Constantine* Team on Why NBC Character Isn't Bisexual, Smoking Cigarettes," *Entertainment Weekly*'s EW.com, July 13, 2014. http://www.ew.com/article/2014/07/13/constantine-bisexual-smoking.

Hibberd, James. "Syfy Plans to Lure You Back with These 5 Shows." *Entertainment Weekly*'s EW.com, October 28, 2014. http://www.ew.com/article/2014/10/28/syfy.

Highfill, Samantha. "MGM Is Once Again Launching the United Artists Media Group." *Entertainment Weekly*'s EW.com, September 22, 2014. http://www.ew.com/article/2014/09/22/mgm-united-artists-media-group.

Hills, Matthew. *Fan Cultures*. New York: Routledge, 2004.

Hills, Matthew. "Media Fandom, Neoreligiosity, and Cult(ural) Studies." *Velvet Light Trap: A Critical Journal of Film & Television*, no. 46 (Fall 2000).

Hilmes, Michele. *Only Connect: A Cultural History of Broadcasting in America*. 2nd edition. Florence, KY: Cengage Learning, 2006.

Himberg, Julia. "Multicasting Lesbian Programming and the Changing Landscape of Cable TV." *Television & New Media* 15, no. 4 (May 1, 2014): 289–304. doi:10.1177/1527476412474351.

Himberg, Julia. *The New Gay for Pay: The Sexual Politics of American Television Production*. Austin: The University of Texas Press, 2018.

Hipes, Patrick. "*Killing Jesus* Premiere Date Set for March 29 on Nat Geo—Full Trailer." *Deadline*, February 18, 2015. http://deadline.com/2015/02/killing-jesus-premiere-date-trailer-national-geographic-channel-1201375969/.

Holling, Michelle A. "El Simpático Boxer: Underpinning Chicano Masculinity with a Rhetoric of Familia in *Resurrection Blvd*." *Western Journal of Communication* 70, no. 2 (July 1, 2006): 91–114. https://doi.org/10.1080/10570310600709994.

Holt, Douglas B. "Distinction in America? Recovering Bourdieu's Theory of Tastes from Its Critics." *Poetics, Changing Representation of Status through Taste Displays*, 25, no. 2–3 (November 1997): 93–120. doi:10.1016/S0304-422X(97)00010-7.

Holt, Jennifer. *Empires of Entertainment: Media Industries and the Politics of Deregulation, 1980–1996*. New Brunswick, NJ: Rutgers University Press, 2011.

Holt, Jennifer. "*NYPD Blue*: Content Regulation." In *How To Watch Television*, edited by Ethan Thompson and Jason Mittell, 271–80. New York: NYU Press, 2013.

Hoover, Stewart M. "Visual Religion in Media Culture." In *The Visual Culture of American Religions*, edited by David Morgan and Sally M. Promey, 146–59. Berkeley: University of California Press, 2001.

Howell, Charlotte E. "God, the Devil, and John Winchester: Failures of Patriarchy in *Supernatural*." In *"Supernatural," Humanity, and the Soul*, edited by Susan A. George and Regina M. Hansen, 13–26. New York: Palgrave Macmillan, 2014.

Hughes, Sarah. "Why *Friday Night Lights* Is One of the Best US Shows of Recent Years." *Guardian*, February 13, 2012, sec. Television & radio. http://www.theguardian.com/tv-and-radio/tvandradioblog/2012/feb/13/friday-night-lights.

Hutcheon, Linda. *A Theory of Adaptation*. New York: Routledge, 2006.

Ifeanyi, K. C. "How Oprah's New Drama *Greenleaf* Is Built on Faith, Flawed Characters…and Tattoos?" *Fast Company*, June 21, 2016. https://www.fastcompany.com/3061105/how-oprahs-new-drama-greenleaf-is-built-on-faith-flawed-charactersand-tattoos.

Ioannidou, Elisavet. "Adapting Superhero Comics for the Big Screen: Subculture for the Masses." *Adaptation* 6, no. 2 (August 1, 2013): 230–38. doi:10.1093/adaptation/apt004.

Itzkoff, Dave. "Comics' Mother of 'the Weird Stuff' Is Moving On." *New York Times*, May 29, 2013. http://www.nytimes.com/2013/05/30/books/comics-mother-of-the-weird-stuff- is-moving-on.html.

Jameson, Freidric. "Postmodernism, or the Cultural Logic of Late Capitalism." In *Media and Cultural Studies: Key Works,* edited by Douglas M. Kellner and Meenakshi Gigi Durham, Revised edition, 482–519. Malden, MA: Blackwell, 2006.

Jaramillo, Deborah L. "AMC Stumbling toward a New Television Canon." *Television & New Media* 14, no. 2 (March 1, 2013): 167–83. doi:10.1177/1527476412442105.

Jaramillo, Deborah L. "The Family Racket: AOL Time Warner, HBO, *The Sopranos,* and the Construction of a Quality Brand." *Journal of Communication Inquiry* 26, no. 1 (January 1, 2002): 59–75. doi:10.1177/0196859902026001005.

Jarvey, Natalie, and Kate Stanhope. "How Mark Burnett and Roma Downey Will Target Faith-Based Audiences with MGM's Light TV." *Hollywood Reporter,* November 21, 2016. http://www.hollywoodreporter.com/news/how-mark-burnett-roma-downey-will-target-faith-based-audiences-mgms-light-tv-949096.

Jenkins, Henry. *Convergence Culture.* New York: New York University Press, 2006.

Jenkins, Henry, Joshua Benjamin Green, and Sam Ford. *Spreadable Media: Creating Value and Meaning in a Networked Culture.* New York: NYU Press, 2012.

Jensen, Elizabeth. "WB's *7th Heaven* a Hush-Hush Hit." *Los Angeles Times,* February 22, 1999. http://articles.latimes.com/1999/feb/22/entertainment/ca-10415.

Johnson, Catherine. *Telefantasy.* London: British Film Institute, 2005.

Johnson, Ted. "New Campaign Addresses Violence in Media." *Variety,* February 27, 2013. http://variety.com/2013/tv/news/new-campaign-addresses-violence-in-media-820084/.

Johnson, Victoria E. *Heartland TV: Prime Time Television and the Struggle for U.S. Identity.* New York: NYU Press, 2008.

Johnson, Victoria E. "The Persistence of Geographic Myth in a Convergent Media Era." *Journal of Popular Film & Television* 38, no. 2 (June 2010): 58–65.

Johnson, Victoria E. "Welcome Home? CBS, PAX-TV, and 'Heartland' Values in a Neo-Network Era." *Velvet Light Trap: A Critical Journal of Film & Television,* no. 46 (Fall 2000): 40–55.

Johnson-Smith, Jan. *American Science Fiction.* Middletown, CT: Wesleyan University Press, 2005.

Joyrich, Lynn. "All That Television Allows." In *Private Screenings: Television and the Female Consumer,* 1st edition, edited by Lynn Spigel, 227–51. Minneapolis: University of Minnesota Press, 1992.

Jurgensen, John. "Oprah Is Back on TV; Oprah Winfrey Takes a Part in *Greenleaf,* a TV Series about a Memphis Megachurch." *Wall Street Journal* (online), June 16, 2016, sec. Arts.

Kackman, Michael. "Flow Favorites: Quality Television, Melodrama, and Cultural Complexity." Flow, 2010. http://www.flowjournal.org/2010/03/flow-favorites-quality-television-melodrama-and-cultural-complexity-michael-kackman-university-of-texas-austin/.

Kaiser, Rowan. "Syfy Is De-Rebranding and It's the Most Compelling Thing on TV." *Inverse,* November 19, 2015. https://www.inverse.com/article/8354-syfy-is-releasing-a-film-de-rebranding-and-becoming-super-interesting.

Kaveney, Roz. *Superheroes! Capes and Crusaders in Comics and Films.* London; New York: I. B. Tauris, 2008.

Keegan, Cael. "Op-Ed: How *Transparent* Tried and Failed to Represent Trans Men." *Advocate,* October 22, 2014. http://www.advocate.com/commentary/2014/10/22/op-ed-how-transparent-tried-and-failed-represent-trans-men.

King, Ursula. *Women and Spirituality: Voices of Protest and Promise*, 2nd edition. London: Macmillan, 1993.

Kissell, Rick. "ABC Family's *The Fosters* Surges in Second Week; Did Controversy Help?" *Variety*, June 11, 2013. http://variety.com/2013/tv/news/abc-familys-the-fosters-surges-in-second-week-did-controversy-help-1200495502/.

Kissell, Rick "History Scores Big with *The Bible* and *The Vikings*." *Variety*, March 4, 2013. http://variety.com/2013/tv/ratings/history-scores-big-with-the-bible-and-the-vikings-1200002918/.

Kissell, Rick. "NBC's *A.D.* Leads Easter Sunday but Can't Match *The Bible*." *Variety* (blog), April 6, 2015. http://variety.com/2015/tv/ratings/nbcs-a-d-the-bible-continues-opens-to-solid-but-unspectacular-ratings-1201466801/.

Kissell, Rick. "NBC's *Constantine* Solid in Premiere Opposite World Series." *Variety*, October 25, 2014. http://variety.com/2014/tv/ratings/nbcs-constantine-solid-in-premiere-opposite-world-series-1201339131/.

Kissell, Rick. "Ratings: *A.D. The Bible* Continues Drops Off, but Still Tops Demos." *Variety* (blog), April 13, 2015. http://variety.com/2015/data/news/a-d-the-bible-continues-ratings-week-2-1201471277/.

Kissell, Rick. "Ratings: Fox's *The X-Files* Tops Monday in Demo, Boosts *Lucifer* to Hot Premiere." *Variety*, January 26, 2016. http://variety.com/2016/tv/news/ratings-the-x-files-monday-premiere-fox-lucifer-hot-1201688915/.

Kissell, Rick. "Ratings: Fox's *X-Files, Lucifer* Down in Week Two, Still Top Night in Demo." *Variety*, February 2, 2016. http://variety.com/2016/tv/news/ratings-fox-x-files-lucifer-down-in-week-two-1201694762/.

Kissell, Rick. "Upscale Viewers Flock to ABC." *Variety* 428, no. 11 (October 22, 2012): 27–27.

Klassen, Chris. "Research Note: Rejecting Monotheism? Polytheism, Pluralism, and *Battlestar Galactica*." *Journal of Contemporary Religion* 23, no. 3 (October 2008): 355–62.

Klein, Amy. "Hollywood Looks for Higher Ground." *Variety*, July 26, 2016.

Knight, W. Andy. Eschatology, Religion and World Order." *Religious Studies and Theology* 29, no. 1 (2010): 1–24. doi:10.1558/rsth.v29i1.1

Kompare, Derek. "'More 'Moments of Television': Online Cult Television Authorship." In *Flow TV: Television in the Age of Media Convergence*, edited by Michael Kackman, Marnie Binfield, Matthew Thomas Payne, Allison Perlman, and Bryan Sebok, 95–113. New York: Routledge, 2010.

Kompare, Derek. "Publishing Flow DVD Box Sets and the Reconception of Television." *Television & New Media* 7, no. 4 (November 1, 2006): 335–60.

Kompare, Derek. *Rerun Nation: How Repeats Invented American Television*. 1st edition. Florence: Taylor and Francis, 2006.

Koonse, Emma. "Rectify Series Creator Ray McKinnon Talks Television, Redemption, and the Future for Daniel Holden." *Christian Post*, July 10, 2014. http://www.christianpost.com/news/rectify-series-creator-ray-mckinnon-talks-television-redemption-and-the-future-for-daniel-holden-123104/.

Kuperberg, Jonathan. "TCA: CW's Pedowitz Says Last Season 'Pivotal' for Network." *Braodcasting & Cable*, August 11, 2015. http://www.broadcastingcable.com/news/programming/tca-cw-s-pedowitz-says-last-season-pivotal-network/143303.

Lafayette, Jon. "Buyers Sense a Competitive Market Ahead." *Television Week* 24, no. 17 (April 25, 2005): 22–24.

Lagerwey, Jorie. "Are You There, God? It's Me, TV: Religion in American TV Drama, 2000–2009." Ph.D. diss., University of Southern California, 2009. http://digitallibrary.usc.edu/cdm/ref/collection/p15799coll3/id/227570.

Launder, William. "Corporate News: Winfrey Network to Add Six Series." *Wall Street Journal,* Eastern edition, January 7, 2013.

Lauzen, Martha. "Diversity in Prime Time: Not a Priority for the Networks." *Television Quarterly* 33, no. 4 (Spring 2003): 34–39.

Lavender-Smith, Jordan. "Networking Families: *Battlestar Galactica* and the Values of Quality." *Flow,* 2009. http://www.flowjournal.org/2009/12/networking-families-battlestar-galactica-and-the-values-of-quality-jordan-lavender-smith-city-university-of-new-york/.

Lentz, Kirsten Marthe. "Quality versus Relevance: Feminism, Race, and the Politics of the Sign in 1970s Television." *Camera Obscura* 15, no. 1 (2000): 44–93.

Levine, Elana. "Toward a Paradigm for Media Production Research: Behind the Scenes at General Hospital." *Critical Studies in Media Communication* 18, no. 1 (2001): 66–82. doi:10.1080/15295030109367124.

Lieberman, David. "Hulu Introduces $11.99 Commercial-Free Option, but Vows to Boost Ad Sales." *Deadline,* September 2, 2015. http://deadline.com/2015/09/hulu-ad-free-service-1201512438/.

Littleton, Cynthia. "Accentuating the Positive." *Variety,* September 17, 2013.

Littleton, Cynthia. "Birth of The CW: UPN-WB Network Merger Deal Rocked TV Biz 10 Years Ago." *Variety,* January 24, 2016. http://variety.com/2016/tv/news/cw-wb-network-upn-merger-announcement-10-years-ago-1201687040/.

Littleton, Cynthia. "Deep Pockets, Family Feel at Mark Burnett's One Three Media." *Variety* (blog), September 17, 2013. http://variety.com/2013/biz/news/deep-pockets-family-feel-at-mark-burnetts-one-three-media-1200614004/.

Littleton, Cynthia. "Easter Week Is Hopping with High-Profile TV Premieres: *Killing Jesus, The Dovekeepers, A.D.*" *Variety* (blog), February 18, 2015. http://variety.com/2015/tv/news/easter-week-high-profile-tv-premieres-killing-jesus-the-dovekeepers-a-d-1201436194/.

Littleton, Cynthia. "Faith & Family: Church & Slate." *Variety,* June 10, 2014.

Littleton, Cynthia. "Fox Aims for Men with Four Drama Series Orders." *Variety,* May 9, 2013. http://variety.com/2013/tv/news/fox-orders-four-dramas-series-for-2013-14-1200478203/.

Littleton, Cynthia. "History, Producers Spread Gospel in 10-Hour Mini." *Variety* (blog), March 1, 2013. http://variety.com/2013/tv/news/history-producers-spread-gospel-in-10-hour-mini-821007/.

Littleton, Cynthia. "Mark Burnett and One Three Media Eye Bigger, Bolder Productions." *Variety,* September 17, 2013. http://variety.com/2013/biz/news/mark-burnett-and-his-one-three-media-eye-bigger-bolder-productions-1200613995/.

Littleton, Cynthia. "Mark Burnett, Roma Downey Promo *Bible* Mini to Faithful." *Variety* (blog), February 8, 2013. http://variety.com/2013/tv/news/mark-burnett-roma-downey-promo-bible-mini-to-faithful-1118065870/.

Littleton, Cynthia. "Mark Burnett's Ties to Trump Put Him in Tricky Situation." *Variety* (blog), January 19, 2017. http://variety.com/2017/tv/news/mark-burnett-donald-trump-1201963228/.

Littleton, Cynthia. "NBC Cancels *A.D.* as Producers Plan Digital Revival for Biblical Drama." *Variety* (blog), July 3, 2015. http://variety.com/2015/tv/news/a-d-the-bible-continues-nbc-cancels-mark-burnett-roma-downey-1201533794/.

Littleton, Cynthia "NBC Execs on Broadcast vs. Cable, Emmy Awards, Thursday Night Struggles." *Variety*, July 13, 2014. http://variety.com/2014/tv/news/nbc-renews-americas-got-talent-ninja-warrior-last-comic-standing-1201261837/.

Littleton, Cynthia. "Proving Herself in the Desert." *Variety*, August 9, 2016.

Littleton, Cynthia. "Roma Downey Pursues Passion Projects, *Bible* Sequel with LightWorkers Banner." *Variety*, September 17, 2013. http://variety.com/2013/biz/news/roma-downey-pursues-passion-projects-bible-sequel-with-lightworkers-banner-1200614054/.

Littleton, Cynthia. "Shows Are Finally Ready to Have a Serious Talk about Religion." *Variety*, May 3, 2016.

Littleton, Cynthia, and Stuart Oldham. "*Variety* Defends Story on *Noah* Survey after Paramount Claim." *Variety* (blog), February 19, 2014. http://variety.com/2014/biz/news/variety-stands-by-story-on-noah-survey-1201111392/.

Lofton, Kathryn. "Practicing Oprah; or, the Prescriptive Compulsion of a Spiritual Capitalism." *Journal of Popular Culture* 39, no. 4 (August 2006): 599–621.

Long, Stephanie Topacio. "Viewers Think *Daredevil* Is Bloody Good, as the Show Takes Netflix's Number One Spot." *Digital Trends*, May 28, 2015. http://www.digitaltrends.com/movies/daredevil-top-rated-show-on-netflix/.

Lopez, Kristen. "Profane or Innocent Fun? Devout Catholics React to *Jane the Virgin*'s Evolving Depiction of Faith." *Remezcla* (blog), January 13, 2017. http://remezcla.com/features/film/catholics-react-to-jane-the-virgins-evolving-depiction-of-faith/.

Loroz, Peggy Sue, and Bridgette M. Braig. "Consumer Attachments to Human Brands: The 'Oprah Effect.'" *Psychology & Marketing* 32, no. 7 (July 1, 2015): 751–63. https://doi.org/10.1002/mar.20815.

Lotz, Amanda D. "Industry-Level Studies and the Contributions of Gitlin's *Inside Prime Time*." In *Production Studies: Cultural Studies of Media Industries*, edited by Vicki Mayer, Miranda J. Banks, and John T. Caldwell, 25–38. New York: Routledge, 2009.

Lotz, Amanda D. *Portals: A Treatise on Internet-Distributed Television*. Ann Arbor, MI: Maize Books, 2017.

Lotz, Amanda D. *The Television Will Be Revolutionized*. New York: NYU Press, 2007.

Lowry, Brian. "*Red Tent* Has Perfect Pitch." *Variety*, December 2, 2014.

Lowry, Brian. "Sudsy *Virgin* Delivers Charm." *Variety*, October 7, 2014.

Lowry, Brian. "Too Big to Fail on Her Own?" *Variety*, June 30, 2011.

Lowry, Brian. "TV: Latest Move Puts Oprah in a World of Her OWN." *Variety*, January 21, 2008.

Lowry, Brian. "TV Review: *A.D. The Bible Continues*." *Variety* (blog), April 3, 2015. http://variety.com/2015/tv/reviews/tv-review-a-d-the-bible-continues-1201461544/.

Lowry, Brian. "TV Review: *Constantine*." *Variety*, October 22, 2014. http://variety.com/2014/tv/reviews/tv-review-constantine-1201331412/.

Lowry, Brian. "TV Review: *The Dovekeepers*." *Variety* (blog), March 29, 2015. http://variety.com/2015/tv/reviews/tv-review-the-dovekeepers-1201460109/.

Lowry, Brian. "The Worst TV Shows of 2015." *Variety* (blog), December 11, 2015. http://variety.com/2015/tv/columns/worst-tv-shows-2015-true-detective-fear-the-walking-dead-texas-rising-1201658055/.

Lubin, Gus. "*Daredevil* Is the Top-Rated Show on Netflix, and These Highlights Show Why." *Business Insider*, May 22, 2015. http://www.businessinsider.com/daredevil-is-the-top-rated-show-on-netflix-2015-5.

Luckerson, Victor, and Matthew Lee. "Netflix Accounts for More Than a Third of All Internet Traffic." *Time*, May 29, 2015. http://time.com/3901378/netflix-internet-traffic/?utm_content=bufferc3f54&utm_medium=social&utm_source=linkedin.com&utm_campaign=buffer.

Lynch, Jason. "Why Some Low-Rated TV Shows Keep Getting Renewed." *AdWeek.* Accessed May 16, 2016. http://www.adweek.com/news/television/why-some-low-rated- tv-shows-keep-getting-renewed-164648.

Lyons, Margaret. "Review: Jason Ritter Saves *Kevin (Probably) Saves the World.*" *New York Times,* October 2, 2017, sec. Television. https://www.nytimes.com/2017/10/02/arts/television/kevin-probably-saves-the-world-review.html.

Maglio, Tony. "Netflix's Push to Own Original Series Fuels Race to 'Out-HBO' HBO." *The Wrap,* April 24, 2015. http://www.thewrap.com/netflix-push-into-owning-original-series-fuels-race-to-out-hbo-the-premium-network/.

Mallon, Thomas, and Pankaj Mishra. "Highbrow, Lowbrow, Middlebrow—Do These Kinds of Cultural Categories Mean Anything Anymore?" *New York Times,* July 29, 2014. http://www.nytimes.com/2014/08/03/books/review/highbrow-lowbrow-middlebrow-do-these-kinds-of-cultural-categories-mean-anything-anymore.html.

Malone, Michael. "TCA: 'Visionary Creators' Wanted, Says Amazon's Price." Broadcasting & Cable, January 11, 2016. http://www.broadcastingcable.com/news/programming/tca-visionary-creators-wanted-says-amazon-s-price/146863.

Mann, Denise. "It's Not TV, It's Brand Management." In *Production Studies: Cultural Studies of Media Industries,* edited by Vicki Mayer, Miranda J. Banks, and John T. Caldwell, 99–114. New York: Routledge, 2009.

Maragh, Raven S. "'Our Struggles Are Unequal': Black Women's Affective Labor between Television and Twitter." *Journal of Communication Inquiry* 40, no. 4 (October 1, 2016): 351–69. https://doi.org/10.1177/0196859916664082.

Marechal, A. J. "LightWorkers Media Options *The Dovekeepers* for Miniseries." *Variety* (blog), September 16, 2013. http://variety.com/2013/tv/news/lightworkers-media-options-the-dovekeepers-for-miniseries-exclusive-1200610855/.

Marechal, A. J. "Olympics Viewers to Get Taste of *New Normal.*" *Variety,* August 11, 2012. http://variety.com/2012/tv/news/olympics-viewers-to-get-taste-of-new-normal-9193/.

Markert, John. "*The George Lopez Show*: The Same Old Hispano?" *Bilingual Review/La Revista Bilingüe* 28, no. 2 (2004): 148–65.

Martinez, Diana. "*Jane the Virgin* Proves Diversity Is More Than Skin Deep." *Atlantic,* October 19, 2015. https://www.theatlantic.com/entertainment/archive/2015/10/jane-the-virgin-telenovelas/409696/.

Martinez, Jessica Hamar, and Cary Funk. "The Shifting Religious Identity of Latinos in the United States." Pew Research Center's Religion & Public Life Project (blog), May 7, 2014. http://www.pewforum.org/2014/05/07/the-shifting-religious-identity-of-latinos-in-the-united-states/.

Martinez, Michelle. "Keeping Betty Ugly: Manufacturing Diversity for Network TV." PhD diss., Arizona State University, 2015. ProQuest, https://search-proquest-com.ezproxy.bu.edu/docview/1681627604/abstract/E296AA09CAB64526PQ/1.

Marwick, Alice E., and Danah Boyd. "I Tweet Honestly, I Tweet Passionately: Twitter Users, Context Collapse, and the Imagined Audience." *New Media & Society* 13, no. 1 (February 2011): 114–33. doi:10.1177/1461444810365313.

Masters, Kim. "Rough Seas on *Noah*: Darren Aronofsky Opens Up on the Biblical Battle to Woo Christians (and Everyone Else)." *Hollywood Reporter,* February 12, 2014. https://www.hollywoodreporter.com/news/rough-seas-noah-darren-aronofsky-679315.

Matthews, Donald G. "Introduction." In *Religion in the American South*, edited by Beth Barton Schweiger and Donald G. Matthews, 1–4. Chapel Hill: University of North Carolina Press, 2004.

Mayer, Vicki. "Studying Up and F**cking Up: Ethnographic Interviewing in Production Studies." *Cinema Journal* 47, no. 2 (2007): 141–48. doi:10.1353/cj.2008.0007.

McCracken, Brett. "Saying Farewell to the Best Show on TV." *RELEVANT Magazine*, July 14, 2011. http://www.relevantmagazine.com/culture/tv/features/26184-saying-farewell-to-the-best-show-on-tv.

McDannell, Colleen. *Material Christianity: Religion and Popular Culture in America*. New Haven, CT: Yale University Press, 1995.

McDaniel, Deanna. "Not Just a Survivor." *Beverly Hills* 9, no. 3 (June 2013): 28–30, 32, 34.

McDermon, Daniel. "*The Leftovers* Recap: What Happened to Gladys." *ArtsBeat*, 1406541640. http://artsbeat.blogs.nytimes.com/2014/07/28/the-leftovers-recap-what-happened-to-gladys/.

Mcgrath, Charles. "The Triumph of the Prime-Time Novel." *New York Times*, October 22, 1995, sec. Magazine. http://www.nytimes.com/1995/10/22/magazine/the-prime-time-novel-the-triumph-of-the-prime-time-novel.html.

McKinney, Kelsey. "How Mark Burnett Created Reality TV—and Donald Trump." Ringer, January 2, 2017. https://theringer.com/mark-burnett-donald-trump-the-celebrity-apprentice-5b1a80ad189c#.6e1309llg.

McMinn, Lisa. "Y2K, The Apocalypse, and Evangelical Christianity: The Role of Eschatological Belief in Church Responses." *Sociology of Religion* 62, no. 2 (2001): 205–20. doi:10.2307/3712456.

McNamara, Mary. "Masada in CBS' *The Dovekeepers*: Bad Storytelling in Every Way." *Los Angeles Times*, March 31, 2015. http://www.latimes.com/entertainment/tv/la-et-st-cbs-dovekeepers-review-20150331-column.html.

McNamara, Mary. "Oprah Winfrey's *Greenleaf* Deserves High Praise, but Her Network May Not Receive Its Full Bounty." *Los Angeles Times*, June 21, 2016. http://www.latimes.com/entertainment/tv/la-et-st-greenleaf-review-20160620-snap-story.html.

McNamara, Mary. "Review: *Rectify* Is a Revelation That Sets a New Standard." *Los Angeles Times*, April 22, 2013. http://articles.latimes.com/2013/apr/22/entertainment/la-et-st-rectify-20130422.

McNutt, Myles. "Limited Series Are a Product of Brand Management, Not Innovation." Carsey-Wolf Center at UC Santa Barbara, 2014. http://www.carseywolf.ucsb.edu/mip/article/limited-series-are-product-brand-management-not-innovation.

Mello, John P., Jr., "Hulu Enters Original Content Biz with *Battleground* Series." *Tech Hive*, February 16, 2012. http://www.techhive.com/article/250089/hulu_gets_into_original_content_biz_with_series_called_battleground.html.

Memmott, Carol. "History Channel Comes Out Shootin'." *USA Today*. Accessed March 31, 2016. http://ezproxy.lib.utexas.edu/login?url=http://search.ebscohost.com/login.aspx?direct=true&db=nfh&AN=J0E269345227512&site=ehost-live.

Menta, Anna. "How *The Good Place* Is Revolutionizing the TV Sitcom." *Newsweek*, October 19, 2017. http://www.newsweek.com/good-place-mike-schur-interview-688754.

Messmer, Marietta. "Transformations of the Sacred in Contemporary Chicana Culture." *Theology & Sexuality* 14, no. 3 (January 1, 2008): 259–78. https://doi.org/10.1177/1355835808091417.

Mian, Bilal. "*Daredevil*'s Charlie Cox on Becoming a Religious Superhero." *Hollywood Reporter*, April 10, 2015. http://www.hollywoodreporter.com/live-feed/daredevils-charlie-cox-becoming-a-787809.

Miner, Brad. "Daredevil and the Devil." *Catholic Thing*, May 18, 2015. https://www.thecatholicthing.org/2015/05/18/daredevil-and-the-devil/.

Mitovich, Matt Webb, and Matt Webb Mitovich. "*Smallville, Supernatural* Returns Delayed a Week." *TVLine*, January 28, 2011. http://tvline.com/2011/01/27/smallville-supernatural-returns-delayed-a-week/.

Mittell, Jason. "Complex TV." *Complex TV*, pre-publication edition. Accessed March 25, 2016. http://mcpress.media-commons.org/complextelevision/.

Mittell, Jason. "Forensic Fandom and the Drillable Text." *Spreadable Media*, December 17, 2012. http://spreadablemedia.org/essays/mittell/.

Mittell, Jason. *Genre and Television: From Cop Shows to Cartoons in American Culture*. New York: Routledge, 2004.

Mittell, Jason. "Narrative Complexity in Contemporary American Television." *Velvet Light Trap: A Critical Journal of Film & Television*, no. 58 (2006): 29–40.

Morabito, Andrea. "OWN Scripts Growth Strategy with Help From Tyler Perry." *Broadcasting & Cable* 143, no. 21 (May 27, 2013): 17.

Moss, Charles. "Daredevil's Greatest Superpower Is His Catholicism." *Slate*, April 10, 2015. http://www.slate.com/articles/arts/culturebox/2015/04/netflix_s_daredevil_show_understands_that_catholicism_is_the_superhero_s.html.

Mullen, Megan Gwynne. *Television in the Multichannel Age: A Brief History of Cable Television*. Malden, MA: Blackwell, 2008.

Murray, Simone. *The Adaptation Industry*. New York: Routledge, 2012.

Napoli, Philip M. *Audience Evolution: New Technologies and the Transformation of Media Audiences*. New York: Columbia University Press, 2010.

"NBC's *A.D. The Bible Continues* Receives High Marks from Faith Driven Consumer: Mark Burnett and Roma Downey's Prime Time Sequel to *The Bible* Miniseries Could Become 'the Most Successful Faith-Based TV Franchise in History.'" *PR Newswire*, April 1, 2015. https://search-proquest-com.ezproxy.bu.edu/docview/1667979456/abstract/34195098A7FF4641PQ/1.

Neale, Steve. *Genre and Hollywood*. New York: Routledge, 2000.

"Netflix Is Now Available around the World." *Netflix Media Center*, January 6, 2016. https://media.netflix.com/en/press-releases/netflix-is-now-available-around-the-world.

Newcomb, Horace. "Religion on Television." In *Channels of Belief: Religion and American Commercial Television*, edited by John P. Ferre, 29–44. Ames: University of Iowa Press, 1990.

Newcomb, Horace. "'This Is Not al Dente': The Sopranos and the New Meaning of 'Television.'" In *Television: The Critical View*, 7th edition, edited by Horace Newcomb, 561–78. New York: Oxford University Press, 2006.

Newcomb, Horace, and Paul Hirsch. "Television as Cultural Forum." In *Television: The Critical View*, 561–73. New York: Oxford University Press, 2000.

Newman, Michael Z. *Indie: An American Film Culture*. New York: Columbia University Press, 2011.

Newman, Michael Z., and Elana Levine. *Legitimating Television*. New York: Routledge, 2011.

Niedzwiadek, Nick. "Oprah Steers Cable Turnaround—OWN Network Rises as Rivals Struggle by Shifting Its Lineup toward Dramas." *Wall Street Journal,* Eastern edition, March 21, 2016.

Nussbaum, Emily. "Open Secret." *New Yorker*, September 29, 2014. http://www.newyorker.com/magazine/2014/09/29/open-secret.

O'Connell, Michael. "*Jane the Virgin* Showrunner Wants *Ugly Betty* Meets *Gilmore Girls.*" *Hollywood Reporter*, July 18, 2014. https://www.hollywoodreporter.com/live-feed/jane-virgin-showrunner-wants-ugly-719620.

O'Connell, Michael. "Mark Burnett Talks about 'Mainstreaming' the Bible in *A.D.*— and His Growing Beard." *Hollywood Reporter*, January 16, 2015. https://www.hollywoodreporter.com/live-feed/mark-burnett-talks-mainstreaming-bible-764431.

O'Hare, Kate. "How Catholic IS *Marvel's Daredevil* on Netflix?" *Patheos*, April 10, 2015.   http://www.patheos.com/blogs/kateohare/2015/04/how-catholic-is-marvels-daredevil-on-netflix/.

Ostrow, Joanne. "How Will NBC's *The Good Place* Tackle Religion?" *Hollywood Reporter*,   September   15,   2016.   https://www.hollywoodreporter.com/live-feed/good-place-religion-explained-mike-schur-interview-927402.

Otterson, Joe. "ABC Head Channing Dungey Says Donald Trump Made Her Rethink Programming Strategy." TheWrap, December 2, 2016. https://www.thewrap.com/abc-channing-dungey-donald-trump-programming/.

Paskin, Willa. "See Me: *Transparent* Is the Fall's Only Great New Show." *Slate*, September 29, 2014. http://www.slate.com/articles/arts/television/2014/09/transparent_on_amazon_prime_reviewed_it_s_the_fall_s_best_new_show.html.

Patten, Dominic. "*The Walking Dead* Ratings: More Cable Records In Live+3 Results." *Deadline*,   October   17,   2014.   http://deadline.com/2014/10/the-walking-dead-premiere-ratings-new-cable-record-season-5-853406/.

Perez, Sarah. "Amazon Studios Now Funding Original Content Series for Amazon Instant Video Service." *TechCrunch*, May 2, 2012. http://techcrunch.com/2012/05/02/amazon-studios-now-funding-original-content-series-for-amazon-instant-video-service/.

Perlman, Allison Joyce. "Reforming the Wasteland: Television, Reform, and Social Movements, 1950–2004," 2008. https://repositories.lib.utexas.edu/handle/2152/3247.

Perlman, Ron. "Me Explaining to @_benipedia_ Why I Prefer Acting While Standing on 1 Foot . . . https://instagram.com/p/3MVRkoonps/." Microblog. *@perlmutations*, May 27, 2015. https://twitter.com/perlmutations/status/603604200321318912.

Perren, Alisa. "The Trick of the Trades: Media Industry Studies and the American Comic Book Industry." In *Production Studies, The Sequel*. Edited by Miranda Banks, Bridget Conor, and Vicki Mayer, 227–37. New York: Routledge, 2016.

Petersen, Line Nybro. "Renegotiating Religious Imaginations through Transformations of 'Banal Religion' in *Supernatural.*" *Transformative Works and Cultures* 4, (July 1, 2010).

Petruska, Karen. "Amazon Prime Video: Where Information Is Entertainment." *From Networks to Netflix: A Guide to Changing Channels*. Edited by Derek Johnson, 355–64. New York: Routledge, 2018.

Petski, Denise. "*Messiah*: Netflix Orders Religious Drama Series from Mark Burnett & Roma Downey." *Deadline* (blog), November 16, 2017. http://deadline.com/2017/11/messiah-netflix-orders-drama-series-mark-burnett-roma-downey-james-mcteigue-direct-1202208898/.

Petski, Denise. "*Preacher* AMC Drama Series Gets Premiere Date." *Deadline*, March 14, 2016. http://deadline.com/2016/03/preacher-amc-drama-series-premiere-date-1201719886/.

Pew Research Center. "'No Religion' on the Rise: 19.6% Have No Religious Affiliation." Pew Forum on Religion & Public Life, October 9, 2012. http://www.pewforum.org/Unaffiliated/nones-on-the-rise.aspx.

Piñón, Juan. "*Jane the Virgin*." *ReVista* 17, no. 1 (Fall 2017): 23–26.

Piñón, Juan. "*Ugly Betty* and the Emergence of the Latina/o Producers as Cultural Translators." *Communication Theory* 21, no. 4 (November 1, 2011): 392–412. Poggi, Jeanine. "The Miniseries, a Onetime TV Mainstay, Poised for an Encore." *Advertising Age* 83, no. 25 (June 18, 2012): 6.

Poniewozik, James. "*Friday Night Lights* Watch (Repost): Let's Go Home." *Time*, July 16, 2011. http://entertainment.time.com/2011/07/16/friday-night-lights-watch-repost-lets-go-home/.

Poniewozik, James. "Streaming TV Isn't Just a New Way to Watch. It's a New Genre." *New York Times*, December 16, 2015. http://www.nytimes.com/2015/12/20/arts/television/streaming-tv-isnt-just-a-new-way-to-watch-its-a-new-genre.html.

Prudom, Laura. "*Supernatural* at 200: The Road So Far, an Oral History." *Variety*, November 11, 2014. http://variety.com/2014/tv/spotlight/supernatural-oral-history-200-episodes-ackles-padalecki-kripke-1201352537/.

Prudom, Laura. "What Every TV Show Can Learn from *Sleepy Hollow*," December 3, 2013. http://theweek.com/articles/455254/what-every-tv-show-learn-from-sleepy-hollow.

"Public Radio Audience Demographics—NPR Profiles." *National Public Media*. Accessed May 18, 2015. http://nationalpublicmedia.com/npr/audience/.

Pulliam-Moore, Charles. "*American Gods*' Jesus Shows What Happens When a God Becomes Too Popular." io9, June 20, 2017. https://io9.gizmodo.com/american-gods-jesus-shows-what-happens-when-a-god-becom-1796255952.

Quinn, Eithne. "Black Talent and Conglomerate Hollywood: Will Smith, Tyler Perry, and the Continuing Significance of Race." *Popular Communication* 11, no. 3 (July 2013): 196–210. https://doi.org/10.1080/15405702.2013.810070.

Rackl, Lori. "Chicago Native Jill Soloway Creates Season's Best New Show, *Transparent*." *Chicago Sun-Times*, September 25, 2014. http://chicago.suntimes.com/entertainment/chicago-native-jill-soloway-creates-seasons-best-new-show-transparent/.

"Ratings—OWN Set to Deliver Its Highest-Rated and Most-Watched Year in Network History." *Futon Critic*, December 16, 2016. http://www.thefutoncritic.com/ratings/2016/12/16/own-set-to-deliver-its-highest-rated-and-most-watched-year-in-network-history-25510/20161216own01/.

"Ratings—*Smallville* and *Supernatural* on the Rise, Performing at or Near Season Highs." *Futon Critic*, October 31, 2008. http://www.thefutoncritic.com/ratings/2008/10/31/smallville-and-supernatural-on-the-rise-performing-at-or-near-season-highs-29378/20081031cw01/.

Reisman, Abraham. "What Daredevil Comics Should You Read When You're Done with the Netflix Series?" *Vulture*, April 11, 2015. http://www.vulture.com/2015/04/what-daredevil-comics-should-you-read-now.html.

Ritman, Alex. "ABC Entertainment Chief: Network Hasn't Paid Enough Attention to 'True Realities' of America." *Hollywood Reporter*, December 2, 2016. https://www.hollywoodreporter.com/news/abc-entertainment-chief-network-hasnt-paid-attention-true-realities-america-952189.

Ritzenhoff, Karen A., and Angela Krewani. "Introduction." In *The Apocalypse in Film: Dystopias, Disasters, and Other Visions about the End of the World*, edited by Karen A. Ritzenhoff and Angela Krewani, xi–xxi. Lanham, MD: Rowman & Littlefield, 2015.

Rivera, Zayda. "Gina Rodriguez Talks *Jane the Virgin*, Similarities to Character: 'I Was a Huge Prude.'" *NY Daily News*, October 9, 2014. http://www.nydailynews.com/entertainment/tv/gina-rodriguez-stars-cw-telenovela-adaptation-jane-virgin-article-1.1968944.

Robinson, Joanna. "How the Emotionally Satisfying *Leftovers* Finale Learned from the Mistakes of *Lost*." *Vanity Fair*, December 7, 2015. http://www.vanityfair.com/hollywood/2015/12/leftovers-finale-damon-lindelof-lost.

Rochlin, Margy. "In *Transparent*, a Heroine Evolves Further Still." *New York Times*, November 27, 2015. http://www.nytimes.com/2015/11/29/arts/television/in-transparent-a-heroine-evolves-further-still.html.

Romano, Andrew. "Hollywood Declares 2014 the Year of the Bible." Daily Beast, January 9, 2014. http://www.thedailybeast.com/articles/2014/01/09/hollywood-declares-2014-the-year-of-the-bible.html.

Rose, Lacey. "FX Chief: 'HBO and FX Absolutely Dominated the Race for Quality in Television.'" *Hollywood Reporter*, January 18, 2015. http://www.hollywoodreporter.com/live-feed/fx-chief-hbo-fx-absolutely-764581.

Rose-Holt, Sundi. "More Than One Kind of Silence in *Rectify*." *Entertainment Weekly*'s EW.com, August 7, 2014. http://community.ew.com/2014/08/07/more-than-one-kind-of-silence-in-rectify/.

Round, Julia. "'Is This a Book?' DC Vertigo and the Redefinition of Comics in the 1990s." In *The Rise of the American Comics Artist: Creators and Contexts*, edited by Paul Williams and James Lyons, 14–30. Jackson: University Press of Mississippi, 2010.

Rudolph, Ileane. "Inside the Resurrection of Religious TV." TVGuide.com, April 18, 2014. http://www.tvguide.com/news/religious-tv-resurrection-1080611/.

Ryan, Maureen. "*Battlestar Galactica* and *Lost*: The Similarities Are Spooky—The Watcher." *Chicago Tribune*, June 9, 2008. http://featuresblogs.chicagotribune.com/entertainment_tv/2008/06/battlestar-gala.html.

Ryan, Maureen. "*Greenleaf*." *Variety*, June 21, 2016.

Ryan, Maureen. "The Man behind the Heroes: Mark Pedowitz Breaks The CW out of Its Niche." *Variety* (blog), October 14, 2015. http://variety.com/2015/tv/features/mark-pedowitz-the-cw-the-flash-arrow-1201617084/.

Rymsza-Pawlowska, Malgorzata J. "Broadcasting the Past: History Television, 'Nostalgia Culture,' and the Emergence of the Miniseries in the 1970s United States." *Journal of Popular Film & Television* 42, no. 2 (April 2014): 81–90. https://doi.org/10.1080/01956051.2013.805118.

Salinas, Brenda. "Is America Ready to Fall in Love with the Telenovela?" NPR.org, November 9, 2014. https://www.npr.org/sections/codeswitch/2014/11/09/362401259/is-america-ready-to-fall-in-love-with-the-telenovela.

Saraiya, Sonia. "TV Review: *Living Biblically* on CBS." *Variety* (blog), February 20, 2018. http://variety.com/2018/tv/reviews/living-biblically-review-cbs-jay-r-ferguson-1202701164/.

Saraiya, Sonia. "Why We Need Narrators: *Jane the Virgin* Has the Best Voice-Over on TV." Salon, October 29, 2014. https://www.salon.com/2014/10/29/why_we_need_narrators_jane_the_virgin_has_the_best_voice_over_on_tv/.

Savage, Christina. "*Chuck* versus the Ratings: Savvy Fans and 'Save Our Show' Campaigns." *Transformative Works and Cultures* 15, (November 12, 2013).

Saval, Malina. "Jeffrey Tambor on *Transparent*: 'People's Lives Depend on This.'" *Variety*, March 18, 2016. http://variety.com/2016/scene/vpage/transparent-jeffrey-tambor-j-j-abrams-man-on-the-land-1201733683/.

Schechner, Sam. "Corporate News: Oprah Winfrey's Network Draws Large Opening-Night Audience." *Wall Street Journal*, Eastern edition, January 4, 2011.

Schechner, Sam, and Christopher S. Stewart. "Media: Oprah Winfrey Network Sets Deal with Comcast." *Wall Street Journal*, Eastern edition, April 2, 2012.

Schneider, Steven. "Why NBC's *Constantine* Will Make You Forget about Keanu Reeves." *Tech Times*, October 24, 2014. http://www.techtimes.com/articles/18659/20141024/why-nbcs-constantine-will-make-you-forget-about-keanu-reeves.htm.

Sciretta, Peter. "HBO Kills *Preacher* Television Series." *Slashfilm*, August 26, 2008. http://www.slashfilm.com/hbo-kills-preacher-television-series/.

Seitz, Matt Zoller. "*RECTIFY* Is Proof That Christian Themes Can Connect with Agnostics and Atheists if the Work Is Good & Isn't Actively Selling Anything." Microblog. *@mattzollerseitz*, June 20, 2014. https://twitter.com/mattzollerseitz/status/479802518839382016.

Seitz, Matt Zoller. "Sundance's *Rectify*, Perhaps the Most Quiet Drama on TV, Is Truly Christian Art." *Vulture*, June 19, 2014. http://www.vulture.com/2014/06/tv-review-rectify-season-2.html?mid=facebook_vulture.

Selznick, Barbara. "Branding the Future: Syfy in the Post-Network Era." *Science Fiction Film and Television* 2, no. 2 (2009): 177–204.

Sepinwall, Alan. "Farewell to *Togetherness*, a Rare Peak TV Cancellation." *HitFix*. Accessed April 16, 2016. http://www.hitfix.com/whats-alan-watching/farewell-to-togetherness-a-rare-peak-tv-cancellation.

Sepinwall, Alan. "Review: Amazon's *Transparent* Clearly the Best New Show of the Fall." *HitFix*, September 24, 2014. http://www.hitfix.com/whats-alan-watching/review-amazons-transparent-clearly-the-best-new-show-of-the-fall.

Sepinwall, Alan. "Review: *The Leftovers* Is Still TV's Best Drama as Season 2 Begins." *HitFix*, September 30, 2015. http://www.hitfix.com/whats-alan-watching/review-the-leftovers-is-still-tvs-best-drama-as-season-2-begins.

Sepinwall, Alan. *The Revolution Was Televised*. New York: Simon & Schuster, 2012.

Shanahan, Mark. "Adaptation: Tom Perrotta Is Growing Accustomed to Seeing His Books on the Big Screen." *Boston.com*, October 18, 2006. http://archive.boston.com/news/globe/living/articles/2006/10/18/adaptation/.

Shaw, Bradley. "Baptizing Boo: Religion in the Cinematic Southern Gothic." *Mississippi Quarterly* 63, no. 3/4 (2010): 445–76.

"*The Shield*." Peabody Awards. Accessed April 11, 2016. http://www.peabodyawards.com/award-profile/the-shield.

Sims, David. "*Ben-Hur, The Passion of the Christ*, and Hollywood's Failed Play for Christian Audiences." *Atlantic*. Accessed January 26, 2018. https://www.theatlantic.com/entertainment/archive/2016/08/why-hollywood-thought-remaking-ben-hur-was-a-good-idea/496868/.

"*Sleepy Hollow* Bosses Find Inspiration in the Bible." *TV Guide*. Accessed January 15, 2014. http://www.tvguide.com/news/sleepy-hollow-alex-kurtzman-roberto-orci-1070348.aspx.

Smith, Jeffery A. "Hollywood Theology: The Commodification of Religion in Twentieth-Century Films." *Religion and American Culture: A Journal of Interpretation* 11, no. 2 (July 1, 2001): 191–231. doi:10.1525/rac.2001.11.2.191.

Smith, Samuel. "*Lucifer* Fox TV Series 'Mocks the Bible,' Says One Million Moms' Petition to Cancel the Show." *Christian Post*, May 29, 2015. http://www.christianpost.com/news/one-million-moms-says-new-fox-tv-series-lucifer-mocks-the-bible-starts-petition-urging-for-shows-cancellation-139742/.

Sobchack, Vivian Carol. *The Persistence of History: Cinema, Television, and the Modern Event*. New York: Routledge, 1996.

Somaiya, Ravi. "Down to the Wire." *Guardian*, April 21, 2008, sec. Media. http://www.theguardian.com/media/2008/apr/21/television.tvandradioarts.

Sottek, T.C. "Netflix Challenges the TV Establishment with Emmy Wins for *House of Cards*." *Verge*, September 22, 2013. http://www.theverge.com/2013/9/22/4759754/netflix-challenges-the-tv-establishment-with-emmy-wins-for-house-of.

Spangler, Todd. "As Netflix Rises, Subscriptions to HBO, Showtime and Other Premium Nets Shrink as Percentage of U.S. Households: Report." *Variety*, January 20, 2014. http://variety.com/2014/digital/news/as-netflix-rises-more-people-are-canceling-hbo-and-showtime-1201065399/.

Spigel, Lynn. "Entertainment Wars: Television Culture after 9/11." *American Quarterly* 56, no. 2 (2004): 235–70.

Spigel, Lynn. *Welcome to the Dreamhouse: Popular Media and Postwar Suburbs*. Durham, NC: Duke University Press, 2001. http://site.ebrary.com/lib/alltitles/docDetail.action?docID=10207659.

Springer, Kimberly. "Introduction: Delineating the Contours of the Oprah Culture Industry." In *Stories of Oprah: The Oprahfication of American Culture*, edited by Trystan T. Cotten and Kimberly Springer, vii–xix. Oxford, MS: University Press of Mississippi, 2010.

Spurgeon, Tom. "Something I Completely Missed about That *Preacher* TV Project." *Comics Reporter*, February 7, 2014. http://www.comicsreporter.com/index.php/something_i_completely_missed_about_that_preacher_tv_project/.

Stanhope, Kate. "Comic-Con: *Lucifer* Series Preview." *Hollywood Reporter*, July 10, 2015. http://www.hollywoodreporter.com/live-feed/comic-con-lucifer-series-preview-807888.

Stanhope, Kate. "Inside *Jane the Virgin*'s Decision to Tackle the Abortion Question (Again)." *Hollywood Reporter*, October 24, 2016. https://www.hollywoodreporter.com/live-feed/jane-virgin-abortion-season-3-postmortem-940867.

Stedman, Alex. "Survey: Faith-Driven Consumers Dissatisfied with *Noah*, Hollywood Religious Pics." *Variety* (blog), February 17, 2014. http://variety.com/2014/film/news/98-of-faith-driven-consumers-dissatisfied-with-noah-survey-shows-1201109347/.

Stein, Joel, and Patrick E. Cole. "The God Squad." *Time* 150, no. 12 (September 22, 1997): 97.

Stelter, Brian. "Hulu Makes History with Emmy Wins." CNNMoney, September 18, 2017. https://money.cnn.com/2017/09/18/media/hulu-emmy-win/index.html.

Stilson, Janet. "Woman on the Verge." *Adweek*, March 23, 2015.

Stone, Brad. "Testing Over, Hulu.com to Open Its TV and Film Offerings This Week." *New York Times*, March 11, 2008. http://www.nytimes.com/2008/03/11/business/media/11hulu.html.

Stone, Jon R. "A Fire in the Sky: 'Apocalyptic' Themes on the Silver Screen." In *God in the Details: American Religion in Popular Culture*, 2nd edition, edited by Eric Michael Mazur and Kate McCarthy, 62–79. New York: Routledge, 2011.

Stone, Natalie. "Mark Burnett, Roma Downey's *A.D. The Bible Continues*: Jesus' Death 'Changed World History.'" *Hollywood Reporter*, April 5, 2015. https://www.hollywoodreporter.com/live-feed/mark-burnett-roma-downeys-ad-786443.

Stone, Natalie. "Roma Downey Reflects on *The Dovekeepers*: 'The Story Is Tragic, but It's Very, Very Touching.'" *Hollywood Reporter*, March 31, 2015. https://www.hollywoodreporter.com/live-feed/roma-downey-reflects-dovekeepers-story-785517.

Stover, Matthew Wooding. "The Gods Suck." In *So Say We All: An Unauthorized Collection of Thoughts and Opinions on "Battlestar Galactica,"* edited by Richard Hatch, 23–34. Dallas, TX: BonBella Books, 2006.

Suebsaeng, Asawin. "One Million Moms Promise Devil of a Time for *Lucifer* TV Show." *Daily Beast*, June 7, 2015. http://www.thedailybeast.com/articles/2015/06/07/one-million-moms-promise-devil-of-a-time-for-lucifer-tv-show.html.

"The Tea Party and Religion." *Pew Research Center's Religion & Public Life Project*, February 23, 2011. http://www.pewforum.org/2011/02/23/tea-party-and-religion/.

Thielman, Sam. "This Fall the Sundance Channel Will Begin Airing Ads." *Adweek*, March 24, 2013. http://www.adweek.com/news/television/sundance-channel-goes-ad-supported-148128.

Tiggett, Jai. "Interview: *Hand of God* Creator Ben Watkins Talks Hollywood's Fear of Religion, Creating 360° Portrayals of Black Women, More." *Shadow and Act, IndieWire*, August 27, 2014. http://blogs.indiewire.com/shadowandact/interview-hand-of-god-creator-ben-watkins-talks-hollywoods-fear-of-religion-creating-360-portrayals-of-black-women-more-20140827.

Todorov, Tsvetan. "The Fantastic: A Structural Approach to a Literary Genre." In *Fantastic Literature: A Critical Reader* edited by David Sandner. Westport, CT: Praeger, 2004.

"Touched by an Angel." Wikipedia, the Free Encyclopedia, June 20, 2016. https://en.wikipedia.org/w/index.php?title=Touched_by_an_Angel&oldid=726176089.

Tripp, Jeffrey M. "Gabriel, Abortion, and Anti-Annunciation in *The Prophecy, Constantine*, and *Legion*." *Journal of Religion and Popular Culture* 27, no. 1 (2015): 57–70.

Tryon, Chuck. "TV Got Better: Netflix's Original Programming Strategies and the On-Demand Television Transition." *Media Industries* 2, no. 2 (December 27, 2015). http://www.mediaindustriesjournal.org/index.php/mij/article/view/126.

Tucker, Ken. "The CW's Identity Crisis: Are *Supernatural* and *Smallville* Better Than *Gossip Girl* and *90210*"? *Entertainment Weekly*'s EW.com, February 26, 2010. http://www.ew.com/article/2010/02/26/cw-smallville-supernatural-smallville-gossip-girl-90210.

Turner, Graeme, and Jinna Tay. *Television Studies after TV: Understanding Television in the Post-Broadcast Era*. 1st edition. Hoboken: Taylor and Francis, 2009.

Turow, Joseph. *Breaking Up America: Advertisers and the New Media World*. Chicago: University of Chicago Press, 1998.

Turow, Joseph. *Niche Envy: Marketing Discrimination in the Digital Age*. Cambridge, MA: Massachusetts Institute of Technology Press, 2006.

"Valenti: TV Reducing Violence." *Variety*, November 8, 1993. http://variety.com/1993/tv/columns/valenti-tv-reducing-violence-115701/.

Valentine, Evan. "*Daredevil* Season 1 Episode 9 'Speak of the Devil' Recap." *Collider*, May 7, 2015. http://collider.com/daredevil-season-1-episode-9-speak-of-the-devil-recap/.

VanDerWerff, Emily. "Mark Burnett, the Reality TV Titan Who Could Hold Donald Trump's Fate in His Hands, Explained." Vox, October 10, 2016. http://www.vox.com/culture/2016/10/10/13220296/donald-trump-apprentice-footage-mark-burnett.

Vespe, Eric. "Quint Talks Neighbors, Deleted Scenes and *Preacher* with Seth Rogen and Evan Goldberg!" *Aint It Cool News*, March 12, 2014. http://www.aintitcool.com/node/66516.

Villarreal, Yvonne. "CW Boss Mark Pedowitz Talks *The Flash* and Broadening Out." *Los Angeles Times*, July 18, 2014. http://www.latimes.com/entertainment/tv/showtracker/la-et-st-cw-boss-mark-pedowitz-talks-broadening-out-genre-sensibility-20140718-story.html.

Villarreal, Yvonne. "TCA '15: With *Dovekeepers*, Roma Downey Looks to Provide Inspiring TV." *Los Angeles Times*, January 12, 2015. http://www.latimes.com/entertainment/envelope/cotown/la-et-st-tca-15-with-dovekeepers-roma-downey-looks-to-provide-tv-that-inspires-20150112-story.html.

Vine, Richard. "Better Than *The Wire*?" *Guardian*, March 18, 2009, sec. Television & radio. http://www.theguardian.com/culture/2009/mar/19/battlestar-galactica-review.

Wagmeister, Elizabeth. "Syfy Cancels *Dominion* after Two Seasons." *Variety*, October 13, 2015. http://variety.com/2015/tv/news/dominion-cancelled-sffy-season-two-1201617277/.

Wagner, Laura. "New York Subway Pulls Nazi-Themed Ads for New Show, *Man in the High Castle*." NPR.org, November 25, 2015. http://www.npr.org/sections/thetwo-way/2015/11/25/457410075/new-york-subway-pulls-nazi-themed-ads-for-new-show-the-man-in-the-high-castle.

Wallace, Daniel B. "Is *Lucifer* the Devil in Isaiah 14:12?—The KJV Argument against Modern Translations." Bible.org, March 22, 2010. https://bible.org/article/lucifer-devil-isaiah-1412-kjv-argument-against-modern-translations.

Wallenstein, Andrew. "Netflix Ratings Revealed: New Data Sheds Light on Original Series' Audience Levels." *Variety*, April 28, 2015. http://variety.com/2015/digital/news/netflix-originals-viewer-data-1201480234/.

Wallenstein, Andrew. "The OTT View-Niverse: A Map of the New Video Ecosystem." *Variety*, April 29, 2015. http://variety.com/2015/digital/news/ott-map-video-ecosystem-1201480930/.

Warren, Christina. "HANDS ON: Amazon's Prime Instant Video." *Mashable*, February 22, 2011. http://mashable.com/2011/02/22/amazon-prime-instant-video/.

Weber, Max. "The Sociology of Religion." In *Introducing Religion: Readings from the Classic Theorists*, edited by Daniel L. Pals, 255–60. New York: Oxford University Press, 2009.

Weisman, Jon. "Emmy Nominations Announced: *House of Cards* Makes History." *Variety*, July 18, 2013. http://variety.com/2013/tv/awards/emmy-nominees-2013-emmys-awards-nominations-full-list-1200564301/.

Wetmore, Kevin J., Jr., *The Theology of Battlestar Galactica*. Jefferson, NC: McFarland, 2012.

Wilkinson, Alissa. "The Ten Commandments Has Been a Springtime TV Staple since 1968, with Good Reason." Vox, April 15, 2017. https://www.vox.com/culture/2017/4/15/15243480/ten-commandments-movie-of-week-passover-easter.

Williams, Oscar. "Social Engagement Now More Important than TV Ratings, Says Fremantle Boss." *Guardian*, January 21, 2015, sec. Media Network. http://www.theguardian.com/media-network/2015/jan/21/social-media-engagement-tv-ratings-fremantle.

Winston, Diane. "Introduction." In *Small Screen, Big Picture: Television and Lived Religion*, edited by Diane Winston, 1–14. Baylor University Press, 2009.

Winston, Diane, ed. *Small Screen, Big Picture: Television and Lived Religion*. Waco, TX: Baylor University Press, 2009.

Wolfe, Elizabeth G. "The Greatest of These: The Theological Virtues and the Problem of an Absent God in *Supernatural*." In *"Supernatural," Humanity, and the Soul*, edited by Susan A. George and Regina M. Hansen, 13–26. New York: Palgrave Macmillan, 2014.

Wolff, Richard. *The Church on TV*. New York: Continuum, 2010.

Wuthnow, Robert. *After Heaven: Spirituality in America since the 1950s*. EBook. Berkeley: University of California Press, 1998.

Index

Tables and figures are indicated by *t* and *f* following the page number

For the benefit of digital users, indexed terms that span two pages (e.g., 52–53) may, on occasion, appear on only one of those pages.

Ingram Content Group UK Ltd.
Milton Keynes UK
UKHW020809110523
421501UK00021B/396